Praise for The Rise of e-Commerce: From Dot to Dominance

'*From Dot to Dominance* is an important and well-timed book about how the humdrum business of shopping was reinvented online. James Roper is a persuasive advocate for the role of collaboration in innovation, who was instrumental in jumpstarting the e-retail industry by methodically tackling every obstacle that blocked its early progress. During periods of rapid innovation, there is always tumult as people try to make sense of it – IMRG's organizing efforts helped make the very complicated and disparate subject and its evolution understandable, and in so doing so saved us online traders much time and many tears. In this book Roper offers a fascinating glimpse at how a motley assemblage of inventions evolved, often in surprising ways, into today's staggeringly powerful e-retail industry. Stuffed with eye-opening facts and statistics From Dot to Dominance is an essential read for anyone who is interested in the evolution of modern retailing.'
Nick Robertson, Co-founder and Ex-CEO, ASOS

'James is an authority on the rise of e-retail. *Dot to Dominance* is a condensed history of the labyrinthine factors that led to the simplicity (for the consumer) of shopping online today. This is approachable and a must-read for those in the retail space.'
Brent Hoberman CBE, Co-Founder and Chairman at Founders Factory, Founders Forum, firstminute capital and Karakuri. Previously co-founded lastminute.com & made.com

'A fantastic historic story of the biggest change to hit retail in the last century told with humour and fact. A must read for how change is always faster than you can imagine.'
Neil Sansom, Ex-CEO, WoolOvers.com / Ex Omni-channel Director, Moss Bros / Ex-Vice President to Consumer, Shell

'With visionary foresight and impeccable timing, James founded IMRG in 1990 to unleash ecommerce's potential. Three decades on, IMRG remains the focal point of UK ecommerce and the authoritative source of its data and insights. This engaging book tells the sweeping history of the tortuous evolution – impossible to understand in the chaos of the moment – that ultimately led to the ease of shopping online today. A must read for anyone interested in the past, present and future of ecommerce.
Justin Opie, CEO, IMRG

'IMRG epitomized my philosophy, "If you are not thinking ahead today then you will not be ahead tomorrow". James' detailed history of e-commerce reminds us all of the prominent role on the global stage that IMRG and the UK played in moving the market ahead, and the massive steps forward that were made in a relatively short period of time. It should be the must read for students, employees and those leading commerce.'
Scott Thomson, Payments Sage: creator of the first Euro Travellers Cheques for Thomas Cook, inventor of the Switch multifunction debit card and 'cashback' for Midland Bank; co-developer of Tesco's Clubcard, and creator of the first e-commerce cross-border payments scheme

'… here is a book that tells the full story of ecommerce over the last 30 years, a concept that was initially met with derision. The UK now boasts the world's highest per capita spend online and the IMRG's learnings, proven by global retail brands it helped incubate, have meant that ecommerce continues to be a true UK success story on the world stage. If history tells us the future, then this is the definitive book to read, keep, refer to and inspire now and for years to come.'
Shiran Liyanage, UK ecommerce technology pioneer

'Tesco.com's pioneering efforts to bring grocery home shopping to the UK was challenging work because we were doing it ahead of others without any insight or models to work from. IMRG changed all that, bringing James's focus and expertise to generate that insight and best practice.'
Nick Lansley, Ex-Head of Innovation, Tesco.com

'James Roper was pivotal to the early lead that the UK won and maintained in eCommerce. James brought the industry together and fought for innovation, security, consumer rights and standards. Unbeknown to most, he's done more than anyone to make shoppers happy to buy online.'
Patrick Wall, Founder and Ex-CEO, Metapack

'… my roles at a senior level in Dixons Group, Argos and Homebase were aligned to the IMRG through membership and participation at meetings and events. As the technology grew and bandwidth improved the 'Roper' dream of total online retailing was getting closer and closer. Despite many challenges and doubters James never once revealed anything but total commitment to his vision of the future for electronic commerce. It was a privilege to be in at the start of this revolution, thanks to the IMRG for being an amazing conduit for learning and development.'
Peter J Jones, Ex-Retail Director: Dixon Stores Group, Argos & Homebase

'Digital could be aptly called "the great disruptor" … When James and Steve Dobson brought this [IMRG] to me in 1991, I immediately saw the potential, having already embarked on the digitisation of the Pathé Newsreel and subsequently the National Sound Archive. But it was James's vision and determination that resulted in the impact that IMRG had on "e-commerce" in retail.'
Dr David Best, Partner, Deloitte

'From the turn of the 20th century eCommerce was on a charge and James and the IMRG were central to its success during its infancy and beyond. It was a learning curve for all of us and if we needed an answer to a question we couldn't figure or to network with people who already had found solutions James knew them! On the mantra that two heads are better than one, IMRG networking events multiplied that by many many heads. From payments to logistics issues many were resolved through the IMRG group meetings and we had fun finding the solutions at the expense of many willing suppliers growing rapidly in this space as well.'
Jonathan Wall, Ex-Group eCommerce Director, Shop Direct / Ex-Marketing Director, dabs.com

'James's unique understanding of online trading, especially e-commerce and e-retail comes from a hands-on perspective. He was there; capturing change as it happened to the way we live, work and trade. His insight goes deep into the founding principles of e-commerce and he has seen how events over 3 decades have changed the world. Dot to Dominance, is the story of events which have led to greatest economic change in the modern world. A must read for everyone interested in the economic future.'
Dr Fiona Ellis-Chadwick, Director of Impact @ School of Business & Economics, Loughborough University

The Rise of e-Commerce

From Dot to Dominance

James R. J. Roper, FRSA

First published in Great Britain in 2023 by
Pen & Sword History
An imprint of
Pen & Sword Books Ltd
Yorkshire – Philadelphia

HB ISBN: 978 1 39906 332 6
TPB ISBN: 978 1 39906 333 3

Typeset by Mac Style
Printed in the UK by CPI Group (UK) Ltd, Croydon, CR0 4YY.

Pen & Sword Books Limited incorporates the imprints of Atlas,
Archaeology, Aviation, Discovery, Family History, Fiction, History,
Maritime, Military, Military Classics, Politics, Select, Transport, True
Crime, Air World, Frontline Publishing, Leo Cooper, Remember When,
Seaforth Publishing, The Praetorian Press, Wharncliffe Local History,
Wharncliffe Transport, Wharncliffe True Crime, White Owl and After
the Battle.

For a complete list of Pen & Sword titles please contact

PEN & SWORD BOOKS LIMITED
47 Church Street, Barnsley, South Yorkshire, S70 2AS, England
E-mail: enquiries@pen-and-sword.co.uk
Website: www.pen-and-sword.co.uk

Or

PEN AND SWORD BOOKS
1950 Lawrence Rd, Havertown, PA 19083, USA
E-mail: Uspen-and-sword@casematepublishers.com
Website: www.penandswordbooks.com

Contents

Author's Note

When Sunday shopping was being legalised in 1993, there were no retail websites and online shopping was considered by almost all of the few people who had even heard of it to be a fanciful idea that would never catch on. I was already three years into running the Interactive Media in Retail Group (IMRG), a small research project that we had set up to try to get people to realise that e-commerce was going to be HUGE, and to help them to get their heads around it.

That year we encountered the internet hands-on for the first time. It didn't seem to make any sense at all. The very idea was just weird. Yet the shrill, screeching, crackling hiss of a dial-up modem heralded the fast-approaching transformation of consumer choice from not so much to EVERYTHING.

Even then I realised that I was going to have to write this book someday, as a testament to the rise of e-retail from its beginnings in 1990, so I began to compile the now-vast archive on which it is based.

I served as IMRG's CEO for more than two decades – my role seemed to be to predict the obvious and then be credited for it when it arrived. During this time IMRG became the world's first and preeminent e-commerce industry association, facilitating, monitoring and mapping the growth of the online shopping industry, and in doing so helping to create a UK and international marketplace that expanded exponentially. IMRG has many great attributes, but its best is the *Group* itself – the thousands of amazing people who have been the IMRG across its thirty-plus years: these individuals made, and continue to make, e-commerce happen.

Nothing was straightforward in the rise of e-commerce. From an up-close-and-personal perspective this book explores the opportunities and challenges, heroes and villains, business successes and failures, and considers the consequences and prospects of the extraordinary global e-retail revolution.

Thank you for spending time reading this book. I hope the e-commerce saga will intrigue you, as it still does me.

Acknowledgements

To my wife, Chrissie Ann Roper, without whose support and encouragement neither IMRG nor this book would have been possible.

Thousands of people teamed up with IMRG on its roving adventure, and I am grateful to every one of them.

Special thanks to all IMRG members and associates: the Interactive Media in Retail Group is a community of activists who made / make e-retail happen – prominent within this cohort are Steve Dobson, David Best, Jo Evans, Harry Bock, Justin Opie, Nick Robertson, Brian McBride, Jason Gissing, Patrick Wall, Scott Thomson, Andrew Starkey, Andrew McClelland, Martha Lane Fox, Brent Hoberman, Jonathan Wall, Daniel Nabarro, Michael Ross, Ulric Jérome, Peter Jones, Tony Kane, Val Walker, David Williams, Alex Murray, Jeff Rodwell, Sean McKee, Neil Sansom, Kevin Cooper, Steve Hinchliffe, James Eadie, Neill Denny, John Burns, Shiran Liyanage, Geoff Page, Ray McCann, Allan Mitchell, Ron Gainsford, Peter Rowlands, Hedley Aylott, Nick Lansley, Charles Prescott, Colum Joyce, Alan McKinnon, Rory Cellan-Jones, Aad Weening, Tim Danaher, Susan Pointer, Jean-Marc Noël, Chris Russell, Martin Gross-Albenhausen, Dieter Junghans, Don Marshall, Tanya Lawler, Jonathan Reynolds, Jon Kamuluddin, Bruce Fair, Tim Woolias, Wendy Derbyshire, Alastair Gilchrist, Wayne Holgate, Kieron Smith, Igor Subow, Kobus Paulsen, Alistair Buckle, Toby Chance…

Thanks also to the national e-commerce associations with which IMRG partnered during my tenure:

AUSTRIA (Dr Stephan Mayer-Heinisch, Präsident, Handelsverband)
BELGIUM (Marc Périn, Director, BeCommerce)
BRAZIL (Ludovino Lopes, President, Camara-e.net)
CHINA (Yao Guanghai, President, CIECC)
CZECH REPUBLIC (Tomas Hájek, Secretary General, ADMAZ)
EUROPE (Susanne Czech, Secretary General, EMOTA)
FRANCE (Marc Lolivier, Délégué Général, FEVAD)
GERMANY (Christoph Wenk-Fischer, Director, BEVH)
GREECE (Yoannis Kourniotis, President, EPAM)
HOLLAND (Wijnand Jongen, Director, Thuiswinkel)
ITALY (Attilio Rubini, Secretary General, ANVED)
PORTUGAL (Alexandre Nilo Fonseca, President, ACEPI)
SLOVAKIA (Juraj Sebo, President, AZIO)
SOUTH AFRICA (Toby Chance, and Arthur Goldstuck, Founder, World Wide Worx)

SPAIN (Elena Gomez da Pozuela, President, Adigital)
SWITZERLAND (Patrick Kessler, President, VSV)
UNITED STATES (Scott Silverman, Executive Director, SHOP.ORG)

All of the Pen & Sword team have been incredibly helpful, but a special note of thanks must go to their Senior Commissioning Editor, Claire Hopkins, who saw potential in my idea, enabled this book project to happen, and skilfully improved my draft to make it eminently more readable than it would have been. I am also hugely indebted to our editor, Chris Cocks, for guiding me through the singular world of book publishing, then helping to set goals and prescribing optimum action.

Cover design and illustration by Richard Bland.

Despite all the help and guidance I have received from so many, it seems unlikely that some inaccuracies and misrepresentations will not have crept unobserved into my work. I ask forgiveness and, as ever, the fault is mine alone.

Whilst every effort has been made to ensure that all appropriate acknowledgements have made, and all necessary permissions to reproduce the illustrations and content have been secured, I may have failed in a few cases to trace the copyright holders. If contacted, I will be pleased to rectify any omissions at the earliest opportunity.

The Rise of e-Commerce Timeline

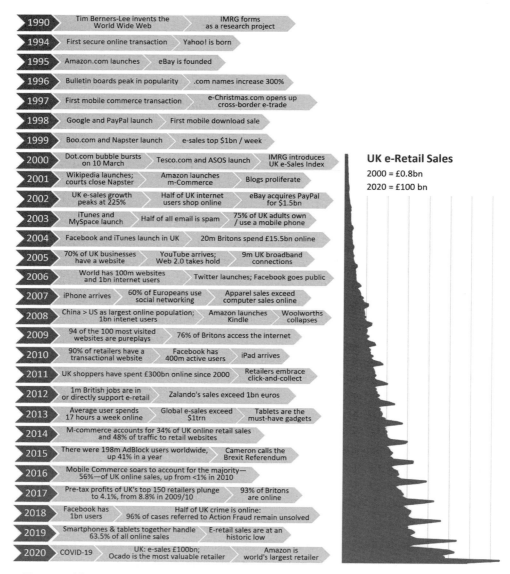

1990 — Tim Berners-Lee invents the World Wide Web — IMRG forms as a research project

1994 — First secure online transaction — Yahoo! is born

1995 — Amazon.com launches — eBay is founded

1996 — Bulletin boards peak in popularity — .com names increase 300%

1997 — First mobile commerce transaction — e-Christmas.com opens up cross-border e-trade

1998 — Google and PayPal launch — First mobile download sale

1999 — Boo.com and Napster launch — e-sales top $1bn / week

2000 — Dot.com bubble bursts on 10 March — Tesco.com and ASOS launch — IMRG introduces UK e-Sales Index

2001 — Wikipedia launches; courts close Napster — Amazon launches m-Commerce — Blogs proliferate

2002 — UK e-sales growth peaks at 225% — Half of UK internet users shop online — eBay acquires PayPal for $1.5bn

2003 — iTunes and MySpace launch — Half of all email is spam — 75% of UK adults own / use a mobile phone

2004 — Facebook and iTunes launch in UK — 20m Britons spend £15.5bn online

2005 — 70% of UK businesses have a website — YouTube arrives; Web 2.0 takes hold — 9m UK broadband connections

2006 — World has 100m websites and 1bn internet users — Twitter launches; Facebook goes public

2007 — iPhone arrives — 60% of Europeans use social networking — Apparel sales exceed computer sales online

2008 — China > US as largest online population; 1bn intenet users — Amazon launches Kindle — Woolworths collapses

2009 — 94 of the 100 most visited websites are pureplays — 76% of Britons access the internet

2010 — 90% of retailers have a transactional website — Facebook has 400m active users — iPad arrives

2011 — UK shoppers have spent £300bn online since 2000 — Retailers embrace click-and-collect

2012 — 1m British jobs are in or directly support e-retail — Zalando's sales exceed 1bn euros

2013 — Average user spends 17 hours a week online — Global e-sales exceed $1trn — Tablets are the must-have gadgets

2014 — M-commerce accounts for 34% of UK online retail sales and 48% of traffic to retail websites

2015 — There were 198m AdBlock users worldwide, up 41% in a year — Cameron calls the Brexit Referendum

2016 — Mobile Commerce soars to account for the majority—56%—of UK online sales, up from <1% in 2010

2017 — Pre-tax profits of UK's top 150 retailers plunge to 4.1%, from 8.8% in 2009/10 — 93% of Britons are online

2018 — Facebook has 1bn users — Half of UK crime is online: 96% of cases referred to Action Fraud remain unsolved

2019 — Smartphones & tablets together handle 63.5% of all online sales — E-retail sales are at an historic low

2020 — COVID-19 — UK: e-sales £100bn; Ocado is the most valuable retailer — Amazon is world's largest retailer

UK e-Retail Sales

2000 = £0.8bn
2020 = £100 bn

Figure 1: The Rise of e-Commerce Timeline. (*Source: James Roper Archive*)

Introduction

'Remote shopping, while entirely feasible, will flop'

Time magazine, 1966

1990–2020: The great retail apocalypse arrived at the dawn of the third millennium. New ways for anyone to find and buy anything from anywhere at any time emerged, evolved and exploded with dizzying speed. Billions of transactions shifted from shops to screens as consumers trawled vast new oceans of abundance online. Legions of retailers failed, unable to compete with the internet's range, convenience and prices. Tens of thousands of town and city centres fell into crisis as their footfall declined and revenues crashed. In 2020 e-retail's ascendency from dot to dominance was complete: an online grocer was the UK's most valuable retailer, and an internet bookseller had become the world's largest shop, its founder the richest man on the planet. This is the story of how it happened.

'Location, location, location'

The three things that matter in retail – Apocryphal aphorism

Retail has always been at the forefront of innovation and affects us all. One new shopping idea after another has taken off and been copied. Yet since trading began, the first and constant key to success was the shop's physical location. Over centuries the courses of our shopping expeditions meandered across a broad retail landscape, tracking shops' changing locations. At one time the place where you bought things was just the house of the man who made them. Then came stall-boards, markets, high streets, independent shops selling factory-made goods, department stores, catalogues, chain stores, supermarkets, out-of-town centres and malls. Supply dominated demand – it was only by looking in the shops (and by reading advertisements) that you could know what things were available. Nobody imagined that the retail location itself could become irrelevant.

The pace of technological innovation had been snowballing for years, but in the second half for the twentieth century, two technologies – *the computer and the internet*, each on a par with the wheel or Guttenberg's printing press for their potential as agents of change and disruption – combined to forge a new and unimagined digital dimension in which the way we live, communicate, learn and shop would profoundly change: *the information realm.*

'Whatever can be done, can be outdone'

Gordon Moore, Co-founder and chairman emeritus, Intel Corporation, 2015

For more than fifty years, Moore's Law set the pace for digital innovation and development. In 1965, when mainframe computers were just beginning to use integrated circuits, Gordon E. Moore published an article in *Electronics* magazine in which he predicted a bright future for the computing industry because transistors were shrinking so fast that every year approximately twice as many could fit onto a chip. By tracking the evolution of integrated circuits to date, Moore extrapolated that computing would dramatically increase in power, and decrease in relative cost, at an exponential rate. This observation became known as Moore's Law, the pace of which he adjusted in 1975 to a doubling every two years. Moore's Law's prediction proved to be remarkably accurate from 1965 to 2013, since when the pace has slowed a little. If automotive technology had progressed at the same rate, cars would go almost 300,000 miles per hour, get over 2,000,000 miles per gallon, and cost only $0.4 cents.[1]

In 1990, Tim Berners-Lee published his formal proposal for the World Wide Web,[2] a plan for a system that would use hypertext, web pages, browsers, and web servers to share documents across the internet. He had first proposed his idea to colleagues at CERN in Switzerland who then worked with him to develop the system for about two years before it became functional. His original goal was to make the sharing of documents easy and universal for scientists and education purposes around the globe, but he had acknowledged the potential for commercial involvement. The creation of the World Wide Web subsequently formed the standard for how we access and use the internet – enabling near-instantaneous global computer communication.

Alexander Graham Bell had invented the telephone in 1876 and demonstrated it to Queen Victoria a couple of years later. Soon, everywhere, copper twisted pair wires dangled overhead, carrying voices from one place to another. For a century the POTS (plain old telephone service) carried analogue voice transmission via a dedicated circuit between two points. Then in the 1980s two American engineers, John Cioffi and Joseph Lechleider, hijacked the Victorian technology to power always-on broadband, cramming an astonishing amount of high-speed data through the copper wires that delivered voice calls to the home without building expensive new networks. This *Asymmetric Digital Subscriber Line* (ADSL) technology would ultimately connect more than 366 million households around the world.

The combination of these elements fomented the digital revolution and a blazing pace of change that impacted almost every social and commercial enterprise. Great advances were made, generating wealth and leisure time for billions of people to enjoy, together with a burgeoning array of new and often cheaper goods, services and experiences that they could buy online.

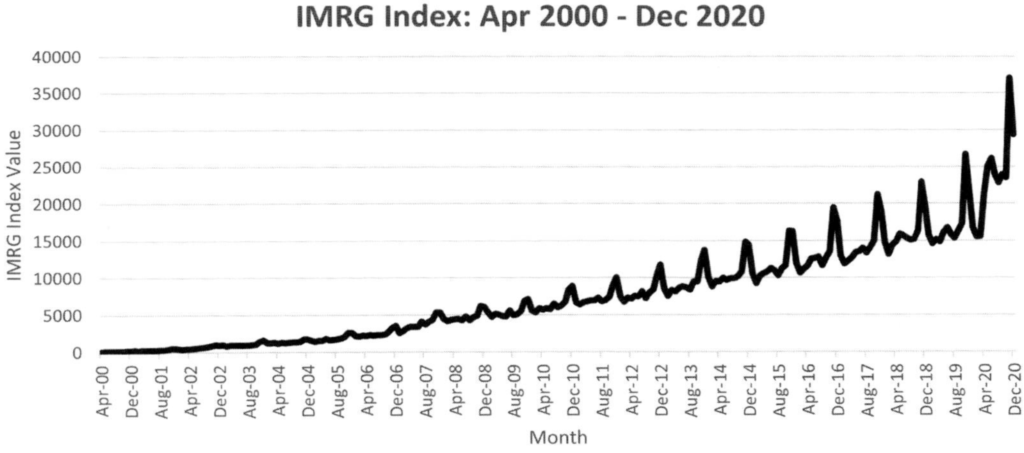

IMRG Index: Apr 2000 - Dec 2020

Figure 2: UK e-Retail Sales, April 2000 to December 2020. (*Source: IMRG Capgemini Sales Index*)

No sector would be disrupted more than retail. By giving rise to the entirely new business function referred to as e-commerce, the digital age transformed and comprehensively rattled the crucial and dynamically evolving links between producers and consumers.

Summary: From Dot to Dominance in 30 Years

'Happiness is not in money, but in shopping'

Marilyn Monroe

Shopping in 1990 was not like it is today. If you wanted to buy, say, a sofa, a suit or a pair of taps, you would have to visit the shops twice: firstly, to discover what was available by asking questions and trusting the word of the salesperson, and a second time to buy the item you had chosen, if it was still in stock. This was not always convenient in Britain, with its unpredictable weather, expensive parking, and the worst transport system in Europe. The shops might be shut when inspiration fired your purchasing quest: most shops were closed on Sunday, the day of rest, while half-day closing, typically but not always on a Wednesday, was both a tradition and required by law. Shop opening hours were commonly 9 am to 5:30 pm, and many also shut for lunch, so for people working normal office hours the opportunities for going shopping could be narrow. John Lewis didn't open at all on Mondays, to give its staff a two-day 'weekend', leaving would-be customers who forgot or didn't know, beginning their week frustrated at JLP's shuttered doors.

Woolworths was a staple of almost every British high street that sold pretty much everything from stationery and Ladybird clothing, to toys and CandyKing *pick 'n' mix* sweets such as Aniseed Balls, Black Jacks, Jellybeans, Liquorice Allsorts, Torpedoes and Flying Saucers. A selection of local shops sold music, but you were most likely to head off to Woolies for a tape cassette or CD of the tune that you had heard on *Top of the Pops*, BBC's music chart TV programme. A trip to Woolies was the pinnacle of many childhood weekends.[3]

For underwear, the predominating outlet was Marks & Spencer, though you had to remember that they refused to take payment by credit card. For jewellery, you could find a bargain at Ratners, at least until 1991 when CEO Gerald Ratner in a speech addressing the Institute of Directors at the Royal Albert Hall denigrated his company's wares as 'total crap'. After this, Argos was the top destination for jewellery bargains.

Buying a holiday would usually involve visiting a high street travel agent – probably Thomas Cook, Lunn Poly, Intasun or Horizon – and thumbing through brochures while queueing to sit at a desk and look at the back of a bulky computer monitor while the agent read out to you flight and hotel options.

British Home Stores (BHS) was faded but still prominent in 1990, selling everything, from clothes and bedding, to lighting and a cup of tea. There were some 20,000 post offices, approaching twice the number that would survive in 2020. Wimpy Bar was the popular burger joint to hang out in. And many people would have been used to stocking up the chest freezer in their garage with multi-packs of pizzas from Bejam, that sold only frozen food until it was bought by its much smaller rival, Iceland, in 1989.

Prior to the arrival of internet shopping, Britain's high streets used to be woefully uncompetitive and anticompetitive. Cynical price-fixing by cartels hit the hapless public in the pocket, meant lower quality at higher prices, and undermined the vast majority of businesses that worked hard to compete honestly.

The few that cheated could reap huge rewards. There were infamous examples of institutionalised sharp practice. Second-hand goods were sold as 'Manager's Specials'. '0% interest schemes', if not paid off in full by the end of the interest-free period, would charge 29.5 per cent APR for the whole of the period. Worthless 'extended warranties' duplicated cover that purchasers already had or even basic rights under the *Sale of Goods Act*. Suspicion hung over carmakers regarding disparities in car prices, and Volvo admitted price-fixing. The competition watchdog investigated banks accused of overcharging customers by billions. And there were ongoing rows over price fixing in the construction and fine arts sectors. Dominant brands could get away with all sorts of things in the 'free' market, leaning on trading partners who might encounter 'supply problems' if they did not provide 'exclusive' opportunities. Allegedly.

1990 high street shop prices could be eye-wateringly expensive. Britain's retailers enjoyed some of the highest profit margins in the world – frequently 40 per cent or more – while their counterparts in Europe and the USA got by on much slimmer yields.

A small number of big organisations dominated and largely controlled the UK's main retail sectors. For example, the consumer electrical goods sector was prevailed over by Currys (Dixons Group) and Comet, whose proposed merger was rejected by the Monopolies and Merger Commission (MMC) in May 1990. A few years later, the world's leading computer chip manufacturer described the

UK's leading electrical retailer's margins as being 'Ridiculous'. The retailer, who at the time probably controlled half of UK home computer sales, countered by saying that it only made about 30 per cent profit on an average PC sale, one of its lowest margins.

TVs and video recorders were so expensive that many people chose to rent them from Rumbelows or Radio Rentals – the latter having 500 stores at its peak. After renting your VHS player, you could pop into your local video rental store to take out a film for the evening. Blockbuster opened its first UK store in 1989, at which time it was reported to be opening a new store every seventeen hours.

Online shopping would upend the cosy world of 'ridiculous profits' enjoyed by the dominant traders, by introducing competition and price transparency. Pre-tax profit margins at the top 150 UK retailers plunged from 8.8 per cent in 2009/10 to 4.1 per cent in 2017/18, according to a report by global professional services firm Alvarez & Marsal, in partnership with Retail Economics.[4]

Every sizeable UK town still had at least one department store in 1990 – Allders, Owen Owen, Trewins, Jessops, Wildings, Fenwick, Arnotts, Bentalls, Rackhams, and hundreds more – the ultimate one-stop-shops for high-end luxury goods, homeware and fashion. But these formidable cornerstones of any successful high street or shopping centre would be hard hit by changes in spending habits brought about by internet shopping. They were to become an anachronism, their format facing an existential threat.

Debenhams epitomised the sorry plight of department stores in 2020. Founded in 1778 as a single high-end London drapers' shop, Debenhams went on to become one of the largest retailers in the UK with, at one point, more than 200 large stores in 18 countries and exclusive partnerships with some of the world's leading designers such as Jasper Conran and Julien Macdonald. Debenhams protracted 'death spiral' ended in collapse, and the venerable brand being sold in late 2020 to the fifteen-year-old British online fashion upstart Boohoo for a knockdown £55 million. But only the Debenhams brand would survive: 12,000 jobs and all 166 shops would be lost, leaving a 14 million square foot hole in the high street.

* * *

'Blinded by witchcraft – elec-trickery!'

*Catweazle, eleventh-century magician in the eponymous
British fantasy television series, 1970*

Retail's computerised reincarnation started slowly. Creating a viable virtual self-service shopping marketplace would require a multitude of new components to be invented, coordinated and adopted, and the economics would only work if deployed at scale. But achieving scale was initially impossible, except in the imaginations of the hopeful e-retail visionaries who, sensing vast potential, cobbled together more than 2,000 self-service kiosk pilots during the 1980s. They developed technology and skills, and gained knowledge, but only a handful achieved rollouts or any kind of commercial success.

'I can never see this internet thing catching on'

CEO of major oil company division, who then closed the division down

When we first encountered the internet hands-on in 1993, it didn't seem to make any sense at all. The very idea was just weird. Yet the shrill, screeching, crackling hiss of a dial-up modem connecting with another modem across the repurposed telephone infrastructure would become a familiar noise to anyone going online or using the internet in the 1990s.

'It's a mad, alien, boffin-invented technobabble'

IMRG comment, 1994

1994 was a pivotal year for e-retail. The potential of the combined power of personal computers and the internet finally began to be realised with the arrival of Netscape Navigator, the first widely available internet browser. With it, secure online shopping transactions were achieved. The following year Amazon.com sold its first book and eBay invented the online auction.

In 1995 Bill Gates gave the world Microsoft's Windows 95, a quantum leap forward for personal computing. Labelled as an upgrade, Win95 was an entirely new operating system and in effect a blueprint for the future of the PC, global networks, home entertainment and much more.

'The Internet is the printing press of the technology era'

Jim Barksdale, CEO, Netscape, September 1996

By July 1996, IMRG was reporting that the number of internet users was doubling every 100 days; around 200 million users were predicted by the end of the year. PCs were becoming capable and powerful; tens of millions of households worldwide were buying them. But we also noted in 1998 what would become a recurring theme: political and business leaders' lack of knowledge and understanding of all things IT – 'On the subject of e-commerce, the average European company director or government minister could get out of his depth on a damp pavement.'

Amazon's first UK website appeared in November 1998, offering 1.2 million titles, six times more than the largest bookstores. As part of its expansion into Europe, Amazon had purchased the UK online bookseller Bookpages.co.uk a few months earlier, and promptly renamed it Amazon.co.uk. Simon Murdoch, Amazon's VP Europe, had established Bookpages in 1996 after being sacked by WH Smith.

With enabling technology and tools in place, and inaugural e-trades having proven the concept of secure online trading to be attainable, the stage was set for e-commerce to boom. As the new millennium approached a dizzying phase of digital trading began. Boo.com, Webvan, Napster, Pets.com and thousands of other internet traders emerged. Online sales rocketed to $400 million a week in 1999. Venture capital and IPOs flooded the market.

*   *   *

Year 2000 arrived, glittering with futuristic promise. The world sighed with relief when the feared Y2K tech bomb turned out to be a dud, then gasped in shock as the dot.com bubble burst in March, ultimately costing stocks $5 trillion in market devaluation.

Boo.com came to symbolise the *dot–bomb* losers. Founded in 1999 by Swedes, the British e-commerce fashion business spent millions of dollars attempting to create a global online shopping portal, which the world was not quite ready for, before going bust in May 2000. But there were winners, too. Ocado, the British online supermarket, was launched as a concept in January 2000 and went on to become, briefly, the UK's most valuable retailer, valued at £21.7 billion in late 2020, as the Covid-19 pandemic disrupted conventional grocery shopping. In June 2000, Net-a-Porter launched from a flat in Chelsea, London, as a magazine format website selling designer fashion, then grew into the world's premier luxury fashion destination, serving customers in more than 180 countries.

Nothing could stop e-retail. Even though the range of products obtainable was limited, website services were unreliable, and home delivery and internet connections often failed; by 2000, consumers were smitten with online shopping, in love with its bargain prices.

2001 witnessed a massive increase in what was available to buy online and soaring internet sales. Tesco.com reported its web trade up 77 per cent in a year. Online car sales leapt tenfold, to 17,000. EasyJet announced that almost 87 per cent of its flights were bought online, up from 65 per cent the previous year. John Lewis, Waitrose and Debenhams refreshed and relaunched their websites.

> *'I'll never forget James [Roper] highlighting the weirdness of grocery e-commerce at an IMRG conference: "Customers buying dozens of products, doing it every week or fortnight, and unexcited about much of their purchases (toilet rolls, anyone?!)"'*
>
> Nick Lansley, Ex-Head of Innovation, Tesco.com, 2020

2002 saw online shopping truly flying – its explosive growth rate peaked at an all-time high of 255 per cent per annum. The IMRG Capgemini Sales Index recorded that UK e-retail sales topped £1 billion in a month for the first time in December. Almost 14 million Britons became internet users that year, as compared with four million a year earlier.

Consumer demand was well ahead of supply. Nothing encouraged consumers to take up internet shopping more than the newly available 'always on' broadband, and millions of households were embracing it. In September 2004 we reported that UK consumers were investing £6 billion a year in PCs and internet connections that gave people their own, personal shopping environments – their *High Street at home* – where merchants might be welcomed or clicked to oblivion on a whim. The British public was investing sixty times more than the top 100 retailers in facilitation of internet shopping; in a very real sense, homeowners were becoming the retailers' landlords. Retailers conventionally talked about *owning* the customer relationship: So, who 'owned' these customers now?

Most traditional retailers turned a blind eye to the internet after the dot.com crash, assuming that the threat had gone away and could safely be ignored. It was only in 2003, when online shopping was growing thirty-one times faster than old school retailing, that any mainstream retail investment in internet trading started to return.

Amazon was setting a blistering pace of innovation – continually raising the bar of consumers' online shopping expectations. Meanwhile 39 per cent of the UK businesses selling online had no 'back-end automation' processes in place at all – fulfilment, shipping, reconciliation, financial management and so forth – resulting in ever-increasing service failures as they struggled to manually process rapidly growing volumes of e-trade.

> *'More people shop online in the UK than in any other country in Europe, and the numbers are rising all the time. Security and consumer rights on the net are as good as the High Street, and there is no reason why millions more cannot start to enjoy online shopping'*
>
> Stephen Timms, Minister for Energy, e-Commerce and Postal Services, in a message wishing IMRG well with its 24/7 DAY 2003 campaign

Three-quarters of UK adults owned mobile phones by 2003, when Apple launched iTunes and only half of all email was spam. Myspace arrived and went on to become the largest social networking site in the world, from 2005 to 2008. Myspace registered its 100 millionth account in 2006 and was at one time valued at $12 billion.

Britain led the e-retailing world during the *noughties*, as the BBC labelled the new millennium's first decade, recording a third of all online sales in Europe. Responding to consumers' persistent concerns about the safety of shopping online, in 2001 IMRG introduced the ISIS (Internet Shopping Is Safe) merchant accreditation scheme. Registered merchants displayed an ISIS logo on their site that hot-linked to their accreditation certificate: this stated the registered

Figure 3: ISIS, the world's first online shopping trust scheme, was introduced by IMRG in 2001 to counter consumer wariness. (*Source: James Roper Archive*)

company's name and internet address (URL), confirmed that the shop subscribed to the ISIS principles, had its site and service reviewed and monitored by IMRG, and had its Business, VAT and Data Protection registrations checked by IMRG.

By Christmas 2004 ISIS was widely embraced by the UK e-retail industry and relied on by millions of shoppers. Hundreds of ISIS-accredited merchants collectively accounted for around two-thirds of all UK online shopping – including the market leaders Argos.co.uk, Comet.co.uk, dabs.com and Tesco.com. Then Kelkoo, Europe's leading shopping search engine, adopted the scheme and displayed merchants' ISIS accreditation within its search results next to the names of ISIS-certified shops. This brought together everything the consumer required to find online what they needed and then buy with complete confidence. It also made small e-retailers both discoverable and trustable, enabling them to compete with large traders on a level playing field in an open marketplace.

Twenty million UK shoppers spent £15.5 billion online in 2004, the year that Facebook first leered out of computer screens, which at the time were still mainly bulky cathode ray tubes (CRTs) – affordable new flat panel displays were just becoming available.

Christmas Present   * </;-)

There was a surge in online shopping each Christmas as busy people with lots to buy and organise opted to avoid overcrowded streets, shop queues and foul weather, in favour of clicking orders at home over a cup of tea or a glass of wine. Throughout the mid-2000s more and more consumers switched to buying online, especially for high-ticket discretionary purchases such as plasma TVs and digital cameras, motivated by the huge choice, rich information and significant savings that the internet could offer.

In 2004, IMRG reported *'Online Shopping's £4 Billion Christmas Cracker'*, with sales estimated to be up 62 per cent on the year before. Some eighteen million Britons shopped on the internet, and a survey indicated that 85 per cent of them (fifteen million) would buy Christmas presents online that year, spending on average £220 each. The value of e-shopping for Christmas 2004 was equivalent to the sales of five London West Ends or nineteen Bluewater Shopping Centres, and growing ten times faster than the high street.

That December, Tesco delivered more than 600,000 online orders, including ten million sprouts and twenty tons of stuffing. Virgin Wines shipped 500 tonnes of wine. Dabs.com's sales director, Jonathan Wall, told us that internet sales of electrical goods surged 42 per cent higher than a year earlier, boosted by sales of MP3 music players.

Clothing sales did spectacularly well. Boden's managing director, Julian Granville, said: 'Over our busiest weekend in December we took over 35,000 orders on the website. Many customers tell us that they prefer shopping online as they can see exactly what's available in their size, they can order anytime of the day or night, and the website carries exclusive sale items.'

> *'Shopping online is like giving yourself an extra week's*
> *holiday each year, thanks to the time you save'*
>
> IMRG *press release, November 2004*

January Sales were an immemorial tradition for the retail sector when shops cleared stock unsold in the *golden quarter* – the three months of October to December when retailers made the most money. In 2003 a few leading e-retailers, notably the iconic British lingerie seller, Figleaves.com, made a surprise move, launching *Sales* in mid-December, as soon as they could no longer guarantee pre-Christmas delivery. This began a process whereby online traders would eventually pull the Sales back as early as October by mobilising innovative marketing events.

* * *

2005: Halfway along online shopping's extraordinary journey from its *year dot* in 1990 to retail domination in 2020, internet shopping reached a tipping point where the majority (51 per cent) of UK consumers purchased something online. E-shopping exceeded £2 billion in one month (November) for the first time ever. IMRG and Royal Mail together estimated that if the UK's 26,000 online shops were bricks and mortar, they would form a high street fifty miles long, offering five million products for sale.

Cyber Monday, introduced in 2005 and usually in late November, together with *Black Friday*, the Friday after the USA's Thanksgiving and the last payday before Christmas, enabled internet retailers to become increasingly successful at competing for consumers' cash by moving up the start of the peak shopping season. Black Friday, a day that was stretched into a week, and ultimately a month or more, was heavily pushed in the UK by Amazon even though Thanksgiving, the fourth Thursday in November in the US, was of little relevance in the UK, being, amongst other things, the day that Americans celebrate achieving their independence from Albion.

The chiefs of one retail sector in particular would go to almost any lengths to impede e-retail's progress. As Christmas 2005 approached, a number of major electrical goods manufacturers introduced *Dual Pricing*, a scheme that forced internet traders to pay far more than bricks-and-mortar retailers for their TVs and other electrical goods, in an attempt to kill online trade (and traders) in the key selling period. IMRG successfully quelled this incursion on fair competition, and permanently discouraged its emulation in other sectors, by threatening high-profile media exposure of the instigators. IMRG never actually identified the implicated manufacturers, but occasionally dropped hints to journalists about how their own online research might identify culprits.

* * *

'…. the creaking infrastructure of the Post Office remains a 19th century solution grappling with a 21st century reality. Investment in better fulfilment is more important to British retailers than almost anything else'

Retail Week editorial, Neill Denny, Editor, 1 October 2004

Neill Denny, the editor of *Retail Week*, and I were having a conversation via email on 24 July 2000 when Neill said, 'the date – you should do something with the date.' I had no idea what he was talking about. 'It's the twenty-fourth day of the seventh month,' he explained, 'and 24/7 is synonymous with 'always on'. 'You should nominate today as *Internet Shopping Day* because 24/7 is what it's all about.' So, we did. We launched ISIS on 24/7 Day 2001, as noted earlier. Thereafter we ran national 24/7 Day events most years until 2007, promoting the industry and inviting the public to 'shop around the clock'.

For 24/7 Day 2006, we branched out with a new GO GREEN, GO ONLINE campaign, raising awareness of the huge potential that the internet-enabled marketplace presented for increasing efficiency and reducing waste. Highlighted research findings revealed savings in retail-building space, retail inventories and vehicle miles. One of our speakers at the final 24/7 Day 2007 event – the *OnLine Green Awards*: OLGAs (up-cycling the BAFTAs concept) – was a Royal Mail director who told us that their vehicles travelled 600 million miles delivering parcels that year, equivalent to a round trip to Mars. A voice from the audience quipped: 'And they were out.'

Figure 4: 'Sorry we missed you' delivery cards were all too familiar in the noughties. (*Source: James Roper Archive*)

> *'With online sales rising at 90 per cent per annum,*
> *why bother to provide a better delivery service?'*
>
> *A retailer, 2005*

Parcel delivery was always the Achilles' heel of e-retail. During the noughties, when carriers would report leaving a 'you were out' card as a 'successful delivery', on the basis that they had got a man to the door, millions of people didn't shop online because of the uncertainty and potential hassle associated with goods arriving when they were out. So, in 2004 we formed an IMRG Delivery Forum that would be instrumental in creating for the UK the most comprehensive, efficient and convenient suite of home delivery services available anywhere in the world.

IMRG partnered with Metapack to make a crucial breakthrough in home-delivery management that would significantly raise the standards of e-retail fulfilment across the entire industry. Launched on 12 November 2007 at the Office of Fair Trading as part of the trading standards institute's *National Consumer Week* opening event, IMRG's new *IDIS Delivery Manager* enabled e-retailers of all sizes to offer their customers a variety of delivery options from multiple carriers and services.

*   *   *

The first implementation of the internet, up to 1999, was described by Tim Berners-Lee as the 'read-only-web'. From the late 1990s, the 'social web' – aka Web 2.0 – began to arrive, enabling anyone to create and publish their own content for free with just a few clicks. Retailers were horrified when consumers' product reviews started to appear online in the late 1990s and actively tried to ban them. However, the arrival of customer-generated product reviews proved to be a major milestone in the development of online shopping.

By 2005, most shoppers read online reviews and considered them essential to their decision-making – millions of web surfers were using blog or social media platforms to interact with each other and post items online. As user numbers exploded, almost all the large influential platforms became commercialised (*Wikipedia*, the free encyclopaedia, is the notable exception), finding ways to convert *connectivity* into monetising potential. Platforms interconnected, and a new infrastructure emerged: a vast ecosystem of connected social media.

Social media became a great equaliser: big brands could be outsmarted, and small brands could make big names for themselves. A pioneering example of viral social media marketing was the *Will it Blend?* campaign, first shown on YouTube in October 2006. In a series of videos, the relatively unknown company, Blendtec, demonstrated their blenders pulverising a mind-blowing array of everyday objects – mobile phones, camcorders, glow sticks, Rubik's Cubes, Bic lighters, glass marbles, television remote controls, car key fobs and more. The mesmerising videos were watched six million times in the first six days.

By early 2009, almost 75 per cent of European internet users were involved in some form of social media. Retailers, eager to follow the crowd, were piling into social networking – US retailer 1-800-Flowers.com became the first brand to produce a Facebook store in 2009. No traders embraced social media more enthusiastically than fashion retailers – ASOS (founded in 2000), Boohoo (founded in 2006) and Missguided (launched in 2009) built their brands on their social networks.

In 2010, the many popular social media platforms included Facebook, LinkedIn, Twitter, YouTube and Flickr. Instagram, the US photo and video social networking service, launched in October 2010, grew rapidly, registering one million users in the first two months, and ten million in a year. Instagram was acquired by Facebook in April 2012, and by June 2018 would have a billion users.

Social media obliged advertisers to rethink their marketing strategies and engage holistic marketing concepts that focused on building customer relationships with more creative, unpretentious and helpful messages, instead of in-your-face intrusions. Some major brands, such as Domino's Pizza, would be completely transformed by social media.

Facebook remained the biggest social media site in 2019 with almost a third of the world's population – more than two billion people – using it every month.[5] More than 65 million businesses used Facebook Pages to promote themselves, and it had six million advertisers. Most Facebook users – 94 per cent – accessed Facebook via its mobile app.

* * *

Early internet security threats were mainly a matter of adolescents causing mischief to impress their peers, but by the mid-2000s these pranksters had been replaced by criminals seeking to make serious money. Criminals switched to the internet from activities such as burglary because it was easy and largely risk-free – the overstretched and under-resourced police generally ignored it. Even when a thief was caught, the penalties for cybercrime were so lenient that they appeared to offer little deterrent. The internet and e-retailing continued to be plagued by crime, and the range and sophistication of online threats proliferated. In September 2018 it was revealed that 96 per cent of cases reported to the UK's national fraud reporting centre, Action Fraud, remained unsolved. In January 2020, Mike Barton, former Chief Constable of Durham Police, speaking on BBC's *Question Time*, commented that half of all crime committed in the UK was actually online.

* * *

Smartphones looked set to become important devices for e-retail transactions even before 2000, yet little to confirm this materialised until 2007 when the first Apple iPhone arrived, followed in 2010 by the iPad. Together the iPhone and iPad unleashed a new reenergised phase of e-retail evolution. More than half of UK online sales were via mobile devices in 2016. The iPhone became the most profitable product of all time, with sales approaching two billion in 2020.

As disruptive technologies go, mobile proved to be a particularly effective one. The rapid take-up of mobile devices by the public thrilled consumers, developers and tech companies but dismayed retailers, brands and governments who had to completely rethink their strategies for marketing, trading and engagement.

The m-commerce market's year-on-year growth rate peaked at 359 per cent in May 2012 as mobile was being adopted as a mainstream shopping channel, enhancing consumers' ability to compare goods and prices wherever they were, including in the high street. The smartphone was becoming the consumer's personal *omnichannel utility*: their very own shopping trolley in their pocket.

* * *

Conventional wisdom had it that online shopping would peak at 15 per cent of total retail sales, but as we powered past that landmark in the hypergrowth of summer 2007, an escape velocity was passed, and retailers found themselves floating out of the known trading universe into uncharted space. Some 27 million British shoppers spent an estimated £35 billion online in 2007, an average of £1,300 each, generating 860 million parcel deliveries.

E- Retail Rockets In June: Total Sales Up 55% – Electricals Up 92%
The IMRG Capgemini Sales Index Report, July 2007

Everything was changing for shoppers as the internet worked its transformation of the possible. Shoppers no longer needed to plan their lives around when the shops were open and, for many, queuing for the till was a thing of the past. Online shopping was becoming normalised, an indispensable component of everyday life.

The range of goods available online was expanding to the point where shoppers expected all products and brands to be obtainable. Yet despite all this, nearly half of the top 100 UK retailers still did not have a transactional website at the beginning of 2007, and their non-store sales were just 4.4 per cent of their total sales.

'Internet now beats Tesco as favourite place to shop'
Evening Standard headline, 17 January 2008

2008 was the year when e-retailers abruptly woke up to the power of shouty Web 2.0 culture and its online society where customers advised each other on what to buy. With it came a new challenge – satisfying the online customer who knew very well that he was king / she was queen and would use every interactive tool at their disposal – blogs, vlogs, email, instant messaging and chatrooms – to remind retailers of that fact.

Google marked its ten years in business with the launch of Google Chrome in 2008. Google was already the dominant search engine, generating 85 billion searches worldwide that year, compared with 25 billion searches on Yahoo! and ten billion on Microsoft Live Search, which would be replaced by Microsoft Bing the following June.

An IMRG survey of internet users revealed that half researched online either 'often' or 'always' before buying goods in all categories via *any* retail channel. More than a third of all online shopping (38 per cent) took place outside normal shop hours, either before 9 am or after 6 pm, the peak being between 7 pm and 9 pm, when most high street shops were shut.

Also in 2008, China overtook the US as the country with the largest online audience – the world's internet population now exceeded 1.5 billion. More than 97 per cent of email messages were Spam, according to a Microsoft security report. Amazon.com surpassed eBay as having the most monthly unique visitors, while Apple's App Store had over 10,000 apps available within six months of launch.

In May 2009, IMRG reported that its Index had grown by 5,000 per cent since its launch in April 2000, estimating UK online sales of over £200 billion during those nine years. By 2010 more than half of consumers were routinely shopping online. UK online sales that had been worth less than £1 billion in 2000 had soared to £58.8 billion in 2010, when 19 million UK homes (76 per cent of homes) had broadband connections, and there were 53 million internet users (of a population of 62.76 million).

*   *   *

In 2009, the government made the first of many connectivity pledges that, in the coming decade, would be proclaimed and spun, then broken or scrapped. The Labour government promised that all UK homes would receive 2 Mbps broadband by 2012 – that didn't happen. In the Christmas week of 2020, with the Covid-19 pandemic raging and most people house-bound for months, UK MPs advised that the government was abandoning yet another broadband target – gigabit-capable connectivity for 85 per cent of the country by 2025 – as only a fraction of the £5 billion promised would be available: Ofcom said at the time that 600,000 people in towns and more rural locations would remain restricted to ten megabits per second or less, which was too slow for business use and would be slow for two or more users at home.

2011: Europe pipped North America as the largest e-commerce market in the world with sales up 19 per cent to €246 billion. The UK was leading the world in online shopping and had export values worth more than three times that of France or Germany, boosted by the global appetite for British fashion, and its having by far the best international parcel delivery network, a legacy of the British Empire's vast postal service network.

The use of mobile internet and m-commerce was rising rapidly all over the world, in emerging as well as mature economies. The number of mobile subscriptions in late 2011 reached 5.9 billion, or 85 per cent of the world population.

2013: Investors were ploughing billions of dollars into large disruptive start-ups, aiming for their new online shops to dominate entire market sectors. Leading the 'let's just buy the market' gamble for separating European online consumers from their cash was the apparently irresistible force of Zalando, the Berlin-based online fashion retailer which had launched in October 2008, that achieved sales worth over a billion euros in 2012. In 2018, Zalando would begin to roll out *Connected Retail*, a bold programme to encompass the whole of the fashion marketplace by enabling brands and brick-and-mortar retailers to integrate their own e-commerce stock into the Zalando platform ecosystem.

Adtech wars: The retail economy – both offline and online – is essentially centred on an 'attention model' whereby traders vie for customer attention in hopes of selling them what they might want. On the face of it, consumers had never had it so good, with the internet bringing more choice, information, services, convenience and better prices 24 x 7 x 365. Yet online abuse, particularly the behaviour of the $600 billion online advertising industry with its rampant appetite for bandwidth and intrusive tracking, led to an arms race, with consumers fighting adtech with ad blockers.

* * *

Q: *How do you justify passing laws that it is not technically possible to comply with?* James Roper, CEO, IMRG, 2007

A: ***That's your problem.*** Viviane Reding, European Commission Vice-President & Commissioner for Justice, Fundamental Rights and Citizenship (formerly Commissioner for Information Society and Media)

The European Commission has always struggled with e-commerce, misunderstanding the technology it regulates, and wilfully neglecting to provide constructive leadership or competent administration. A classic example of EC ineptitude was when it tried to ban cookies, having failed to understand what they are or do. (Some websites, including the EC's, use hundreds of cookies.) Instead, the EC introduced the so-called *cookie law* (the e-Privacy Directive) which forced all websites in the EU to gain *informed consent* before they could store or retrieve information on a visitor's web-enabled device. The well-meaning but breathtakingly stupid cookie law – which evolved into the General Data Protection Regulation (GDPR) – condemned everyone for years to an impaired internet, a nightmare of *I accept* pop-ups that people almost immediately became conditioned to dismiss without reading, frustration, much wasted time, a huge cost to the online retail industry – and zero improvement to privacy.

GDPR has been heavily criticised as a case of regulatory failure – ineffective, costly, unenforceable, and spoiling user browsing experience – reminiscent of the UK's 1865 'Red Flag Act' that limited all road locomotives to a 4 mph speed limit (2 mph in the city), stipulated a crew of three, and required an additional man with a red flag to walk in front of vehicles hauling multiple wagons.

* * *

2015: IMRG membership now included 2,500 retail organisations and 130 solution providers; our 15-year-old Index had tracked an estimated £640 billion spent online in the UK since 2000. Some 10,000 physical retail stores had been empty for more than three years, and tens of thousands more were at risk as their costs rose and productivity fell. It was increasingly obvious that these brick-and-mortar shops could no longer bear the same costs and lengths of commitment to rent and business rates negotiated when most retail sales were store based. Councils and landlords were contributing to the demise of high streets by ignoring the fundamental transformation taking place in shopping.

Recall Boohoo, the British online fashion upstart that bought the iconic Debenhams for a knockdown £55 million in 2020? Boohoo, an IMRG member since its foundation in 2006, lit up our radar in November 2015 when it was the fastest riser in the IMRG comScore Top 50 Online Retailer chart, up eleven places to 37th compared to a year earlier.

In 2017, around 93 per cent of the UK's 65.5 million population were internet users and 87 per cent shopped online – over 57 million e-shoppers. Department stores recorded the biggest growth in online sales in January, their sales increasing by almost 20 per cent year-on-year, due largely to their late arrival at the online shopping party – too late.

* * *

The UK government didn't appear to understand – in any holistic sense – what was going on in e-commerce, or the long-term implications of ungoverned digital intervention. The conspicuously mixed results of unimpeded market forces ranged from twenty-something billionaires to neutralised law-enforcement agencies, and from Black Friday excesses to devastated high streets. Britain's government also demonstrated continually that when it came to implementing IT, it just didn't realise what it was doing, or learn and apply lessons. But squandering huge opportunities that the internet presented for the nation is surely the UK government's most incomprehensible dereliction of digital duty, examples of which we shall look at in the chapter *Unruled e-Britannia*.

* * *

2020 was a leap year in every sense. From day one, 2020 was defined by the Covid-19 pandemic which caused global social and economic disruption. The UK economy shrank by 9.9 per cent, the largest fall in 300 years. A string of household names collapsed, including Arcadia, Debenhams, Topshop, Miss Selfridge, Dorothy Perkins and Cath Kidston. Adding to the turmoil, Britain leapt into the unknown when it formally withdrew from the European Union on 31 January (though still with no agreement for living, working and trading together), *Brexit* ending 47 years of EU membership.

E-retail was not in a strong position heading into 2020: the growth trend had seen a general decline for years, and in 2019 was at an historic low, retailers experiencing myriad issues. But when the Covid-19 pandemic hit, closing stores and incarcerating the public in their own homes, online shopping was more than ready to span the hiatus.

The pandemic precipitated an abrupt mass shift to digital, and the worst year for high street job losses in 25 years.[6] People used to shopping online did so more, while millions adopted the habit for the first time, particularly the older community who were most at risk from Covid-19. Fifty-four major UK retailers failed, affecting 5,214 stores. There was a total of 16,045 store closures.

> ### *'[Amazon] is now the key enabler for most of Western society during this crisis'*
> *Christopher Rossbach, Chief Investment Officer, J. Stern & Co, July 2020*

The biggest retail winner from the Covid-19 pandemic was Amazon; its UK revenue soared 51 per cent to £19.5 billion, up from £12.9 billion in 2019 and £10.7 billion the year before that. Jeff Bezos invested heavily and was willing to forgo profits to seize the unique opportunity to grab market share while most of Amazon's brick-and-mortar rivals were closed.

*   *   *

> ### *'A nation of shopkeepers'*
> *Adam Smith, 'The Wealth of Nations', London, 1776*

E-retail's effect on high streets was inevitable: with better retail productivity fewer shops were needed. But for most people the term 'shopping' took on meaning far beyond the simple exchange of goods and money. Shopping was central to the human condition, inseparably enmeshed in all manner of human behaviour. And high streets had for centuries been the crucible in which the normalising power of social interactions played out, upholding the functions of all the other institutions in society.

Our world was changing faster than ever before. Over thirty years, we had witnessed massive digitalisation and technology advancements in many aspects of our lives. Having access to digital infrastructure became absolutely critical for almost everything – from sourcing information to communication and social interaction, from transport to watching TV and banking. Mobile devices were no longer just for communication, but also served as a gateway to a universe of applications and services. A digital divide – between those with and without internet access – remained but was narrowing.

In the early days especially, the internet had been seen overwhelmingly as a force for global good. Some postulated that globalisation and the interdependence it wrought, would bring world peace. Others hypothesised that the productivity gains of the new digital economy would end recessions. But, as ever, malign forces circled, corrupting and abusing the brilliant internet, spoiling it for everyone.

This chapter skimmed across some of the headline events of e-retail's emergence and rise. Now let's look at a curated slice of the backstories and breakthroughs, twists and turns, strategies and shenanigans, barriers and blunders behind the startling front-page banners.

1985: Before the Apocalypse

'We think it's the most innovative shopping system to date. It incorporates today's most sophisticated technology and translates it into easy-to-use selection and purchase procedures'

Harry S. Bock, vice-president for information services, Florsheim Shoe Co., Chicago, USA, November 1986[7]

I was captured into orbit around the origins of e-retail in April 1985. It didn't take a mental giant to see the potential – though its incubation proved tricky: before it became easy, it was bafflingly difficult.

In the spring of 1985, I was the sales director of a small design and multivision studio in London called Slideshop AV, part of the Heavyweight Group. One of our freelance designers mentioned an unusual project that he was working on for another studio, New Media Productions (NMP), and suggested that I might like to see it. 'Hairstyle' as we knew him for his long trendy golden locks, described a computer-controlled multimedia programme he was producing artwork for. Intrigued, I went over one evening to have a look.

NMP was a creative production house that explored the latest technology to create new ways of communicating. Their open-plan studio occupied a long, spacious loft in a Victorian barn-of-a building at 79 Parkway, Camden, north London. I met managing director Dick Fletcher who showed me a motley collection of wired-together boxes, at the centre of which was a large TV monitor and a flat case with a drawer that slid out to reveal a shimmering silver plate, twelve inches in diameter, that I was informed was a videodisc, read by a laser.

NMP had been commissioned by the American publisher, Grolier – publisher of *Encyclopaedia Americana*, the US equivalent of the UK's *Encyclopaedia Britannica* – to produce a pilot chapter of a laser-disc version of *Encyclopaedia Americana*. The pilot disc was to contain all manner of media in order to see what it looked like on laserdisc and how it might be organised and presented in a consumer-friendly way. The idea was to consider the possibility of replacing the thirty-volume print set of *Encyclopaedia Americana*, which occupied yards of shelf space, with some laserdiscs, just inches wide.

Though still a work-in-progress, much of the pilot had been completed. The interactive multimedia programme contained text, still and animated graphics, various formats of film and video, photographs, music, audio effects and narration, scans, data and computer code, all controlled by an IBM Personal Computer. Dick demonstrated the many options for navigating the content using a keyboard, trackball, mouse or touchscreen, and explained how it could be hooked up to other computers via the telephone network.

I was amazed. It was brilliant. The potential for this amalgamation of capabilities was obviously huge, and my enthusiasm for NMP's work obvious. I remarked that I wished multimedia had been around when I was growing up in the countryside with very limited access to resources. 'If wishes were horses, then beggars would ride,' Dick said, quoting the old Scottish proverb. 'Why don't you join us as our business development director and help us promote this?' I accepted Dick's job offer that week.

Interactive multimedia was very exciting; however, it proved to be extremely difficult to sell in 1985. People would be blown away by our demonstrations of the capabilities, but then struggle to arrive at practical, commercial applications for it, and were horrified by the costs. Everything was expensive – the design, production and programming, and in particular the costly equipment that had to be coaxed to work together, not always successfully. Everything about multimedia was in a state of flux – the many technologies employed were all evolving rapidly, so a wrong choice of kit might make an entire development programme redundant. There was either an absence or a confliction of standards: for example, PAL, the TV standard in the UK and most of Europe used 625 lines of data to make up a screen image, whereas in the US and Japan the NTSC TV standard used only 525 lines, and it was in these latter two countries where most of the latest (and incompatible for us) equipment was being invented and manufactured. There was also an abundance of hype.

The ideal target applications for multimedia were obviously large-scale rollouts, where the high initial production and equipment costs could be mitigated across volumes of users, but such commissions remained elusive, and there were no installed networks of equipment out there to publish for. It soon became apparent that we were at the bottom of a very steep learning curve.

NMP suffered a major blow when we were offered – and began gearing up for – a £5.5 million contract from Grolier to produce the initial ten of twenty-four videodiscs planned to comprise the first interactive audio-visual encyclopaedia of human knowledge. NMP was a small, specialist start-up, and for us this contract had been a huge win that would fully engage the company with years of work. But then Grolier changed its mind and cancelled the order because the fastest evolving consumer market for interactive media was in Japan, where the preference was for an entirely different technology platform: the 12cm-diameter CD-ROM, not the 30cm laserdisc we were using. A CD-ROM version of the *Encyclopaedia Americana* was not actually published until 1995, ten years later.

*   *   *

Convergent Communications was the UK's leading interactive media production company of the day, focusing on information technology-based communication solutions, and I was fortunate to be invited to join them as business development director in September 1987.

Convergent was particularly successful in the finance sector, where changes to British banking laws in the 1980s allowed building societies to offer banking services equivalent to normal banks, and vice versa. A result of this was the need to rapidly reskill thousands of finance sector personnel at a time when training typically involved bussing staff to teaching centres for several days at a time. Rising to the challenge, and borrowing some innovative ideas that were working well in the US, Convergent devised revolutionary self-learning solutions whereby people could use multimedia workstations located in their own offices to gain skills in bite-sized sessions, whenever convenient – say, twenty minutes in their lunchbreak, or a couple of hours after work. Clients including Halifax and Bradford & Bingley Building Societies queued up to commission our self-learning programmes. Convergent estimated that in 1988 it had a third of the UK's available and viable market for interactive multimedia software production.

By this time, I was developing ideas about how the retail industry might benefit from interactive media. I persuaded Currys, the home electronics and household appliances division of Dixons Retail plc, to commission a pilot project from Convergent: the *Currys Cooker Selector*. Currys' 570 shops across the UK came in a wide range of different shapes and sizes, with correspondingly irregular selections of cookers on display, dependent on space available. The idea was that, by installing our proposed interactive *Cooker Selector*, suddenly every store would be able to present and sell every model and variation in the entire range. Our plan was for touchscreen kiosks to be placed in stores for use by both customers, on a self-service basis, and by staff. Eventually six kiosks were deployed. Unfortunately, Currys, already the dominant white goods retailer with arrogance to match, lacked any real commitment to the initiative. The project was severely underfunded, which led to inconclusive results and its discontinuation.

Anticipated technology developments further stifled market growth, and I parted company with Convergent in 1990, on good terms, but extremely frustrated by the lack of any real progress towards realisation of the potential of interactive media in retail, which I was increasingly convinced would be huge.

* * *

In these pre-World Wide Web days, the nascent e-retail market focused on stand-alone kiosks. Entrepreneurs hoped their friendly designs and simple human interfaces would attract people to select and buy from ranges of goods larger than could be stored locally – the kiosks were usually located within a shop or a mall. However, the reality was that kiosks were just boxes containing a confusion of technology – personal computers, touch-sensitive screens, card readers, laserdisc players, printers, modems, trackballs, speakers – that could and very often did crash, jam, overheat, run out of paper, and generally go wrong. If a cleaner accidentally pulled out a power plug, someone would probably have to visit the site and reboot everything. It was all horribly complicated and uncertain.

Nevertheless, by now we e-retail enthusiasts were impelled by our vision of the future of automated shopping, convinced that this phase of technology teething troubles would pass and that when it did a new era of liberated consumerism would begin. That vision might have been a bit fuzzy round the edges, and it wasn't at all obvious how some of the key elements would work, but we were certain that it would eventually materialise and have far-reaching consequences.

During the second half of the 1980s a handful of other significant UK interactive retail pilots came and went – Sears *Home Lighting Centre*, Levi's *Jeans*

Screen, Safeway's *Electronic Cookbook*, Rover Cars *IMR Kiosk*, NatWest's *InfoPoint*, Forte Hotels *Information Point* – but these achieved little, and very few kiosk networks were implemented. A notable exception was Zanussi, whose chain of 75 *Satellite* white goods demonstrator terminals in electrical retailers had since 1986 consistently increased sales by up to 30 per cent.

But one gold standard IMR kiosk exemplar did exist: Florsheim Shoes' *Express Shop*. This breakthrough initiative proved beyond any shadow of doubt the potential commercial viability of the interactive retail medium if it was correctly specified and adequately resourced.

Florsheim Shoes: irrefutable proof of concept

Florsheim Shoes of Chicago was the USA's biggest manufacturer and retailer of men's shoes. It launched its shoe kiosk programme in 1981 and eventually installed a network of 550 *Express Shops* nationwide. Harry S. Bock, marketing director (later vice-president) explained: 'The economics are unbelievable. You sell something you don't have. You deliver direct to your customer. You have his money right away and you don't have to pay your supplier for the product for at least 30–60 days. Returns are extremely low – experience shows averages of only 1.3 per cent – for both men's and women's shoes. Over a period of ten years, these units obviously pay for themselves over and over.'

In the early 1980s, Bock had been called into the office of his company president who advised him that customers were complaining that they were unable to

Figure 5: The Florsheim 'Express Shop' began to be deployed circa 1985: 500 were eventually installed across the US. (*Source: Harry Bock, Vice-President, Florsheim Shoes / James Roper Archive*)

purchase the shoe styles being advertised. Florsheim manufactured the styles, but stores could not carry all of the 14,289 different combinations of the 350 styles in every size, width and colour.

Shoe retailers strived to maximise their investments and increase their inventory return by keeping to the centreline of the size and width scales. They stocked the minimum number of styles, sizes and widths to satisfy the maximum number of customers. However, they were only catering to about half the market as an equal number of consumers were outside that centreline of sizes. Harry's team came up with the idea of stand-alone kiosks that could be installed in shopping malls and stores, showing all the combinations.

The Florsheim interactive kiosk was created, manufactured and customized by ByVideo Inc. of Sunnyvale, CA, and operated for over six years in Florsheim retail locations across the US. Each unit cost $10,000 to $15,000.

In 1987, Bock commented: 'In 1981 they said interactive video would never sell shoes, now they say it can only sell shoes.' The problem was that Florsheim's achievements were unique; no other retailer was getting even close to scoring this level of success.

Harry Bock would become a good friend of IMRG. We first met at Florsheim's headquarters in Chicago, and Harry took me for dinner at his club, halfway up the Sear's Tower – he later presented to IMRG members in London, and we stayed in touch over many years. As Harry would say: 'We think of the Florsheim Express Shop as the world's smallest shoe store with the world's largest selection of shoes.'

Part I

1990–2000

'You can burst into flames for all I care'

Dr David Best, Partner, Touche Ross Management Consultants'
Advanced Systems Division, 6 February 1991

1990 was a remarkable year. Wrecking cranes began tearing down the Berlin Wall at the Brandenburg Gate, marking the end of the Cold War. Nelson Mandela was released from prison in South Africa after 27 years of incarceration. Construction workers drilled through the final wall of rock to join the two halves of the Channel Tunnel and link Britain with France – joining the UK to Europe for the first time since the Ice Age, some 8,000 years ago. Margaret Thatcher resigned, ending more than 15 years as Conservative leader and 11 years as UK prime minister. The Human Genome project formally began. The Hubble Space Telescope launched during a Space Shuttle Discovery mission. 'The Simpsons' was seen for the first time on FOX TV. And we began a modest research programme that led to the founding of IMRG.

On a personal level, 1990's most significant event was the birth of our son, James Lawrence Christian, on 14 March. At around 6 am my wife, Chrissie, woke me and told me she thought it was time to head for the hospital. Unfortunately, the exhaust pipe had fallen off our car the previous evening so we made the journey from Boxmoor to St Albans early that morning in what must have sounded like a very low-flying Lancaster bomber – apologies to everyone we woke. A healthy 7lb 4oz James was born at 3.10 pm.

Meanwhile, an event of supreme significance for e-retail was happening, though we did not know about it at the time, and only realised the implications much later: Tim Berners-Lee published his formal proposal for the World Wide Web.[2] He was knighted in 2004 by Queen Elizabeth II for 'services to the global development of the Internet'. He never patented his invention.

The Interactive Media in Retail (IMR) research project

I had for years been researching and assembling a database of every interactive retail project I could find worldwide to help understand and support the case for such

Figure 6: My delegate badge for TIME (The Interactive Multimedia Event), 17 October 1990. (*Source: James Roper Archive*)

systems: by mid-1990 my archive contained records of more than 2,000, nearly all of which were small pilots. Whereas many people sensed retail opportunities that information technology appeared to present, almost every project was failing. Worse still, most projects were naively repeating the same mistakes over and over again: there was no documentation of what had been learned, and no sharing of (often-embarrassing) experiences. Consequently, there was almost no progress.

It became increasingly obvious to me that thorough, structured research was needed to identify and capture what retailers perceived might be the potential for interactive retail systems. The findings could then be used to inform collaborative, pre-competitive development towards unlocking IMR's potential.

On 17 October 1990, at a new industry conference and exhibition, *TIME 1990* (The Interactive Multimedia Event), I was discussing these ideas as usual with any attending business acquaintances who would listen. Some were enthusiastic and contributed useful suggestions. One, Chris Marsh, the proprietor of a small media company, Recent Productions, offered to work on this with me.

A plan emerged: if we could get a raft of sponsors to fund an IMR research project, retailers could be invited to complete a questionnaire and thereby exclusively qualify to get a copy of the final report, and also be registered as a member of the IMR Group (IMRG) – all free of charge to retailers, but only if they completed the survey.

The National Interactive Video Centre (NIVC) in Stephenson Way, Euston, was very helpful and its director, Angus Doulton, kindly allowed us to operate out of their offices. During our residence there, the NIVC became the European Multimedia Centre.

By the end of 1990, after an intense round of lobbying retail suppliers, we had secured a quorum of a dozen potential sponsors, vocally led by Barclays Bank who particularly liked the idea. From 7 December we were busy mailing out to retailers detailed research questionnaires, seventeen pages long (overlong due to sponsors insistence that a battery of precise questions be included), with a return deadline of 28 February 1991. Questionnaires were sent to 450 senior executives, usually the marketing or merchandising director. We hoped to secure seventy returned questionnaires, and in fact received back seventy-seven, though unsurprisingly not all fully completed.

The founder sponsors of IMRG were Barclays Bank, British Telecom Research Laboratories, British Telecom Visual Communications, IBM, Mars Electronics International, NCR, Philips Interactive Media Systems, Pioneer Laser Technology, Siemens Nixdorf, and Sony Broadcast and Communications.

Barclays was an enthusiastic supporter of IMRG and keen for the research and development work to continue. Steve Dobson of Barclays, who later became IMRG's first chairman, suggested that we try to form a relationship with one of the major consultancy firms, and set up a meeting for us with Dr David Best, a partner in Touche Ross Management Consultants' (TRMC) Advanced Systems Division, on 6 February 1991. Dr Best quickly assimilated the situation and asked us what we needed. We agreed that our primary requirement was for 'a home' for IMRG, which Dr Best kindly offered in the form of desk space in TRMC's offices, in return for TRMC becoming an IMRG sponsor. A smoker at the time, I asked Dr Best if it would be OK for me to smoke in TRMC's offices. 'You can burst into flames for all I care,' he retorted. Over the following weeks we engaged with Dr Best's team, and Chris Marsh and I set up IMRG's office in Hill House, TRMC's headquarters in Shoe Lane, just off Fleet Street in central London.

TRMC remained very generous to and supportive of IMRG, enabling us to significantly raise our ambitions, and continued to host the growing organisation within its offices for the next eight years (1991–1999). We were in illustrious company: local hearsay had it that senior TRMC partners could leap over tall buildings in a single bound. In 1995, Touche Ross became Deloitte via a merger, and thereby one of the 'Big Four' accounting organisations and the largest professional services network in the world by revenue and number of professionals.

Although there had been few actual IMR implementations thus far, the much-hyped topic was generating significant interest amongst retailers who wanted to understand both the opportunities and threats it might pose. IMRG's aim was to simplify the process of understanding and implementing IMR for all concerned, and to share what had been learned from work already done.

One of the TRMC team who routinely worked with us was Chester Wallace, a management consultant in the retailing practice with seventeen years' experience working for Boots and Argyll Foods, where he had been merchandising director. Chester also managed the monthly analysis and reporting of the British Retail Consortium's then new monthly *Retail Sales Index*, the retail industry's official key performance indicator. Chester made important contributions to IMRG's work, not least the two charts below, from the introduction of the first IMRG Report:[8] *IMR and the Retail Profit Model*, and *Improving the Shopping Experience*. These charts succinctly captured the aspects of retailing that interactive media could impact – i.e. almost all of it.

The original findings of the 1990/1 IMR research project – two large binders containing all the details, copies of the completed surveys, and data – together with the first IMRG report were presented to the sponsors on 27 September 1991 at

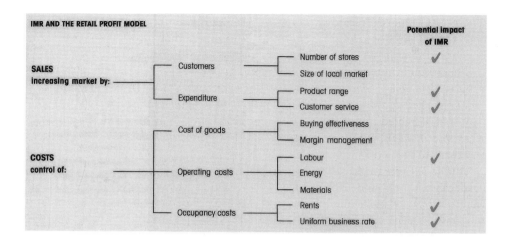

Figure 7: Chester Wallace's charts in the first IMRG Report, 1991: 'IMR and the Retail Profit Model', and 'Improving the Shopping Experience'. (*Source: James Roper Archive*)

TRMC's offices. The thirty-six-page report contained case study examples of the use of IMR, a set of good practice guidelines, and a summary of the survey results.

In October 1991, a larger presentation of the findings was held for the retailers who had completed and returned questionnaires. About eighty retailers attended. Normally a vociferous bunch, the attendees sat through the presentation in silence. At the end, when copies of the IMR report were distributed, the retailers remained tight-lipped. Questions were invited, but none was forthcoming – no delegate made any comment. Was it just too early for them to have views, or did this signal how far out of their comfort zones these retailers were? Were they being guarded, overwhelmed or underwhelmed? We could not tell. It was strange.

* * *

The IMRG report's research findings held few surprises for us, but it was a unique and sizeable poll of relevant senior retail executives that provided an important benchmark against which changing opinions could be measured over time.

The research identified the most popular putative use of interactive media as being an '*in-store product guide*': this was unanimously voted for. An '*electronic store window*', a '*test-bed for new marketing strategies*' and a '*moving poster*', were all possible uses that attracted more than 70 per cent of the vote. The least favoured options were '*shop in a box*', with just 35 per cent, and '*multifunction vending machines*', with less than 30 per cent.

Our focus was on kiosks as the internet was still largely unheard-of outside academia. All respondees opted for touchscreen as the interface of choice rather than buttons, joysticks or a mouse / rollerball. Sixty per cent favoured small desk-mounted screens compared with 40 per cent who preferred large free-standing displays. Seventy-eight per cent of respondees preferred single distributed screens, rather than banks of them.

With regard to the potential benefits of IMR, retailers consistently ranked top '*product information without staff*', followed closely by '*consistently deliver information*', '*staff product knowledge*', '*position products correctly*', '*product demonstration*', '*cut queues*' and '*training*'.

Other than sales, retailers considered '*customer loyalty / satisfaction*' the most important factor, and were more interested in using IMR to give non-product information than to use it to achieve transactions without salespersons.

Major concerns were '*low acceptance by customers and staff*', '*difficult integration with current systems*', '*poor security*' and '*the investment being superseded by newer technology*'.

Asked about their willingness to invest, 56 per cent indicated they would fund a pilot project themselves, while a whopping 72 per cent indicated that they would co-fund a project with others. Forty retailers indicated interest in participating in syndicated projects such as '*product presenters*', '*through-the-window*' facilities and '*staff sales aids*'.

These last points were key insights for us that led us to establish a programme of syndicated *IMRG Pathfinder* projects in the following years, developing 'generic' solutions that avoided the need for much of the time-consuming and costly 'bespoke' work usually required.

Retailers under pressure to try new ideas

During the 1980s consumers had been relatively affluent, living for the present, motivated by experimentation and impulse buying – as evidenced by there being 14,000 products toting the high-flying luxury brand name: Gucci. Increasing consumer credit had fuelled strong retail sales growth, but the decade ended with a rapid decline in shoppers' expenditure. The number of large UK retail grocery outlets continued to shrink, having halved from over 100,000 to 50,000 between 1971 and 1987.

In the early 1990s there was a global recession in which the combined effects of high interest rates and the threat of unemployment led to a collapse in consumer spending. Central Statistical Office figures showed that consumers saved 10 per cent of their disposable income in the last quarter of 1991 compared with just 4.1 per cent at the beginning of 1988 – shoppers had money but were not inclined to spend it.

People also valued time as much as money, especially as increasingly both adults in a household were working. US research showed that the average number of visits to shopping malls each month fell from 3.1 in 1980 to two a decade later, and the number of hours spent shopping weekly slumped from twelve to four.

For retailers, the main issues confronting them in 1991 were static or declining sales, steadily rising store occupancy and operating costs, a heavy burden of debt, demographic change, and increased difficulty in recruiting, motivating and retaining staff.

All this forced retailers to carefully examine every available means of reducing costs, improving the productivity and profitability of their existing assets, and to look for new opportunities for increasing efficiency and gaining competitive advantage in the distribution of their goods and services.

Furthermore, consumers were becoming familiar and comfortable with technology such as personal computers, fax machines, cellular telephones and satellite television channels, and they expected retailers to use technology to improve the speed and convenience of retail services.

Yet despite this, there was a widespread perception that the first generation of interactive media had not fulfilled its promises. Retailers were deeply uninterested in the IT aspects. IMRG research showed that few appreciated the ability of IMR systems to serve customers out of hours, at remote locations or at home. Hardly any had thought of IMR in the role of a counselling tool, helping sales staff to serve customers.

Nevertheless, a Frost & Sullivan report ('The European Market for Multimedia Products & Services') estimated the overall multimedia market to have been worth $2 billion in Europe in 1991, and projected that it would increase at a real average annual growth rate of 13 per cent, to reach $3 billion by 1996.

Computer technology had already become a vital ingredient in successful retailing, and patterns had emerged in the way retailers adopted new technology. For example, EPOS (Electronic Point of Sales) systems had first appeared in 1981, taking advantage of then new personal computers. Retailers struggled with EPOS for a decade, during which many pilots were tried and abandoned. Eventually a few of the majors rolled it out. Others soon followed and EPOS became commonplace, an everyday fact of retail life and a necessity.

IMR was increasingly being perceived as a vital area for strategic development. IMR had been through a decade of pilots, so was it now poised for its day in the sun?

Technology Soup

'Foolproof and incapable of error'

Self-description by the HAL Nine Thousand computer, the sentient villain in Stanley Kubrick's 1968 science fiction film '2001: A Space Odyssey' (fans noticed HAL was a one-letter shift from the name IBM – both Arthur C. Clarke and Kubrick denied that this was a dig at the computer company)

The integrated circuit (IC) chip had been invented in the late 1950s. There is no consensus on who invented it, as several people made essential contributions over a number of years, though Jack Kilby of Texas Instruments was awarded the 2000 Nobel Prize in physics 'for his part in the invention of the integrated circuit'.[9] ICs contain tiny transistors, of which 99.9 per cent are the metal-oxide-silicon (MOS) transistor type. MOS transistors are the most frequently manufactured artefact in history, with an estimated 13 sextillion (13 followed by 21 zeros) having been produced between 1960 and 2018.[10]

These semiconductors are the brains of modern electronics and the primary components of personal computers, mobile phones and most consumer electronics. Semiconductors have driven advances in communications, computing, transportation and countless other applications.[11] The scaling and miniaturisation of MOS transistors has been the driving force behind the growth of the semiconductor industry, which recorded sales of more than $481 billion in 2018.[12]

In 1971 Intel, producer of silicon 'microchips', introduced the world's first microprocessor, a development that changed much of the industrial world. A decade later, IBM launched the Intel microprocessor-based *personal computer* (PC) which became the worldwide business computer hardware standard. By the early 1990s desktop and portable systems were delivering computing performance hundreds of times that of the original PC and approaching that of mini- and mainframe computers.

This power, together with advances in telecommunications, data storage capacity, and the digitisation of pictures, video and sound, allowed many types of information to be stored, processed and shared electronically. These elements, and peripheral devices such as touch-sensitive screens, were the building blocks for automating customer-oriented shopping operations – *interactive media in retail*.

Home computers

'There is no reason for any individual to have a computer in his home'

Ken Olsen, CEO, Digital Equipment Corporation, 1977

Computers first invaded UK homes in the 1980s, when futuristic machines such as the Sinclair ZX81, Commodore 64, BBC Microcomputer and Apple II with a millionth of the power of a modern smart phone provided a laughably primitive experience by modern standards. Britain, always one of the earliest European countries to adopt new technology, had the highest level of computer ownership in the world in 1983.[13]

By the early 1990s home computing was still a daunting adventure with crashing software, chunky text on large cathode ray tube monitors that monopolised much of your desk, and the nightmare of impossible-to-configure dot matrix printers that instead of your short paragraph would spew out 50 sheets of paper with one letter on each. But things were changing fast and starting to impact everyday communications, entertainment, education and work. The scale and speed with which consumers began to embrace computing took both hardware and software companies by surprise.

'Santa bombarded with requests for PCs' ran a headline in the *Sunday Times* on 20 November 1994. A Gallup poll had found that buying a personal computer was second only in Santa's postbag to flying abroad on holiday. It beat a mountain bike, a sound system and a designer outfit as the ultimate present. Those who most wanted a PC were aged 35–44 and living in London and the southeast. The survey concluded that families with children aged 11 to 15 were most likely to ask for a computer – email was the main motivation for most people. 'Don't be surprised by this, as email is cheap, fast, easy and powerful. It does not levy any extra cost in time or money when posting overseas; email sent to America and Japan can arrive within two minutes of pressing the carriage return key.'

Compaq sold more personal computers than any other company in 1994, mainly those of the company's highly successful *Presario* domestic range, overtaking IBM as the world's leading PC supplier. Compaq had 10.3 per cent of the world PC market while IBM and Apple each had 8.5 per cent.[14]

Only one leading PC company grew faster that year: Packard Bell, which concentrated solely on home PCs. Packard Bell doubled its worldwide shipments, growing its market share to 4.9 per cent, propelling the company into fourth place in the world's PC-makers' league, ahead of big brand names such as Dell, NEC and Gateway.

Compaq had ridden the rising tide of home PCs well, but even it underestimated demand and suffered from stock shortages in the run-up to Christmas 1994, as did other manufacturers. IBM, its great rival, was estimated to have lost sales of around $100 million through over-conservative forecasting of demand for its Aptiva home range.

Several companies, including Compaq, Packard Bell and ICL, were also looking at developing PCs that would double as full-screen TV sets.

The gadget glut

By the early 1990s, a spate of new technology and domestic multimedia systems was arriving, each jockeying to be the next 'big thing' and establish its proprietary design as a de facto standard through market dominance. The major tech suppliers were looking to repeat the same fantastic level of growth witnessed in the 1970s and 1980s, but instead of the increasingly saturated business market, they were looking for this growth in fast-moving consumer goods. Silicon chips' ability to motorise innovation seemed limitless. But the glut of gadgets and standards rivalries confused the market and led to inertia.

New devices launched in 1991/2 included *CDTV* (Commodore Dynamic Total Vision) from Commodore, and *CD-I* (Compact Disc Interactive) from Philips. These were both derivations of the 12cm (4.7") CD and marketed as all-in-one multimedia devices. However, the anticipated demand for such appliances failed to materialise and neither device enjoyed any real commercial success.

In February 1992, Sony announced that it would have a new hand-held CD-ROM player that would run Microsoft's MS-DOS – quickly dubbed the *BookMan* – in US shops by Christmas. Within weeks of the Sony announcement, Apple announced that it would work with Sharp on the introduction of its *PDA* (Personal Digital Assistant) technology.

These developments represented the next generations of computer technology: *personal digital assistance* (envisaged as a combination of the telephone and the *Filofax*), and home-based interactive entertainment and education systems.

Just-in-time: telecommunications

Intel, with a 1991 turnover close to $5 billion, predicted that, as the pace of competition picked up, we would come to the threshold of 'just-in-time business' where getting the right information to where it is needed quickly would become the prime competitive advantage, and that this would be facilitated by a worldwide interactive communications infrastructure, allowing all forms of data to be easily shared and moved from anywhere to anywhere: an environment in which interaction took place naturally, despite barriers of space and time.

It was calculated that telecommunications alone could generate up to 7 per cent of world GDP by the end of the 1990s, and the range of possibilities was expanding rapidly. In March 1992, at the World Administrative Radio Conference, the global radio frequencies regulatory body added yet another powerful ingredient into the interactive media mix when it announced approval of frequency allocation for global satellite-based voice and messaging systems.

Global satellite systems were planned which would enable telephone calls from anywhere on earth, as well as global messaging and tracking services. An ambitious example was a plan put forward by Iridium, a subsidiary of Motorola which was itself a major manufacturer of silicon chips, to launch sixty-six satellites to enable customers to use pocket phones anywhere in the world.[15] Over the next five years, at least nine similar projects would apply for licences.

Iridium – Motorola Corporation's $5 billion debacle

The Iridium constellation of 66 low-Earth-orbit satellites was planned in the mid-1980s. But the system was archaic by the time it was deployed in 1998, offering global communications from a brick-size, $3,000 phone at charges from $6 to $30 a minute. By August 1999, Iridium was bankrupt, however it was salvaged by the Pentagon and flies still, six groups of eleven 1,412-pound satellites orbiting Earth every 100 minutes.[120] Motorola, itself one of the big players in the cell phone revolution that made Iridium obsolete, should have known better.

A direct relationship was anticipated between the development of telecommunications and overall growth of economic activity, and this motivated the European Community telecommunication policy of the day. It had three major aims: promotion of an integrated pan-European infrastructure; stimulation of a homogenous European market for services and equipment; greater competitiveness among European industry.

In the UK, dozens of companies were starting to chip away at profitable niches within the deregulated UK telecoms market, and were using new technologies and approaches to help them do so. Examples of this included: 'radio tails', which were telephone aerials on the roofs of houses to transmit telephone calls using radio signals to and from local exchanges; VSAT, offering roof-to-roof communications via satellite; *mobile communications* – three groups were licensed to form *Personal Computer Networks*, a service competing with the two existing cellular services (Vodafone with 700,000 subscribers, and Cellnet with 550,000). Also, *capacity resellers* were emerging, who bought bulk capacity on trunk lines to provide customers with phone services.

E-retail Takes Shape: The Early 1990s

'If you're competitor-focused, you have to wait until there is a competitor doing something. Being customer-focused allows you to be more pioneering'

Jeff Bezos, Amazon

Some significant IMR investments began to be made in the early 1990s. For example, Sears Roebuck, one of the largest retailers in the US, after years of testing various interactive media applications, announced plans in January 1992 to eliminate 7,000 jobs and achieve annual cost savings of about $50 million, through a $60 million investment programme in automated customer service facilities. The development of 28,000 new Point of Sale terminals and 6,000 automated customer service 'mini-kiosks' also enabled 676,000 square feet of back-office space to be converted to selling space.

Again, in the US, TV Answer Inc. invested some $30 million to launch a two-way television system to enable viewers to order advertised goods, check bank balances, transfer funds and pay bills, even order a pizza – all without using a telephone. This took advantage of the US Federal Communications Commission's authorisation, on 16 January 1992, of the use of radio spectrum for the application of two-way interactive video and data services.

Zanussi, whose UK network of 75 *Satellite* IMR counter-top terminals in electrical retailers had for several years consistently increased sales by 25 to 30 per cent, as previously mentioned, now installed over 500 of its new *Optima* information terminals, and then a further 250 units.

Dozens more multimedia trials and developments were coming to light throughout Europe across a broad spectrum of applications including travel, pharmaceutical, utilities, public information, postal services, grocery, electronic home shopping, home entertainment, music and real estate.

In France, a network of over 100 *Audiocatalog* systems, a digital interactive music catalogue, had been installed in record stores and was being used 900,000 times a month. Customers could select, by artist or album, from 2,000 records, then listen to a music sample and view the record cover. Each interactive terminal had a colour screen, two sets of headphones, and a touchscreen. The catalogue was updated weekly by a central computer which distributed data via ISDN telephone lines to individual sites.

Retail automation using card payment systems, a vital ingredient of IMR, was reported to be increasing rapidly in France, Japan and the USA. In Norway, Statoil, the major fuel retailer, had 500 stations open 24 hours a day in 1992, but very few of them were manned all the time: card readers and PIN pads on or next to the pumps allowed customers to pre-authorise purchases and serve themselves.

Smart cards were also beginning to appear. It was expected that by 1995 over 100,000 Paris parking spaces would be 'smart', following the introduction in November 1991 of *Paris Carte*, a system in which reusable value cards, like phone cards, were being sold in Tabacs. British Gas was planning to convert 700,000 domestic coin-in-the-slot gas meters to smart card readers over the coming five years. Under the British Gas *Quantum* scheme, 6,000 read-write terminals were to be installed in newsagents, post offices and corner shops, which would load the cards with cash and tariff information, and download details of latest meter readings. A successful *Quantum* trial in Newcastle upon Tyne, in which 25 new meters were installed in the St Anthony region, was being extended to 800 meters, and three further pilots were planned for Manchester, London and with South-East Gas.

Also in the UK, the Greater Manchester Transport Executive set out to replace conventional travel cards with a smart system. This project was planned to ultimately involve 40 different bus operators, 700,000 users and 800 retail outlets. Although UK consumers were by then familiar with simple prepaid phone cards, the prospect of national schemes with reusable cards was new and offered exciting possibilities to use spare capacity for other purposes, including retail applications.

1992: IMRG – From Research to Development

'Woolworths' new touch screen approach, launched in May 1993, enables shoppers to call up details of 12,000 CDs, 4,000 videos and 9,000 audio cassettes, and then to see and hear clips from their chosen titles. Apart from being highly entertaining, the system can track down a title from just the artist's name'

Demonstrated at the first IMRG / CBI conference on 23 July 1993, Woolworths' kiosk was the state of the art of interactive media in retail. This was one of a dozen live demonstrations we provided to give delegates hands-on experience with IMR – many for the first time. At the time Woolworths was the largest seller of music and videos in the UK.

The original IMR sponsorship had been for just one phase of research and reporting. However, many of the participating sponsors and retailers wanted the work to continue and asked us to come up with plans for its continuation. A joint proposal was drawn up by IMRG and TRMC to operate IMRG as an annual programme, and on 18 April 1991 this idea was presented at a meeting with the sponsors, whose support and funding was a prerequisite.

The proposal was in two parts: a core programme for the benefit of all members, and optional syndicated *Pathfinder* projects, referred to earlier, that would address areas of specific interest. The core programme aimed to increase awareness of IMR, to help members keep up to date with developments, and provide administrative and management infrastructure for sector development.

The proposal was accepted by a quorum of five sponsors, with others showing robust interest, so we all committed to getting on with a twelve-month programme of work that focused on research, discussion, marketing, disseminating regular reports, setting up pilots and establishing standards.

Figure 8: This 30-cm roundel was displayed by IMRG sponsors on their exhibition stands. A wit asked why the person was pointing out of an aeroplane window. (*Source: James Roper Archive*)

The workplan included two syndicated projects: a *Multimedia Pathfinder* package, with a fixed price pilot, and an *Electronic Home Shopping* collective. In the year to April 1992, IMRG increased its membership by 35 per cent to 105 retail members.

An IMRG members' seminar on *Electronic Home Shopping* (EHS) held in early 1992 identified several significant potential implications for the retail sector if a large installed base of multimedia terminals in homes was to materialise. Domestic multimedia systems could not only be used to carry electronic catalogues, but also – with communication links in place that many such devices were being designed to accommodate – would be capable of providing a complete retail service, including product selection, ordering, payment, and arrangement of delivery or collection.

It was also recognised that home multimedia could blur the boundaries between entertainment, information and retailing. For example, a multimedia *DIY book* might explain how a home development project could be undertaken, calculate the materials needed, provide a shopping list, promote a supplier able to fulfil the order, enable purchases, and then provide online help while the job was in progress.

*   *   *

Numerous barriers still hindered IMR progress in 1992. IMRG analysed more than 200 successful and unsuccessful interactive media projects to reveal the main factors which had combined to hold back wider acceptance of IMR. There were four:

1. a lack of understanding of the benefits that multimedia could provide in the retail environment, which led to poorly defined pilot projects that did not have the full backing of senior management
2. a lack of measurable objectives for the implementation of IMR, and a consequent failure of initial systems to collect meaningful performance information with which to justify further investment
3. the tendency for multimedia projects to be led by companies' IT departments and to concentrate on technical issues rather than on delivering real business benefits
4. poor project management, which often led to long development cycles, higher than expected costs, and systems which did not deliver the benefits expected of them.

IMRG worked to help retailers avoid such barriers, coordinating the vast experience, knowledge and resources of its collective membership, which by this time included retailers, FMCG brands, tech vendors, banks, carriers, law firms, consultancies and an army of other specialist IMR facilitators.

This unique forum enabled people to work in a pre-competitive, collaborative environment that was dedicated to the implementation of successful projects. The approach was vitally useful in this hugely complex and rapidly evolving domain where people didn't know what they didn't know.

*   *   *

IMRG's first office at TRMC in 1991 was in Hill House, a substantial 1970s office building that was beginning to look tired. Our glass-walled room was on a corner of the first floor, immediately above the main entrance.

Across the road was a large, derelict, 1960s office block that filled our view. One day in 1993, I noticed a man walking down the street who stopped at the door of this hulk of a building and nailed a noticeboard on it – a sign which turned out to be a demolition notice. Over the coming months, we watched this eyesore being dismantled until there was nothing left but a hole in the ground some three floors deep. Everything was cleared, all except for a previously invisible-to-us pub at the far side of the plot on Farringdon Street, the Hoop and Grapes, that had been built around 1720, which remained, perched precariously like a last slice of a cake, encased in scaffolding and steelwork.

Slowly, a spectacular new Portland stone and granite-clad building arose on the site, seven storeys high, resembling an elegant ocean liner. As the building neared completion in 1995 we were told that TRMC had leased it and that we would shortly be moving into what would become IMRG's handsome and happy home for most of the next several years: Stonecutter Court. [On 29 January 2019 planning permission was granted for the demolition of Stonecutter Court and the erection of a new thirteen-storey building on the site – a condition was the retention of the old Hoop and Grapes Public House.]

IMRG was shuffled about within TRMC's (latterly Deloitte's) various other London offices from time to time as it grew and TRMC's accommodation requirements fluctuated. One such temporary home that we occupied for a while was around the corner in Peterborough Court, Fleet Street, an imposing Art Deco temple to journalism and the former home of the *Daily Telegraph*. Peterborough Court's façade of Portland stone dates from 1928, but behind this was a lavish new office block, occupied largely by Goldman Sachs, with whom we shared the space in 1993/4.

*   *   *

IMRG continued to operate as an annual programme for the next two years, presenting sponsors with a new proposal towards the end of each year. IMRG established itself as a unique source of independent and authoritative information about the commercial use of interactive media. Several retailers informed us that our information had been a critical factor in supporting their decisions to invest in interactive media, including Argos, Dixons, Sears, Marks & Spencer, Thresher and Woolworths. IMRG also worked on numerous research and development projects with retailers including Allied Lyons, BhS, British Rail, London Underground, TSB, Nationwide and the Post Office.

In April 1993, Chris Marsh's company, Recent Productions, went into bankruptcy and was liquidated, so Chris parted company with IMRG.

IMRG engaged in numerous joint marketing initiatives with organisations including the *Design and Art Directors Association, AIC Conferences, INTECO*, the *British Interactive Multimedia Association*, and the *Centre for the Study of Financial Innovation*. However, our main promotional events at the time were joint conferences and exhibitions with the *Confederation of British Industry* (CBI) held each year in 1993, 1995 and 1996 in their theatre and reception area in *Centre Point*, in London's West End.

By 1994 the number of IMRG sponsors had risen from the original five to eighteen, and our membership, comprising mostly of retailers, increased from seventy-five to 138. The level of interest in interactive multimedia was rising, as was illustrated almost daily by announcements of major investments in infrastructure and applications. This led to an insatiable demand for qualitative and quantitative information about multimedia from potential users, not only in retail, but also in many other sectors of commerce and industry, particularly *advertising, finance, travel, television, cable* and *telecommunications*.

People interested in the issues associated with software, application development, design, and consumer acceptance of multimedia were gravitating to IMRG with requests were for unbiased information, for the findings of the IMRG's ongoing research programme, and for live commercial initiatives, especially those in which they could participate. In addition, many organisations wishing to sell products

Figure 9: The three IMRG / CBI conference and exhibitions held in 1993, 1995 and 1996 were IMRG's main promotional events. (*Source: James Roper Archive. Images used with permission from the CBI*)

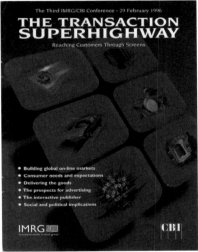

and services to IMRG members sought opportunities to use the association as a channel to inform the market and precisely target clients, their acquisitive behaviour requiring careful stewardship at times!

As the primary forum for IMR activists in the UK, our brief was continually expanding, and our workload increasing. International enquiries were flooding in, and conversations were being held with a view to establishing satellite IMRG operations in Italy, France, Spain, Holland and Australia.

A second IMRG report was produced on the state of IMR in the UK and the views of IMRG members as recorded in our 1993 annual survey. This revealed that over half the respondents were planning interactive media activity, and nearly a third already had an interactive media budget.

At the time, all communication with the IMRG community was via phone, fax or post. Most member organisations would have several people on our circulation list, so sending out reports involved photocopying and binding hundreds of copies, each to be mailed with individual, signed letters in envelopes with transparent address windows. On a regular basis, every photocopier on every floor of one or more TRMC building would be commandeered for the task, with the mailroom sending multiple trollies to collect a hill of sacks bulging with IMRG's outbound post.

*   *   *

In early 1994, it was decided to put IMRG on a long-term commercial footing, and to produce a range of additional products and services that would be sold to sponsors and members at reduced rates, and to non-members at commercial rates. A small team would be recruited to deliver the expanding programme of work.

The consensus was that IMRG should become a legal entity with potential for international expansion. Various options for its structure were considered – forming a charity was mooted but rejected as being too complicated and expensive. In the end we set up IMRG Limited as a standard £2 private company and I agreed to own its equity. As our chairman, Steve Dobson of Barclays, said to me at the time, with a wry grin: 'We sponsors will always control IMRG, because if you disappoint us, we will simply leave, and you'll be out of business.' It was a good call that has worked well ever since.

The new *IMRG Limited* announced several innovations, including a quarterly journal, however the most dynamic and visionary element to be introduced was an *online information service*, either via CompuServe or alternative internet access provider. The aim was to improve communications, massively reduce the management team's workload, and place sponsors in direct contact with an appreciably wider audience. The risk was that not all of our membership community was online, but we planned to turn this to everyone's advantage by making IMRG digital membership *a reason to go online*, encouraging and helping anyone who needed a nudge to join the growing community of *netizens* exploring the *cybersphere*.

Not everyone was thrilled by interactive media's potential. Our 1994 mouse mat 'hedgehogs tried their hardest to uninvent the wheel' nodded at the point, but also alluded to the inevitability of progress.

In 1994, IMRG moved temporarily to Friary Court, another of TRMC's offices, this time in Crutched Friars, a street in the City, near the Tower of London. Friary Court was a monster office block, clad in Swedish red granite, sited on the former home of the *Crutched Friars*, who did not hobble about on crutches but instead were members of the House of the Holy Cross, the Latin for cross being '*crux*'. The Crutched Friars had held a staff with a cross and wore a cross on their habit.

It was at Friary Court that Jo Tucker (latterly Jo Evans) joined IMRG as our managing director, a post she held for the next sixteen years until she retired in 2010. Prior to this, Jo had been helping to organise IMRG activities and events in her role as PA for Mike Braithwaite, one of the senior TRMC partners and responsible for stewarding our relationship. Jo had become interested in IMRG and its potential, and correctly recognised that we urgently needed help with organisation and management, at which she was brilliant. Jo's skill and hard work were largely responsible for IMRG's success in the coming years.

We also brought on board John Burns, who for many years had been with ICL, an IMRG sponsor. John, a Canadian from Thunder Bay, was a super guy and very fit – he had recently been trekking in the Himalayas. John said to me one day: 'The great thing about the internet is that if there is only one other person in the world interested in the same thing as you, you'll be able to find them.' Some months later John was scheduled to represent us as a speaker at an event in Cannes, but when the cab came to take him to the airport, he said he didn't feel well enough to go. Within hours John was in a coma, and tragically, just a few days later, died of suspected Legionnaires' disease. We were devastated.

The Wibbly Wobbly Web

> *'There's so much free content [online], it's going to be extremely hard to get people to pay'*
>
> Mark Andreessen, co-founder of Netscape, February 1996

Our first hands-on experience of the internet was in 1993 when Geoff Page, business development manager of Pipex, invited us to their offices on the Cambridge Science Park to see it in action. Pipex (later UUNet) was the UK's first commercial internet service provider (ISP) and in 1992 began operating a 64k transatlantic leased line. Geoff's demonstration involved us tapping a key on a PC keyboard. A sonar-like 'ping' sounded, followed a short time later by a second 'ping'. Geoff announced proudly: 'We've just pinged an internet server at the McMurdo Station in Antarctica.' The pings measured the round-trip time of a message via a computer network echoed back to the source. It was a real 'so what?' moment for us. But Geoff was persuasive in explaining how the internet worked and its vast commercial potential – especially for retail. With his encouragement and help we launched the first IMRG website in March 1994.

The shrill, screeching, crackling hiss of modem dial tone was familiar to anyone going online or using the internet in the 1990s.[16] The dial-up modem may have monopolised the analogue family phone line – it was one or the other; use the phone or go online – but it was the gateway to the strange new digital world. The frustration of having the internet disconnect every time the phone rang did not enhance the experience.

Tim Berners-Lee had created the first web server while working at the *European Organization for Nuclear Research* (CERN) in late 1990. Test operations began on *ARPANET* (Advanced Research Projects Agency Network), a forerunner on the internet, around 20 December that year. The US military's ARPANET was the first wide-area packet switching network with distributed control that supported government projects, universities and research establishments. Its role over time had expanded to serve most of the world's largest universities and the research arms of many technology companies. ARPANET was officially decommissioned in 1990. The first web content search engine, *Archie*, fired up a few months later, on 10 September.[17]

The creation of the World Wide Web (WWW) made near-instantaneous global computer communication possible, at least theoretically. But in the early days setting up internet access often turned into a nightmare, developing as it had from a mishmash of academic interconnections. It was slow, prone to sudden and erratic glitches, and seemed always to have a rather high proportion of vital servers out of action. There wasn't much to access anyway. Mass market shopping by such a system would obviously be impossible.

Before the widespread adoption of the internet and the World Wide Web there were several pioneering online services such as *CompuServe*, *AOL*, *Delphi* and *Prodigy*. These were proprietary closed-system collections of services. For a fee, subscribers could access a range of amenities such as chat, messaging, software libraries, news, weather, shopping, bulletin boards, games, polls, expert columns, banking, stocks, travel, and a variety of other features.

CompuServe was the first major US online service provider, dominating the sector in the 1980s, and peaking with three million users in April 1995. *CompuServe UK* launched Britain's first national online shopping service on Thursday, 27 April 1995 with what was claimed to be the UK's first secure online transaction, the purchase of a book from the WH Smith shop by Paul Stanfield, the consultant who had originally proposed the online mall idea. Space was sold to major retailers including Tesco, Virgin / Our Price, Great Universal Stores / GUS, Interflora, Dixons / PC World, Past Times, Innovations, Sainsbury's, WH Smith and Jaguar Cars. A million UK shoppers could access these online shops and it was the UK retailers' first major exposure to online shopping. However, CompuServe, with its closed system, or 'walled garden' as these curated selections became known, was slow to react to the rapid development of the open World Wide Web and it was not long before major UK retailers started to develop their own websites independently of CompuServe.

WWW: four breakthroughs

In the mid-1990s, there were four significant developments that each contributed hugely to unleashing the economic potential of the internet as the global network of networks.

In 1994, Tim Berners-Lee founded the *World Wide Web Consortium* (W3C) to 'Lead the Web to Its Full Potential'. *W3C* became the main international standards organisation for the World Wide Web, located at the *Massachusetts Institute of Technology Laboratory for Computer Science* (MIT/LCS), with support from the European Commission and the *Defence Advanced Research Projects Agency* (DARPA), which had pioneered the ARPANET. W3C's promotion of internet openness, interoperability, transparency and vendor neutrality was instrumental in the web's rapid global adoption.

The second significant development was when VeriSign introduced *SSL* (Secure Sockets Layer) secure transaction technology in 1994, which extended the internet's potential from being just an astonishing communications tool into a supercharged global transaction medium as well. SSL is all about encryption of data, like credit card numbers and personal information, and remains the de facto standard for e-commerce transaction security.

Thirdly, until the spring of 1995 the United States government controlled some of the internet's infrastructure, and under the rules of the National Science Foundation, commercial activity on the internet was technically forbidden. In May 1995, the agency relinquished all sponsorship of the internet's network backbone, and thus, too, these restrictions on commercial use of the internet. Email use began to take off as soon as these constraints disappeared.

Netscape Navigator

Netscape Navigator was the first widely available internet browser and the fourth significant development to help unleash the internet. Released in 1994, its share of the web browser market peaked in 1996 at more than 90 per cent. Netscape's IPO on 9 August 1995 is universally considered to be the official start of the dot.com era. The original Netscape Navigator was voted *The Best Tech Product of All Time* by PC World in 2007 due to its impact on the internet.[18]

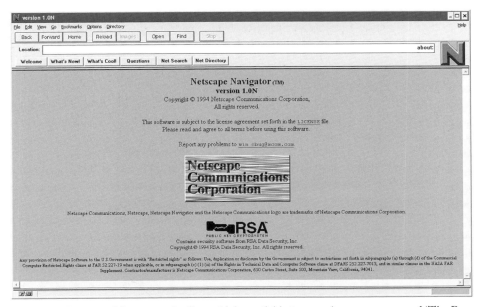

Figure 10: Netscape Navigator, the first widely available internet browser, was voted 'The Best Tech Product of All Time' by *PC World* in 2007. (*Source: James Roper Archive*)

Marc Andreesen, prior to co-founding Netscape, was leader of the team that wrote the *Mosaic* web browser in 1993 at the *National Centre for Supercomputing Applications* (NCSA), a unit of the University of Illinois. Mosaic was a breakthrough browser development that supported multiple internet protocols, provided an intuitive point-and-click interface, and was reliable. It added graphics to otherwise boring text-based software, and ported code across from the specialised Unix operating system onto the popular Microsoft Windows software. Mosaic brought the internet alive, with photos, sound, video, search tools and hypertext links, and made it fun.[19]

Andreesen and four colleagues left the University of Illinois and joined forces with Jim Clark, one of the founders of Silicon Graphics, Inc. (SGI), to form *Netscape Communications Corporation*, in 1994. Together they produced the all-new (but based on Mosaic) browser, Netscape Navigator, that was initially provided free of charge to all non-commercial users, and rapidly became the dominant web browser during the explosive growth period of the 1990s.

Microsoft, which had been uncharacteristically slow to appreciate the internet's potential, barged muscularly into the browser space in 1995 with *Internet Explorer*, first released as part of the add-on package, *Plus! For Windows 95*, and originally based on a licensed version of Mosaic. Internet Explorer soon became available as a free download in service packs, and pre-loaded on new PCs, going on to become the most widely used web browser, cresting with around 95 per cent usage share in 2003.

Bundling Internet Explorer for free enabled Microsoft to rapidly overtake Netscape as the dominant browser, though this led to the US Department of Justice filing an antitrust suit against Microsoft on 18 May 1998 to determine if this constituted monopolistic action. The suit, which Microsoft lost, was brought following the collapse of Netscape, the remnants of which were acquired by AOL in 1999. The Netscape browser's market share plummeted to less than 1 per cent in 2006. AOL officially announced that support for Netscape Navigator would end on 1 March 2008.

Netscape Navigator had been a ground-breaking innovation that created an explosion in technology businesses, the first dotcom millionaires, and a brand-new information, advertising and retail environment. In November 1992 there had been 26 websites in the world:[20] by August 1995 there were 10,000, and by 1998, millions.[21] In 1995, there were 56 million internet users worldwide and global

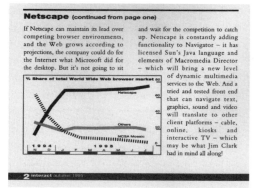

Figure 11: Extracts featuring Netscape from IMRG's newsletter, *Interact*, Autumn 1995. (*Source: James Roper Archive*)

e-retail sales were approaching $300 million. A decade later, there would be nearly a billion users and global e-retail revenues would exceed $150 billion.

Netscape joined IMRG as a sponsor in 1995 and I had lunch with Jim Clark during an event that I was chairing for ICL, at which Jim was a speaker. I was in awe of Netscape and what it was achieving, but few of the delegates seemed to have any awareness of it, so I had the great pleasure of an uninterrupted hour chatting with Jim at around the zenith of Netscape's success. Netscape was then the hottest company on the internet, with over 70 per cent of the browser market, and its position seemed unassailable; therefore, I was taken aback by Jim's bleak view of their prospects. With prescient foreboding he told me that Netscape was at great risk because the major organisations who would most benefit from their services – banks, governments, utilities and so forth – would be too slow to recognise the potential and commit to contracts, leaving Netscape starved of cash and vulnerable.

1994: The First Secure Online Shopping Transaction

'Even if the N.S.A. [US National Security Agency] was
listening in, they couldn't get his credit card number'
Dan Kohn, CEO, Netmarket, August 1994

The many progenitors of online shopping as we know it today include terminal-based services like France's Minitel[22] and Germany's Bildschirmtext[23] that sold train and air tickets in the 1980s. As mentioned earlier, there were also online services such as Prodigy, CompuServe and AOL that early hooked-up American shoppers could use. But these transactions weren't secure – payment was typically made through an account, or by phone or fax.

In 1971/2 students at Stanford University bought marijuana from students at the Massachusetts Institute of Technology (MIT) via ARPANET, according to a Shopify video,[24] which goes on to explain that that can't be the first online sale because it was illegal, no actual funds were exchanged, and it looked more like an instant messaging conversation than the way we buy online today.

Then in May 1984, a 72-year-old British grandmother from Gateshead named Jane Snowball bought margarine, eggs and cornflakes at home using a TV remote control via Videotex from her local Tesco. Jane's groceries were then delivered to her door where she paid by cash. The inventor, Michael Aldrich, who enabled this as part of a council initiative to help the elderly, explained that they had taken a domestic TV and turned it into a computer terminal with a phoneline connection, utilising a Mullard Lucy chip set that was being mass-produced for BT's teletext service, *Prestel*, and Minitel. 'That was the big leap,' Aldrich proclaimed.[25] Three retailers were involved in the Gateshead shopping experiment, Tesco, Greggs and Lloyds Pharmacy, and Mrs Snowball was selected to test the system because she had broken her hip. But this also wasn't the first secure online shopping transaction as no money changed hands online. Videotex was already being used by companies to do business, notably by the travel industry, but the slow, clunky set-up wasn't even close to catching on as a popular home shopping medium. It would be another decade before the breakthrough came that opened the floodgates to what would become a multitrillion dollar industry.

Ten Summoner's Tales

At noon on 11 August 1994, the college graduates that founded *NetMarket* in Nashua, New Hampshire, USA, conducted what is generally considered to be the first ever secure retail transaction on the internet, though some argue that Pizza Hut or The Internet Shopping Network may have just pipped them.

NetMarket was one of the earliest web start-ups, founded by 21-year-old chief executive Dan Kohn with three Swarthmore College classmates. One of Kohn's friends, Phil Brandenberger, that day purchased the CD *Ten Summoner's Tales* by Sting via the NetMarket website. He paid $12.48 plus shipping costs using his Visa credit card and the transaction was protected by commercially available data encryption technology, designed to guarantee privacy. A *New York Times* article the following day that chronicled the transaction credited the company with making e-commerce history.[26]

NetMarket, which described itself as *a shopping mall in cyberspace*, had been selling products such as CDs, flowers and books for several months on behalf of various merchants that leased space, including *Noteworthy Music*, the local store that sold the Sting CD. But this was the first time they had offered *digitally secure* transactions.

Whereas this was a key milestone for online shopping, the solution NetMarket used was no slick consumer experience. It would only work on the small minority of computers running Unix and X-Mosaic software and required the user to have already downloaded a data encryption programme called PGP, for *Pretty Good Privacy*, that required technical proficiency to configure and operate correctly. And as Dan Kohn said in the Shopify video, 'It was just way too hard to set up internet access.'

Kohn, who had come up with the idea for NetMarket during his junior year abroad, at the London School of Economics, commented that they had tons of reaction: 'You're doomed, this will never work, AOL is going to own e-commerce.' But he made a comment that chimed exactly with IMRG's view at the time: 'It just required a tiny a bit of imagination to say, hey, this stuff could get easier over time.'

Dan Kohn was just 21 years old when he celebrated with a champagne toast conducting the first secure online transaction. He lived to see his innovation change history forever but died aged only 47 in 2020 due to complications from colon cancer. Kohn was revered in technology circles around the world. He went on to be the Executive Director of the Cloud Native Computing Foundation, and latterly was General Manager at Linux Foundation Public Health where he leveraged open-source software to help public health authorities fight COVID and future pandemics. The Linux Foundation's in memoriam page for Kohn says: 'Dan was one of the great open-source leaders of our time, a brilliant mind –

devoted to giving back to the community.' Dan Kohn, ecommerce pioneer: 20 November 1972–1 November 2020.

*   *   *

People and businesses were alarmed by the growing number of security breaches on the internet in 1994, and therefore reluctant to transmit sensitive information online. Iron-clad security was obviously essential if commercial transactions were to become common on the internet, in order to make data communications immune to wiretaps, eavesdropping and theft. But the development of standard data encryption software had been hindered by government regulations and software patent disputes. The Clinton administration was pushing for a US national standard, based on the *Clipper* system, which the government had software keys to open and read. PGP, that NetMarket used, was considered to be as strong as Clipper, but was not controlled by the government. Federal export limits on strong encryption software also hamstrung early e-commerce efforts, as companies grappled with a safe method to collect payments online.

Another remaining problem was that the United States government still controlled some of the internet's infrastructure. As previously mentioned, commercial activity on the internet was technically forbidden until the spring of 1995, when the National Science Foundation relinquished all sponsorship of the internet's network backbone.

Standards were needed for incorporating encryption into web browsers. These began to appear the following year when Netscape introduced a version of its browser that integrated the Secure Sockets Layer (SSL) security protocol, which created a connection between a desktop computer, or client, and a server, over which data could be sent securely. This was recognisable by the web address beginning with 'https' rather than 'http'. Microsoft also adopted the SSL protocol for its Internet Explorer browser, further cementing it as a standard way of securing data online.

The Star-Spangled Banner Ad

'The advertisement is the most truthful part of a newspaper'

Thomas Jefferson, Founding Father and third US president

1994 also spawned a host of other game-changing internet innovations, including Yahoo! Search and what a decade later would be the ubiquitous banner ad.

One of the first-ever banner ads on the web (there are several contenders for being the first) was an advertisement for AT&T, designed by Tangent Design, that was unveiled on 24 October 1994 on *HotWired*, the online forerunner of *Wired* magazine.[27] It asked viewers: 'Have you ever clicked your mouse right HERE?' with an arrow pointing to text that read 'YOU WILL.' Once viewers clicked on the banner ad, they were directed to displays of some of the world's greatest art museums.

For more than four months, 44 per cent of people who saw the banner clicked on it, proving itself to be one of the most effective forms of advertising ever invented.

CLICK HERE CLICK HERE CLICK HERE CLICK HERE

The banner ad first appeared in 1994

The ad was part of an ongoing campaign that AT&T ran about futuristic technical wonders. The ads asked if you had *paid tolls without stopping your car, navigated using a map projected on a dashboard screen, borrowed books from libraries thousands of miles away,* or *tucked your baby in from a phone booth?* All ended with the same promise: 'You will.'

'At a time when people wondered what the web was all about, [the banner ads] demonstrated how AT&T could transport people through space and time via the Internet – just as AT&T had done 100 years earlier with the first long distance telephone network,' Joe McCambley, who helped create the first banner ads, explained in a *Harvard Business Review* article in 2013.[28] People loved and shared the experience. 'It was the first time I heard the term *viral* applied positively. We were onto something,' McCambley said.

Banner ads caught on quickly and enjoyed a brief golden age of *content and utility* in which pioneering digital advertisers set out to create advertising that was *so useful that it was a service – helping* rather than *selling.*

The established advertising agencies were slow to catch on, but they were rudely awoken in 1998 by soaring internet ad revenues. Before long, the medium was subsumed to deliver the only thing big agencies understood – *SALES MESSAGES!!!* – but with added reach and frequency.

It was around this time that we first started seeing ads featuring www addresses appearing on city buses, shopping bags, everywhere. Before long entire truck fleets were being turned into rolling billboards, their vehicle sides displaying giant ads for websites.

The Internet Advertising Bureau (IAB) was founded in 1996, and just two years later reported that 1998 US online advertising revenues had doubled to $1.92 billion, surpassing that of outdoor advertising, at $1.58 billion. In an IAB statement issued in New York on 3 May 1999, chairman Rich LeFurgy said: 'It is easy for us to forget that the Internet, as a viable advertising medium, is barely four years old, and it is astounding, that in such a relatively short period of time, its growth is now measured in billions of dollars'.[29]

Banner ads ignited a chain reaction whereby monetised clicks diverted the whole advertising industry in an entirely new direction. However, what most of the advertising industry failed to appreciate was that people went online to get things done, and banner sales messages that offered no utility, help or value were simply a nuisance. Tricking users to click on banners and shrinking them to fit on mobile devices just made matters worse, breeding resentment and ultimately a major backlash, that we shall look at later.

Meanwhile, in the UK…

'Customers were ahead of us – saying not if but when'

John Wheeler, IS Director, Sears, UK, 1992

1994 was a tough year for UK retail. The economic slump continued and with it the threat of unemployment. Retail sales were weak and volatile. Perpetual 'Sale' notices in shop windows were making shoppers ever more cynical. The UK was effectively an e-commerce technology bystander, awaiting usable tools to emerge from the US where all of the major developments were taking place.

By 1994 retailers were beginning to recognise that digital technology might bring about significant opportunities and threats for them. The IMRG membership was growing. We were tackling the issues central to the development of e-commerce, encouraging retailers to learn how to use digital capabilities that would evidently soon become business-critical for them. We flagged worldwide retail innovations and illustrated with examples how quickly change could arise in this complex and mercurial environment.

IMRG syndicates formed to research and propose viable solutions for payments, copyright and security. Our teams identified and published guidelines for successful IMR implementation. These activities would lead to IMRG establishing e-retail standards and accrediting suppliers, as framed in the IMRG Code of Practice, which we would publish in 1997.

Our fledgling internet site was live, and we were tentatively sending our very first emails. *Would they get there? How would we know?*

Kiosk kings

While all this e-commerce stuff was interesting and pointed towards change in the future, most of IMRG's hardnosed UK retailer members were focusing on the short-term and what they considered to be the concrete, immediate, predictable now, paying little attention to strategy, fundamentals and long-term value creation. Some told us that if an IMR marketplace ever did take off then they would jump in hard and dominate in that channel too. As a result, the modest amount of IMR activity happening in the UK was still focused almost entirely on kiosks. The few exceptions included QVC, launching its first home shopping TV channel in the UK, and BT, announcing that it was ready to start trials of video-on-demand down existing telephone lines.

Argos continued trialling its *Purchase Point* kiosks in 1994. Argos was Europe's largest catalogue store chain with sales that topped £1 billion in 1992, selling a wide range of consumer durables from more than 300 UK outlets. The customer *Purchase Points* were claimed to be the first of their kind in the UK, with ICL touch screen units that linked straight into the store's computerised stock system

Figure 12: Woolworths was the largest seller of music and videos in the UK in 1994. (*Source: James Roper Archive*)

and facilitated instant ordering, payment and collection. Ray McCann of ICL, who was IMRG's chairman at the beginning of that year, kept us posted on the project's progress.

Woolworths claimed its interactive computer system to be a world first when it was launched during the spring of 1993, and in 1994 began rolling it out. Woolworths, with 790 stores, was the largest seller of music and videos in the UK. Part of the Kingfisher Group, it contributed £78 million to the 1992 group profit of over £200 million. Its IMR systems enabled shoppers to call up details of 12,000 CDs, 4,000 videos and 9,000 audio cassettes, then see and hear clips from their chosen titles. IMRG produced a case summary within its 1994 annual report that noted: '*The system, as well as being highly entertaining, enables shoppers to quickly and easily track down a title, even if they only know the artist's name. It is also an ultra-efficient ordering system for the more obscure titles not held in stock by the store. Using the computer, customers can select the albums or videos of their choice, and if they're not in stock they simply pay for them at the checkout in the normal way, and then the item is mailed to their home free of charge, usually within seven days.*' Woolworths' Trading Controller for Entertainment, Charlie McAuley, commented: 'Interactive computers have been tried in-store by other retailers before, but there has never been anything as sophisticated as this, with its facility for offering full audio as well as high-quality moving images.'

Woolworths UK had been founded in Liverpool on 5 November 1909. At its peak in the late 1960s it had 1,141 branches. On 26 November 2008 trading in Woolworths shares was suspended and it entered administration. Deloitte subsequently closed all 807 stores with 27,000 job losses

Sears Childrenswear, the UK's leading childrenswear retailer, continued the rollout of its MUMs (*MUltiMedia information systems*) in 1994, their having been very well received by both customers and staff. MUM self-contained kiosks were installed in eight Pride & Joy stores, and several of its 289 Adams Childrenswear outlets. The aim was to provide a one-stop-shop offering a comprehensive range of products from maternity wear, babywear, toys and toiletries through to safety products, nursery furniture and pushchairs. IMRG's case summary of the time explained: 'MUM has enabled Pride & Joy to extend the range of merchandise that it can offer: different colourways, different products, even a manufacturer's entire range can all be displayed within a modestly sized store, and without the associated stock holding cost. By using multimedia, products and their specific features and uses can be presented in detail. The message is simple: *If you need advice, just ask MUM.*'

Other kiosk pilots running in 1994 included Boots, Peugeot with a Philips CD-I-enabled kiosk for dealerships and motor shows, Ladbrokes trialling its automatic betting system, Vantage Chemists which rolled out 50 kiosks, Home Real Estate whose 120 *Home Vision* kiosks across Denmark had been successfully selling homes since 1990, and the Consumers' Association *Which? Plant* kiosks installed in a mock garden shed.

Barclay Square's virtual mall

Following hard on the heels of CompuServe UK's launch of an online shopping service on 27 April 1995, in June Barclaycard launched *Barclay Square*, another early attempt to create a virtual shopping mall, as a way to explore the potential of sales on the internet.[30]

While shoppers may have been nervous of shopping online, so too was the bank. For Barclays, the two major challenges at the time were connecting website pages to payment capabilities, and trust: Barclay Square set out to address both. The participating retailers, all customers of Barclays Bank including Interflora, Toys 'R' Us, Eurostar, Victoria Wine and Argos, joined Barclays on a steep learning curve. For example, Barclays had to hire a photographer to provide digital pictures as the retailers had none. And they soon learned that forcing visitors to register their details on arrival severely hindered take-up.

Simple shop pages presenting a few products were set up for each retailer, with shopping baskets that connected to Barclays' payment capabilities. Barclay Square also claimed to have conducted Britain's first secure online payment.

There was a high level of interest in the Barclay Square initiative: 14,000 people passed through its virtual doors in the first twenty-four hours of business. But a Barclays spokeswomen said at the time that they could not yet say how many people went on to buy anything as 'It takes a few days to process the credit card transactions.' Actual purchases remained stubbornly low. Some months later *The Independent*, reporting Argos' results, said that its store on the Barclay Square *virtual shopping mall* had performed poorly, selling *hardly anything* in the first few months of business, according to Argos' chief executive Mike Smith. He said in the article, dated August 14, 1995: 'I think this kind of electronic shopping might be six or seven years away from widespread customer acceptance.'

*   *   *

The fourth IMRG survey, *Selling Through Screens*, set out to identify the prevailing issues that motivated or deterred adoption of interactive media for marketing and transactions. The survey was completed in Q2 1995, with questionnaires being returned by 140 organisations that collectively operated through 18,000+ sales outlets worldwide (11,500 in the UK and 6,500 in the rest of the world) with annual sales turnover in excess of £475 billion.

The four most common reasons given for not using interactive media were:

1. We have a major investment in stores which we do not wish to write down
2. We are delaying until the UK cable infrastructure has greater penetration
3. We will make a commitment when competitive pressures require it
4. We are waiting for smart cards to become widely available.

Shortage of development finance in the retail industry was also identified as a significant problem. Other difficulties included: *development times were too long*; *inability to accurately represent products because of low/poor image resolution*; *customer education*; *ease of operation/interface, in terms of both design and integration with business systems*; *visibility of screen image in daylight/sun/reflection from overhead lights*; *printers*!

WH Smith: Self-help books, anyone?

'I don't have email'

Tim BIythe, Head of Corporate Affairs, WH Smith Group, 1998

Having a long-term strategy was essential for success with IMR, but retailers were almost entirely absorbed with short-term issues. This misalliance led to many lost opportunities and some calamitous mistakes. Of all retailers, WH Smith should have seen and seized the internet retailing opportunity, but instead was about to make what was surely one of the biggest mistakes the UK e-retail sector would ever witness.

In 1995, at around the same time that Amazon.com was selling its first book, Britain's largest bookseller, the venerable 200-year-old WH Smith, had sales of some £1.5 billion through its 900+ stores. That year, Terence Cudbird, then WH Smith's Group Business Development Manager, told me that 80 per cent of WH Smith's product portfolio could be digitised, and therefore WH Smith could be threatened by disintermediation by suppliers, new channels of distribution, substitution of products, and new competitors including international challengers.

In 1966 WH Smith had originated a 9-digit code for uniquely referencing books, called 'Standard Book Numbering' or SBN. It was adopted as international standard, ISO 2108, in 1970, that was used until 1974, when it became the ISBN scheme.
ISBN enabled internet book sellers such as Amazon to set up.

WH Smith was not new to electronic commerce. Their in-store service, *WH Smith Bookfinder*, had won the 1994 BT Retail Technology Award, and was the precursor of WH Smith's first online bookstore which launched on CompuServe UK in April 1995, offering 250 popular books and CD-ROMs available for search and home delivery (the overall bestseller was *The Joy of Sex*). In fact, the UK's first ever secure online transaction was almost certainly a book bought from WH Smith sold on CompuServe UK.

Allan Mitchell, WH Smith's development manager who had created and was responsible for *Bookfinder*, was a man of considerable vision who had worked for WH Smith for more than fifteen years. He built arguably the best interactive media team in Europe with twenty-four staff at its peak. Critically, Mitchell had done the crucial and difficult R&D work to enable WH Smith to exploit at will any electronic channel – internet, kiosks, interactive TV, etc. Mitchell told me that by January 1996, online sales per week were the equivalent of about 33 per cent of store take from the same population, with 25 per cent of orders being taken from overseas.

But WH Smith was going through a difficult phase during 1995/6 and appointed a new chairman, Bill Cockburn, to sort the company out. Cockburn only worked for WH Smith for a few months, but during his tenure he sacked the entire interactive media team to *be rid of non-core operations, to save money*, and *to avoid the risk of cannibalising store sales*, in the belief that it would be years before

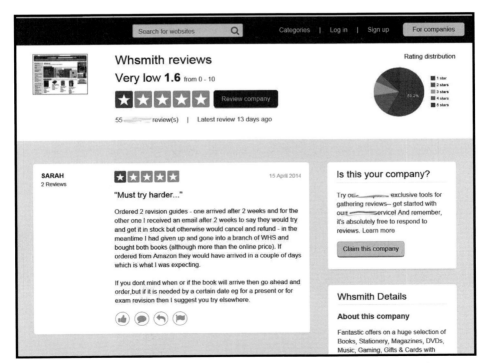

Figure 13: WH Smith's website attracted criticism: this consumer review of 28 April 2014 was typical. 'Very Poor'—scoring one out of ten in 58.2 per cent of the last fifty-five reviews. (*Source: James Roper Archive*)

online selling became important. They could think about that later. One of the people Cockburn sacked was Simon Murdoch who went on to establish the online retailer *Bookpages*.

Amazon announced on 27 April 1998 that it had acquired Bookpages to become a fundamental component of its expansion into the European marketplace, and promptly renamed it Amazon.co.uk.

On 8 June 1998, spurred on by Amazon's purchase of Bookpages, WH Smith bought Europe's leading online book business, *The Internet Bookshop* (iBS – www.bookshop.co.uk), for £9.4 million in what was then by far the largest internet commerce investment by any European retailer.

But WH Smith's management team never seemed to understand e-commerce and failed to invest in or drive its online business.

More than two decades later, in May 2019, a BBC News item indicated that management problems at the bookseller endured when it reported that WH Smith has been ranked the UK's worst High Street retailer for the second year in a row, according to a *Which?* survey of 7,700 shoppers. The poll, which covered 109 retailers, rated the chain *very poor* for value for money and in-store experience. A WH Smith spokeswoman commented: 'This survey… is neither statistically relevant nor meaningful relative to our loyal customer base.'

1995: Convergence

> *'So sudden has been the upsurge of the World Wide Web – effectively since late 1994 – that corporate and investment America is staring wild-eyed at this new phenomenon which they barely understand'*
>
> The Convergence Report, Dialogues 2000, October 1995

Tropical storms and hurricanes regularly buffet the east coast of the US then reappear as dominant, local weather systems over the UK. In a similar way, the North American experience of technological, commercial and social developments often provided a model of how changes would impact corresponding industries in the UK some one or two years later.

To provide an early warning of turbulent changes on the way for enterprises in the UK as a result of the convergence of the telecommunications industry and the computing industry, the UK Department of Trade and Industry (DTI) funded a six-person study visit (I was one of the six) to more than forty US and Canadian companies active in the space during July 1995. These key companies visited included:

- **Telcos and Cablecos** such as Bell Canada, Videotron and Nynex
- **Speech processing technology and systems suppliers** such as Voice Processing Corp., Brite Voice Systems, Wildfire, Octel and Rhetorex

- **Computer hardware and software companies** including Silicon Graphics, Sun Microsystems, EDS, Creative Labs., Apple computers, Oracle and Microsoft
- **Online service providers** like Delphi, AT&T Interchange and Prodigy
- **Internet enterprises** including Netscape, e-Shop and Sony.

Mervyn Jack, director of CCIR at the University of Edinburgh, set up the expedition, with help from Roger Essam and his team at Forrester Research of Cambridge, Massachusetts. Mervyn then led the visit along with experts from BT (Mark Hewett, manager of network voice applications, and Fred Stentiford, head of dialogues for network services), GUS Home Shopping Network (John Andrews, electronic retail director), the Royal Bank of Scotland (Les Cashin, research consultant) and me, representing IMRG (James Roper, managing director).

The team presented its findings at a packed IMRG event in October 1995, where it also published its 48-page *Convergence* report, compiled by IMRG's editor, Ian Thompson. The report provided a detailed analysis of how the two technologies upon which much of the world's commerce and industry was dependent – telecommunications and computing – was on a global scale creating a revolution in the way we live and the way we do business. It noted that in the US, convergence was already impacting enterprises which were being forced to reposition themselves to accommodate the implications of convergence through *co-opetition* – in other words cooperation and collaboration, even with competitors, customers and suppliers – to create new opportunities and to sustain market positions in the new electronic world.

To the US companies interviewed, the location and significance of the point of the convergence depended on their attitude, vested interests and position in the value chain for a market sector. To some, the convergence was happening in the personal computer, which was then shipping with a modem installed. To others, the key convergence point was the server, or the network, or the user interface. The important thing was that the magnitude of the convergence meant that all these points of view were equally correct.

The challenge facing every organisation – public or private, large or small, global or local – was to understand the factors that were driving convergence, and how to position their organisation to take advantage of the new opportunities. The report's message was aimed primarily at technology exploiters – government, retailers, bankers and businesspeople – who might not yet realise that their organisation was part of the expanding sector that comprised telecommunications and computing.

The threat was that interactive online channels enabled the buyer to go directly to the maker, in a process of *dis-intermediation*, that completely changed the value chain in many sectors. The report stressed that retailers, distributors and intermediaries that failed to add value by exploiting the potential of the new electronic media, might find themselves cut out entirely. Driving the growth of interactive technology was people's desire to communicate – accelerating its development and forcing its proliferation – just as the telephone did in the 1950s.

In the US, the pace of this convergence meant that networking and information technology was already becoming mission-critical for almost all types of enterprise.

The desktop computer, once littered with a variety of plug-in devices for separate functions, was being transformed into a multimedia terminal combining telephony, fax, video, email and computing. The systems behind this desktop convergence were also converging, with powerful, open-architecture server products pushing telephony closer to the database.

New open standards were set to revitalise the telecommunications sector and were already transforming the voice processing industry. Applications that employed the telephone as the user interface were attractive for many reasons – simplicity, a huge installed user base, and widespread acceptance of telephone-based services. Advances in *Computer Technology Integration* (CTI), voice response and recognition technology were boosting uptake of integrated messaging, intelligent call routing, voice dialling and call answering which, in the past, had been supplied as discrete systems.

Messaging had traditionally been divided into two domains: communications in *real-time*: person-to-person telephony and video conferencing, and *non-real-time*: voicemail, email, letter and telegram. Convergence was evident at all points within and across these domains, all converging at the desktop, and the establishment of common interface standards was allowing cross-system and network communications.

Speech recognition technology was recognised as the key to the evolution of future easy-to-use telephony systems. Apple computer, in collaboration with IBM, AT&T and Siemens had created the *Versit* programme to define interoperability standards for computer and telephony interconnection. Meanwhile, Microsoft was also creating its own interface standard for telephony – *TAPI* (Telephony Applications Programmer's Interface). Speech recognition was described as having 'advanced considerably in the last few years'; however, the US telcos that employed voice dialling reported that only 5 per cent of customers made use of it, typically using around four words out of a potential twenty-word vocabulary. It would be another fifteen years before speech recognition became a major growth-enabling factor for e-commerce.

Strengthening consumer interest in convergence was evidenced by the increasing penetration of PCs in the home. In the US, at Christmas 1994, PC sales exceeded TVs sales (by both volume and value) for the first time. Also, more PCs and associated applications were sold to private individuals than businesses, of which the home PCs had higher functional specifications. By May 1995 40 per cent of US homes had a PC, the majority capable of supporting multimedia applications and features. Technophobia was being eroded by user-friendly *point-and-click* interfaces, such as those provided by Apple and Microsoft.

The internet was of course noted as a crucial point of convergence, but one which still needed new browser tools, faster access and better services if it were to develop into a fully fledged commercial consumer network. In the first three months of 1993, the internet generated five gigabytes of data traffic: in 1995, five gigabytes were being generated every hour. In April 1993 there were fifty servers; in 1995 there were 50,000.

Netscape, then a start-up which we interviewed in their temporary offices in Mountain View, California, was recognised as being in the forefront of driving the internet's commercialisation. Netscape had started out by creating a better World Wide Web browser and widely distributing it as shareware. Seven months later Netscape Navigator was the de facto standard for web browsing, with more than 90 per cent of a market estimated at nine million people.

Enterprises were just waking up to the opportunities of having their own home page and selling advertising space on it. An example of this was Netscape itself, whose homepage was attracting six million *hits* per day and was charging other vendors for links and advertising space on its pages.

However, the Convergence report stated, 'Surprisingly, none of the on-line service providers or Internet technology companies are amassing vast fortunes,' and noted:

- **Netscape** has been giving away its web browser free of charge so that now the majority (75%) of Internet users are Netscape-friendly. That leaves the company with a distinct market advantage: when it comes to enterprises deciding on which server application software to use – Netscape looks good. However, with losses of $4.3 million on sales of $16.6 million, the jury is still out on Netscape's long-term strategy.
- Online service provider **Prodigy**, into which IBM and Sears have reportedly poured $1 billion since 1984, has yet to make a profit.
- **CompuServe**, the world's largest online service provider, earned only $6 million on sales of $104 million in 1994.

In 1995, internet service providers' biggest problem was churn, with typically 30–50 per cent of customers leaving within the first three to six months. Boredom, hunger for greater excitement, and the desire for novelty were contributory factors. In addition, there was a new generation of consumers: techno-literate, accustomed to instant fulfilment and gratification, and with high-tech expectations created by movies, arcade games and CD-ROM multimedia applications. To this community the internet was slow, especially when graphics, text and sound were transmitted at a meagre 14.4 kilobytes per second.

For improved speed of response, ISDN (Integrated Services Digital Network) technology, then ten years old, was a relatively expensive option in terms of support and installation. ISDN take-up had been slow due to lack of software applications that exploited its ability to simultaneously transmit voice, video data and other network services over traditional phone networks. ISDN was seriously challenged by other broadband technologies, notably cable, which was proliferating in the US, with ten times the bandwidth. The Convergence report commented that while a shake-out would happen, it was too early to anticipate the outcome.

Apparent lack of interest by the telecommunications companies in internet operations appeared to be because the telcos were essentially the internet in the first place. The vast majority of all internet data traffic passed along the communications pipes (ultimately) owned by the telcos, who seemed to consider the internet as just another dial tone for them. There was no urgency for the telcos to provide added value as they benefitted from all innovations surrounding the internet anyway.

At the time, about 10 per cent of US households were hooked up to online services, including the internet. Online customers were typically male (75 per cent) and predominantly in the 18–35-year age band, though the proportion of women users was rising. This was significant because, statistically, females traditionally did 60 per cent of the shopping. Prodigy took great pride in the fact that some 42 per cent of its users were female and promoted itself as the *family* service provider.

Prodigy was originally intended to sell online, with its profit being a charge made on each individual sale. But in the light of five years' experience, Prodigy had found that *The consumer driver is people wanting to talk to each other.*

The magic moment for online service providers was when the customer bought something via their channel, particularly things that they could download, such as music, data or information. The hope was that first single purchase would turn into a habit.

But nothing was quite in place. The content providers were all rushing to build and differentiate their services, and it was difficult for them to keep up with the changes. Most online selling channels were simply price lists with ordering done separately, by telephone. Consumers were confused and would remain so until a simple *click here to order* user interface emerged.

The Convergence report went on to examine the prospects for online services (the walled gardens of proprietary services) vs the open internet, the pros and cons of selling online, security, client-server architectures (Sun dominated the internet server market in 1994 with a 56 per cent share), UNIX vs Microsoft Windows operating systems, interactive television, and the outlook for retail kiosks, amongst much else. It concluded with the following prophetic observation.

The Convergence Report, Dialogues 2000, October 1995

'New players with vision are coming along, assessing the new capabilities, exploiting opportunities and redefining their businesses as they move on. New sectors are springing up and new products and services are arriving to sustain them. Many billions of dollars are being pumped into communication and technological advancements in the expectation that the masses will be either converted by the opportunities presented or dragged along by commerce's relentless search for profit, new market opportunities and reduced costs. And as in the past, there will be casualties. Major corporations that thought their profits secure and their markets unassailable, will stand on the sidelines wondering what happened to their customers and their once-mighty businesses.

'Convergence causes change. Change is happening – and happening fast.'

---

*This is the closing statement of the Convergence report,
compiled by IMRG's editor, Ian Thompson*

Windows of Opportunity

'We always overestimate the change that will occur in the next two years and underestimate the change that will occur in the next ten. Don't let yourself be lulled into inaction'

Bill Gates

Setting the scene for a packed IMRG/CBI conference, The Transaction Superhighway, on 22 February 1995 was keynote speaker Bruce Bond, managing director for National Business Communications at BT (British Telecommunications). Bond pointed out that a superhighway had to be something very broad and very fast, and as internet users were only too well aware the net was quite the reverse – narrow, slow and erratic – therefore mass-market shopping by such a system would be impossible anytime soon. There was much work to be done.

During the morning coffee break of the 1995 IMRG/CBI conference, we digitally photographed senior retail delegates. Then, just before lunch, we projected on-screen the new IMRG website, featuring their mug shots, taken just minutes earlier. This was a light bulb moment for many in the audience, as they began to realise the implications for retail.

Apart from unreliable online connectivity, online shopping's other main challenge was that personal computers were expensive, slow, crashed a lot and were generally inadequate.

Windows 95

Microsoft played a huge part in the development of e-retail, especially with the launch of Windows 95, which was a quantum leap forward for personal computing.

Microsoft had entered the computer operating systems (OS) sector in 1980 and by early 1995 dominated the world PC software market with seventy million users and growing by two and a half million a month. Apple with its Mac OS 7.7, and IBM with its rival OS/2, were left trailing far behind with eleven million and five million users each. Microsoft's office-suite bundle, *Microsoft Office* introduced in 1990, had also been a huge success and taken around 80 per cent of the desktop software market while the traditional software behemoths such as Lotus (*Notes*) and Novell (*WordPerfect*) watched in dismay as their revenues plummeted.

Apple had popularised the idea of graphical, easy-to-use computers, however Microsoft had picked up the idea and adapted it for the mass-market PC-compatible computer. But Microsoft's Windows 3.1 disc operating system (DOS) was now old and unfriendly: a cobbled-together fudge of components that was overdue a radical overhaul.

Windows 95 finally arrived more than a year late, labelled as an upgrade, but actually an entirely new operating system. With more than eleven million lines of code compared with the three million lines in its predecessor, it was in effect a blueprint for the future of the PC hardware itself. Bill Gates' huge ambition now encompassed the entirety of modern computing, from applications to communications, from home entertainment to global corporate networks.

Windows 95 was Microsoft's first entirely graphical PC-based operating system, with DOS relegated to a minor role inside the system, mainly to promise some backward compatibility with older applications. It introduced a host of improvements, many borrowed from other innovators, to make it easier to use, and new technical features to make working on a PC faster, more reliable and more flexible than ever.

Its many innovations included *plug and play*, a hardware recognition standard for peripherals such as printers, and a powerful messaging service, *Microsoft Exchange*, that provided a single *inbox* for electronic mail, faxes and voice messages. It also gave a free gateway to a new dial-up online service, the *Microsoft Network* (MSN), available in 40 countries at launch. With monthly minimum fees of around £5, MSN aimed to help email become as commonplace as the then ubiquitous fax machine. MSN also took the company into new online information services and the coming area of electronic finance.

Such a radical new product as Windows 95 with global ambitions would obviously encounter teething problems, so some months before the launch, in an entirely unprecedented exercise in public *beta version* testing, Microsoft issued 400,000 copies of trial software to volunteers around the world, to throw up problems of compatibility with existing applications and hardware.

One thing that this trial demonstrated, very publicly, was that all the extra features in Windows 95 were greedy for PCs' resources and to fully enjoy its benefits millions of users would need to upgrade to computers with more muscle; a 66-megahertz PC and a 486 processor with at least eight megabytes of memory was recommended. This, together with Windows 95's intolerance of old applications and hardware, would guarantee billions of dollars of new business for PC makers and software houses – but only if take-up was as hoped for, which was not certain.

Gates was betting the ranch on the success of Windows 95, but he had to: a major potential threat to the duopoly of Microsoft and the chip giant Intel was set to arrive the following year in the form of an open architecture *PowerPC* chip developed by IBM, Motorola and Apple. Users of the new open PowerPCs would be able to choose to run any one of a number of operating systems on it, not just Microsoft's Windows. On the other hand, if Gates' huge gamble worked, sales of Windows 95 and related products were expected to generate nearly $3 billion in revenues for Microsoft over the coming year.

Win95's move to 32-bit technology enabled applications to run more quickly than conventional 16-bit ones and made the PC much more versatile. If an application crashed it would no longer bring the whole system down, and 32-bit allowed several different applications to run at full speed simultaneously.

Plug-and-play was a game changer for consumers. At the time it was common to spend hours setting up PC peripherals such as printers and CD-ROM drives, and a single installation error could make the device unusable. Plug-and-play promised to enable you to plug a device into your PC or network and work with it straight away. Making this work was a formidable task for Microsoft because IBM PC compatibles that Windows 95 ran on came from a range of manufacturers and embraced a vast number of different chips, technical standards and types of hardware. Microsoft had to write plug-and-play code into the operating system, and then share it with dozens of hardware manufacturers so they could build it into their products and thereby be entitled to display a *Windows 95 compatible* tag.

Many still familiar things that Windows 95 introduced include the *Desktop*, the *Start* menu button, the *Taskbar*, the *Explorer* file manager, the *shortcut* to a file and the ability to drag its icon between folders or onto the desktop, *power clicks* using the right mouse button to bring up a *properties* screen, software *wizards* to walk you through common jobs, and online help facilities.

One awkward niggle with the old Windows 3.1 was that you could only use eight-character filenames, that were too short to be useful: Windows 95 fixed that issue too, enabling 255-character-long filenames.

Multimedia sound, video and animation were all part of Windows 95: a new *AutoStart* facility played CD-ROM titles, music CDs and a new breed of enhanced CDs as soon as they were inserted into the PC. Furthermore, new video compression chips and software were expected to make high-quality TV pictures possible before long.

To help seed the multimedia market, Microsoft had for some years been producing educational software titles on CD-ROM, and with the launch of Windows 95 their sales had boomed. *Encarta*, Microsoft's multimedia encyclopaedia was published in 1993 and by Christmas the following year was outselling rival paper-based titles many times over. Its *Magic School Bus Explores the Human Body* shipped more than 100,000 copies in the run-up to Christmas 1994 in the US alone.

Yet another radical area where Windows 95 supercharged progress was the convergence of personal computers and telephony. TAPI (Telephony Application Programming Interface) was a component developed jointly by Microsoft and Intel that effectively enabled the telephone to become a soft application on the PC. This unlocked an entire suite of programmable telephone functions such as *voice mail, conference calling, call forwarding, queue management* and *virtual secretaries*.

Windows 95 gave roving computer users a desktop *briefcase* that could be used to synchronise files automatically between a desktop and notebook PC. If the user dialled into their office network through a modem and let Windows log them on to their system, it would update their mail and file directories automatically.

*   *   *

A few weeks before the launch of Windows 95, Bill Gates announced that they were building internet access into the product and providing international high-speed internet feeds – at last, there would be a cheap and easy way onto the *information superhighway*: fun for all the family! Internet Explorer was first released as part of the add-on package, *Plus! For Windows 95*, but soon became available as a free download in service packs, and pre-loaded on most new PCs. As noted earlier, Internet Explorer was originally based on a licensed version of Mosaic, the browser developed by Marc Andreesen at the National Centre for Supercomputing Applications that had popularised the World Wide Web and the internet. Internet Explorer would go on to become the most widely used web browser, peaking with around 95 per cent usage share by 2003.

Start Me Up

On 24 August 1995, Windows 95 launched with an unprecedented industry-wide marketing campaign aimed at persuading nearly 100 million PC users worldwide to adopt a new generation of technology and spend an estimated $20 billion over the coming twelve months on new computers and related products. A host of TV commercials featured Windows 95's theme song, the Rolling Stones' *Start Me Up*.

Hundreds of companies joined Microsoft in a billion-dollar blitz of advertising and publicity events worldwide that would reset the pace of growth for the entire $130 billion personal computer industry. More than 280 personal computer manufacturers, representing about 80 per cent of the worldwide PC market, committed to pre-installing Windows 95 on machines, and hundreds of new compatible applications programmes were released.

Microsoft predicted sales of Windows 95 would be in the region of thirty million in the year ahead, of which twenty million would be bundled on new computers. Sales were strong, with a million copies shipping worldwide in the first four days, and seven million in the first five weeks.

After the Windows 95 launch there was an inevitable backlash as hype met reality. Media reports claimed that Windows 95 was riddled with glitches. Sales slumped to 20 per cent of the launch week's while many companies said that they would not buy Windows 95 for at least a year, when the bugs had been fixed. In fact, while there were many minor problems, there were few major defects – it didn't crash systems or corrupt data and was stable. Windows 95 was soon the most popular operating system, selling forty million copies in the first year.

*   *   *

In 1996, all seemed set for IMR to finally take off as a mainstream shopping channel. Little did we know how many more obstacles, complications and diversions lay ahead, or that it would be years before online shopping would become mainstream.

What's in a (Domain) Name?

'The Domain Names Server (DNS) is the Achilles' heel of the Web.
The important thing is that it's managed responsibly'

Tim Berners-Lee

A domain name is a string of characters that identifies the location of something on the World Wide Web – such as a website or where to send email. Back when the internet was small and non-commercial, domain names were abundant and had negligible value. Domain names were assigned on a first-come, first-served basis, regardless of an applicant's right to have any particular name: this approach had the advantage of being cheap to administer as nobody had to monitor behaviour or enforce any rules.[31] But disputes were inevitable when more than one person wanted a particular domain because, as each series must be unique, it can only have one owner. This would lead to horrendous problems later when the value of digital real estate skyrocketed.

The internet's domain naming and addressing scheme came into being in 1981. The first commercial internet domain name was *symbolics.com*, registered on 15 March 1985, and, incidentally, now hosts an online internet tribute museum.[32] In 1992, less than 15,000 domains had been assigned. By early 2015, 294 million domains had been registered.[33]

During the 1990s battles raged over domain registrations and property rights between technologists, brand and name owners, governments, and rights advocates. The Clinton administration decided to pass the knotty issue of regulating the burgeoning internet to the public sector by instigating the *Internet Corporation for Assigned Names and Numbers* (ICANN) in 1998. ICANN is a non-profit organisation responsible for the Domain Names System (DNS), accrediting the many domain name registrars worldwide, and responsible for keeping the internet secure, stable and interoperable.

In response to lobbying from trademark owners and celebrities, Congress passed the *Anticybersquatting Consumer Protection* act in November 1999, which made it slightly easier to resolve disputes where it was established that a domain name holder acted in bad faith.[34] Over the years, ICANN and the courts have increasingly balanced competing claims in favour of legitimate property rights owners.

A famous legal action about the ownership of domain names was focused on *sex.com*, which was registered with Network Solutions on 9 May 1994 by Gary Kremen, an entrepreneur who invented online dating, but did not develop the site.[35] On 18 October 1995 Network solutions was conned by a fake fax into transferring the domain to Stephen M. Cohen. Cohen then produced a website that attracted

IMRG Newsletter Summer 1996

For some time, the InterNIC registration body has been handing out domain names on a first-come, first-served basis. This has led to instances such as McDonalds paying out an undisclosed sum to charity after an enterprising journalist had registered the name before the hamburger giant, as a publicity stunt. Then there were the students who registered Windows95 (and 96, 97, 98, 99 and 2000) and put up sites just to embarrass Microsoft. Now the InterNIC has stated that it will look into the circumstances of disputed names, and may compel owners to surrender a domain if the aim is merely to sell it on to a more 'rightful' owner. In addition, since the .com domain category is almost fully subscribed, there are plans to offer a number of others – .inc, .corp, .ltd, .pic etc. So anyone buying up domain names with a view to making a killing later, beware. You may be wasting your time and money.

This extract from the IMRG quarterly newsletter 'Interact', Summer 1996, describes the chaotic nature of early internet domain name allocations

up to twenty-five million hits per day and reportedly made $50,000 to $500,000 per month. Kremen set out to recover the domain and a five-year legal battle ensued, which Kremen won in November 2000, when Network Solutions was ordered to return the domain to him. Cohen was ordered to pay $65 million, though he apparently never did, claiming poverty, while Network Solutions settled for an undisclosed sum. Sex.com was reportedly sold to Escom LLC in January 2006 for $14 million, widely cited then as the most expensive domain name price.

A couple of personal experiences illustrate some of the domain name issues. In the mid-1990s I was surprised to come across a www.boots.com website that instead of displaying the wares of Boots, the UK's leading pharmacy-led health and beauty retailer, as I had expected, was the site of a German fetish outfit, featuring bondage gear, stiletto jackboots, whips and various other items in shiny black leather. Intrigued, I tried to find Boots on the internet, without success, but did unearth a lot of footwear and weirdness. I arranged a meeting with Boots' marketing director at their headquarters in Beeston, Nottingham, and showed him on my laptop a presentation of websites that internet users seeking his company online were likely to find. He told me that he was unaware of any of this, but showed no surprise, or concern, or even appreciation for me taking the trouble to bring this to his attention. He just said, 'So what?' In the coming months I continued to monitor www.boots.com and before long it redirected to Boots. Some years later a director of Boots told me that the company had paid a lot of money for the www.boots.com domain and the board had instructed that I was never to be allowed to know how much.

In 2001 the Barbadian government asked me to conduct a digital SWOT (strengths, weaknesses, opportunities and threats) analysis of their country, then flew me out to Bridgetown to present the results. The Caribbean island of Barbados had been a British colony until 1966, when it became an independent state and Commonwealth realm. Its economy had transformed to be based on tourism and the offshore sector, so its presence online was becoming consequential.

My research started, of course, with typing Barbados.com into a browser, only to discover that it together with the dot com URLs Jamaica.com, Trinidad.com, Martinique.com, Dominica.com, StLucia.com and most of the other Caribbean islands had been acquired by a US start-up travel agency that was using them to tout its vacation packages. I flagged this to the Barbadian government who, unaware of the fact, asked me if it mattered. 'Yes, it does,' I advised, 'because that is where many people interested in Barbados will head first, and will assume that the website on which they land is an official site.' At the time of writing, nineteen years later (2020), the Barbadian government still hadn't acquired Barbados.com – it was being offered for sale at a domain brokerage service.

Payment

'Banks feel they should control and regulate money on the Internet, which seems to be out of touch with what's happening'

Tom Donnelley, financial adviser, IBM, March 1995

There were two big problems with the internet as a putative channel for trading – payments and security. Payment systems could not be deployed until security was cracked, because security was essential to protect the exchange of sensitive data, authorization and verification. Technologies such as RSA encryption and firewall servers to protect internal systems from hackers, were emerging in the mid-1990s, but these placed a significant burden of time delay on the already glacially slow internet, then a low-bandwidth medium of 14.4 MB at best.

Cash was the number one method of paying for shopping in the mid-1990s, followed by cheques, neither of which was of any use for shopping online. Plastic payment cards looked promising, but there was no satisfactory acceptance procedure for their use on the internet. Payment cards had been introduced in the US in 1950 by Diners Club, and in 1966 Barclaycard introduced the first credit card in the UK. Spending by Visa and Mastercard had risen rapidly between 1986 and 1994, from £13 billion to £38 billion. By late 1995 around 40 per cent of Britons held some 28 million credit and charge cards, while more than half of adults had a debit card: cards accounted for 12 pence in every £1 spent with UK retailers.

In 1995, Mastercard announced that it would enable the internet's thirty million users to make secure payments from their home computers for the first time. *Hooray! At last*, we thought. But it turned out that credit and debit card holders would have to buy Netscape software that was being developed to encrypt transactions, and was not expected to be available before mid-1996. Visa reported that it was developing a similar service, in cooperation with Microsoft. 'This is obviously the killer issue at the moment,' a Barclays Bank spokesman commented.

As noted earlier the first secure UK payment online was claimed for a book bought on Barclays' virtual shopping mall, *Barclay Square*, in 1995. The bank had lobbied security agencies to be able to use the strongest encryption available – 128-bit rather than the 40-bit that it was normally offered – though most people, including Barclay's staff, had no idea what encryption was or why it was needed.

Plastic payment cards were not widely used for smaller transactions at the time, therefore Barclay Square was challenging shoppers to make the double leap to buying online and with a credit card. The site sold hardly anything in the first few months, after which sales remained stubbornly low.

Nevertheless, with the online shopping concept proved, Barclays concentrated on moving on from manually capturing card numbers, keying the numbers into machines later, then sending an email to the shopper saying, 'yes it's been authorised, we'll send you the goods in due course', to becoming a payment gateway, with fully automated payments, confirmed in near-real time.

*   *   *

Electronic commerce could not scale up until there were simple, inexpensive, private and secure ways to make payments over the internet. The e-retail industry's ambition was to have a global system enabling people to use payment accounts anywhere in the world, with one common method of account holder identification, secure in the knowledge that there was a very high level of protection against all forms of fraud.

Several alternative payments contenders emerged in the 1990s, notably *DigiCash*, a digital equivalent of paper cash and coins, founded by David Chaum in 1989. DigiCash Inc. operated for several years, and its *ecash* solution won the European Commission's 1995 Information Technology Award for innovative technology. In October that year the Mark Twain Bank of Missouri instituted ecash accounts from which users could withdraw sums to buy goods online, and Deutsche Bank launched a similar pilot in May 1996. But DigiCash failed to break into the mainstream and declared bankruptcy in 1998.

PayPal appeared with the first version of its new electronic payments system in 1999, and rapidly established itself as a trailblazing challenger to the financial establishment. Joining forces with Elon Musk the following year, PayPal went public in 2002, raising over \$61 million. Soon after, the company was acquired by eBay for \$1.5 billion and would go on to become the default payment method used by most eBay users.

Credit cards were the principal means used for online payments, but they had two main drawbacks: many people were reluctant to send unsecured credit card information over the internet, where it might be intercepted, to a merchant whom they might not know; secondly, transaction costs were relatively high, which made credit cards unsuitable for small purchases, especially micropayments, such as a few pennies for accessing a page of information.

3D Secure (3DS)

On 1 February 1996, the payment industry announced its response to the inadequacies of online card transactions: *3D Secure* (3DS), a protocol using digital certificates and designed to be an additional security layer that triangulated the *three domains* involved – the retailer, the card scheme and the bank. The first iteration of 3DS was *Secure Electronic Transaction* (SET), developed by Visa, Mastercard and various other companies.

IMRG reported at the time that Visa and Mastercard were adopting 3DS and expected to work out a standard credit-card payment form (or forms, plural, if they couldn't agree) that online merchants would be able to offer to shoppers by Q3 1996. That didn't happen. The first SET specification was not published until May 1997. Delays continued. In December 1997, the major credit card companies and other e-commerce leaders including Microsoft, Netscape and IBM formed a company called *SET Secure Electronic Transaction LLC* (SETCo) to maintain and implement the SET specification, administer compliance, and foster its global adoption.

After great fanfare at SET's launch, the banks and card schemes essentially declined to make it available. The payments industry was extremely risk averse, and profited anyway from shopping transactions whatever channel was used, so pursued online capabilities with negligible urgency. More deadlines were set and missed. E-retailers were left highly exposed to fraud, and liable for fraud losses.

In April 1998, IMRG commented: '...merchants have abandoned hope that Visa and Mastercard's SET e-retail payments solution will ever be of any more use than a chocolate fireguard – it's been permanently *six months away* since mid-1996, we are now told it will arrive as a *mainstream consumer solution* in October (1998).' SET ultimately failed due to lack of support.

The second iterations of 3DS – Verified by Visa (VbV) and Mastercard SecureCode – would not arrive until 2002, and even then, would not be rolled out.

The Pay Barrier

At speeds close to the speed of sound, there is a large, sudden increase of drag, known as the sound barrier. When test pilots plummeted from the sky on first encountering this invisible and enigmatic obstacle, it shocked the world. In the late 1990s, at a point in online retail close to the transaction, there was a large, sudden increase in consumers' reluctance to input their credit card details, which IMRG came to describe as *The Pay Barrier*.

Consumers had negligible financial exposure when shopping online, but of the many reasons not to buy via the internet that the media constantly stoked public fear with, *lack of credit card security* was the stock justification they reached for. Stern warnings were issued to shoppers: if they had any queries or concerns, they should telephone the company before giving them their card details to reassure themselves that it was legitimate. Also, they should keep a record of the retailer's contact details, including a street address and a non-mobile phone number, and !!!*beware*!!! if these details were not available on the website. And if a shopper was foolhardy enough to place an order, they should print out the details together with copies of the retailer's terms and conditions and returns policy. Later, the government would advise people to only shop online with retailers they knew, undermining almost entirely the fundamental point of the activity.

Even regular web users admitted illogical nervousness made them unwilling to enter their credit card details for the first time, and instead opt to pick up the phone to complete an online transaction. It was all just so radically new!

A growing number of European companies had online turnovers that measured in millions of pounds; however, for many, having a website remained just a publicity stunt – a novelty in which they invested a token sum. Financial directors, many of whom had been carried along against their better judgements, could be relied upon to soon blow the froth off this *new media market*, and reveal that the new-born industry wasn't wearing any clothes. They demanded ROI at least equal to competing demands on capital, as well as a credible business case for any further funding. This necessitated online investment to be directly and measurably linked to profit.

A European *new media* industry was rapidly emerging to service cyberspace investments, but few of its practitioners appeared to understand that the promising US model would not work in Europe, or how the Eurocentric environment was fundamentally and confusingly different. Before long they (and their customers) were arriving at the inevitable conclusion that any future income would require an ability to deliver profitable online transactions, and Europe's catch-22: lack of payments infrastructure curtailed transactions / lack of transactions curbed investment in payments infrastructure.

Overcoming the Pay Barrier remained one of the main challenges facing the online retail industry in Europe for the next several years. And like the sonic boom heard by those on the ground when a pilot goes through the sound barrier, the breaking of the Pay Barrier would produce its own violent shockwaves as consumers lunged through to shop online faster than traditional retailers could imagine.

1997: e-Christmas.com

'Christmas will never be the same'
Hugo Lunardelli, Microsoft Europe, Paris, 1997

In 1997 IMRG helped to organise and lead a large-scale international 'Pathfinder' project called e-Christmas that kick-started cross-border e-retailing and gave the UK a significant advantage in global online trading. IMRG won the Chartered Institute of Banking / BT Financial Technology Innovation award for 'Delivering Solutions through Partnership' for e-Christmas the following year.

During the mid-1990s online shopping was beginning to take off, but buying goods online from another country was impossible. Online trading systems to handle

Figure 14: The e-Christmas website logo, 1997. (*Source: James Roper Archive*)

payments, shipping, taxes and tariffs, time zones, currency conversion, languages and local legal requirements simply did not exist. Sending an email from, say, London to Paris would involve the message being first sent to and then back from the MAE-West servers in California because European countries only had internet connection with the USA and not each other.

Microsoft approached IMRG in early 1997 with an idea for an international Christmas shopping website that would tackle the challenges and provide practical trading experience for a wide range of European stakeholders. UPS, HP and KPMG were recruited to help, and a $7 million budget was raised.

After months of frantic activity, that November the e-Christmas.com website went live, bringing together 131 merchants in nine countries, offering 1,900 gifts in eleven currencies and six languages (French, German, Italian, Dutch, Spanish and English). For the very first time, consumers could shop online for presents from any participating retailer and have them delivered to any of twenty-seven countries, with all relevant taxes and tariffs and shipping requirements taken care of and paid for at the time of order.

There was a strong business argument for e-Christmas. In 1997 internet commerce was taking off rapidly in the US while Europe was lagging. Some 14 per cent of US households were using the web compared with only 2 per cent in Europe, and among businesses the gap was much wider. If European consumers, coming to the net later than their US cousins, found US web services ready and willing to take their custom, we could expect to see a growing e-trade imbalance in favour of the US, unless Europe had more to offer.

This US dominance was not surprising. The US had a single homogenous market, one language, one currency, a common approach to banking, fulfilment and marketing, and a government which strongly encouraged electronic commerce. European online merchants faced many challenges: multiple languages, currencies, taxes, address formats, shipping costs, internet infrastructure and bandwidth anomalies, and a minefield of irreconcilable bureaucracy. All this plus high risks and, so far, negligible sales prospects. Small wonder few European merchants were going online and millions of new European internet users who wished to shop on the web were buying from elsewhere.

French Prime Minister Lionel Jospin's decision to abandon the Minitel system, which had been blamed for holding back adoption of the internet in France, was one small step in the right direction. But far more radical action was required. Many European businesses and retailers had had enough of theory and were crying out for an opportunity to actually trade online and thereby learn about the best way to support electronic commerce. Europe also needed practical aid in the form of resources, tools, a consumer base, standards, codes of practice, certificate authorities, an information channel for small and medium enterprises, and purposeful leadership.

European consumers were largely unaware of the possibilities and benefits of online shopping. E-Christmas set out to demonstrate the internet's purchasing potential by providing an exciting, convenient and safe online service with a diverse range of gifts that shoppers worldwide could choose and buy from, and send gifts anywhere in the world.

E-commerce was profoundly different from anything the traditional retailers were used to in that its transaction chain involved many more partners in the process. As well as a buyer and a seller, the operation required a set of third parties to supply internet connections, financial gateways, hosted web services, payments security, digital certificates for authentication and non-repudiation, fulfilment and shipping services. Although complex, these essential services are mostly invisible to the customer, who is presented with a simple screen interface.

Cross-border Payments

One of the first obstacles IMRG identified almost proved to be a showstopper: cross-border online payments were impossible due to the lack of a suitable payments system. VISA and Mastercard's SET protocol remained unavailable. And this was two years before the *euro* was adopted, on 1 January 1999, as the 'single currency of the European Monetary Union' by eleven member states, so e-Christmas also had to deal with a range of currencies including German marks, French francs, Italian liras, Spanish pesetas and Dutch guilders together with their fluctuating exchange rates and political and legal idiosyncrasies.

Scott Thomson of QPQ rescued the situation by creating from scratch an entire *e-Christmas Payments Scheme*. Scott had been IMRG's chief payments expert for several years and was well known and respected as a serial inventor of advanced payments solutions: his impressive achievements included creation of the first *Euro Travellers Cheques* for Thomas Cook, invention of the *Switch* multifunction debit card and '*cashback*' while working for Midland Bank; after setting up his own consultancy, QPQ, in 1992 he had helped develop Tesco's *Clubcard*.

Scott set out a highly creative overall payments strategy for e-Christmas to control the processes associated with acquiring, implementing and managing the entire e-Christmas payments mechanism, ensuring that they collectively formed a single and cohesive structure and integrated with the many other necessary project elements – for example, the timing of customer debit in relation to the timing of the shipment of their goods.

Scott's payments plan short-circuited payments and security concerns. The banks' inflexible approach to acquirer agreements and the less-than-competitive commission rates charged for *Card Not Present* transactions were circumvented by sheer competitive pressure that Scott introduced.

QPQ, as payments agent and catalyst, ensured that all the various individual negotiations and developments were coordinated and the extremely tight deadlines were met; also that the scheme in its totality had a consistency of approach. Scott authored specific *e-Christmas Payments Scheme Rules*, to which all parties had to agree to abide by contract. This encompassed everything from tailor-made merchant agreements, to be suitably adapted for each acquirer, through to standardised selling and operating procedures for use by all participants.

For almost all the retailers involved this would be their first experience of commerce on the *net*, so it had to be simple to understand and easy to use. The scheme also had to accommodate the assumption that the majority of buying consumers would probably be US-based residents in a variety of time zones.

As the first practical European online trading model, e-Christmas had to cut through the *myths* and deal with practical issues arising from implementation. Scott's payments scheme was a triumph that had real and lasting value, enabling participants and many other stakeholders to use the structure as a prototype design for the future.

Taxes, Duties and VAT

The aim was to charge each e-Christmas shopper a single amount in the currency of their choice that included the cost of the gift(s), shipping and any taxes and duties in order to avoid the recipient of the gift having to pay anything at the time of delivery. Working out what that cost would be in near-real time across 27 countries for every item offered for sale on the site was no trivial matter. This was achieved by UPS creating a *pricing engine* that computed up front

1997 VAT rates in EC countries:	
Austria	20 %
Belgium	21 %
Germany	15 %
France	20.6 %
Ireland	21 %
Italy	19 %
Netherlands	17.5 %
Portugal	17 %
Spain	16 %
UK	17.5 %

every possible destination and currency scenario for every one of the 1,900 gifts on offer. The buyer was shown these costs and was able to pay, all in one transaction. Behind the scenes complex arrays of mechanisms were set up to produce waybills and convey the parcels and money to their correct destinations.

UPS's integrated tracking infrastructure let both the merchant and the shopper see the flow of the goods in the UPS system until delivery was completed.

It was complicated. For example, all trade between European Community (EC) countries attracted VAT at a range of rates from 15 per cent to 21 per cent. But for goods shipped from an EC country to a non-EC country, say the USA, no VAT needed to be added. However, if a non-EC resident bought an e-Christmas gift to be sent to someone living within the EC, then VAT did have to be charged.

For certain goods different rules applied, and each country tended to have its own specificities. For instance, the USA required an additional fee of $25 per shipment for *textile products, footwear, headwear* and *furniture*.

Most countries also had de minimis thresholds for the value of imported goods below which no duty or tax was collected, and these too varied.

1997 EC de minimis thresholds for distance sales		
EC Member State	**ECU**	**National Currency**
Belgium	35.000	1.500 BF
France	100.000	700 FRR
Germany	100.000	200 DEM
Ireland	35.000	270 IEP
Italy	35.000	54.000 ITL
The Netherlands	100.000	230 NLG
Spain	35.000	4.549 ESP
United Kingdom	100.000	70 GBP

Code of Practice

IMRG had for several years been working to identify and overcome the outstanding e-retail industry barriers, so was familiar with the broad array of elements and activities that had to be aligned for online shopping to work well. For e-Christmas, IMRG summarised its collective wisdom into a code of practice – an operational guide that all participating merchants were required to sign up to. The *IMRG Code* enabled merchants to fully understand their obligations and gave their teams a comprehensive checklist of exactly what they had to do, when and why.

The IMRG Executive 1997, which administered the first IMRG Code of Practice:

Arcadia (Burton) Group, BT, Compaq, Deloitte & Touche Consulting Group, DHL, Ernst & Young, Forrester Research Inc, Hughes Olivetti Telecom, The Post Office, IBM, iCat, IKEA, Intel, Kingfisher Group, Lloyds TSB, Marks & Spencer, Microsoft, MicroTouch, Module Communications, Mouse Power, Netscape Communications UK, Nokia, On Demand Information, Unipower, UUNet UK

The IMRG Code became a key e-Christmas deliverable, enabling major advances in defining many critical areas. After e-Christmas, the Code continued to be developed as a scalable framework for the ecommerce industry in Europe.

Figure 15: IMRG introduced a gold hallmark on 17 November 1997, for use by any online merchants that signed up to the IMRG Code. (*Source: James Roper Archive*)

IMRG then introduced a *Hallmark* for merchants that signed up to the IMRG Code. The Code provided a benchmark for consumer service which merchants could apply (many merchants used the Code as a website developers' checklist) and against which consumers could comment or criticise. The aim of this was to facilitate a growth of trust in e-retailing. IMRG began to follow up consumer complaints about merchants trading electronically, whether or not the merchant was displaying the IMRG Hallmark. This provided the basis for another IMRG world-first: the UK e-commerce trust scheme, *Internet Shopping Is Safe* (ISIS), which the government would help to launch in 2001.

131 retailers from 9 countries and their 1,900 gifts

At its peak, e-Christmas presented 131 retailers from nine countries offering 1,900 seasonal gifts, including some of Europe's leading stores such as Brinkmann of Germany, Hamleys of the UK and Casino of France, together with high-profile brands such as Aer Lingus, Berlitz, BMW and Kraft Jacobs Suchard.

There were also many gifts reflecting Europe's diverse national and regional heritage: traditional corkscrews and knifes from *Couteaux Laguiole* of France, handmade Belgian lace from *Louise Verschuren*, and traditional Celtic jewellery from *Ogham Crafts* of Ireland.

Seasonal food, Christmas hampers, chocolates and decorations were available from *Emil Reimann* of Germany, *Bewleys* of Ireland, *Bettys & Taylors* of Harrogate and *Thorntons* of the UK. Unusual gift ideas included fine art calendars for 1998 from Italy's *Castiglioni*, home weather stations from *Meteo* of France, and German cuckoo clocks from *Eble Uhren-Park*. Clothing offers included stylish weatherproof jackets from *Mulberry* of the UK, bathrobes by *Descamps* and lingerie from *Princesse TamTam*, both of France.

The e-Christmas site was live from 10 November 1997 through to 8 January 1998. It attracted over 250,000 visitors and more than 14,000 individuals registered with e-Christmas, the majority of whom, it turned out, were not US visitors. Just over 500 online transactions were successfully completed during the eight-week period.

KPMG closely observed the entire e-Christmas project and in early February 1998 published a report on its comprehensive audit and analysis of all quantitative and qualitative data gathered. This detailed report included statistics on traffic and transactions. It also reviewed the experiences of every type of participant including consumers, retailers and the various technology and delivery partners, who had each to overcome challenges or contend with issues within their own areas of interest.

E-Christmas took place amid the *browser war* between Netscape Navigator and Microsoft's Internet Explorer for Windows. Navigator remained free of charge for non-commercial use and had 72 per cent of the web browser market in October 1997[36] while take-up of Internet Explorer was growing fast. When the first several boxes of the *KPMG e-Christmas Report* (describing the Microsoft-initiated project) arrived, I was horrified to see that the designer had placed a large background watermark image of the iconic Netscape browser across almost every page. The print-run was scrapped overnight and replaced with copies sporting an Internet Explorer 4 watermark, just hours before the formal presentation of the e-Christmas results.

The primary goal of e-Christmas was *knowledge creation and sharing*, as had been identified consistently throughout the project. However, in the first week of February 1998, *The New York Times* ran a story which effectively trashed the e-Christmas project and European ecommerce in general on the basis of some statistics, taken in isolation, from KPMG's report – in particular that only some 500 internet transactions had been completed on e-Christmas.com.

'Was e-Christmas a success or a failure?' Phil Dwyer of New Media Age asked in his article 'Getting airborne' of 12 February 1998. Dwyer argued that the US press has failed to understand how much the project has achieved by focusing on the number of buyers the project attracted, in tones which suggested the small numbers involved branded the exercise a failure: 'It was predictable, but none-the-less a depressing reaction. How, after all, could *The New York Times* have been expected to understand the complexity of the task which the e-Christmas consortium had undertaken? Ecommerce takes place in the US in an entirely different context: one currency, no borders (the majority of sites still refused to sell their goods to anyone outside of the US), a single tax regime, and a single language.'

Dwyer emphasised that the point of the exercise was discovery by comparing it with 17 December 1903, when Wilbur and Orville Wright were running around a field in North Carolina attempting to prove that a jumble of wood, metal and canvas could defeat gravity and fly. There were no headlines in the newspapers the next day declaring transatlantic flight a failure, or questioning man's ability to get to the moon. 'How much was sold on e-Christmas.com was only slightly more relevant than the number of passengers carried on the Wright Brothers' maiden flight,' he concluded.

E-Christmas discovered a great deal about using the web to do business in Europe: what users wanted, what retailers needed to think about when they went online, and the logistical and tax implications of doing business in a global market. It also revealed just how challenging were the many technical issues and the infrastructure problems which Europe faced.

E-Christmas accelerated the progress of cross-border shopping by years and marked the end of the beginning for e-commerce in Europe.

* * *

Many Christmas websites with consumer propositions for seasonal gifts had been appearing since September that year, all of which had experienced teething troubles, or worse. IMRG reviewed eleven of them, including IBM's French e-mall *SurfAndBuy.com* that launched on 15 October 1997 to '*demontrer son savoir-faire en commerce electronique*'. IBM, which was said to have a $200 million budget for e-commerce awareness, had spent $2 million on *SurfAndBuy.com*, positioning it as 'an e-commerce experiment, enabling merchants to try out selling on the internet'. SurfAndBuy got off to a rocky start with an *unfortunate press conference*, having to close after getting just 712 visits (10,000 hits) in 90 minutes due to lack of bandwidth to handle that traffic. SurfAndBuy attracted 70,000 visitors during the first month and made some 200 sales, although the IMRG *Mystery Shopper* commented, 'I think that the site should be renamed *SurfAndSurf* as there is hardly anything to buy.'

Approaching 2000 – The End of the Beginning

'e-Commerce has taken off way beyond even our own optimistic projections'

David Risher, Senior Vice-President, Amazon.com, 1998

Consumers' use of the net was rising fast as the new millennium approached. Japan's 1998 Nagano Olympic Winter Games' website registered nearly 650 million hits from around the world during the sixteen-day event in February – more then treble the 187 million scored by the USA's 1996 Atlanta Olympics two years earlier. The official Buckingham Palace website, which became a focal point for condolences and information after the death of Princess Diana on 31 August 1997, drew 100 million visits in its first year, making it one of the most popular websites in the world.

Email use grew rapidly after restrictions on commercial use of the internet were revoked in May 1995, and was boosted by a series of UK national postal strikes that began on 6 August 1996. These crippled mail deliveries and led to a threefold increase in the use of email. At the time UUNET Pipex reported being approached by 1,000 small companies a week, primarily interested in establishing an internet presence for email. The August 1996 IMRG report noted: 'Although email is in no position yet to challenge the one million fax machines in British offices and homes, the postal strikes have given it its first real chance to show its potential.' The number of email accounts worldwide grew by 83 per cent in 1999, to 569 million, 40 per cent of which were in the US where two-thirds of the workforce was using email. One in four US families had at least one email account.

E-retail was progressing, albeit in a haphazard way, its path still littered with obstacles. Europe was a fragmented collection of domestic markets each doing their own thing and lagging years behind the US, where most of the fifty million people who had transacted online so far lived. US businesses wishing to ride the electronic roads to big profits were making significant investments: a third of US websites surveyed in 1997 had budgets of between $100,000 and $1 million; a tenth of US webmasters expected sales to top $1 million that year – 40 per cent expected their revenue to come from selling products online.

Retailers' expectations

Whereas consumers were flocking online to shop, most UK retailers still considered internet trading to be extremely risky. It threatened to cannibalise their existing trading channels, was susceptible to generating unhelpful peaky demand, was a poor distribution channel for overstocks and ends-of-ranges, and was becoming afflicted by growing consumer and criminal fraud. It was also plagued by hysterical media reporting, suffered an acute human resource shortage, and was being undermined by inappropriate regulation and an apparently delinquent capital market. Instead of helping, the banks hit merchants with unpredictable *chargebacks*. Governments advised retailers that they were on their own and passed more laws to protect consumers who were not at risk anyway from what those new laws covered.

Early in 1997, IMRG held an *Electronic Home Shopping* workshop for its retailer members on the theme of 'Advances and Developments in the Retail Sector' that focused on the internet. The workshop posed a series of questions which delegates could vote on anonymously using handheld clickers, then the results were shown, as in the set of slides in the *Colour Plates* section.

The workshop revealed several interesting presumptions, some of which changed significantly as the session progressed. Most delegates believed that competitors' use of the internet would become threatening – but at the outset they assumed that competition would come from their own sector, whereas by the end of the morning they realised that new market entrants would pose the main ascendant danger.

Early in the workshop, most attendees were unconvinced that people would buy much online – the aphorism had it that *shoppers like to see and touch goods*. But as we worked though the most likely forthcoming scenarios, they increasingly accepted the internet's large potential for market disruption.

It was interesting to note delegates' low expectations that they would buy white goods via the internet – this turned out to be one of the first sectors to move massively online, driven by the fact that such commodity items could be viewed in a store and then bought cheaper online. On the other hand, attendees revealed high expectations that they would purchase cars and property on the web, sectors in which the internet invariably remained little more than an influencer for many years. But even in 1997 it appeared obvious to most of our retail members that buying music, software and travel would soon migrate online, though the distribution formats envisaged then were cassettes, discs and high street travel agents – paradigms that would soon become largely obsolete.

*   *   *

US internet shopping during the Christmas period of 1997 was estimated to be worth $1 billion, with almost a quarter (24 per cent) of US web users actively shopping online, according to market researcher @pian. The top five *Web Purchase Retail Categories* showing the greatest percentage growth were (1) airline ticket reservations, up 301 per cent, (2) stocks and mutual funds, +291 per cent, (3) computer hardware, +111 per cent, (4) car rental, +105 per cent, and (5) books, +94 per cent.

Mystery Shopper

'The IMRG mystery shopper is on the prowl, dedicated to digging the dirt, detecting any online scams, and reporting back with extreme criticism or praise depending on the experience of online shopping'

To help people understand *what good looked like* (and *bad*!) apropos e-retail websites we unleashed the *IMRG Mystery Shopper* in March 1997. Our anonymous mystery shopper rated a different sector each month and published commentary on their experiences, shopping at more than 3,800 e-retail sites before being retired in 2001. By then we considered the mystery shopper's 'job done' as both retailers and consumers were becoming familiar with shopping online and had a pretty good idea of what to expect.

Over those five years the many sectors reviewed included clothing, mobile phones, airline tickets, shoes, edutainment, CDs, insurance, cars, holidays, Christmas sites, days out, wine, distance learning, football sites, events, hotels, books and auctions. Every month a dozen or so sites in the sector under review would be scrutinised, each being described and given a star rating based on the following guide:

IMRG Mystery Shopper Ratings Guide:
***** Excellent, well thought out, looks great, lots of useful features and good customer support
**** Very Good, but just falls short in some areas
*** Average. Some redeeming features, but the overall experience was nothing special
** Poor, not particularly well thought out
* Absolutely awful! Don't waste your time

Site	Comment	Rating*****
Cellphones Direct	This site is not only very basic, it is out of date and I could not access information on phones, tariffs or ordering. A message appeared saying "File Not Found" for all the categories, except FAQs. The Accessories section is under construction and it appears the site was last updated on 26/9/96! I could only find an e-mail link for the site designers, Contact Consultants, so I sent a message advising of the problems. I received a reply the following day saying they are no longer responsible for this site and they think the company has been taken over. Don't even bother to visit this one. *www.cellphonesdirect.com*	*

Figure 16: This Cellphones Direct review from the May 1998 IMRG Mystery Shopper Report typifies the live online dabbling many companies indulged in at the time. (*Source: James Roper Archive*)

Contact: Jo Tucker

IMRG Limited
Stonecutter Court
1 Stonecutter Street
London EC4A 4TR
Phone: +44 (0)171 303 6603
Facsimile: +44 (0)171 303 5881
e-mail: market@imrg.org
Web: http://www.imrg.org

Press Release

A MYSTERY SHOPPER SPECIAL REPORT

The Web Sites of The Times' Top 100 UK Companies.

Q. "What do you get if you sit the average consumer in front of the Web sites of the UK's top 100 companies?"
A. "World Wide Weariness."

Today the IMRG releases its Mystery Shopper review of the sites of the UK's top 100 companies, as listed by The Times. Only 2% of companies were awarded the highest rating of five stars, BT and Tesco. And as a small blessing only 2% achieved the lowest rating of one star, National Power and Thistle Hotels. However there are nine companies that cannot be rated as they are without a site at all, most surprising amongst these is Yorkshire Water.

The IMRG feels that the general level of understanding and commitment demonstrated is woefully inadequate, and that given the increasingly high profile of the web, this amounts to communications negligence. As a shareholder in any of the poorer performing consumer companies, there is little to be confident about in these companies' ability to meet the demands and grasp the opportunities of this rapidly evolving consumer channel.

The IMRG believes that the reasons for the disappointing quality of these online communications are
however there are a number of key issues that can be distilled.

- Almost nobody is doing this well on their own. External partnersh
  companies to 'think outside the box'.
- The technology community is giving conflicti

Figure 17: In March 1998 IMRG published a special mystery shopper report on the websites of the UK's Top 100 Companies, as listed by *The Times*. (*Source: James Roper Archive*)

In March 1998 we produced a *special mystery shopper report* on the websites of the UK's Top 100 companies, as listed by *The Times*, that provided an insight into how the country's leading organisations were engaging – or not – with their internet presence as the world was moving online.

Our general feeling was that these premier league organisations were mostly making second and third division efforts. Only two companies were awarded the highest rating of five stars, BT and Tesco. Only two achieved the lowest rating of one-star, National Power and Thistle Hotels. However, there were nine companies that could not be rated as they were without a website at all.

IMRG commented that the general level of understanding and commitment demonstrated was woefully inadequate, and that given the increasingly high profile of the web, this amounted to communications negligence. Steve Johnston, development manager at IMRG, said 'given that the first US-based transactional websites are into their fourth year of trading, it is sad to see such a spread of mediocrity and brochure-ware in the UK.'

The mystery shopper exercise began with a telephone call to the listed switchboard number for each company to determine if the firm had a website and where it was located. You might think that if anyone should know this information it would be the main contact number for the organisation, but this was not our experience. Even when this information was immediately available there was often a problem with the staff communicating '*some of the terribly complicated punctuation that formed a modern-day URL: those arcane and rare things that are two full stops, one on top of the other'*. When the firm's communication staff did not know what a colon was, there was little hope for a sensible description of the 'forward slash'; 'column' was our favourite. On this subject, when discussing email addresses, we encountered some pleasing variations of the 'at' symbol (@), which varied from the French and Italian versions – *le petit escargot* (little snail) and *chiocciola* (snail's shell) through to some we hadn't heard before: *cabbage*, *strudel*, *vortex*.

We also attempted to locate the sites through guesswork – *maybe it's www. thames-water.com* – and through the search engines – *www.britishpetroleum.co.uk* – with several surprises. Using Yahoo! to locate BP you would, at the time, have encountered a site at the address www.britishpetroleum.co.uk, which to all intents and purposes appeared to be the official BP site. On closer inspection this site had, behind every link, a tirade of abuse from a disgruntled BP customer who had had the spoiler ripped off his Rover by one of their car washes. This was a no-holds-barred tirade, and was quite extensive, with copies of correspondence, photos, etc. All BP had to say about not purchasing the domain and other similar ones themselves, was that they 'didn't think they were relevant'.

It was clear from our experience that very few of the companies making sites available to the public had thought it through carefully. For many companies, this was the first time that information was being made available in this uncontrolled and open way, and frequently it would have been the first time ever that corporate information was being published for general consumption, beyond the annual report.

*   *   *

Amazon was setting the gold standard for e-retailing with brilliant service that continued to improve, and soon included 'single click purchasing'. Amazon.com had gate-crashed the UK retail scene soon after the repeal of the Net Book Agreement (NBA) in March 1997, a regulation that fixed the price of books in the UK. Repeal of the NBA spurred significant book sales growth for large stores and chains, book clubs and supermarkets at the expense of independent retailers. It also fostered the appearance of online booksellers. Based on Amazon.co.uk's almost instant success, most people assumed that the maverick online trader was having an easy time, but the truth was that it faced intense competition from an overabundance of challengers including HMV, Bol.com, Streets, Blackstar, Play247, Tesco, Jungle, PC World, Software First, Dixons, Comet, Game, dabs, Empire Direct, Borders, Marks & Spencer, Argos, Currys, Woolworths, Dell, John Lewis, Ottaker's and Blackwells.

Amazon.com's IMRG Mystery Shopper review, July 1997

☆ ☆ ☆ ☆ ☆

This site has 2.5m titles. You can search by author, title or subject. Categories include business, sci-fi, romance and children's books. The New User Guide gives advice on navigating and how to order. Full descriptions and reviews of each book as well as customers' comments. I ordered a child's book and received an email immediately confirming the order. Further email received within hours confirming order had been shipped. There are three shipping options for international orders: Standard with delivery in approx 6 weeks, $4 per shipment + $1.95 per book; DHL Worldmail with delivery in 7/14 working days, $7 per shipment + $5.95 per book; or DHL Worldwide Express with delivery in 1 to 4 working days, $30 per shipment + $5.95 per book. I opted for the Worldmail service and received the book 5 working days later. An excellent site with an extensive range of books, easy to navigate and secure ordering.
http://www.Amazon.com

Amazon.com's IMRG Mystery Shopper 'five star' review, July 1997 (just prior to the launch of Amazon's UK site – Amazon.co.uk). This was the only one of thirteen book sites reviewed to score five stars.

Impact on retailers' stock market value

In 1998, the value of Europe's four-year-old e-retail market remained tiny. Even in the UK, where e-commerce was developing faster than elsewhere in Europe, the value of UK online retail sales for 1998 was guestimated to be only *a few hundred thousand pounds*, though nobody really knew the market's value or growth rate because data was unavailable – companies were cagey about their sales figures, and the payments companies then had no way of discriminating sales by channel.

However, several IMRG members reported UK Christmas 1998 sales up 400 per cent on the previous year, and we were hearing anecdotal information about some startlingly good individual performances. An IMRG survey, 'How was your e-commerce Christmas?', revealed online merchants' experiences as:

1. Beyond our wildest dreams   15%
2. Better than expected   42%
3. On target   35%
4. Disappointing   5%
5. Pathetic   3%

High street retail sales were slumping towards the end of 1998, with supermarket giant Safeway saying that it was expecting its toughest Christmas for years.[37] Heavy media reporting of the relatively buoyant e-sales market prompted a rapid increase in price competition and obliged established traditional retailers to begin to invest more seriously in the online channel. E-commerce was also beginning to impact retailers' stock market values.

> ### Dixons stock value doubled on news of its internet activity
>
> Dixons, the UK's dominant high street electrical retailer, was the first UK electrical retailer to launch an online shopping site on the internet, shortly before Christmas 1997. Following its 1998 launch of Freeserve, Britain's first free internet access service, Dixons' share price doubled, adding almost £3 billion to its market capitalisation.

Retailers were being forced to overcome their 'cannibalisation inertia', having reluctantly recognised that they would lose customers to online traders anyway if they didn't sell online themselves. Dixons, the UK's dominant high street electrical retailer, had been the first UK electrical retailer to launch an online shopping site on the internet, shortly before Christmas 1997, its site boasting a 2,000-strong product range and the promise of next-day delivery. Dixons' stock value jumped on the news.

The following year, experiences like those of Dixons Group and WH Smith – whose mere tentative touch of the magic lamp, that the internet was becoming, immediately conjured the awesome spectre of the ecommerce genie and stock market magic – would compel other mainstream retailers to re-evaluate the alchemy of retail.

Freeserve and the free access bandwagon

On 22 September 1998, Dixons launched *Freeserve*, Britain's first free access service to the WWW. Corporate development director John Pluthero said: 'We wanted a presence on the internet. With a history of bringing new technology to the mass market, we should play an active role.' Mark Danby, Freeserve's general manager, commented that 'the sources of value for us are really threefold: advertising and sponsorship on the site, ecommerce on the site, and a tiny cut of the telephone call revenue'.

At this time consumers' access to the internet was still via an agonisingly slow modem that monopolised the phone line. An estimated one million UK households had internet access, paying around £10 a month for a 56k dial-up connection.[38] Freeserve lowered the overall cost of using the internet as users didn't have to pay for access, although they still had to pay for the cost of the phone call.

Just eight weeks after the Freeserve launch Dixons announced that it had clocked up 475,000 subscribers to its internet access service, of which 40 per cent were newcomers to the net. Freeserve thereby became the number two ISP in the UK behind AOL, which had 500,000 subscribers, and ahead of the long-serving CompuServe with its 400,000 subscribers. By the following March (1999), more than twenty different companies had jumped onto the UK's free internet access service bandwagon including Tesco, Virgin Net, BT and Barclays Bank.

Just four months after Freeserve's launch, Dixons' managing director, John Clare, claimed 'surprise' that 900,000 UK citizens had subscribed to their free internet service, now estimated to be worth £1.7 billion. In a weak retail market, this success helped Dixons' stock to rise to a record high of 958p, a rise of 44p, against hopes of large profits from third-party agreements and advertising. Meanwhile WH Smith's shares soared by 33 per cent, adding almost £400 million to the company's market value during the first two weeks of 1999, on ambitious hopes for its fledgling internet division.

However, the lesson of e-commerce pioneers such as Netscape and Amazon was that the relationship between investment, turnover and profit was changing, as margins became razor-thin, and value became increasingly oriented to the customer, instead of to the business. Leading electronic commerce operations were setting goals to focus on value, not volume; customer acquisition and retention, not hierarchy and structure; measured input to the business in terms of ideas, not output in terms of hours logged or widgets in the warehouse.

And while Amazon was setting ever-higher standards of service, it was also warning of ever greater losses. One of IMRG's retail members lamented at the time, 'This does little to support the argument for web investment. Our board wants to make money, not lose it! Amazon says the expense of adding infrastructure, warehousing, inventory, and marketing efforts are likely to lead to more rapidly growing losses.'

For years, the final retreat of the e-commerce sceptic was the maxim 'even Amazon.com haven't made a profit yet'. This assertion would not be sealed off until 22 January 2002 when Amazon.com finally announced its first ever profit of $5 million in the fourth quarter of 2001 – an investment return of just 1 cent per share on revenues of more than $1 billion. Though very modest, this profit proved that Jeff Bezos' unconventional business model could work.

Sex drive

> **'The military had the money to create it [the internet],**
> **and the sex industry has the money to expand it'**
>
> *Rod Collen, graphic designer, IEG, 1998*

For all the fuss about electronic retailing, the sector was still in its infancy, and apart from a few early starters, most organisations had yet to successfully re-orient themselves to exploit the new online media. One early starter was the sex industry, ever quick to recognise and adopt new methods in what is probably the only retail environment where customers are never in short supply.

In 1998, *SEX* had become the biggest electronic retailing sector by far, and sales were booming. Revenues were fuelling investment and pushing the envelope of online retailing technologies far more than in any other area.

The sex industry was pioneering a range of innovations: payment systems that were easy to use, secure and discrete; better, fast-downloading graphics; new compression techniques to *stream* live video; state-of-the-art database management;

new network marketing models; and the transition to Interactive TV, as Wired. com's article by Frank Rose, 'Sex Sells', explained.[39] 'If widgets sold as good as sex, I'd be selling widgets,' commented Seth Warshavsky, the leading US online sex mogul. 'But, unfortunately, they don't. It [online sex content] is cheaper to produce than mainstream content, and it's easier to sell,' he added.

It seemed he was telling the truth. Forrester upped its online sex industry revenue estimates from $185 million to $500 million, and Forrester's Mark Hardie said he knew of at least three sex sites doing better than $100 million a year. Other people in the business suggested that figure was way too low, estimating worldwide revenues for sex sites – the majority of which were US based – at a whopping $1.2 billion to $3 billion. Back in the UK, one leading payments provider told the IMRG that 60 per cent of their transaction volume was associated with sex sites. Whereas most commercial sex sites were amateur ventures that collected a penny or two for each click on an ad banner, the professional operations made big money through a combination of subscription fees and sales of goods and services.

While sex was often regarded as a source of mild titillation and dirty jokes, it had always represented big bucks. Sex was estimated to be an $9 billion industry in the US alone – bigger than the Hollywood movie industry or the music business. It was the backbone of hotel pay-per-view systems, cable providers and long-distance telecoms carriers. Every major internet service provider admitted that sex sites, which they hosted for a fee, were a substantial part of their business, and New York City market researchers *Media Matrix* reported that in 1997 some 30 per cent of online US households visited an adult site at least once a month. According to their research, the audience was professionals logging on at work, with a predictable demographic lurch that was 90 per cent male, 70 per cent domiciled in the US, and 70 per cent aged between 18 and 40.

There were clear precedents for this. Early adoption of many consumer technologies had been driven by sex, including cable and pay-per-view TV, camcorders and VCRs. The first Laserdisc ever pressed was a blue movie title, and the format's failure was laid at the door of Sony and Philips (which jointly controlled the technology) who refused to permit its use for X-rated media. By the time DVD arrived, Sony had learned its lesson, and handed out DVD players and large-screen TVs to all the top adult film distributors.

But the internet was heaven-sent for the sex industry, with huge advantages over earlier technologies. The *product* was an impulse purchase, with immediate delivery, anonymity and instant gratification. It was safe, cheap and available. In the US, phone-sex operators led the move to the internet: convergence technologies gave them more flexibility, better quality, and a way to bring their highly interactive offerings bang up to date, as it were. For them, the internet was the telephone with pictures. As a result, their revenues soared, far more than magazine publishers and video producers who had simply moved their products online.

The emergence of the internet as a consumer channel coincided with US legislation aimed at blocking phone-sex activities, forcing operators to seek other, less-regulated channels. 900-number calls had been all but outlawed – in September 1995, the Federal Communications Commission had issued an advisory against the use of 10XXX numbers (a system that phone-sex entrepreneurs used to route calls via enterprising third world countries, with charges of up to $3.99 a minute or more). In effect, these moves limited phone-sex operators to 800 and 900 numbers, requiring a credit card number that few people were prepared to give out.

Warshavsky, a 25-year-old Seattle entrepreneur who headed up online porn empire, *Internet Entertainment Group* (IEG) Inc., expected to gross $50 million via the internet in 1998, up from $20 million in 1997 – its second year in existence. Warshavsky joined the phone-sex industry in 1990, when he was 17, and started his first business, *J&S Communications*, by running up a $7,000 credit card bill. By 1995, with annual revenues hitting $60 million, he was a major player in the business. His first website, *CandyLand*, had been launched in January 1996, and by the end of 1997 he had invested some $3 million in IEG sites – enough to pay for twelve SGI servers, twelve Pentium-based video servers, two Oracle servers for credit card processing, two T3 connections, and forty-eight PCs for point-to-point videoconferencing and long-distance telephone billing. Warshavsky was also spending $1 million a year on promotions. IEG's flagship site, *ClubLove*, drew far less traffic than brand-name sites like *Penthouse* and *Playboy*, yet was regarded as more lucrative than all of these.

Warshavsky's success was based on his ability to wholesale live video to hundreds of other sites across the web, including *Penthouse*, with whom he signed a five-year exclusive deal. According to figures issued in late 1997, he had business arrangements with some 1,400 adult sites – around 5 per cent of the market. About 1,100 were taking part in IEG's *ClickBucks* programme, running banners for IEG sites and collecting 2.5 cents for every hit. Several hundred more had signed up for IEG's *turnkey* products, running live video they couldn't afford to produce themselves, and keeping 35 per cent of the revenue.

During 1996, IEG claimed 400,000 subscribers to twenty-nine sites. Noting his customers' discomfort with sending credit card numbers over the internet, and an annoying habit of denying charges, Warshavsky launched a company called *Interfund Financial Services* in 1997, to facilitate the payment process. Through IFS, customers could submit an encrypted credit card number via dedicated lines, put their charges on their phone bill, or even have their bank account debited directly. 'If you're going to take money from somebody, you want to make it the easiest thing in the world,' Warshavsky explained. A point that many mainstream retailers needed to learn.

All the big online sex operators agreed on the need to keep the sites free of kids, for two obvious reasons: to keep within the law, and because minors were just not profitable enough. In the US, some had been urging Congress to pass *constitutionally sound legislation* that would prevent minors from accessing adult sites without infringing free speech. And sex sites benefitted from the fact that technology for screening out minors was the same as technology for collecting money.

The *Communications Decency Act* of 1996 (CDA), which was the first notable attempt by the United States Congress to regulate pornographic material on the internet, even acknowledged credit cards as an acceptable screening device as they were not supposed to be issued to anyone under 18. If children got their hands on their parents' cards, that was considered to be the parents' problem.

Like other publications, US websites had to meet the Supreme Court's obscenity test, which meant they must abide by contemporary community standards, could not appeal to a prurient interest in sex, and must show some serious scientific, literary, artistic, or political merit (the *SLAPS* test). As usual, obscenity guidelines were practically impossible to interpret, let alone police. In practice, this meant no *hardcore* material, for example genital penetration.

But such material wasn't hard to find on sites based outside the US, especially from the Netherlands, the Nordic countries and Italy. Predictably, the not-so-long arm of the law was ineffective at reaching beyond national boundaries, and it was expected that European sites might soon overtake the revenues of their US counterparts by providing *harder-core* material that commanded high prices from the mainly American customer base.

Uncontrolled sexually oriented activity on the web was a growing problem that threatened the development of the internet as a consumer trading channel. The sexually oriented vocabulary that some netizens used, with its multiplicity of meanings for even the most innocent word, made it virtually impossible for anyone regularly using the internet to avoid running into offers of X-rated material or worse. The problems for young people were a matter of particular concern. If you naively typed into search engines words such as *toy*, *game*, *sport* or *fantasy* you could soon find yourself being offered a torture chamber for rent instead of the Lara Croft doll you were looking for.

Many sites asked 'Are you 18? Yes or No' – but this was hardly a deterrent. Advertising in magazines was also problematic – for example, the online magazine *Sugar and More* featured *Position of the Month*. IMRG was informed about a number of school students who were accessing sexually orientated sites (some no doubt innocently!) after following URLs advertised in newsstand magazines. One UK teacher commented, 'The only totally safe control is total monitored access with disabled download and disabled printing.' And the use of software to block certain words was of limited value – as the Arsenal, Cockfosters and Scunthorpe United football teams discovered to their cost; you couldn't teach arts, science, sport or religious education without using sexually oriented words.

In the interactive TV world, the only sex-related content with any reach was branded offerings, such as *Playboy*, or those that made it into the channel guides, which was why players like Warshavsky worked so hard to cement deals with *Penthouse* and other big brands. At the time, internet video images were tiny and fuzzy, and on 28.8 modems they were hopelessly jerky as well, yet this already accounted for more than 65 per cent of the traffic on Warshavsky's websites and was forming the basis for his lucrative series of partnerships. 'Right now, it's a novelty. But when the mediums converge and you have true interactive TV, it's going to be unbelievable,' Warshavsky commented. In the meantime, he was moving into the mainstream by launching non-sex ventures such as *Formlawyer.com* – an online bankruptcy site where for $79, users could go through the entire filing process online. Presumably this venture was aimed squarely at Warshavsky's competitors.

The adult movie industry, which in 1998 generated around $6 billion from video sales and rentals, had definitely got the message about the potential of video-on-demand via the web, with its ease of distribution and its potential for circumventing obscenity laws. The big US players, whose home ground was the San Fernando Valley, part of the northern Los Angeles sprawl, had the money, the invention and the nerve to exploit it. Not even sober institutions like the investment publication *TheStreet.com*, were safe from their attentions, as it discovered when *WallStreetSex. com*, a little-known Californian adult entertainment site that mixed blue photos with stock quotes, blatantly copied the look of its site, including its logo, graphics and colours. The idea was that office workers could disguise the fact that they were looking at sex material by pretending to be checking the stock market. TheStreet.com launched in November 1996 and charged $6.95 to $9.95 per month for access to news and commentary about investing. The bogus site combined real-time financial information with erotic chat rooms, sex videos, and a *trading pit* that was really a store filled with adult toys and lingerie.

The e-retail battleground was shifting like never before, and in ways that no retailer would have guessed just a few years earlier. When *Playboy*'s site launched in 1996, it logged an inordinate number of hits from *nasa.gov* and *senate.gov*. The writing was on the wall that retail skirmishes would soon be taking place on the beaches of Work Force Connectivity where workers surfed, credit card in hand, for thrills, toys and Viagra. Clinton's sexual shenanigans, and the internet publication of *The Starr Report* which investigated them, provided workers with yet another legitimate reason for online *research* of sexually oriented material, a connection not lost on the leading online sex operators, who immediately set about exploiting the opportunity.

The retail mantra *location*, *location* and *location* assumed novel meanings in the wired world. And one location that was becoming more and more important was the office worker's PC screen. However jerky, slow, unreliable and low-fi, there was clearly a large number of people who subscribed to Andy Warhol's dictum that 'Sex is more exciting on the screen and between the pages than between the sheets.' Or as IMRG's managing director, Yorkshirewoman Jo Tucker, commented, 'There's nowt so queer as folk.'

1998: Email or die

'I haven't time to faff about with computers'

Senior UK Travel Industry Executive, 1998

This section is an extract from the introductory 'Comment' article of the October 1998 IMRG Report, reflecting attitudes at the time to the newfangledness of the internet and its inseparable twin, email.

Have you heard the one about the entire company board at an internet workshop who couldn't find a search engine between them? Or the one in which twelve chief executives together couldn't figure out how to work a printer, and were rescued by the tea lady – who turned it on? How about the Head Teacher of a 'forward thinking' school who emailed the message, 'I've written this to you but I'm not sure I've done it right so you probably haven't got it anyway'?

Eavesdrop conversations on almost any plane or train these days and you will hear real-life 'jokes' like this featuring senior management making fools of themselves due to their lack of knowledge and understanding of all things IT. On the subject of e-commerce, the average European company director or government minister could get out of his depth on a damp pavement.

But not knowing which way up the PC goes is just a symptom of the real problem, which is that these people are throwing away Europe's future prosperity, as illustrated by this sorry tale: IMRG met recently with one of the UK travel industry's most senior figures who told us 'electronic commerce will not have any noticeable impact on the travel trade in the foreseeable future.' The comment seemed a little odd, given that consumers are adopting the purchasing of travel faster than any other sector online. I mentioned to him that the online travel market is on track to make $3 billion of sales worldwide this year, and the figure is forecast to grow to $29 billion in 2003, at which time it will represent some 12 per cent of total industry revenues.

He discounted this as mere *projections* and challenged me for some facts. I shared with him some recent reports: over two million people have already bought air tickets on the internet, according to the airlines, and a recent easyJet promotion in *The Times* generated 13,000 flight sales on the first day, of which 40 per cent were via the internet, according to easyJet's Commercial Director. He remained unimpressed, dismissing this as a trifling, inconsequential number of people. To him these were mere nerds, and the whole thing a fad.

My curiosity roused, I asked this guiding light of the travel industry if he used the internet. 'I've seen it,' he replied. 'It was very slow.' 'How about email?' 'Of course not! I haven't time to faff about with computers.'

Personally, I avoid writing letters like the plague because it is so slow. All the fuss of folding paper and addressing envelopes and sticking stamps and waiting at least a day for the addressee to receive it just seems increasingly ludicrous when the purpose is to convey a message or information. And you don't need to be a mental giant to realise that if one person receives a message immediately by email and another person receives the same message a day or more later by a post, that the person receiving the email has a significant time advantage in which to extract value from the contents of the message. Similarly, if one person looks at an advertisement online just after it has been placed, or is immediately notified of its availability by email, and a second person looks at the same ad in a printed newspaper some hours later, then the second person is more likely to find the flight, house, car or job long gone.

It is often argued that sales volumes are still not large enough for mainstream businesses to worry about e-commerce. In the UK this year, less than £0.5 billion of consumer transactions will take place via the internet. But, whereas the turnover of the <500 trade-enabled UK web sites is a closely guarded secret, it is clear that an alarmingly large proportion of these sales is being won by overseas competitors. The key points here are that this is not new money – it is trade being lost by local suppliers – and that the prospects for growth in internet sales are phenomenal for players in otherwise static or declining markets. No other change-agent presents businesses with similar potential for growth or decline.

A pertinent question, therefore, is: Why do normally sensible people self-induce myopia for e-commerce? Why do senior businesspeople today continue to justify their own ignorance and inaction in respect of the fourth channel? Why don't they wake up?

We could, perhaps, blame government for not providing intelligence or even basic tools – e.g. templates, boiler-plate contracts, tax-breaks – for businesses to use, but government doesn't even understand the basic issues let alone know what to do. The UK government claims leadership in *the digital age*, but only when the cameras are rolling and there's a headline to be grabbed. Throughout Europe, governments are nodding sagely and saying things like 'we favour a light touch regulatory regime for the internet, and we will keep new legislation to a minimum' – for which read 'we haven't a clue.'

The fact is that, in Europe, government, trade bodies and most industry leaders, despite the rhetoric have abandoned those businesses trying to engage in e-commerce. The entrepreneurs are on their own and will just have to muddle through the free-for-all that is e-commerce today as best they can, hoping that US and other foreign competitors don't grab too much of their market before the financial pain goads a sensible response from Europe.

So, what to do? Well, to understand the *networked economy* that is e-commerce, you have to be on the network. The single most important first step for any organisation that is not fully switched on to e-commerce is to insist that all directors, managers and appropriate workforce use email, the internet and electronic documents – themselves, now, often, every day. And when I say *use* email, I don't mean have a secretary use it, print out emails that they then mark up and hand back to the secretary to deal with – they must do it themselves. It's about being in charge of an open email account and receiving and responding to communications in real time. The crucial differences with email communication boil down to just two key catalysts: (1) The immediacy of control that is personal and empowering, i.e. I decide. I do. It's done; and (2) Its position *between conversation and writing* that almost needs new vocabulary to enunciate fully, i.e. when an issue is being managed and resolved, it is like having the telephone line open all day to your counterpart, and whenever you want to say something it gets heard straight away, but without the inconvenient interruption that insists that both of you deal with it at precisely the same moment in time. And you are not confined to just one telephone line.

By using the internet themselves, your people can see at first hand the new value propositions that are being created, and how. And I don't mean just go online and look at the pretty websites – they must use them to buy online: buy their Christmas presents, book their annual vacation, choose their next car, order their groceries...

Commercial operation at these speeds can generate vertigo in the seasoned executive, and to many *traditional* unwired execs the responsibility and instant decision-making that is unavoidable with email can be very intimidating. To the rest of us, however, it is profoundly liberating. There is no doubt that professional extinction threatens those who will not engage with the pace of networked business.

I remember four years ago commenting that virtually every US businessperson we encountered had an email address on their business card and was offering us email as their primary means of contact. Then, about three years ago, we started to hear Americans boasting, as we saw it, that they couldn't remember the last time they had written a physical letter. It was not until this year that we began to hear similar comments from European businesspeople. And they were not boasting, they were smart.

Late last year we gambled that the time was right for the IMRG to move wholeheartedly to electronic channels for virtually all communication and interaction with our members. The main issue was, of course, our members' willingness to receive information this way, together with their availability of access to email and the web. It felt a pretty brave decision at the time – especially given that we only had email addresses for some 30 per cent of our members and, through unfamiliarity, they would often get their own details wrong, with the dots in the wrong place and so forth. But now, I'm delighted to say, we have an email address for every single IMRG member. And they work!

This move to online communication has streamlined the IMRG's entire operation and has transformed our lives – no more staying late to stuff envelopes. In particular, it transformed our ability to work with the international community. Just last week we welcomed a new contributor in Beijing, who joins the IMRG's expanding network of regular contributors in Germany, France, Spain, Sweden, Greece, Italy, South Africa, Canada, the US and Australia.

If you just don't have an e-commerce vision for your business yourself, one solution is to hire someone who does. Chelsea Football Club recently provided a great example of doing this the smart way. Chelsea FC found that a host of unofficial Chelsea football websites had sprung up in recent years, so when they decided to create their own site, they enlisted help from IBM and examined all of the unofficial sites. They then employed the guy who ran the best of them to run their new official site, so everyone is happy.

No alternative, however, is as good as doing it yourself. Nobody will understand the needs of your business as well as you and your senior managers do, so get yourselves out there learning how to negotiate the fourth channel. Email, and fly!

James Roper, Chief Executive, IMRG, London 1998

1999: Television is dead. Long live television

A US Gallup poll in 1939 showed that 87 per cent of Americans weren't interested in having a TV. By 1953, 52 per cent had one

Television had dominated consumers' leisure time for half a century, but in 1999 the TV industry's power and influence was being challenged. The bulky appliance had displaced the living room hearth as the heart of the home – cathode ray tubes' phosphorescent glow substituting for fireplace flicker. TV was most people's primary channel for news, entertainment and more. Would television now become consumers' primary gateway to The Network, or be relegated to a place of minor import, just one of many strands of media available through the internet's ubiquitous screens?

The traditional evolutionary view was that TV would become the main consumer portal to the internet. To the television establishment, it all seemed so logical: Interactive Television promised hundreds of channels, digital video and audio, together with new revenue-generating interactive services and games delivered via cable, satellite and terrestrial broadcast. Pundits estimated that by 2003 some 50 million internet-enabled TVs would be in place in one of four online households in Europe and America, providing email, shopping and web access, their penetration having increased sevenfold in five years.

Since the mid-1990s, the television industry had dabbled with The Network opportunity. Oracle's Larry Ellison and TCI's John Malone convinced credulous journalists that we would all soon be shopping, banking and emailing from our TV sets. But early interactive TV offerings revealed the many cultural, technical and interface challenges the medium faced. When in *TV mode*, consumers didn't want to *interact*. At best, the medium only delivered a very lightweight version of *interactivity* compared with internet access via a PC – the classic example given was the pizza ad with an 'Order Now' button. And the interactive TV interface was pretty awful, as anyone who had tried to surf with an air mouse or email with an infrared keyboard would testify. With a few notable exceptions such as CNN and the BBC, the television industry had so far failed to gain any meaningful foothold on the internet, and for most of the traditional TV players it seemed to be already too late.

The cash that had funded the television industry was rapidly drying up as advertisers sought fresh ways to grab attention. Procter & Gamble was reallocating up to 80 per cent of its $3 billion annual advertising budget to the web, largely away from television. Numerous other major advertisers, including Coca-Cola, AT&T, Levi Strauss, Nike and McDonalds, were cooperating to 'accelerate development of digital into the next mass medium'. The fat fees that TV operators used to negotiate on the golf course were going to lean and hungry new media players.

Advertisers' funds were enabling enormous improvements in online offerings, and the rapidly enhancing services were attracting a flood of new consumers. In Europe, some 60,000 new internet users were signing up each day, as the customers followed the money. US households with an internet connection were watching on average 15 per cent less television than households that didn't have access to the web (7.5 hours per day). Between 4:30 pm and 6 pm on weekdays, this figure climbed to 19 per cent less TV.

Would it be 'interactive television' or 'television on the network'? The share of TV sets within total consumer electronics spending had fallen from 65 per cent to 14 per cent in the past thirty years, with VCRs, CD players, PCs and communications devices taking the balance. It was estimated that by 2005, 63 per cent of US households would buy digital set-top boxes, while only 6 per cent would own an IDTV (Integrated Digital TV set). This implied that the TV set would increasingly serve simply as a particular type of screen – a large, high-definition terminal – through which people would access the net for leisure activities.

We were speeding towards a wired world in which the device you chose to access the internet at any given time would be determined by your circumstances and the application you wished to use. Already there were numerous different types of devices providing access to the net in variety of locations – PCs, TVs, kiosks, mobile phones, PDAs and so on – and the range of screen / location choices was expanding. A mobile phone might not be very satisfactory for watching a movie, but fine as a network access device to check flight times or when your new car would be delivered.

A body blow to television was the advent of free and low-cost web access terminals. AOL, Microsoft and Prodigy joined a growing number of players offering to give US consumers PCs that were effectively free, in exchange for (typically) a three-year commitment to use their services. The *iToaster* net terminal, priced at $199 (£121), was an internet-only BeOS-powered computer which PC-manufacturer Microworkz unveiled in July 1999. European retailers soon followed suit, selling this type of sub-£200 internet-optimised computer. Dixons' chairman, Stanley Kalms, announced that Dixons was planning by Christmas to sell stripped-down computers 'without spreadsheets or other software' to be used solely for surfing the web. 'They may not even be called computers, just access machines. And they will come down in price.'

One might have expected that television regulators, observing the profound threat facing the TV industry, would be bending over backwards to help. But no, the TV regulator's galaxy revolved around scheduling and the proportion of advertising per hour, and this did not comfortably accommodate the concept of *interactivity*.

Distracted by the concept of television being 'an appliance' as well as a medium, TV regulators originally (in 1998) argued that if the 'TV appliance' delivered 'the internet' then they should 'regulate the internet' too. In July, Australia made headlines with the passing of absurd censorship legislation to govern the distribution of illegal and offensive content on the internet. Through the provisions of the *Broadcasting Services Amendment (Online Services) Bill 1999*, the national Senate authorised the Australian Broadcasting Authority, ABA, to patrol the internet for objectionable content, and to require offending ISPs to remove the content from their servers. But as previously noted in the December 1998 revision to *Advertising Breaks Code* of the UK's Independent Television Commission (UK TV regulator), 'it will not always be possible or appropriate to seek to apply rules based on a traditional, single stream, sequential model'. Having finally acknowledged the impossibility of scaling that particular 'Everest', most regulators became nervous about even embarking up the internet's foothills.

Television regulators were driven by their remit to ensure that consumers could easily tell the difference between 'advertising' and 'editorial content', and with logic reminiscent of the middle age's religious argument about how many angels could stand on the head of a pin, they were engaged in bizarre debates about where 'television' and 'the internet' met. Only when this riddle was solved to their satisfaction would they feel able to define their responsibilities, and so take a formal position – sometime next year. Possibly. Unless some other unexpected factor emerged before then.

You could see the regulators' dilemma: politicians were afraid that 'little Jimmy' would gain access to hard core pornography via the internet on the TV in the front room. Governments' nanny instincts immediately went into overdrive at the very idea. And so the regulators opted to do (for them) the safe thing – nothing – which was hardly conducive to TV operators making strategic investment decisions.

Television was considered to be a *lean back* viewing experience, while the internet was more *lean forward*, akin to 'a chat across a table' – i.e. the traditional human format for one-to-one discussion, teaching and, crucially, trading. So why didn't TV operators make the leap to become network barons? Because they failed to understand the opportunities that interactive media presented, and they didn't see themselves as being in *that business*. Fossilised in the intractable mud of its traditional commercial and delivery formulae, the television industry expected the quart of interactive services to be forced into the pint-sized TV set.

So, would the internet kill television? Not exactly – though it would continue to divert its advertising revenue. TV viewing grew faster than ever during the following decade, peaking in the US in 2010, when the average household watched *the box* nearly nine hours every day. And the coming of ever larger and increasingly affordable flat-panel TVs in the 2010s further boosted TV's appeal. The John Lewis Retail Report 2013, *How We Shop, Live and Look*, said that the company's sales of *80-inch and above* televisions increased by 319 per cent, compared with a mere 1.5 per cent growth of 32-inch to 38-inch sets (sales of even smaller-size TV decreased by more than a third). It also noted that *tablets* were the must-have gadgets of 2013, with shoppers buying 152 per cent more than the year before, while sales for *Netbooks* fell 45 per cent. Many of those tablets would be used by people surfing the internet while at the same time watching their supersized television sets.

Unlike the ill-fated video cassette recorders, DVDs, MP3s, compact discs and many other now obsolete technologies, television's rumoured death in 1999 was greatly exaggerated. Long live television.

Seeds of the dot.com Bubble

> *'The four most dangerous words in the English language are 'This time it's different'*
>
> Sir John Marks Templeton

As the new millennium approached, the internet was facilitating industries which had not previously existed. Investors were besotted with the digital lucky dip, dollar signs flashing in their eyes, but they could not know if a start-up would pioneer a valuable new business paradigm, or flop.

One winning bet started out in 1996 as an algorithm first known as 'BackRub', a search tool developed at Stanford University, California, by students Larry Page and Sergey Brin. They turned their PhD research into *Google* in 1998 and gave away its core product 'search' for free. Though far from being the first search engine (that was the *Archie Query Form* of 1990, followed by many others, including *Yahoo!*, *Infoseek*, *Lycos* and *WebCrawler* in 1994 alone), Google was soon to become one of the world's largest media companies. The name Google began as a misspelling of the word *googol*, the number 1 followed by 100 zeros, and was chosen to convey the vastness of information it intended to provide.

Among other interesting developments materialising was the online auction, a completely new business model that connected millions of people who wanted to sell, buy or trade around the world, enabled by the real-time interaction capabilities of the internet.

eBay was originally founded by Pierre Omidyar in California on 3 September 1995 and started out as *AuctionWeb*. Unlike traditional auctions, there was no auctioneer. One of the first items sold on AuctionWeb was a broken laser pointer for $14.83. Astonished, Omidyar contacted the winning bidder to ask if he understood that the laser pointer was broken. The buyer explained by email, 'I'm a collector of broken laser pointers.' AuctionWeb was soon renamed eBay and became the first online auction site allowing person-to-person trading. eBay experienced phenomenal growth and in January 1997 hosted 2,000,000 auctions. eBay was one of the most talked-about sites on the web in 1998.

Jack Ma founded the China-based B2B marketplace site, *Alibaba*, on 4 April 1999 in Hangzhou, Zhejiang. Alibaba Group would go on to become one of the most valuable companies in the world: at the close of Alibaba's IPO on 19 September 2014 – that raised close to $22 billion – the company was valued at $232 billion.

*   *   *

In 1999 it was extremely difficult to get e-commerce financing in Europe. Entrepreneurs were abandoned by the investment community and faced an almost hopeless situation. IMRG commented at the time that European e-commerce investors would want to see sunshine and a forty-day drought forecast before they would lend you an umbrella.

It was not much easier for mainstream players: the chief executive of a major European retail group complained to us that, although he knew exactly how to position his brand online, if he made the decision one day to spend the money necessary to properly e-facilitate his business, he would lose his job the next because the analysts just wouldn't wear it.

In the US, the situation was reversed. In this 'new economy' it didn't seem to matter that most of the internet stocks were nowhere near close to turning a profit. Venture capital and IPOs were flooding the market. Internet retailers, each striving to be the Amazon of their sector, were losing fortunes, and able to afford to because venture capital – almost $13 billion in 1998 according to Venture One, a San Francisco research firm[40] – was financing the birth of e-commerce.

'The share values of most US internet companies doubled last month, and the talk on Wall Street is of "internet mania". Some web stocks are trading at an unprecedented 60 times historic earnings…' the IMRG Report of May 1998 observed.

The prevailing online retailing strategy was to spend whatever it cost to acquire customers, and the leading US merchants were spending on average an astonishing 65 per cent of revenues on marketing and advertising, compared with less than 5 per cent of sales invested by traditional retailers. And it was not enough just to advertise on the web if you wanted to be a serious player. *eToys.com* learned this when it got a surprisingly large sales response from its first print and TV ads that carried the tag line 'We bring the toy store to you', a not-so-subtle dig at Toys 'R' Us. Even Amazon then spent an estimated $29, on average, to acquire a new customer.

eToys.com paid $3 million for a two-year deal to become an 'anchor tenant' on America Online, and also gave 25 per cent commission on orders referred by some 5,000 third party internet sites, such as USA Today and Ameritech. 'Some people thought we were crazy,' said Toby Lenk, eToys' founder and CEO, who previously worked for Disney as head of strategic planning for the theme parks. 'But this business is all about getting customers. If we sell $40 worth of toys, $10 is a reasonable acquisition cost.'

Venture capital money alone wasn't enough for this long-haul game, so nearly every hot US web company, including eToys, was planning an Initial Public Offering (IPO). Their aim was to provide cash to build the business, and eventually they would have enough loyal customers so that they would no longer need to spend as heavily on marketing, and then profits would come. At least, that was the plan.

eToys.com became emblematic of the dot.com bubble of 2000, that we shall come to shortly. eToys was conceived by the Californian start-up studio *Idealab* in 1997. On the first day of eToys' IPO in 1999, shares were issued at $20 and closed at $76. The company's value quickly shot up, before going bankrupt and closing in 2001. The domain is now owned by Toys 'R' Us.

Boo.com, a British e-commerce fashion business mentioned earlier, was another brand that came to symbolise the dot.com.bomb: founded in 1999, bust in 2000. The underlying e-commerce technology in which boo.com had invested £70 million was bought by Dan Wagner for a reported figure of $250,000, and this formed the basis of Venda – one of the first cloud-based, enterprise-class e-commerce platforms – used by many retailers, when setting up to sell online.

Spam – email's foot-and-mouth

> *'Spam email presents one of the biggest obstacles to the development of e-commerce by undermining the legitimate use of email for customer relationship management'*
>
> Jo Tucker, MD, IMRG, March 2001

Advertising is a key part of trading. Digital marketing offers advertisers massive leverage over traditional forms through lower costs, real time communication, measurability, multiple formats, easy targeting and vast reach. Yet these benefits contain the seeds of their own downfall if misused – as they all too often are.

Unsolicited Bulk Email (UBE) – aka *junk email* – is known as *Spam* after the Monty Python TV sketch 'Spam',[41] first shown in 1970, where a couple go into a café and everything Mrs Bun is offered contains spam. A group of Vikings break into a chorus of the *spam, spam, spam song* and soon all you can hear is the word 'spam'. SPAM is a brand of cooked ham, trademarked in 1937 by Hormel Foods Corporation of Austin, Minnesota, of which more than eight billion cans have been sold worldwide. The analogy to modern-day spam applied, Hormel said, because unsolicited email is seen as drowning out normal discourse on the internet. Hormel tried to sue tech companies over their trademark, but eventually gave in and even sponsored the Monty Python musical *Spamalot*.

The internet and its binary, email, are the most significant communication innovations of our time. The first email systems emerged in 1960. ARPANET's promotion of software portability made the Simple Mail Transfer Protocol (SMTP) influential and one of the still current email protocol standards, together with POP3 and IMAP.

Fast, cheap, and more or less universally popular, email is the ideal medium for online marketing. In the early 2000s, around 90 per cent of web users went online primarily to view and send email. Inevitably, this immensely powerful, free, global, anonymous communication medium with no effective policing would be abused by some. By 2003, half of all email was spam, as noted earlier.

Junk email shifts the costs of advertising from the advertiser to the recipient, like a telemarketer calling you collect. The economics of junk email facilitated massive exploitation and because junk emailers could send an email to millions of people at practically no cost, the volume of junk email increased exponentially from the mid-1990s, threatening to stifle the internet as an effective means of communication. Botnets – networks of virus-infected computers – sent up to 80 per cent of spam. Email boxes everywhere were bombarded with ubiquitous, unavoidable, and repetitive advertisements for $ex, V!agra, Di3t P!!!s and a host of other products, deliberately misspelled to evade spam blockers. It was very annoying.

The public were advised never reply to a spam as a 'remove' request simply told the spammer your email address was active, and you would be spammed even more. Some *commercial marketers* would even honour a 'remove' request, whilst passing the address onwards to another entity as a 'confirmed live'.

One spam email sent to vast numbers of recipients could turn into hundreds, even thousands of megabytes of data, costing individuals and their internet service providers countless millions in lost time, lost money, extra staff hours, damaged equipment, lost productivity, and lost business opportunities.

Technology alone couldn't stop the scourge of spam. As long as there was an economic incentive to send junk email, users and ISPs would need some legal recourse to stop the growing flood. Many efforts were made to outlaw spam, for example the *Coalition Against Unsolicited Commercial Email* (CAUCE) was founded in May 1997, by a group of concerned internet users, to advocate for anti-spam laws in the US.

Highlighting the enormity that the spam problem had become by 2002, the European Commissioner with responsibility for information technology, Erkki Liikanen, said that spam had cost European businesses an estimated €2.25 billion in lost productivity that year, as he appealed for international cooperation to fight it.[42] European Commission (EC) legislation banning unwanted email was due to come into force in November 2003[50] – the *Directive for Privacy and Electronic Communications* – but given the global nature of the internet, it was expected to have little effect: most spam came from the United States and China and would be outside the law's reach.

In 2005, Ferris Research estimated the worldwide cost of spam to be €39 billion.[43] By 2009, the cost had rocketed to €91.6 billion according to a European Commission report published that November, which noted that spam accounted for more than 90 per cent of total email traffic.[44]

As spam's runaway growth continued, the debate over opt-in versus opt-out raged on. The anti-spam community believed that any email that wasn't opt-in was spam. But many marketers rejected this interpretation, arguing that sending messages not explicitly asked for was OK as long as they were relevant, and people could easily opt out. By 2014, an average of 54 billion spam messages were being sent every day, according to Cyberoam.

TRUST! A Virtual, Technical and Political Minefield

'We have to democratise the new economy.
We must ensure that it is open to all'

Tony Blair, UK Prime Minister, Knowledge 2000 Conference, 7 March 2000[45]

The famous 1993 cartoon, 'On the internet, nobody knows you're a dog', resonated with consumers in the early days of e-commerce when schoolboy pranksters could pretend to be banks plausibly enough to trick gullible novice internet surfers into emailing through their credit card and PIN numbers. Throughout the 1990s the media revelled in alarmist stories of scams, misrepresentations and downright abysmal service.

In the late 1990s there were still no official guidelines for setting up and running a website. Even major organisations were 'just making it up as they went along', with consumers suffering any resulting inconvenience and risk. In late 1997, UK law firm Eversheds reported that 83 per cent of UK companies it surveyed had planned and implemented their websites without taking on any legal advice. Even those that did take advice often provided appalling services, either because they didn't know any better, or because they thought that merchants could do as they liked and 'practice' in public, using consumers as guineapigs.

"On the Internet, nobody knows you're a dog."

Figure 18: This cartoon by Peter Steiner appeared on page 61 of the 5 July 1993 issue of *The New Yorker*. It is the most reproduced cartoon in the magazine's history.[124] (*Reprinted with permission from www.CartoonStock.com*)

> **'It's official: Most UK e-tailers break the law:**
> **eight out of ten often fail to protect consumers...'**
>
> *Deirdre Hutton, Chairman, National Consumer Council, 19 September 2001*

In 2000, shopping via the internet remained a fraught experience for both consumers and merchants, brimming with opportunities to make costly and embarrassing mistakes. Year after year, *lack of consumer confidence* was identified by the IMRG membership as the primary factor inhibiting consumer take-up of internet shopping and preventing those who did shop online doing so more and for higher value items.

Tony Blair: 'The e-generation is with us'

Tony Blair, the country's youngest leader since 1812, had become the UK Prime Minister on 2 May 1997, aged 43. In 1999 Blair declared that he was going to *make Britain the best place in the world to do e-commerce* and created three new offices to make it so: *E-Commerce Minister, Minister of State for E-Commerce* at the Department of Trade and Industry, and the *E-Envoy*. IMRG's membership in effect *was e-commerce*, so of course we engaged closely with Blair's e-team and were invited to make strategic recommendations for Great e-Britain.

Alex Allan took up his post as the first the E-Envoy on 1 January 2000 and one of his initial tasks was to help Blair launch IMRG's Greenwich Electronic Time (GeT) – more on that later. Alex Allan was only in the post of e-Envoy for a few months, during which time the e-envoy's aspirations were moderated from *making e-Britain Great* to *getting government departments and services online*. Allan was succeeded by Andrew Pinder, in October 2000, who ran the e-Envoy Office until it was wound up in September 2004.

TrustUK

Patricia Hewitt became the Minister of State for E-Commerce at the Department of Trade and Industry (DTI) on 28 July 1999. She invited IMRG to work with the government to provide 'authoritative advice with one voice', acknowledging that *lack of consumer confidence* was the e-commerce industry's biggest problem, and that the situation was exacerbated by the media and a horde of *experts* giving conflicting advice on *how to stay safe online* – advice that was confusing and often plain wrong.

An 'Alliance for Electronic Business' (AEB) had been set up in 1998 with Colin Lloyd, the longtime CEO of the British Direct Marketing Association, as its chief executive. Colin's catchphrase at the time was the Erasmus quote, 'In the land of the blind, the one-eyed man is king.' The AEB's role was to bring together various business, industry and government organisations – Advertising Standards Authority, British Bankers' Association, Confederation of British Industry, Mail Order Protection Scheme, National Consumer Council, Department of Trade and Industry, and so forth.

The AEB seconded IMRG in early 1999 to be part of its *Consumer Protection Working Party*. IMRG found participation in this group an uphill task due to others' lack of relevant experience and focus (one government representative routinely fell asleep at meetings), and we had to provide much of the leadership. IMRG developed and put forward a detailed plan for establishing a world-leading e-commerce trading framework to enhance the competitiveness of Britain's merchants, and I proposed that it be called *TrustUK*.

To my dismay, while the name *TrustUK* was adopted, it was gifted to the Consumers' Association (the publisher of *Which?* that had recently set up the *Which? Web Trader* accreditation scheme) and all other aspects of IMRG's plan were ditched. TrustUK was launched by Patricia Hewitt at the DTI on 16 February 2000 as an e-commerce codes accreditation scheme. A press release stated: 'Nearly 90 per cent of internet users [87 per cent] want independent certification saying a site is safe for online shopping.'

TrustUK – which was endorsed but not funded by government – was a joint venture between the Consumers' Association and the AEB, in consultation with the Office of Fair Trading. TrustUK would *accredit codes of conduct to make sure that they provided good protection for online shoppers.* In other words, it was *a code of practice for codes of practice* that, for a fee, would allow its badge to be displayed alongside certified badges.

The TrustUK plan was deeply flawed and unworkable, as I advised the IMRG Senate at the time: 'Whereas one could expect some slight imperfections in the first iteration of such a multi-participant plan, unfortunately TrustUK is littered with show-stoppers, and these are not its main problems.' It failed SMEs, focused on maintaining the status quo, added no value, and was little more than a box-ticking exercise.

TrustUK launched its *e-hallmark* on 18 July 2000. Three years later it had only two member organisations – the Association of British Travel Agents and the Direct Marketing Association – and just 75 merchants signed up to the scheme. TrustUK reported a loss of £4,183 on turnover of £7,500 for 2003, and at the time of writing (2020) remains a dormant company.

* * *

The UK government could easily have solved the e-trust problem by providing an identity verification mechanism to enable consumers to validate that shops were who they claimed to be and okay to shop with – as they did in the high street. Alternatively, the government could have endorsed the industry's efforts and helped IMRG to nail the trust issue. They did neither.

Worse still, rather than either grasping the nettle or standing back and letting the industry get on with self-regulation, the government became a loose cannon, randomly firing off absurd missives. For example, in October 2000 the government issued guidelines recommending that consumers should only shop online with merchants they knew, completely undermining a primary benefit of internet shopping: choice. Then in 2001 the government published five *Safe Internet Shopping Tips* of which the first one was wrong – it stated: 'PAYMENT: In the EU, the card company must refund you if your credit or debit card is used fraudulently.' – in fact, consumers' rights to refunds were neither automatic nor uniform.

* * *

Several independent e-ID cross-referencing schemes emerged, all attempting to address the 'internet trust' issue, and each floundered for one or more of three reasons: (1) *lack of consumer awareness* – they were unable to gain critical mass and traction; (2) *lack of funding* – their business model, typically based on marketing returns, proved unsustainable; (3) *they were too expensive* and so failed to serve the SMEs who most needed such schemes but could not afford high fees. An example of the latter was the European Commission-backed scheme, *Euro-Label*: http://www.euro-label.com. This cost the best part of £1,000 per annum to facilitate each merchant with what Euro-Label considered to be a 'proper audit', so while being well intentioned, it was too expensive for retailers to gain accreditation by and therefore attracted little take-up, rendering it of negligible use to consumers as it offered so few shops to choose from.

Trust schemes that had been and gone by 2003 included:

- **Which? Web Trader:** Operated by the Consumers' Association, publisher of *Which?* magazine, this was the mainstay of the UK government's TrustUK programme. Which? Web Trader closed at the end of January 2003, saying that it had become too costly to run, having operated since July 2000. The scheme confused and alienated many merchants because Which? had relationships with electrical, car and other retailers whose discounted services for Which? readers it promoted heavily.

- **ShopSmart:** Barclaycard bought the ShopSmart shopping price comparison site for £1 million in April 2001 and proceeded to subsume its *Indigo Square* shopping portal as a combined operation. After teething problems, Barclaycard took full control of ShopSmart in September 2001, but was unable to make the service work and closed the site down at the end of 2002.

- **SafeDoor:** Securicor PLC introduced SafeDoor, a secure shopping portal, in January 2001 and promoted it with a £7 million marketing campaign that March. The aim was to allay fears about online credit card fraud by operating a system whereby e-retailers were paid for their goods and services, prior to customers' credit cards being debited, thereby shielding customer identity. Securicor closed the scheme in May 2002 having recorded a loss of £11.8 million in the previous year.

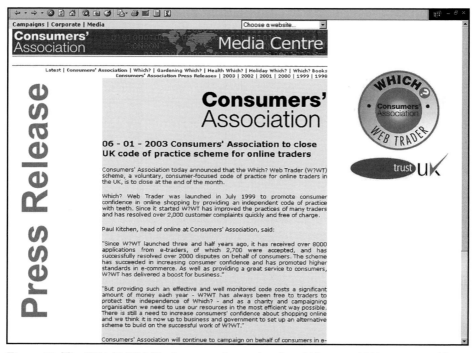

Figure 19: The Which? Web Trader trust scheme closed on 31 January 2003, as reported here. (*Image used with permission from Which?*)

Meanwhile, the IMRG membership continued to flag *lack of trust* as the primary factor inhibiting take-up of internet shopping. So, in 2001, having abandoned any hope of the government actually taking pragmatic steps to *make Britain the best place in the world to do e-commerce*, IMRG launched its own Internet Shopping Is Safe (ISIS) trust scheme, which was quickly adopted by hundreds of e-retailers, and helped foster the sector's fastest ever growth period, as we shall see.

Summing up the '90s

The '90s was the decade when tech shrank the world. The World Wide Web came from non-existent to Wall Street obsession. PCs dramatically improved and were adopted by consumers en masse.

The Microsoft Windows operating system became virtually ubiquitous on IBM PC compatibles. Its high performance and pervasiveness helped standards to emerge that gave consumers true multimedia at home – music, video, primitive streaming and online shopping – and businesses a platform on which to begin to trade online.

Mavericks experimented with everything. Some of the crazy ideas even worked. IMRG became a lightning conductor for e-commerce energy, illuminating the strange new environment; a forum for synergy between experimentation and something actionable.

From a few million people using online services, by the end of the decade more than half of the population in some Western countries had internet access, and more than a quarter had cell phones. Many were tentatively shopping online.

This Web 1.0 'read-only-web' era spawned a startling new digital world where the laws of physics and traditional metrics didn't apply; its infinite unreal estate and virtual addresses were soon deemed to be worth billions.

As the wondrous new millennium approached, the bug in the e-commerce ointment was dysfunctional behaviour on the stock market. Investors looking for supernova IPOs from wildly wasteful start-ups poured cash into highly speculative companies with little or no potential for profitability, showing yet again that people never learn – they just keep on blowing ever bigger economic bubbles.

Part II

2000–2010

2000: The New Millennium! Bug, Bubble, Bust and Boom

'Almost every dot-com idea from 1999 that failed will succeed'

Marc Andreessen, co-founder of Netscape, 2000

Five years earlier, many people had not even heard of the internet, but by 2000, some 30 per cent of Britons were on it, and seven million had shopped online. Not to be left behind, Labour's Prime Minister Tony Blair sent his first email and browsed his first website a few days before the end of the twentieth century.

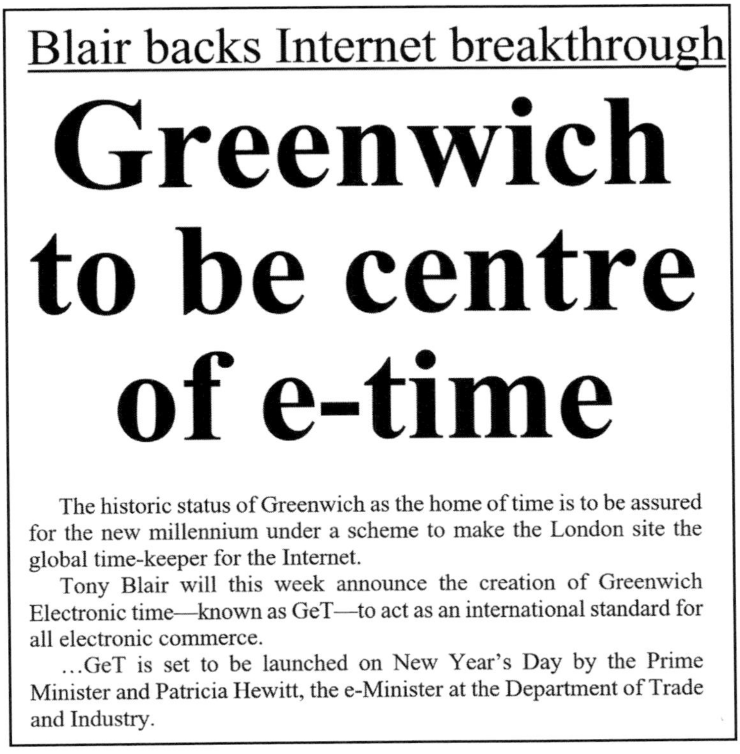

> ## Blair backs Internet breakthrough
>
> # Greenwich to be centre of e-time
>
> The historic status of Greenwich as the home of time is to be assured for the new millennium under a scheme to make the London site the global time-keeper for the Internet.
>
> Tony Blair will this week announce the creation of Greenwich Electronic time—known as GeT—to act as an international standard for all electronic commerce.
>
> ...GeT is set to be launched on New Year's Day by the Prime Minister and Patricia Hewitt, the e-Minister at the Department of Trade and Industry.

Figure 20: 1 January 2000 – *The Times'* front page lead story on 28 December 1999 was that Tony Blair was to announce IMRG's Greenwich Electronic Time (GeT) scheme. (*Used with permission from The Times / News Licensing*)

Wow! What a party! All over the world, the millennium arrived with a big bang, and street, square and beach parties attended by millions of revellers. Holiday companies, airlines and hotels complained about trade being lower than expected, but champagne makers, fireworks companies and cleaners (hopefully on overtime!) all had a bumper season.

It had been predicted that a huge problem in the coding of computer systems – *the Millennium Bug*, or Y2K (Year 2000) as it was dubbed – would create havoc as the date switched from 1999 to 2000. Aeroplanes would fall out of the sky, elevators would plummet, utilities would fail and cash machines would hurl out money if the doomsters were to be believed. The root of the problem was that early computer systems with tiny memories had abbreviated four-digit years to two digits to save space, so computers still using this format might crash when confronted with the ascending number assumption switching from 99 to 00. After several years of international alarm, feverish preparations, and expensive programming corrections – an estimated $300 billion was spent on Y2K compliance worldwide – the new millennium breezed in, digitally fuss free.

On New Year's Day 2000, Tony Blair launched IMRG's Greenwich Electronic Time (GeT) as the universal time standard for the internet. Government and Industry had joined forces to synchronise time for internet users worldwide to Greenwich Mean Time, he declared, and would provide tools to set online transactions, delivery agreements, customer service and email across time zones to a uniform time standard. 'It's a stroke of genius,' commented one senior Whitehall source. 'It plays to the Prime Minster's whole thing about making Britain the best in the world for e-commerce, and it goes nicely with the millennium and Greenwich.' More later on how lack of government follow-through scuppered this programme, consigning forever GMT to be a mere *time zone*: unknown to most, GMT's role as the worldwide *Time Standard* had been usurped by UTC (Coordinated Universal Time), supervised by the Paris-based *Bureau International des Poids et Mesures* (BIPM).

The FT's main headline was 'Yeltsin quits and hands power over to Putin'. The financial markets' first news of the new year was £100 billion wiped off the Financial Times Stock Exchange 100 Index (aka FTSE, the collective name for the 100 largest UK companies by value) overnight. *We told you so*, said the 'back to mono' pundits, *there go your technology stocks – overvalued, overhyped and over here.* But two weeks later this was being regarded as merely an 'adjustment' as the FTSE bounced back.

The second piece of financial news was AOL's midnight swoop on Time-Warner, swallowing up the media giant in a $366 billion deal, at the time the biggest in history. This proved to be the high-water mark of the dot.com bubble. In fact, AOL was the last major net company without a media partner – practically all the world's large media companies had already formed new media alliances: NBC/Cnet/Snap; Fox/BT/News Corp; CMGI/Compaq/AltaVista; USA Networks/Lycos/Ticketmaster; AT&T/Excite@Home/MSN; and CBS/Marketwatch/Sportsline.

Christmas trading results came in, revealing that Britain's 17 million internet surfers had spent some £200 million online. Amazon claimed UK sales of £26 million for Q4 1999, compared with £4.9 million a year earlier, at the time Amazon.co.uk's first quarter in business in Blighty. While sales were up overall, some internet retailers made heavy losses – collectively £75 million according to one estimate – due to lack of scale, heavy marketing costs, online discounting, and inefficient filling of orders, with many goods delivered late.

> *'Like "the horseless carriage", "etailing" is a silly name,*
> *and the sooner it goes away the better'*
>
> Jo Tucker, Managing Director, IMRG, 2000

In the US, online Christmas 1999 revenues approached $7 billion. AOL reported that its 25 million US members alone had shelled out in the region of $2.5 billion. Amazon.com, the most visited shopping site, reported fourth-quarter sales up more than 150 per cent on the previous year at $650 million (up from $253 million a year earlier), but with no narrowing of its loss level, which had ballooned to $720 million in 1999. It also reported that during the last seven weeks of 1999, 2.5 million new customers had shopped at Amazon.com, and it forecast sales of $4 billion for 2001, up from $1.64 billion in 1999.

Dotpocalypse

The long-anticipated burst of the dot.com bubble finally came on 10 March 2000, when the technology heavy NASDAQ Composite index peaked at 5,048.62 (intra-day peak 5,132.52), more than double its value just a year before. Excessive speculation in internet-based companies had begun in 1995 and two years later the Nasdaq was attracting record amounts of capital. By 1999, 39 per cent of all venture capital was going to internet companies. That year 295 of the 457 IPOs were related to web outfits, and then in the first quarter of 2000 there were a further ninety-one.

The dot.com crash lasted through to 9 October 2002. Its many casualties included Webvan, Pets.com, eToys.com, WorldCom, Global Crossing, ClickMango, Boxman, Dreamticket.com, wowgo.com, swizzle.com, intersaver.co.uk, Sportal, Loaded and Beenz.

Some 80 per cent of bricks and mortar start-ups also suffered the slings and arrows of outrageous fortune then failed, so a sprinkling of dot.com retail crashes should have surprised nobody. The issue was that dot.coms failed so very extravagantly: Boo.com had collapsed after spending $188 million in venture capital in just six months.

A classic example of this excessive speculation was *Kibu.com*, a site for teenage girls that focused on 'fashion, music and boys' which closed in March 2000 just forty-six days after its launch. Described at the time as *just another of the many overfunded and under-thought-out initiatives in the kids and teens market*, Kibu, based in a trendy part of San Francisco, had thrown a flashy launch party and was reported to have sent staff to an all-day conference with a consultant to try to come up with a mission statement.[46] Netscape co-founder Jim Clark and several other high-profile investors had poured $22 million into Kibu.com.

Other companies *only just* managed to scrape through the mayhem, including Cisco, whose stock value fell 86 per cent. By the end of the crash, stocks had lost $5 trillion in market capitalisation since the dot.com peak.

Amazon.com also came close to being one of the casualties with its share price plunging 75 per cent before the Christmas 2000 retail bonanza delivered a customary fillip to its stock. Amazon had grown fast using cash raised in its IPO on 15 May 1997, in the middle of the dot.com boom. Several of the companies it had invested in failed, but Amazon showed no sign of scaling back its ambitions and focused on getting existing customers to buy more – Amazon derived almost two-thirds of its sales from repeat customers. Amazon.com's rubber brand continued stretching every which way to cover more and more of the things consumers were looking for online.

Amazon.co.uk dominated the UK e-retail space and was the first European e-commerce site to reach two million customers, in the summer of 2000, a doubling of its customer base in less than eight months. Amazon.co.uk was ranked number one in Europe as the most visited shopping site, followed by Amazon.com (the US parent) and Amazon.de (its German site).

This was a period of severe disruption, not just in financial markets but also in how companies traded. The internet gave businesses a newfound flexibility to try out new business models, and its pioneers deserved better help that they were getting from many analysts and the money markets they served, who stood to benefit enormously from online innovators' efforts.

To counter the 2000 stock market crash, the US Federal Reserve eased credit availability and drove interest rates down to lows not seen in many decades. These low interest rates fuelled growth of debt at all levels of the economy, particularly private debt to purchase more expensive housing. A real estate bubble soon followed.

> *'It is astonishing how much money was wasted chasing dreams in a vacuum. However, the core concept remains valid: networked screens will constitute 'the marketplace' and transform the way all of us shop'*
>
> IMRG Comment article, February 2001

Stock market valuations lurched from 'way too high' to 'way too low'. Particularly unhelpful was the analyst herd's pursuit of a 'formula' for e-commerce success, as they tried to identify familiar patterns within the enigma that the nascent interactive markets remained. 'Subscriptions' had been 'It' – then 'advertising' and 'affiliate marketing'. 'Intranets' and 'extranets' had won and lost favour. After that 'content' became 'King' and 'exchanges' were esteemed. Unsurprisingly they couldn't find a magic recipe: most analysts didn't even understand the interactive market as a medium in which a 'formula' would operate. If they had swapped their microscopes for telescopes, they might have begun to get the e-marketplace into focus, for it was several orders of magnitude larger and more far-reaching than they seemed able to appreciate. The digisphere needed to be viewed and evaluated on its own extraordinary terms. It would take years, not days, to show whether the land being grabbed was fertile, desert or swamp.

Dangerous stuff that t'internet!

The public was constantly warned of the internet's perils. Not a week passed without a new round of scare stories about glitches, rogues and scams – and yet another report being published highlighting the risks of shopping online. Scaremongering commentators insisted that internet customers could have no idea who the online upstarts were, or where physically they might be. *Were they foreign? Were they real?* Predictably, consumer confidence remained the e-retail industry's biggest challenge.

According to a National Consumer Council survey of 3 August 2000, only 3 per cent of UK adults regularly shopped online for *fear of releasing credit-card and personal details*, the *lack of opportunity to check goods before buying*, *delivery problems* and the *risk of fraudulent suppliers*.

On 12 October, under the headline *Net shopping 'pitfalls' warning*, the BBC reported that a Trading Standards Institute survey of 102 companies found that almost 40 per cent of goods ordered did not arrive on time, and 17 per cent were not delivered at all. Officers said *some of the biggest names in retailing are not getting their customer service right*. This was because *systems crashed, companies vanished, items were out of stock or simply forgotten*, and *poor or misleading descriptions*.[47]

Europe had not experienced very much online crime at this point, and though media puff focused on the threat from sloppy service and the occasional rogue merchant, the far bigger issue was rogue consumers. Word travelled fast on the net, and while Europe's businesses and governments were taking their time to respond to its new opportunities, Europe's villains could be relied upon to catch on in a flash. And the *Distance Selling Directive* was about to open up yet more opportunities for rogue consumers.

All of the old favourite crimes were moving online, and internet fraud was about to replace 'gas station crime' as the 'crime of choice', particularly of the young. IMRG commented at the time, 'Coming soon to a computer near you are theft, hacking, deception, cheating, duplicity, use of stolen payment cards, denial of receipt, bogus returns, ordering for delivery to false addresses, e-vandalism, and all the rest. But our primary concern is the new generation of tricks that are constantly being invented on and enabled by the internet. What will the cyberfraudsters dream up next?'

> *'Hang a thief when he's young, and he'll no' steal when he's auld'*
>
> Scottish proverb, often cited by IMRG's payment adviser, Scott Thomson of QPQ (QPQ stood for quid pro quo – 'something for something' in Latin)

Only a collective and concerted effort by all of the responsible market players – merchants, police, banks, card schemes, carriers and governments – had any hope of effectively confronting the threat from online fraudsters, as the IMRG Payments Forum had been flagging for years. But this was not happening. E-retailers were abandoned in the rising tide of consumer crime by the intransigence and complacency of the only people who could help them.

And speaking of banks behaving badly, NatWest Bank went to the wall on 11 February 2000 having surrendered to a £21 billion takeover bid from the Royal Bank of Scotland, ending 342 years of independence: staff numbers would be slashed by 18,000, equivalent to a fifth of the two banks' combined 90,000 workforce. Strangled by its own bureaucracy, scorn was heaped on NatWest from every direction. Millions of customers had been fed up with its hopeless online banking solution and horrible automated telephone response system, looping endlessly – *you now have five options...* NatWest, the self-proclaimed 'Number 1 business bank', had been notorious for stifling progress through its unwillingness to provide funding for innovation. But nobody was more fed up with NatWest than its retailer clients whose online trading efforts were undermined by its abysmal online payments and security services.

The Distance Selling Directive 2000

> *'It's the key to free motoring – you simply order 52 new cars during the year and keep each one for a week. But what about the 'fair trading rights of merchants?' And which poor sod is going to feature in the 'test case.' Personally, I am fed up with politicians who have no qualms about knowingly issuing impracticable rules, so long as they 'scan' well in the media'*
>
> A senior lawyer (and IMRG Member), London, October 2000

Consumers already had far stronger legal protection when shopping online than in traditional retail transactions, nevertheless the European Commission took it upon itself to beef up its distance selling regulations, opening up yet more opportunities for rogue consumers, and massive cost implications for e-retailers.

The *Distance Selling Directive*, first mooted in 1998, came into effect on 4 June 2000, making it compulsory for e-retailers to provide online shoppers with a seven-day 'cooling off period', during which the consumer was entitled to withdraw from the contract with a full refund – even after goods were dispatched. In the UK, the Directive was interpreted in the *Regulations* as requiring the retailer to provide a refund to the consumer as soon as possible and in any case within 30 days of the notice of cancellation being given regardless of whether or not the item had been returned to the retailer and of its condition. E-retailers failing to comply would be liable to hefty fines. The inevitable result was widespread abuse by unscrupulous consumers, such as clothes being worn for a weekend, then returned for a full refund including delivery costs.

The retailer's only available remedy was a right of action against the consumer for breach of statutory duty. But the commercial reality was that the costs of taking such action against a consumer would almost always exceed the value of any claim, so in practice the remedy was worthless. All this placed a disproportionate regulatory burden on entirely genuine and legitimate businesses who performed contracts exactly as requested by the consumer, and was ultimately detrimental to consumers by significantly restricting their access and choice by deterring retailers from making their full range of goods and services available online, particularly higher value items.

Several merchants told IMRG that they were simply ignoring the 'largely unworkable' Consumer Protection (Distance Selling) Regulations 2000.

The Rise of the e-Retailers

'We were lucky that the UK fashion scene is unparalleled. I don't profess to be a big fashion person, but I've walked up and down global high streets and I've never seen the variety we've got in London'

Nick Robertson, Co-founder and CEO from 2000 to 2015, ASOS

Rising to the e-commerce opportunity, a growing band of determined retailing entrepreneurs was emerging to service the rocketing demand. Some of these upstarts would soon eclipse the old guard and become the new establishment.

On 19 January 2000 came news that London-based Lastminute.com was to receive major funding of £31 million from investment agreements with seven giant companies including Sony and the British Airports Authority. Online travel specialist Lastminute.com had been founded in October 1998 by Martha Lane Fox and Brent Hoberman, since when it had attracted over 600,000 members and branched into new areas including online auctions and gift retail. This investment, and partnerships with companies from the international media, entertainment, and travel industries, would consolidate the company's bid to become a global player in the e-commerce marketplace.

Ocado, the British online supermarket, was launched as a concept in January 2000 and founded as a business that April by former merchant bankers with Goldman Sachs, Jonathan Faiman, Jason Gissing and Tim Steiner. Ocado was to have no stores and make all home deliveries from its warehouses. Ocado started trading as a business in partnership with Waitrose in January 2002, and would go on to become the UK's most valuable retailer amid the Covid-19 mayhem of late 2020, valued at £21.7 billion.

Tesco announced on 19 January 2000 that its online grocery shopping business was the biggest in the world and profitable, and that 2,000 new shoppers were signing on with *Tesco Direct* every week. Tesco began internet operations in 1994 (with a CDROM-based off-line system that would only connect to download stock lists and send orders) and started an online shopping service named Tesco Direct in 1997. Now, with annualised sales of £125 million and 250,000 registered users, Tesco Direct was poised for further expansion which would create 7,000 jobs. By the end of the year, 90 per cent of the UK population would have access to the online service, available from 300 of Tesco's 640 stores, and its range was to be expanded to offer non-food items like books, clothing, gifts, furnishings and banking services. 'We are now the biggest online grocery business in the world, and that is fact,' said Tesco.com's chief executive, John Browett. Its nearest rival was Peapod, which then had 100,000 e-customers. Peapod is a US grocery business and one of the earliest internet start-ups that had launched its website in 1996.

EasyJet claimed to be selling $1 million (£650,000) per day over the internet in May 2000, representing 61 per cent of its flights. Self-styled in 1998 as 'The Web's Favourite Airline' (a play on BA's tagline 'the world's favourite airline'), easyJet had been established by Stelios Haji-Ioanniou at the age of 33 in 1995, using a low-cost business model pioneered by the US operator Southwest Airlines. Initially, easyJet flight booking was by telephone only and all the aircraft were painted with the booking telephone number. When his team suggested trialling direct online sales in December 1997, Stelios replied: 'The Internet is for nerds, it will never make money for my business!' But a trial, using a different telephone reservations number on the website to track effectiveness, was an immediate success, and a website offering real-time online booking went live in April 1998, the first such website for a low-cost airline in Europe. Internet bookings were priced cheaper than booking by telephone to reflect the reduced call centre costs: as a further means of encouraging use of the website, aircraft were repainted with the web address.

As easyJet approached its flotation on the London Stock Exchange on 5 November 2000, analysts expressed cynicism about its *new economy* business model that focused on giving its customers the best deal rather than maximising investors' profits. By this time, 80 per cent of easyJet's 5.5 million passengers booked via the internet, saving 30 per cent of the costs incurred by airlines that booked through conventional channels, and the company planned to be the first airline selling 100 per cent of its tickets online. EasyJet had already revolutionised flying within Europe for ordinary people by making low fares to more destinations more easily available to a larger market. EasyJet recorded a pre-tax profit of £22 million for the year ended 30 September 2000, and in the event, the floatation was seven times oversubscribed, opening with a healthy premium.

John Lewis had launched a minimal website, *Johnlewisnow.com*, in 1999 selling a limited selection of items such as chocolate, linen and ties, and handled just twenty orders a day. In February 2001 John Lewis bought the UK arm of troubled US hi-fi and gadget website Buy.com for $4 million (£2.9 million) and used its technology and people, plus a further £27 million of investment, to turbo-charge its internet offering, which was relaunched as *johnlewis.com* on 8 October 2001. Now with some 5,000 products available, John Lewis immediately *clicked* with digital audiences and in the run-up to Christmas was taking 1,000 orders online per day. John Lewis went on to become a dominant e-retail leader – by early 2013/14 JohnLewis.com's annual online sales reached £1 billion, a quarter of the department store division's turnover.

e-Motor Mania

Automobile Association research in the 1990s identified that UK consumers would rather visit a dentist and have a tooth drilled than open a conversation with a car salesman. People so hated the car selling experience that many would visit dealer showrooms when they were shut. If ever an industry had a customer relationship problem, the motor industry was it.

To the European car buyer's rescue now came a rapidly growing list of new online entrants including banks (e.g. Royal Bank of Scotland with *Jamjar.com*), software companies (e.g. Microsoft, with a European version of *CarPoint*, its US car sales portal), consumer groups (e.g. the Consumers' Association with its *carbusters.com*), car clubs (e.g. The AA with its *Autotrader* partnership), and a host of other opportunists (e.g. Richard Branson with his *Virgincars.com*: Tesco too joined in, announcing plans to sell cars online). All saw a wide-open opportunity for almost anyone to profitably sell cars except those lumbered down with an existing car sales infrastructure and mentality.

Royal Bank of Scotland made the strongest of these internet plays in Europe at the time by launching Jamjar.com in July 2000, which promised to save its customers at least 10 per cent on the price of new cars and 25–30 per cent on *special offer* cars in a marketing campaign costing insurance division Direct Line £15 million. Jamjar.com's marketing included national TV, radio and consumer interest magazine advertising, and sponsorship of a new television motoring show, *The Real Car Show*. Jamjar.com clocked up over three million page impressions and over £1 million of car sales in its first week of trading.

Virgin Cars launched in May 2000, claiming to give its UK customers savings of up to 40 per cent. Instead of the usual ten-minute spin up the road, they would deliver the customer's chosen model to their door and leave it with them to test drive for 24 hours – or even a weekend.

By mid-2000, the internet was said to influence half of all the US's eighteen million annual car purchases, with double the number of buyers researching their purchase online than two years earlier. Consumers saw the benefits of online car buying as saving time and money – $490 on average on the purchase of a new vehicle – providing better information about vehicles and promotions, and helping in making comparisons. Only 1 per cent actually bought their vehicle online, however 7 per cent of those surveyed said they were 'very likely' to buy their next new vehicle online and a further 12 per cent were 'likely' to. Microsoft claimed that CarPoint, originally launched in 1996 with close links to Auto-By-Tel, attracted some six million US visitors, and was generating more than $650 million (£450 million) in car sales, each month.

Car finance was a huge and highly lucrative business that gave manufacturers a whole set of levers with which to cut deals and shape their marketing offers. The vast majority of car finance was arranged within the dealership. It followed that if the dealer was cut out of the sales cycle, so might be the manufacturer's opportunity to promote and sell finance. Suddenly the bargaining power was shifting from the car manufacturer to the well-informed consumer.

The stakes were high. Ford Credit, the world's largest automotive finance company, provided vehicle financing in forty countries to more than ten million customers and more than 11,500 automotive dealers – with net finance receivables of $156 billion for the first half of 2000.

We can loan you enough money to get you completely out of debt

Sign on a bank, 2000

In view of RBS's Jamjar venture, was the answer to the question 'What do we need banks for?' going to be 'to buy cars from because the car manufacturers are so inept at selling them'? Some people were quick to quip that banks should focus on being better at banking rather than competing with their own customers.

Magic: Harry is chosen

On 8 July 2000, the biggest single order in the history of e-commerce thus far took place when *Harry Potter and the Goblet of Fire* was published in both the US and UK on the same day, strategically a Saturday to avoid conflicting with schooltime. The fourth in the series of J. K. Rowling's novels chronicling the life of the young wizard and his friends had a combined first printing of over five million copies. On the day of issue Amazon.com and Federal Express shipped 250,000 copies of *Harry Potter and the Goblet of Fire* to US homes, while Royal Mail delivered 500,000 copies to front doors throughout the UK.

The first book in the series, *Harry Potter and the Philosopher's Stone* had an initial print-run of just 500 copies in 1997, whereas the seventh and final novel, *Harry Potter and the Deathly Hallows* sold eleven million copies within twenty-four hours of its release. A magical coincidence no doubt was that the sixth book in the series, *Harry Potter and the Half Blood Prince*, was published on the tenth anniversary of Amazon.com starting to sell books online in July 1995 – it sold nine million copies within a day of its publication (many via Amazon). Harry Potter is the best-selling book series in history, having sold more than 500 million copies worldwide in eighty languages by 2018 – the vast majority bought online.

ASOS: The UK e-retail legend

ASOS.com is an online-only fashion and cosmetic retailer and the peerless British e-retail success story. Founded in London in 2000, just as most dot.coms were struggling to survive, ASOS pioneered online retailing and by 2019 had become one of the largest and most famous fashion e-commerce sites globally with sales approaching £3 billion. The Duchess of Cambridge, Samantha Cameron and First Lady Michelle Obama have all worn ASOS's own-label designs.

ASOS was established on 3 June 2000 by Nick Robertson, Andrew Regan and Quentin Griffiths, with a £2.8 million loan. The idea was to sell items inspired by celebrity style from films and television, but at a low price point, its acronym standing for *As Seen On Screen*. Originally ASOS wasn't fashion-specific – the first product it sold was a pestle and mortar – but, as Nick Robertson put it: 'We decided to follow the pound. Fashion had a higher margin than anything else, and own brand had an even greater margin'.[48]

Before founding ASOS, Nicholas John Robertson had no background in the clothing industry, though as the great-grandson of Austin Reed it would seem that fashion was in his blood. As its CEO from 2000 to 2015, Nick led ASOS's directorial approach, applying expertise and insight into consumer behaviour he had acquired while working previously in advertising. Nick started his career in 1987 with the advertising agency Young & Rubicam, and in 1991 moved to Carat, the UK's largest media planning and buying agency. In 1995 he co-founded Entertainment Marketing, a small marketing services business. Recognising that presentation was the key to fashion sales, Nick soon brought the ASOS PR team in house.

A condition attached to the loan used to establish the company was that it had to be floated, to enable the investors' exit, so in 2001 ASOS went on to AIM, the London Stock Exchange's junior market for smaller and growing businesses. The timing was terrible, dot.coms having just gone disastrously pear-shaped. Looking back in a 2017 *Drapers* article, Nick commented: 'For the first three or four years we thought, "What have we done? We're in a floated company, our results are rubbish, and sales aren't great. It was bloody stressful – we had no money, and we couldn't go back and raise any more. So we just had to make it work. We ran it on an absolute shoestring; we didn't pay salaries for a month. Nobody else in the space operated like that."'

In the early days, ASOS offered products for every age group and even had a children's section at one point. They realised that they weren't clear on their proposition: Nick said 'We had £400 handbags on our site, but we'd decided to focus on twentysomething fashion. And guess what: 0.1 per cent of twentysomethings can afford £400 handbags. So they were out, gone.'

Over the first four years, ASOS worked to grow its young fast fashion sales, inspired by what Topshop at Oxford Circus was doing with the latest clothing trends, and what Amazon was doing with its website and ever-expanding product range. ASOS provided truly stress-free shopping along with an audacious delivery proposition: free worldwide shipping and free returns. ASOS focused on distribution efficiencies, localisation and a strategic international plan to scale globally.

ASOS innovated constantly to stay ahead of competitors, presenting the widest possible range of options to purchase, ship and track orders, and best-in-class navigation and usability. It established a strong base of brand-loyal customers with its customer-first policies, responsiveness, engagement, and personalized marketing. It was early to tap into social networking sites including Myspace, Twitter and Facebook, and to collect, aggregate and display comments about the company. This brave move demonstrated its authenticity and transparency, and retained customer interest while also developing a sense of community.

ASOS joined IMRG shortly after it started trading, and Nick was actively involved with us for many years. At one IMRG Senate meeting at Goodenough College, Bloomsbury, the conversation among the several senior retail directors attending centred around how market research and data analysis guided trading decisions. Nick was uncharacteristically quiet, so I pressed him for comment: his view was that, while data was important, gut instinct was more so for a retailer. On another occasion he joined our *Vente à Distance* (VAD) event as a speaker at the Grand Pallais, Lille, France: he essentially told the audience of mainly catalogue retailers that they were out of date and would soon be out of business – to my amazement they loved his presentation.

IMRG and Hitwise launched our *Hot Shops List* in May 2006. This ranked by popularity, as indicated by visits, the top 50 UK e-retailers. On the first *HSL*, ASOS scraped in fiftieth. By November 2008 they had climber to fourteenth, and in May 2009 they were up to ninth place, above easyJet, Topshop, River Island and John Lewis.

In June 2010 ASOS reported a £20.3 million profit on sales of £223 million that had grown 80 per cent every year for the previous nine.[49] That year, customers in the USA, France and Germany were enabled to order items from the ASOS website. The following year, websites were launched to serve customers in Spain, Italy and Australia, and ASOS chose the Australian city of Sydney to open its first non-UK office. In 2013, ASOS launched online stores for both Russia and China.

Between April 2015 and April 2016, over 20 per cent of the UK population placed an order with ASOS, many of whom were using its new seamless mobile app.

ASOS listened hard to its free-thinking and non-conforming Generation Z customers. It broke barriers with inclusive *genderless fashion*, replaced terms such as 'beauty' with 'face+body' and removed gender-specific sections for clothing and accessories. Its models were 'real' people, not pretentious, unrealistic glamouristas.

In 2019, ASOS was shipping 80,000 orders per day to its 20.3 million active customers in all 196 countries from fulfilment centres in the UK, US and EU. Retail sales that year were £2.733 billion, up 13 per cent on 2018,[50] though it reported in April that profits had plunged 87 per cent for the first half of the year after a difficult time caused by heavy discounting and website traffic issues.[51]

2020: ASOS.COM / ABOUT / WHO WE ARE

We believe in a world where you have total freedom to be you, without judgement. To experiment. To express yourself. To be brave and grab life as the extraordinary adventure it is. So we make sure everyone has an equal chance to discover all the amazing things they're capable of – no matter who they are, where they're from or what looks they like to boss. We exist to give you the confidence to be whoever you want to be.[122]

Nick, who was awarded an OBE for his achievements in the world of fashion retailing in late 2011, once claimed that ASOS's success was down to 'luck at every junction' – they were in the right place at the right time. In reality ASOS's phenomenal achievements are the result of a consistent, brilliant, passionate and exceptionally executed e-retail strategy, and the ethos elucidated, as I write, on the homepage of asosplc.com thus: *'We focus on fashion as a force for good, inspiring young people to express their best selves and achieve amazing things. We believe fashion thrives on individuality and should be fun for everyone.'*

Bricks & Clicks: Hello, Hello, Is Anybody There?

'When you've seen one shopping center you've seen a mall'

José Manuel Moreira Batista, private trader and investor

Most traditional retailers sighed with relief when the dot.com bubble burst, then largely stopped investing in e-retail for years as the threat from dot.com upstarts appeared to recede. Few realised how quickly the commercial viability of brick-and-mortar stores was eroding. Networked digital services were remorselessly driving prices down and competition up.

Conventional retailers had two great advantages when trading online. Firstly, consumers trusted their familiar, reliable brands, and knew where to find them if something went wrong. Secondly, they had powerful leverage with manufacturers to block online competitors' access to products. A survey in 2000 by *Goldfish* (British Gas' venture into the credit card business) claimed that traditional retailers were consistently offering 12.7 per cent lower online prices than pure dot.coms, and that prices for similar goods on the net could vary up to 40 per cent.

However, most retailers and product manufacturers still had no web presence at all in 2000, nor any e-commerce strategy. Those that did often presented little more than online brochures or were merely web-enabling a *nine-to-five* retail experience. The IMRG Report of August 2000 included findings of a Gartner Group study showing that 100 per cent of large retailers failed to achieve a ranking of *excellent* or even *good customer service* on the web: only 28 per cent even acknowledged that email enquiries had been received. Research published by Deloitte & Touche indicated that not enough British enterprises were getting the message.

Online sales may have been rising fast, 'but is anyone making money', retailers would ask. Dixons Stores Group announced its e-commerce turnover for the 28 weeks to 11 November 1999 had been up by more than 600 per cent to £10.8 million, though its internet services division's losses more than doubled to £4.4 million for the period, reflecting 'significant' new web start-up costs.

Meanwhile, consumers were embracing the internet enthusiastically and investing in their own *online shops at home* by way of buying PCs, software and internet connectivity. In a very real sense, homeowners were becoming the retailers' landlords, and were beginning to take control of the marketplace.

2001 was a year of strong and accelerating growth for e-retail. Sales that had previously been doubling year-on-year, grew 133 per cent to £4 billion as the surviving dot.coms and a few major brands swept up the online shopping opportunities so expensively developed and lost by the IT and investment communities. Around two million UK businesses – 80 per cent – had a website, and 540,000 were trading online. But most retailers were noticeably absent from this community.

2002 saw online shopping truly flying. IMRG commented that retail was being re-forged in the crucible of social change and that consumer demand for multichannel retail services was well ahead of supply. Also, that a second e-gold rush was inevitable – probably soon – and analysts wouldn't be allowed to steal the shovels this time. In 2003 there was a noticeable increase in activity associated with e-commerce IPOs, mergers and acquisitions. Facilitators, such as website developers and parcel carriers, were seeing strong client interest in improving their e-retail services, for which there was urgent need.

My High Street at Home

We noted earlier that in September 2004 UK consumers were investing sixty times more than the top 100 retailers in facilitation of internet shopping – investing £6 billion a year in PCs and internet connections that gave people their own, personal shopping environments.

Meanwhile, Britain's 100 most profitable high street retailers, who accounted for half of the online shopping trade, were collectively investing a meagre £100 million per annum on website infrastructure and development, which equated to less than £8 per online household. And within this group there was distinct polarisation between those who 'got it' (e-retail) and those who didn't. Of the £100 million these 100 retailers were collectively investing, half was accounted for by just seven companies, who were taking internet shopping seriously and spending £5 million or more per annum on it. Brands in the 'definitely got it' group included Tesco, Argos and Comet.

At the 'don't get it' pole was a cluster of 40 of the top 100 retailers who were spending next to nothing on online shopping functionality. Their websites were mainly 'placeholders' that typically offered a few marketing messages and a list of where their shops were – sometimes not even that. Brands that fell into this category included BHS, DFS, H&M, House of Fraser, JJB Sports, Matalan, Monsoon, Safeway, New Look Group, Primark, Selfridges and Somerfield.

Between the investment extremes were some fifty merchants – i.e. half of the top 100 – who had 'ticked the internet box' and were 'showing willing'. We described this group as the 'traders reaching for the moon with a stepladder'. They likely let shoppers buy a few items online from them – some might even have a database populated with little pictures of products, each with its own 'add to basket' button. But their online brochures generally added little value and were either 'out of the box' solutions or looked like they were. Brands that fell into this category included Hamleys, Harrods, River Island and WH Smith.

By providing the PC, the internet connection, the electricity, the desk and the floor space, the consumer was effectively providing their own digital High Street. All a retailer had to do was have a website, make useable content available, and then service the sales that came in.

Learndirect

It was increasingly perceived as a basic requirement for all businesses to have an effective internet presence, however there was a critical shortage of human resources for building and managing websites. The scale of the problem in 2001 was emphasised by an estimate that 400,000 man-years of work was required simply to set up the websites that Europe's SMEs then needed.

In 1998 the New Labour government had a *big idea* for 'upskilling' the UK workforce by creating a University for Industry (Ufi) with a remit to use new technology to transform the delivery of skills and learning. Two years later the Ufi launched *Learndirect*, to deliver learning online. One of Learndirect's first acts was to commission IMRG as a partner to produce an online course, 'The IMRG Guide to Practical e-Retailing', based on our code of practice.

Two years later, after much work and £500,000 had been invested in developing the Learndirect course, *The IMRG Guide to Practical e-Retailing* was close to completion. Then, out of the blue, we were dumbfounded to be told by Learndirect that we were not allowed to change the IMRG Code of Practice at all for at least a year as only then could the online course be updated. Meanwhile, the government was implementing its lurid *eCommerce Directive*, which our research indicated would cost businesses £11 billion to meet its demands, some of which were impossible to implement, unnecessary and / or counterproductive as they were at odds with best practice. The fast-evolving nature of e-retail, and our need to continually update our Code in response to change, meant that we could not comply with this *no-can-change* condition, so Learndirect scrapped the entire *Guide to Practical e-Retailing* project.

A highly critical government review in 2005/6 found that the Learndirect programme, which had by then received £930 million in public funding, was failing. In 2017, Ofsted inspectors gave Learndirect the lowest possible rating, leading to the Department for Education pulling all Learndirect contracts and funding.

Connectivity: Broadband and the Gigabit Society

'BT is looking to invest more capital than the UK spends on roads to build the digital network that the nation needs'

BT executive, 2000

Slow connection speeds and pay-per-minute fees had throttled e-retail growth. Finally, in 2000, high-speed domestic broadband connectivity – the 'always on' internet service – arrived in the UK and was the game changer we expected it to be.

The first UK home broadband service was installed in Basildon, Essex, by Mark Bush in early 2000, making him NTL's (now Virgin Media) sole broadband customer during its testing period.[52]

Telewest launched the first commercial home ADSL (asymmetric digital subscriber line) service on 31 March 2000, in Goldsmith Road in Gillingham, Kent. Demand for the £10 per month *SurfUnlimited* service was so great that the

Telewest's support lines were swamped, and parts of its network were crippled by the surge in traffic. The initial UK broadband connections were mainly provided by BT, NTL, Telewest and Kingston Communications, offering maximum speeds of 512 kilobits per second.

Within days of each other in March there were announcements from Freeserve, NTL, AltaVista, Telewest and Virgin that 'free', or at least *unmetered*, internet access schemes were to be launched. Fully aware of a forthcoming ADSL offer from BT, these other ISPs and cable operators were racing to introduce 'always on' access plans to compete head-to-head with BT. The unlimited access tariffs were overcomplicated and hard to compare, ranging from about £30 per year, to £10 per month, to around £30 per month for BT's ADSL service.

Meanwhile, BT was boasting that it was set to 'alter the internet landscape' with high-speed internet access over copper phone lines. Customers taking advantage of its service would be offered video on demand, interactive gaming and online shopping. Months later than originally slated, June 2000 saw 400 phone exchanges upgraded in major UK cities, including Manchester, London and Leeds, making ADSL available to six million homes. A further 100 exchanges would be modified, covering an additional sixteen towns and cities by the middle of the year. Half of the UK's homes were expected to have broadband availability by mid-2001 and BT hoped to reach 70 per cent of the population by 2002. The number of UK ADSL subscribers was estimated would rise from 1,500 in August

---

Copper telephone lines are reinvented as internet connections

Graham Bell invented the telephone in 1876 and demonstrated it to Queen Victoria a couple of years later. Soon, everywhere, copper twisted pair wires dangled overhead, carrying voices from one place to another. For a century the POTS (for plain old telephone service) carried analogue voice transmission via a dedicated circuit between two points. In the 1980s two American engineers hijacked the Victorian technology to power always-on broadband. John Cioffi figured out that an astonishing amount of high-speed data could be crammed through the copper wires that delivered voice calls to the home without building expensive new networks—the key was to use digital signals that have non-continuous electrical signals rather than analogue signals that are continuous. Joseph Lechleider turned Cioffi's dream into the reality of modern broadband by sending large amounts of data in one direction and smaller amounts in the other to overcome interference—this Asymmetric Digital Subscriber Line (ADSL) technology ultimately connected more than 366 million households around the world. The old network has served us all well—the same bit of copper wire brought us our phone, TV and internet services—but by 2025, BT Openreach plans to shut the copper down and replace it with a Fibre Optic Broadband Network. Fibre connectivity transmits data far quicker, has fewer reliability issues and allows more flexibility because of its breadth and speed.

1999 to 489,000 (around 7 per cent of all internet subscribers) by November 2000, according to Online Research Agency.

In June 2000, BT Cellnet launched the world's first 'always on' mobile network when it introduced GPRS (general packet radio service) technology that was expected to revolutionise the way people used the internet. Initially available only to businesses, GPRS enabled travelling workers to form wireless connections between their laptops and their head office computers. Consumers would get access to the technology by the first quarter of 2001, with the launch of mobile handsets that were permanently connected to the internet. Users could access WAP (Wireless Application Protocol) websites and receive email without first having to dial into an internet service.

Fast connections made using the internet a lot easier than it used to be, and the main barriers and objections simply evaporate: no agonising minutes waiting while data squeezed along a congested pipe, and most of all, no worrying about the cost of phone bills at the end of the month.

The fastest domestic broadband services were via dedicated cables and the nation found itself with muddy shoes as streets were dug up and lines laid. Homeowners often wanted their internet connection at the back of the house: the traditional method adopted by piece-rate fitters for achieving this involved tying the end of the cable round the shaft of a hammer and throwing it over the roof, with predictable consequences for many conservatories and windows.

By 2001, 9 per cent of UK households had broadband connections, though the take up in northern Europe (where many more people lived in apartment blocks, which are easier to connect) was often faster: by then some 30 to 40 per cent of homes in Germany and Sweden were connected to broadband.

* * *

Tesco, the first high street retailer to offer bundled '*internet, home telephone and mobile packages*', launched a new broadband service in the summer of 2004, following trials by a group of parents and children from a primary school in Barking, east London. The 512 kilobits-per-second service was made available in the supermarket's 700 stores and online via its internet service, priced at £19.97 per month, slightly less than BT's basic broadband offering. Customers were offered unlimited downloading as part of the deal.

Carphone Warehouse opened 200 new stores in its 2004 financial year, taking the total to 1,424. Its retail revenues leapt by a quarter, thanks to 23 per cent growth in mobile phone connections, of which it sold 2.06 million in the thirteen weeks to 25 December. Pre-pay sales were 33 per cent higher.

Freeview, the digital terrestrial television service owned by the BBC, BSkyB and Crown Castle, was installed in five million UK households – one and a half million terrestrial set-top boxes sold in the three months leading up to Christmas 2004, including 400,000 for BskyB's free-to-air satellite service, *FreeSat*, which launched in October.

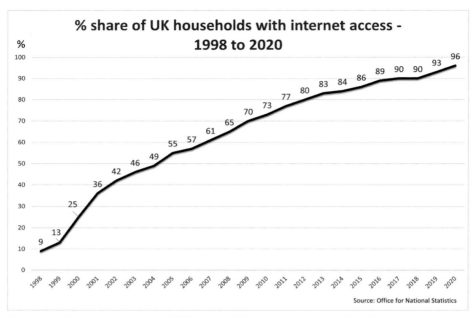

Figure 21: This chart shows how UK household internet access grew from barely any to almost total (9% to 96%) in a little over two decades. (*Source: ONS*)

AOL's 2.3 million UK customers spent more than one billion hours surfing the internet that year. Worldwide, 100 million subscribers were on the AOL Instant Messenger service, sending 2.5 billion messages every day.

Towards the end of 2004, BT announced that it had nearly six million wholesale broadband customers and was connecting a new broadband customer in the UK every ten seconds – in four months it had connected a million ADSL customers and was adding around 8,500 customers daily. Over 95 per cent of homes and businesses in the UK had the ability to access broadband services and by the following summer this figure would reach 99.4 per cent. In addition to the four million ADSL broadband customers – 40 per cent of whom accessed it directly through BT, while the rest used an ISP that bought broadband lines wholesale from BT – there were also around 1.7 million broadband cable subscribers in the UK. By the end of 2005, the number of UK broadband subscribers would reach eight million.

Details started to emerge of BT's plan to build a Next Generation Network through its *21st Century Network* (21CN) programme, with converged voice and data networks to become a mainstream technology in the UK. Britain's broadband standards body agreed to support a new technology that would transmit information on BT's existing copper wire network thirty-five times faster than then current ADSL technology by the end of 2005. ADSL2+ would send data at up to 18Mb per second and enable suppliers to offer convergent communications, such as VoIP, multichannel TV, shopping and video on demand, all through the existing network infrastructure.

Under pressure from Ofcom, the communications regulator, in January 2006 BT established a separate business division called Openreach to ensure that rival operators had equal access to its network cables that connect most UK businesses and homes to the national broadband and telephone network. Most of the UK's leading internet providers provided services via BT's national infrastructure, including Sky, TalkTalk and PlusNet, amongst others.

Broadband numbers were boosted significantly in 2008 when one and a half million new customers acquired connections, many attracted by the higher speeds being achieved that could reliably stream video. Virgin Media began a major rollout of fibre optic broadband that year, offering a 50MB package, claiming to be twice as fast as BT's best internet speeds.

Shop Around the Clock – 24/7/365

'There's loads of nice things you can buy on the Internet!'

Sir Elton John, London, 2001, Royal Mail Christmas advertising campaign

A communications revolution was happening in 2000 and consumers were loving it. Mobile phone sales were soaring worldwide and the internet user base was expanding exponentially, boosted by faster connections, new transaction-enabling technologies and a massive increase in what was available to buy online.

IMRG Index for UK e-Retail Market

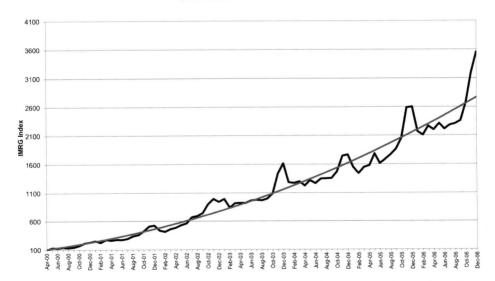

Figure 22: This chart shows the 3,553 per cent growth in UK e-retail sales during the eighty-one months from April 2000 to December 2006—the monthly value rose from £87 million to £3.624 billion. (*Source: IMRG Capgemini Sales Index*)

Europe led in the field of mobile communications. The European digital television market was growing faster than in the US, as was internet penetration. More than three million Britons came online in 2000 alone, 40 per cent of whom were women, swelling the connected community to almost fourteen million. Of the UK's 11- to 16-year-olds, 78 per cent were online. Over 40 million Brits had cell phones by the end of the year, having purchased five million between October and December.

For these 'internauts', as the French dubbed them, it was taken for granted that they could email friends or chat with someone on the other side of the world, almost instantaneously. 'Always on' communication was creating new possibilities for nearly everything from learning to shopping, from forming new friendships to remote gaming with your new-found distant pals. An *instancy* culture was evolving, changing expectations and driving a 'new economy'.

Email was 30 years old in 2001

Ray Tomlinson brushed his hand across a keyboard and sent something insignificant like 'QWERTYUIOP' as the first email in late 1971. He used the '@' symbol to indicate the location of the email recipient because he knew he needed to use a symbol that would not appear in anyone's name to avoid confusion – the logical choice was the 'at sign' as it represented the word 'at' as in a particular user is sitting @ this specific computer. The @ symbol subsequently became the de facto delimiter in email addresses, separating the user's name from the domain name. Tomlinson commented: 'It's possible I saved the at sign from extinction since some were considering removing the at sign from the keyboard.'
In 2001 more than ten billion emails were sent and received every day.

Connectivity was everywhere, and via a proliferation of new devices. Interactive TV had appeared to brim with potential for seven years, with little sign of progress, until *Open*, Britain's first nationwide interactive TV service, launched on 12 October 1999 and processed 127,767 shopping orders before Christmas, with peak sales of over £1 million per week. Soon 40,000 people were using TV banking with HSBC. Domino's Pizza was selling two and a half times as many pizzas through interactive TV than via the web, and some 3 per cent of its weekly sales was online, worth more than £1 million in the first half of 2000.

Most games consoles now had internet connections. A portable MP3 player with enough memory to hold 150 CDs, *The Digital Jukebox*, was released by Creative Technologies in August 2000. Panasonic unveiled the first DVD recorder in December, enabling discs to be recorded, played back and edited on personal computers. Whatever next? Maybe the interactive fridge and internet armchair would dominate the home market after all.

A worldwide downturn in PC sales saw market growth slowing to less than 15 per cent in 2000, with just 134.7 million units purchased, indicating market saturation in some areas. The US PC market had grown steadily for years, peaking at 21 per cent per annum in 1999, but now US growth slowed to 10.3 per cent. In a disastrous December for home computer retailers, sales fell 24 per cent from the previous year, despite a 7 per cent drop in the average PC price, to $846.

A rapidly growing number of consumers were recognising that they were the primary beneficiaries of e-retailing with its greater choice, convenience and lower prices, and were simply ignoring the relentless media hype about the risks. The proportion of European consumers buying online doubled during 2000, rising in the UK to 12 per cent of the adult population, or around five million people.

*   *   *

The low point of 2001 was 9/11. Everyone remembers where they were when they heard the appalling news of the series of terrorist attacks against the US on the morning of Tuesday, 11 September. I was coming from a meeting with our data partner, Forrester Research, whose offices were just by the stretch of Tottenham Court Road where consumer electronics shops cluster. Window displays of hundreds of large screen TVs were all showing the same surreal pictures of the iconic twin towers of the World Trade Centre complex in Lower Manhattan. Around each shop window was a growing crowd of passers-by, all staring in stunned silence at one tower blazing from a gaping hole near the eightieth floor of the 110-storey building. As we watched, a passenger airliner sliced into the other tower, causing a massive explosion that showered burning debris onto the streets below. It was immediately clear that America was under attack. Both towers collapsed within an hour and forty-two minutes. In my pocket was a lucky guardian angel medallion, bought at the south tower's *Top of the World Trade Centre* observation deck that I, like thousands of others, had visited a few months earlier. We would discover later that almost 3,000 people were killed in the four coordinated attacks that day.

With apparently no horror now either out of bounds to terrorists or unimaginable to the public, September 11 redefined 'safe'. Merchants reported that the very possibility of terrorist threat seemed to be driving some shoppers online. Stephen Cochrane, managing director of shoe-shop.com, told IMRG: 'Since the horrific events of last month, we have noticed a marked increase in weekend sales: the first weekend was 45 per cent above any other previous weekend. We think this is because people are not travelling into cities when they don't have to, preferring instead, to shop in the safety of their own homes.'

2002 saw the UK's biggest single year rise in both the number of internet users and the value of online sales, as millions of families bought PCs and subscribed to more competitively priced broadband services. Some fourteen million Britons became internet users that year, compared with four million a year earlier, and e-retail's all-time growth rate peaked at 225 per cent in 2002.

Half a billion people were online at home worldwide in 2002, and a third of them shopped online. Europe had more internet users than the US. The UK recorded a third of all e-retail sales in Europe, with internet trade worth an estimated £507 million in May alone.

In 2003, a growing army of people were boycotting the crush, inconvenience, stress and uncertainty associated with trips to high street stores. 'I hate Christmas shopping, it's a chore,' agreed 53 per cent of 1,000 consumers polled by ICM.

IMRG Comment – Christmas, December 2001

A new survey reveals that many consumers would rather swim the Channel naked at night, eat slugs or pierce their nipples with rusty nails than go down the shops Christmas Shopping. For them it's not 'news' that the UK has the worst transport system in Europe. Their experience is that the physical 'retail theatre' is just too full of dramas, tragedies and comedies of error they can well do without – battling with crowds, wrestling with packages, traffic jams, full car parks, treacherous slushy pavements, eye-level umbrellas, bomb scares, pick pockets, shops not having what they need when they finally get there, and opening times that force everyone to shop at the same time – when it's convenient to the shop, not the shopper!

The media's appetite for any story combining 'internet' and 'shopping' was insatiable at Christmas. They would publish almost anything we issued in a press release, including this flippant comment, which accompanied one of our many e-Christmas sales forecasts.

Iwantoneofthose.com reported its *Top 10 Cool Stuff* for Christmas 2003 as follows: Portable DVD, DV4000, Voice Commander, Kameleon 6-in1 remote control, Mini keyring camera, Airzooka, Mini Battling tanks, Hot Bears, The Walking Hand of Doom, Battle Tank.

Online boomed while the high street bombed. Britain's 16 million internet shoppers splurged £2.5 billion online during November and December 2003, up 70 per cent, and some 7 per cent of all UK retail sales. Meanwhile most high street retailers were having a miserable time, caught in a double trough of low trading volumes and a pre-Christmas sales fever that piled intense pressure on their profit margins. BRC reported annual growth of just 2.3 per cent for total retail in December.

Perpetual e-Payment Pain

'Honesty pays, but it doesn't seem to pay enough to suit some people'

Ken Hubbard, American cartoonist, humourist, and journalist

Plastic cards were used for almost all internet shopping transactions in 2000, but the entire system was deeply flawed. E-retailers were facing a growing threat from credit card fraud, which had soared by 40 per cent the previous year, largely because organised gangs were targeting the internet, amid clear evidence that 90 per cent of fraudsters were getting away with theft. The banks remained, at least publicly, in denial that there was a problem at all – for them, of course, there wasn't so long as they continued to deflect all responsibility and exposure back onto the merchants.

By mid-2000, 85 per cent of UK adults held one or more of the 120 million plastic cards in circulation, more than double the number of people that had been using them five years earlier. Over five billion UK transactions were made with plastic cards in 1999, including £140 billion spent in retail, according to APACS (Association for Payment Clearing Services). Even Marks & Spencer finally caved in and started accepting credit cards in their high street stores for the first time that year.

Card not present (CNP) fraud on internet transactions was low in 2000, accounting for only around 2 per cent of all card fraud losses. Most internet theft involved using fraudulently-obtained card details – aka *counterfeit fraud* – to make CNP transactions. And most cases of counterfeit fraud involved 'skimming', a process where the genuine data in the magnetic stripe on one card was electronically copied onto another, without the legitimate cardholder's knowledge. Skimming normally occurred at retail outlets where a corrupt employee copied a customer's card details before handing it back. The cardholder was usually unaware of the fraud until a statement arrived showing purchases they had not made.

CNP fraud occurred when neither the card nor its holder was present at the point-of-sale, as was obviously the case in internet transactions (and those conducted by telephone, fax or mail order). Retailers who accepted this type of transaction were forced by their bank to accept responsibility for any fraud loss, because their bank's outdated security mechanisms were based entirely on the card being present.

This meant that different payment methods bore confusingly different levels of risk for both shops and shoppers. And the increase in payments via the internet saw a disproportionate growth in payment disputes, fraud and chargebacks. Evidence was mounting that rogue customers were denying legitimate transactions, and the banks and card schemes were passing their share of the risks and problems (and whatever else they could get away with) on to hapless merchants.

Card skimming jumped from 20 per cent of counterfeit fraud in 1996 to over 60 per cent in 1999, as criminals acquired more sophisticated technology. To neutralise this scourge, *smart cards*, which contained a microchip with highly secure memory and processing capabilities, began to be introduced.

Britain led the international deployment of smart cards in 2000 with a £300 million roll-out that APACS described as the biggest fraud prevention milestone ever achieved by the card industry. Smart cards, recognisable by the gold-coloured contact plate on the front, had been developed in close cooperation with the major international card schemes: Europay, Mastercard and Visa (EMV), and the UK debit card scheme Switch. The technology identified genuine cards, making counterfeiting much more difficult – and hugely expensive – for the criminal.

Along with smart cards came extension of the use of PIN (Personal Identification Number). Consumers were already familiar with PIN from using them at cash machines, where they identified the cardholder: on an average day in 1999 there were around five and a half million cash withdrawals from ATMs (1.97 billion that year).

As the combination of *chip and PIN* technologies made the high street much harder to rob, thieves looked for softer targets – online.

*   *   *

Under the bizarre and outdated CNP (Card Not Present) rules, beleaguered internet merchants could be presented by their bank with a 'chargeback' (i.e. lose their money) up to six months after a transaction, with no explanation given and no course of redress (the banks hid behind their 'client confidentiality'). Merchants were unable to know how best to protect themselves, and against what, because they were not given any information, or even allowed to know whether they were suffering from 'real' fraud or some other problem (e.g. the consumer had just maxed out their card). Even when an online transaction was authorised as required, sometimes the credit card company would bounce it back to the bank who would then hit the retailer with a chargeback, encouraging dishonesty amongst honest customers. Few shoppers could be expected to contact a retailer because a transaction had not appeared on their card statement. Furthermore, many cards remained valid and in circulation long after the cardholders had denied a transaction.

One IMRG member lamented: '*Caveat Emptor* [let the buyer beware] is the traditional market maxim. Change that to *Caveat Vendor* [let the seller beware].'

Payment: top priority for 2002

Each January IMRG canvassed its membership regarding their top priorities, to guide our focus for the year ahead. In 2002, *payments* topped the list by a significant margin, as shown in the table below.

PRIORITY LIST OF KEY E-RETAIL ISSUES FOR IMRG TO ADDRESS IN 2002
(as voted by members)

	%
Payments (chargebacks, new solutions, etc.)	**72**
Consumer confidence	54
Legislation (e-commerce directive, etc.)	50
Rogue consumers	41
Delivery (physical product)	38
Bandwidth - broadband	36
Interactive TV (t-commerce)	36
M-Commerce	26
Accurate Timing for Network activities	20
International market issues	19
Insurance	19
Training	10

Figure 23: IMRG canvassed its membership annually regarding their top priorities. In 2002, all of the top four were associated with payments and security. (*Source: James Roper Archive*)

E-retailers could not solve the fundamental online fraudster problem on their own, so were doing whatever they could to mitigate the risks of trading online. The card schemes' *Secure Electronic Transaction* (SET) was still unavailable, viewed by the banks as too cumbersome to implement. The rival security protocol, *Secure Sockets Layer* (SSL) – a standard technology that established an encrypted link between a server and a client – was being adopted instead and helped somewhat.

Security issues were exacerbated by the absence of online fraud detection systems, and a police force ignoring this type of crime as being too new and too small for them to bother with.

The e-Retail Payments Charter: May 2000

With the banks and card schemes continuing to fail to provide the secure payment solutions e-retailers desperately needed, IMRG decided to illuminate the problems as brightly as we could, and to apply carrots and sticks in the form of positive and negative publicity about organisations' behaviour, in an attempt to accelerate progress.

Led by Scott Thomson, we launched an *IMRG e-Retail Payments Charter* that set out standards to which those involved in the debit and credit payment cycle should adhere, with the common objective of assisting in the elimination of fraudulent transactions and card misuse. The aim was also to eradicate much of the industry's administration costs.

The standards embodied in the charter were self-regulating and policed by all, under the auspices of the IMRG Senate. Where breaches could not be amicably settled between parties, the option was available for that party – e.g. card issuer, card acquirer, card scheme, retailer – to state categorically that they were unwilling or unable to conform, and to refer the matter to PayCom (the regulatory body arising from the then recently published Cruikshank Report on competition in the UK banking industry, following an independent review commissioned by the government in 1998).

Publicity was given to those organisations signing up to the e-Retail Payments Charter and thereby accepting its core principles – *as well as those who elected to opt out*.

The principal conditions of the charter were:

- All properly authorised payment card transactions will be applied to the cardholder's account
- 'Requests For Information' instigated by the cardholder are required to be in writing
- Transactions, where appropriately denied, will result in that associated card being immediately withdrawn from circulation
- Cards not withdrawn and subsequently misused become the liability of the card issuer
- All card acceptors (retailers / service providers) will assist (e.g. through production of documentation) in the immediate investigation of transactions

- All card acceptors will ensure that the narrative relating to a card transaction clearly identifies to the cardholder the organisation / company to which the transaction refers
- 'Card Not Present' is accepted as a valid transaction type.

Security Alert – **Fighting Online Fraud**. We also introduced a new security toolset in late 2002: *IMRG Security Alert*. This was a fraud avoidance scheme that enabled e-retailers to safely share with each other *hot lists* containing fraudsters' details. This meant that, for the first time, if one retailer took a fraud hit, they could at least warn other traders with actionable information. The service was entirely complementary to all other major anti-fraud schemes and went live in October, in time to help protect merchants during the imminent Christmas shopping period. Security Alert won solid backing from the e-retail industry and was rapidly taken up by many leading merchants including Argos Direct, Blockbuster, Carphone Warehouse, Digital Wellbeing, Dvd.co.uk, figleaves.co.uk, Greenfingers.co.uk, lastminute.com, Ocado, Petplanet.co.uk, Screwfix, Thinknatural.com and Zoom.

> *'Too expensive… largely ineffective… ready for change'*
> Paul Hanks, Technical Director, TriRidium, 2002,
> commenting on card dispute handling

Card Dispute Handling was also a major problem with internet payments in 2002. E-retailers were finding themselves ever more exposed to risk from dishonest consumers repudiating transactions (it weren't me, guv, honest!). The banks and card schemes could have easily closed down 80 per cent of these if they had really wanted to, but instead they simply bounced the losses back to the merchants as chargebacks. NatWest (aka colloquially by some of our members as *NatWorst*) was not the only culprit involved in this payment ambush, though it was considered by many to be the most obstructive.

The processes and procedures surrounding chargebacks had hardly changed over the past twenty years. No standards existed for the retrieval of dispute information, with each acquirer operating on an independent basis. Each dispute was treated as a single entity and no concept of *repetitive card holder disputes* existed.

Without exception for the retailer, disputes were paper intensive and required significant manpower to process. APACS reported that the number of requests for copy voucher retrievals was increasing month by month, leading to a processing backlog and increased write-offs for retailers.

Genuine customers suffered too, by having their orders rejected by retailers' overcautious fraud detection protocols that presumed hazards if the divination of arcane clues scored high.

IMRG argued the case for establishing an e-retail industry solution that could pull together the disparate array of front- and back-office systems and processes of the payment card industry, to dramatically reduce costs and risks.

Verified by Visa and Mastercard SecureCode

Hopes were raised yet again in 2002 that Visa and Mastercard were finally getting round to making internet payments acceptably safe for merchants when they launched new branded versions of 3DS – *Verified by Visa* (VbV) and *Mastercard SecureCode*.

On 1 April 2002, Visa promised that retailers who adopted VbV would from that date no longer be liable for any CNP repudiation chargebacks, regardless of whether the cardholder had used VbV or not – *their liability would shift to the issuing bank*! However, by late October, no merchants had yet been able to adopt VbV, no matter how much they wanted to or tried. Two years later (in 2004) we were still reporting VbV and SecureCode 3DS schemes as being new and in the process of arriving.

But there was still much wrong with these early forms of 3DS. Initially they used a pop-up password entry form, even though pop-ups were notoriously favoured by fraudsters and scammers, and problems arose with pop-up blockers that many consumers had installed on their PCs. Then inline-frames ('iframe') were introduced, but these had no address bar or telephone number, so shoppers had no way of verifying who was asking for their password. And the design of the forms did not match those of the merchant, or Visa, or the bank – instead, they looked cheap and untrustworthy.

Shoppers were obliged to register a password with their bank before 3DS could authenticate transactions: to solicit a password, most banks simply interrupted the first time the customer tried to shop online with their 3DS-enabled card, possibly asking for an authenticator, such as date of birth. From the shopper's perspective, the shop suddenly looked dodgy by asking for personal details. Almost immediately criminals launched rafts of copycat phishing websites, impersonating the 3DS form to ask for banking details. Some banks *forced* 3DS activation by preventing the purchase, which was hardly the best way to get either informed consent or a well-considered password. And by setting up a password, customers were deemed to have accepted new terms and conditions – an opportunity that some banks took to set terms shifting all liability to customers![53]

Even in 2020 – 18 years later – banks were still 'too often' blaming customers for falling victim to fraudsters, according to the Financial Ombudsman Service in December, having received 6,603 complaints between April and September about how banks dealt with fraud and scams, up more than a third on the previous year. It commented that 'the voluntary code was not working as intended'.[54]

Shopping Comparison Sites

> *'Comparison is the thief of joy'*
>
> Theodore Roosevelt

Shopping comparison sites were key drivers in the growth of online shopping, particularly in the industry's early days. These vertical search engines didn't sell goods themselves, but instead helped shoppers find and compare product offers, especially prices and delivery terms, on aggregated listings from many different retailers, while earning their revenue from affiliate marketing agreements. In the UK, it was estimated that shopping comparison sites earned approaching £1 billion in affiliate marketing revenue in 2005.

> 'The future of shopping on the Net exists in prototype today at BargainFinder http://bf.cstar.ac.com/bf/. Using an agent process, BargainFinder searches through the catalogs of eight online music stores and finds the best price for the CD of your choice. One click takes you to the store with the bargain... If buyers can always get the best price, how do sellers react? When last checked, three of the eight stores were blocking the agents out.'
> *Wired* magazine, 1995[126]

An early shopping comparison site was *BargainFinder*, created in 1995 as an experiment by Anderson Consulting (now Accenture). *Wired* magazine commented at the time that this prototype represented the future of shopping on the internet. BargainFinder alarmed retailers and some prevented it from accessing their product listings.

The first commercial shopping comparison site, *Jango*, was built by a Seattle start-up and acquired by the *Excite* web portal in 1997. A number of other shopping comparison agents emerged at around the same time, including *Junglee*, a pioneer from the San Francisco Bay Area that was soon acquired by Amazon.com. *PriceGrabber*, founded in 1999, was bought by Experian for $485 million in 2005. *Time* magazine listed another contender, *NexTag*, as a world top-50 website in 2008, though a decade later this would be gone.

Google launched its own shopping comparison service *Froogle* in December 2002, using its web crawler to index product data from vendors' websites rather than paid submissions. Froogle was monetised by Google's *AdWords* keyword advertising platform. Modified and rebranded *Google Product Search*, the service was prominently featured in Google search results in the UK and Germany from January 2008. Rebranded again as *Google Shopping* in May 2012, the service was switched to a 'pay-to-play' model later that year whereby merchants had to pay to list their products. The switch to paid listings was controversial, considered detrimental to smaller retailers; Microsoft's *Bing* called Google out for using 'deceptive advertising practices' in an advertising campaign known as 'Scroogled'.

The European Commission began an investigation in 2010, which concluded in July 2017 when European Commissioner for Competition, Margrethe Vestager, fined Google's parent company Alphabet €2.42 billion for breaching EU antitrust rules. Google was found to have abused its market dominance by giving illegal advantages to its own shopping comparison service from as early as 2008, thereby undermining other sites and driving some out of business, and depriving 418 million EU citizens of the full benefits of competition, genuine choice and innovation.

ISIS: The UK Online Shopping Trust Scheme

'I would never have shopped at dot2shop.com's website
without the reassurance of seeing the ISIS logo there.
I had never heard of them before. But their service was great!'

Consumer to IMRG, October 2003

IMRG's Internet Shopping Is Safe (ISIS) trust scheme was launched on 24 July 2001. By Christmas 2004 there were hundreds of ISIS-accredited merchants who collectively accounted for two-thirds of all UK internet shopping outlets. ISIS was instrumental in accelerating the growth of e-retail in the UK and was one of IMRG's most significant contributions to the online shopping industry. Its origins were the IMRG Code of Practice, published in 1997 as part of the collateral created for e-Christmas.

Figure 24: ISIS, the UK's online shopping trust scheme, was introduced by IMRG in 2001. (*Source: James Roper Archive*)

While many of the perceived problems associated with internet shopping were exaggerated and already obsolete, the labyrinthine nature of the channel required that it be navigated with care and in a prescribed manner. In the early days, many problems encountered by novices were due to their ignorance of the most basic information – equivalent to lack of road sense to look both ways before crossing.

Recall that several other attempts to address the lack of consumer confidence in shopping online proved ineffectual: the European Commission-backed scheme, *Euro-Label*; the UK government-backed *Trust UK*; *Which? Web Trader*; Barclaycard's *ShopSmart*; and Securicor's *SafeDoor*.

ISIS was determinative because it created a practicable and continually evolving set of e-retail standards, so consumers knew what to expect and merchants knew exactly what they needed to do – both parties were then helped to achieve their goals.

ISIS was launched on 24/7 DAY 2001 – IMRG's *always on shopping day* (24 July – the 24th day of the seventh month). ISIS provided online shoppers with three things:

- SAFE SHOPS LIST – a register of vetted e-retailers who subscribed to the ISIS principles
- TOP TEN TIPS for online shoppers
- INTERNET SHOPPING GUIDELINES – practical guidelines for shopping safely online.

The campaign was launched with the support of hundreds of companies, and with the following statements prised from the UK government:

E-commerce Minister Douglas Alexander said:

> *'This campaign shows what retailers can do to get the safe shopping message out to the public. Industry initiatives like this can enhance consumer confidence in e-commerce and are very much to be welcomed.'*

The government's E-Envoy Andrew Pinder said:

> *'Educating consumers about how they can shop online with confidence and safety is a vital part of the Government's objective of making the UK the best place in the world for e-commerce. Government, industry, and consumers must all take a part in this process, and therefore we are happy to support IMRG's campaign.'*

The online shopping environment was improving rapidly thanks to the efforts of committed merchants and facilitators throughout the world who by then had several years' experience under their belts. But shoppers were still nervous – in 2002 two-thirds of consumers were still not buying online. And webstore builders were still making daft mistakes – equivalent to putting shelves out of reach or the door in the middle of the ceiling.

IMRG converted its *ISIS Safe Shops List*, that had initially operated in a basic 'look up' form, into a dynamic service enabling consumers to easily check with just one click the status of any participating merchant's ISIS registration. Shoppers who contacted IMRG by email or phone to raise issues were responded to immediately, and every legitimate problem was dealt with and resolved. Merchant participation was low-cost at just £125+VAT per annum for accreditation and ISIS Listing – even so the scheme was quickly self-funding thanks to the large volume of merchants who came onboard.

By Christmas 2004 there were hundreds of ISIS-accredited merchants who collectively accounted for two-thirds of all UK internet shopping outlets. Many happy customers reported exceptionally good service from ISIS-accredited merchants. For example, a dabs.com customer told us they were pleasantly surprised when a computer accessory ordered at six o'clock on the evening of 23 December was delivered by Parcelforce at 8:30 am on Christmas Eve morning – only fourteen hours later!

The ISIS management team received just twenty-two customer complaints between 1 November 2004 and 5 January 2005, of which twenty were successfully resolved to the consumers' satisfaction within two or three days, and the remaining two were resolved within a few weeks.

*   *   *

The IMRG Code, that all members were required to comply with, was straightforward, reflecting common principles long established for high street shopping:

- All services provided should be legal, decent, fair, honest and truthful
- All services should be operated with a sense of responsibility to customers and to society; they should be conducted equitably, promptly and efficiently and should be seen to deal fairly and honourably with customers. Suppliers should avoid causing unnecessary disappointment
- Reasonable care should be taken to avoid causing offence on the grounds of gender, race, religion, disability or any other form of discrimination or unacceptable reference
- All services should respect the principles of fair competition generally accepted in business
- No IMRG Member should bring electronic commerce into disrepute
- Any unreasonable delay in responding to the IMRG Executive's enquiries may be considered a breach of the IMRG Code
- IMRG will, on request, treat in confidence any private or confidential material supplied unless the Courts or officials acting within their statutory powers compel its disclosure
- The IMRG Code is applied in the spirit as well as in the letter.

The IMRG Code was originally based on the Committee of Advertising Practice Code's core principles[55] – *legal, decent, honest and truthful* – to which we added the term 'fair', in light of the power consumers wielded in the *new economy*. A few of our members were unhappy with this addition and one – a law firm – resigned, on principle, saying that it was often their role to be *unfair*: we were happy to see them go, as it reinforced our point nicely.

*   *   *

ISIS was especially helpful to small merchants. It helped them to be discovered by the many shoppers who referred to the *Safe Shops List*, and it gave people confidence that their site and service was honest, reliable and of good quality.

Proving the online merchant's identity is a fundamental requirement of internet shopping that had remained an intractable problem for years. The non-face-to-face nature of the internet shopping medium, involving as it does both distance and the graphical representation of stores, goods and processes, needed a robust, independent identity verification mechanism to be in place, and properly managed: this was required both to enable consumers to validate that shops were who they claimed to be and were OK to shop with, and to provide a framework in which to deal with shops that were not consistently up to scratch for whatever reason.

ISIS solved the verification problem by means of its distinctive logo which indicated merchants' participation in the scheme. When a consumer saw an ISIS logo, they could click on it to view that organisation's *ISIS accreditation certificate*, which stated the registered company's name and internet address. This certificate confirmed that the shop subscribed to the ISIS principles, had its site and service reviewed and monitored by IMRG, and had its Business, VAT and Data Protection registrations checked by IMRG.

Whereas ISIS made no guarantee to the consumer about the listed merchants or trading with them, legislation and the payment schemes did. In the event of a problem, ISIS provided consumer advice and guidance on what to do and who to contact, and might, at the discretion of the IMRG management team, intervene on the consumer's behalf with a merchant.

If the ISIS support team could not quickly resolve a dispute with an ISIS-registered merchant (they usually resolved problems within two days) then they would assist in forwarding the matter for resolution by the appropriate authority – e.g. Trading Standards, the police, their payments service provider or other appropriate organisations – while continuing to monitor the situation and support the consumer, as necessary.

Most consumer problems associated with internet shopping arose from simple mistakes or oversights. IMRG's experience was that ISIS could generally resolve issues very quickly through clear, neutral mediation.

One example of how far the ISIS team would go out of their way to help shoppers started out with a phone call from a distressed lady on 16 December 2003. Her cooker had packed up, so, with Christmas looming, she had ordered a new one on 7 December from an e-retailer who was *not* ISIS-accredited. Payment for the cooker was taken the following day. After ten days of failing to get any information about her order, the lady was contacted by the merchant and told that they were out of stock, and it would take a further seven days for her money to be reimbursed – i.e. 23 December. The lady – a single parent with three kids, no cooker, and not enough time or money to buy another one – was distraught. The ISIS team joined up the dots and arranged for an IMRG member to deliver a new cooker to her before Christmas, with payment deferred till mid-January.

ISIS took a major step forward in October 2004 when Kelkoo, then Europe's leading shopping search engine, introduced a new service that displayed merchants'

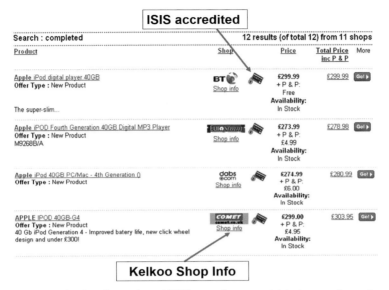

Figure 25: Kelkoo displayed merchants' ISIS accreditation within its search results – extract from the IMRG Trust Online White Paper, November 2004. (*Source: James Roper Archive*)

ISIS accreditation within its search results next to the names of ISIS-certified shops. This brought together for the first time, everything the consumer required to find what they needed online, and then buy it with complete confidence.

By 2013 the domestic UK confidence issue was essentially resolved and IMRG was increasingly focused on helping members with their cross-border trade. The leading European trustmark for online shops at this time was Cologne-based Trusted Shops, which had more than 13,000 accredited retailers across Europe, and was ahead of its competitors by a considerable margin. After extensive discussions with Trusted Shops' founder and managing director, Jean-Marc Noël, we agreed to merge the ISIS scheme with the German mark and invited all ISIS-accredited merchants to join Trusted Shops. As of late 2020, Trusted Shops has 30,000 shops across 40 nations and is assuring 900,000 orders per day.

Data: Sipping From the Firehose

'Data is the new oil'

Clive Humby, British data commercialisation entrepreneur, 2006

Nobody in Europe had a clue as to the value or nature of online trade in 2000. Merchants refused to share intensely sensitive sales intelligence with each other. Financial institutions were unable to attribute transactions to channels. All we had were analysts' guestimates of the market size and dynamics, based on ad hoc snippets of data and consumer surveys. An evidence-based business case was required to secure capital, but no reliable statistics were available – yet another e-commerce catch-22.

Lack of reliable 'hard' market trading data was becoming a major problem for the e-retail industry in 2000. Retailers and facilitators wishing to engage seriously in the digital marketplace would need to commit large-scale funding, but after the dot.com crash – and most of the *dot lot* gone – speculative investment capital for e-commerce all but dried up in Europe. Doubters rallied round the stock rationalisations for avoiding e-retail investment, even though these had been exposed as oversimplifications, out of date, or plain wrong.

The issue was complicated by the absence of a specific definition of what 'retail' even was. The term retail traditionally referred to the sale of most physical goods, however reporting was inconsistent, with an assortment of stakeholders recording different things in dissimilar ways. The Office for National Statistics (ONS) used definitions for 'retail' that had been framed in 1948 – consequently these excluded digital (i.e. virtual) goods and services, software, downloads, travel and event tickets amongst many other core e-retail categories, rendering them largely useless for quantifying online shopping. The BRC (British Retail Consortium) tracked and reported on what its members sold (largely groceries). EC data collection methods produced statistics that were years out of date and based on narrow retail classifications – the justification for this was to 'ensure consistency over time'.

Before internet shopping arrived, the primary retail performance indicator was '£s per square foot'. But now e-retailers urgently needed to be able to weigh, balance and contextualise the many interdependent digital opportunities, threats, trends, drivers, factors, issues, barriers, incomes and costs. A fresh approach was conspicuously needed.

'If you can't measure it, you can't improve it'

Peter Drucker, Management Guru

Under pressure from members, IMRG agreed to find a way to provide meaningful data to support their commercial decisions. We decided to define 'retail' for the purposes of our metrics as everything that shoppers were buying online, with a few exceptions such as gambling, pornography and mortgages that would have unhelpfully skewed results. We also anticipated that the physical and digital worlds would become inseparably interwoven, and therefore an entirely new measurement framework was required to make sense of the unfamiliar social and economic landscape we were entering.

At a workshop held on 17 July 2000, IMRG agreed to conduct a data pilot, to run between September 2000 and February 2001. Participating retailers were asked to supply their back-dated sales data from March 2000. At a follow-on workshop on 1 March 2001, definitions were confirmed, and it was agreed to roll out the data programme. By July 2001, some thirty contributors had reported online sales worth £469 million.

'An e-retail sales survey, conducted by an independent and trusted body, would bring some long-awaited reality into an over-hyped world. Argos will be happy to participate, and hope others will follow and join the IMRG scheme'

Peter Jones, Operations Director, Argos, March 2001

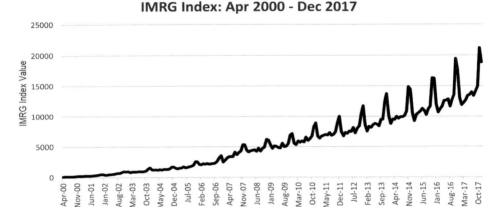

Figure 26: IMRG Index Chart 2000–2018. Note how the Christmas peaks increase massively each year. (*Source: IMRG Capgemini Sales Index*)

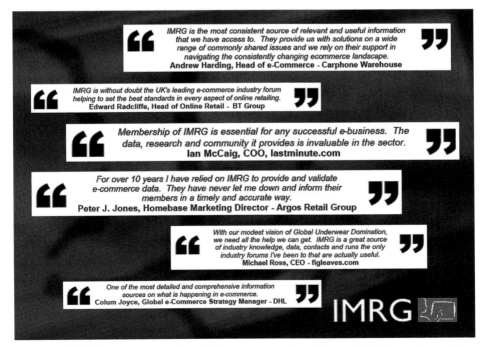

Figure 27: IMRG presentation slide of client quotes on data, 16 June 2004. (*Source: James Roper Archive*)

	Internet users millions	Broadband homes	e-Spend £ billions	e-Spend Y-o-Y Change	e-Shoppers millions	Avg £ e-spend/per head/annum	Parcels millions
1999	9	0%	0.3	+167%	1.8	167	
2000	15	0%	0.8	+167%	3.5	228	
2001	19	0.4%	1.8	+125%	6	302	
2002	33	6.5%	6.4	+255%	12	533	
2003	38	11%	11	+72%	16	688	
2004	39	21%	14	+32%	20	727	
2005	42	29%	19	+32%	24	816	
2006	42	38%	30	+57%	25	1,208	540
2007	46	52%	35	+17%	27	1,304	820
2008	48	58%	44	+25%	28	1,564	860
2009	52	68%	50	+14%	30	1,667	900
2010	53	71%	59	+18%	33	1,782	1,000
2011	54	74%	68	+16%	37	1,843	1,350
2012	56	75%	78	+14%	40	1,950	1,100
2013	57	75%	91	+16%	41	2,195	1,200
2014	59	77%	104	+14%	42	N/A	1,300
2015	60	80%	115	+11%	43	N/A	1,400

Figure 28: This table shows key UK internet and e-retail trends between 1999 and 2015. In 2002 IMRG recorded the biggest single-year rise in both internet users and online sales value. In 2015, over 92 per cent of the UK population was using the internet. (*Source: James Roper Archive*)

IMRG Capgemini e-retail Index Sector Classification

The IMRG Capgemini Index records UK online retail sales of the products and services listed in the Index Sector Classification, as set out below.

INDEX SECTOR CLASSIFICATION These products and services bought online by UK consumers are recorded by the IMRG Capgemini Index	EXCLUDED FROM INDEX Online spending by UK consumers of these items is excluded from the IMRG Capgemini Index

Beer / wine / spirits
Books
CDs / tapes / records
Clothing / footwear / accessories
Computer hardware / peripherals / consumables
Consumer electronics
Digital downloads (e.g. music, software)
Flowers
Food, beverages and household supplies
Furniture
Garden / DIY
Health and beauty
Home appliances (e.g. washing machines)
Household goods (e.g. kitchenware, bedding)
Jewellery / watches
Software
Sporting goods
Tickets (e.g. cinema, theatre, events)
Toys
Travel (e.g. flights, holidays, hotels, car hire)
Video games
Videos / DVDs
	Adult
	Auctions
	Cars / motor vehicles
	Gambling
	Gaming
	Houses / real estate
	Telecom services
	Utilities (e.g. water, heating, electricity)
	Financial services, e.g.
	- CREDIT: mortgages, loans, credit cards,
	  overdrafts
	- INVESTMENT: savings accounts, funds, stocks &
	  shares, bonds, life assurance, pensions
	- INSURANCE: car, home, life

About the IMRG Capgemini Index:

The IMRG Capgemini Index tracks 'online sales', which we define as 'transactions completed fully, including payment, via interactive channels' from any location, including in-store. These sales are predominantly internet-based today, but the Index remains ready to record e-retail sales conducted via whatever interactive channels the market may embrace in the future.

Figure 29: IMRG Capgemini Sales Index Sector Classification indicating the products and services that were – and were not – included in the sales it recorded. (*Source: James Roper Archive*)

After extensive consultation and a further series of workshops we created the *IMRG e-Retail Sales Index*, which was soon adopted as the primary performance indicator of the UK online shopping industry.

Over the following years, IMRG's Index survey was extended to cover all of the most relevant e-retail data and trends, using reliable aggregating performance measurement criteria and tools, across all primary types of merchant, main subsectors and interactive channels. Participating organisations were identified to each other and publicly in order to help promote the survey. Wherever practicable, IMRG aligned definitions used with industry norms, to provide consistency for contributors and optimise the usefulness of the survey, though this was not always possible.

IMRG E-COMMERCE BENCHMARKS (2008)

WEBSITE PERFORMANCE
- Visitor bounce rate
- Basket abandonment
- Checkout abandonment

CUSTOMER ACQUISITION & RETENTION
- Active customer retention rate
- New customers %

COMMERCIAL
- Average selling price per item
- Average order value

ORDER FULFILMENT
- Percentage of total orders cancelled due to fraud
- Percentage of units returned
- Number of items / products per order

GEOGRAPHICAL SPLIT
- Percentage of sales within the UK
- Percentage of sales within the EU
- Percentage of sales rest of world

MARKETING PERFORMANCE
- Pence per Click ROI
- Affiliate ROI
- Online marketing ROI
- All marketing ROI
- Revenue split by marketing method (last click)
  - Paid, Affiliate, Email, Natural, Direct, Social, Display, Other
- Visits split by marketing method (last click)
- Paid, Affiliate, Email, Natural, Direct, Social, Display, Other

ORDERS SPLIT BY MARKETING METHOD (LAST CLICK)
- Paid, Affiliate, Email, Natural, Direct, Social, Display, Other

CHANNEL
- Percentage of sales via mobile
- Percentage of visits via mobile
- Percentage of click-and-collect sales (completed online)
- Percentage of reserve & collect sales (completed in store)

Figure 30: This table is a condensed summary of the IMRG Capgemini Sales Index benchmark definitions used in its quarterly reporting in 2008. (*Source: James Roper Archive*)

The IMRG Index established a metrics framework for the key performance indicators of online retailing that was subsequently adopted worldwide.

For several years, the IMRG Index data collection, processing, analysis and reporting remained a manual operation, conducted largely by IMRG's project development manager, Gareth Donovan, by means of emails and a desktop PC. By late 2007, the data sets were becoming huge and barely manageable as the number of retailer participants and sub-categories grew, so we enlisted Capgemini to help support and expand the programme in return for renaming it the IMRG Capgemini e-Retail Index.

As the online shopping sector grew in value and influence, all enterprises involved in the business of retailing needed to understand to a fine level of insight the market's performance and dynamics, and in particular what the points of competitive advantage were that justified a price positioning that was not the lowest in the market. To meet this growing demand IMRG continually increased the frequency, volume, granularity and analysis of the regular data outputs we provided.

Multichannel trading became increasingly convoluted as a growing array of physical and digital touchpoints could potentially be involved in the shopper's journey towards a purchase. The introduction of smartphones and social media into the mix compounded the complexity, increasing the number and nature of shopping interactions. Each touchpoint had a cost and a value contribution to each sale: complex formulas were contrived for calculating these. And to address the quantification issue, we first had to develop a lexicon of vocabulary – common terms and definitions around the digital topics of retailing and e-commerce. As the accuracy and precision of IMRG's measurements increased, along with our standardised scales such as website performance and channel splits, new possibilities were revealed for our members to explore.

*   *   *

The issue of inconsistent reporting of e-retail statistics continued to be problematical. Below is a selection of UK e-retail market values and their definitions

UK e-Retail 2015	Publisher	Definition
£43 billion	Office for National Statistics (ONS)	Online sales of physical goods
£33.9 billion	British retail Consortium (BRC)	Online sales (including mail order and phone) sales of non-food transactions which take place over the Internet, or via mail order or phone
£111.4 billion	IMRG	Sales of goods and services completed online (including online in-store)
£46.8 billion	Verdict	Physical goods

Figure 31: A selection of UK e-retail market values and their definitions published in 2015 by ONS, the BRC, IMRG and retail analyst Verdict. (*Source: James Roper Archive*)

published in 2015, by the Office for National Statistics (ONS), the BRC (British Retail Consortium), IMRG and retail analyst Verdict (now GlobalData). IMRG subsequently ceased to publish estimates of e-retail market and sector values.

On a number of occasions, the quantity of BRC's data contributors was so small that its participants were able to calculate the value of their competitors' sales. BRC largely reported groceries because that is what its members mainly sold: however, in May 2018, TESCO, the UK's biggest retailer, left the BRC for three years.

Music: Downloads Kill CDs

*'Music gives a soul to the universe, wings to the mind,
flight to the imagination, and life to everything'*

Plato

The traditional global music industry had been in turmoil for years. In the 1990s the CD had reigned supreme, their sales peaking at two billion in 1996. The music sector was infatuated with CDs because they were so popular and profitable – cheaper to produce and distribute than vinyl records and selling at up to double the price – so unsurprisingly the industry did all it could to resist CDs demise.

But the CD was doomed by the proliferation of PCs and digital recorders that allowed consumers to burn discs for free. And then MP3 came along, enabling music to transcend physical formats altogether. Napster's arrival in June 1999 sounded the death knell for CDs, its online service letting people freely share their MP3 files.

Despite intense music industry resistance, the internet quickly became the primary channel for music distribution in the early 2000s as consumers gravitated to the simple convenience and value for money it offered. Digital downloads would soon largely displace the old consumer channels to market.

During 2004, a spectacular boom in music downloads saw 200 million music tracks downloaded in the four big digital music markets – the US, UK, France and Germany. This resuscitated the UK singles market, with downloads outselling all traditional physical formats.

In January 2004, Coca-Cola led what rapidly became a bandwagon when it launched online music download site, *MyCokeMusic.com*, with more than a quarter of a million tracks available, the largest collection of legal downloads on the internet at the time, together with an alternative *official singles sales chart*. The site sold 150,000 downloads in its first month. Before the year was out, Microsoft in partnership with HMV, as well as Tesco, easyGroup and even Oxfam had all launched download music services. BMG (Bertelsmann Music Group) with a view to selling its entire catalogue online, acquired Napster, which had closed its service in June 2001 and gone bankrupt in 2002 after losing a court case for copyright infringement. Napster was reborn as a legal downloading service in May 2004 and before long had the UK Post Office, Dixons and *The Sun*, amongst others, selling its vouchers.

In June 2004, Apple's *iTunes* arrived in the UK, Germany and France, having secured rights deals with all major record companies. It had already sold more than 70 million songs in the US in its first year since an April 2003 launch. Apple's CEO, Steve Jobs, demonstrated his astute grasp of the music business by also launching the year's 'must-have' gadget, the *iPod* range of portable players and storage devices. By the end of 2004, iTunes had achieved an 87 per cent market share, with sales of 200 million songs and six million iPods.

Key to Apple's success had been the proprietary AAC file format and a Digital Rights Management (DRM) scheme, known as *FairPlay*. These specified technology and guidelines that governed what consumers could do with their music or other digital assets once purchased. For example, they prevented songs bought from iTunes being played on anything but the iTunes environment or an iPod, and also restricted Microsoft format songs to being played only on Microsoft digital music players (for the moment). Record industry trade bodies in the UK (BPI) and the US (RIAA) backed DRM schemes since they maintained rights and payments structures for artists and provided a satisfactory degree of copy protection.

By the end of 2004, a million songs were available to buy from legal download sites in a market worth $330 million (£175 million) globally. Between twenty and twenty-five million portable players were sold that year.

It's ironic that online shopping all started just a decade earlier with a CD – NetMarket's sale of *Ten Summoner's Tales* by Sting – a format that e-commerce would subsequently wipe out and go on to replace as the dominant distribution method for all entertainment.

The digital download industry was, along with airline ticketing, considered to be one of e-commerce's first real commercial breakthroughs. It incorporated online delivery of a software product, with built-in quality, protection, and a secure payments system. Now that digital music downloads had become a viable business, there were clear opportunities to extend these to other technologies, especially mobile phones, and to other sectors, particularly film and video.

Happy Click Mouse   * </;-)

'When times are good, people shop online to save time –
when times are tough, people shop online to save money'
IMRG, 2005

Just ten years on from the first ever secure internet transaction there were a billion internet users worldwide and half of those in the developed world were making regular online transactions, especially in the run-up to Christmas. Global e-retail revenues exceeded $150 billion per annum. IMRG estimated that UK e-trade value was £19.6 billion, equivalent to five London West Ends.

In 2004 the retail sector faced the toughest trading conditions in decades, with annual growth in total retail sales at just 2.5 per cent. E-shopping's rise – at 20 per cent per annum in the festive season – was outperforming the high street eightfold.

Web shopping was fun, safe and an increasingly rewarding experience. Brits' annualised online spend had doubled to £770 each, according to Visa, and for the first time women were spending more than men. Online shopping was proving durable across all seasons, sectors and economic climates.

Internet grocery sector sales more than trebled, while travel bookings grew by 159 per cent in a year. Debenhams announced e-sales up 90 per cent and that it was droppin its mail order catalogue as a result. Alliance & Leicester was closing 46 branches because 80 per cent of its customers were banking over the web, the telephone or via cash machines. The speed and scale of this expansion was all the more remarkable because, while ample growth potential remained in existing sectors, opportunities in many key retail areas such as high-end fashion and real estate had yet to be addressed commercially.

People had scoffed that clothing and footwear would never sell online. Yet over £644 million worth of UK fashion goods were clicked into digital shopping baskets in 2004, an annual increase of 37 per cent, representing 9 per cent of all British internet shopping.

Half of the UK population shopped online that Christmas, when Royal Mail still handled 60 per cent of their 90 million Yuletide parcels. Ann Summers' marketing manager, Kevin Barnes, told us: 'Business was up 66 per cent over the same period last year, with the new Platinum Rampant Rabbit proving to be a *hopaway* success.'

E-retailers became much more effective at timing and promoting their sales for Christmas 2004. Many launched their sales as soon as they were unable to guarantee pre-Christmas delivery – typically around 15 December, resulting in revenues remaining strong through to the end of the month. This was the beginning of a market-changing trend in which each year e-retailers found new ways to pull sales forward, luring consumers' cash before high street retailers could.

Top products searched on Kelkoo, Christmas 2004

1. DVD Recorders / Portable DVD players
2. Digital cameras over 3.2mp
3. MP3 players / Mini iPod
4. LCD TVs
5. Nokia mobile phones
6. Dyson (vacuum cleaners)
7. Xbox
8. Trampolines
9. Coffee makers / grinders
10. Sofa beds

The most popular product searches that Christmas included *The Da Vinci Code* (book), *Shrek 2* (DVD), *Eminem Encore* (music track), iPod, Playstation 2 (games console), Nokia 6230 (mobile phone), Timberland boots and Burberry scarves, GHD hair straighteners, trampolines and George Foreman grills.

Christmas 2005 saw e-shopping exceed £2 billion in one month (November) for the first time ever, up 50 per cent on the year before. IMRG and Royal Mail together estimated that if the UKs 26,000 online shops were bricks and mortar, they would form a high street fifty miles long, offering five million products for sale. Meanwhile, actual high street annual sales for the same period grew by just 0.9 per cent, according to the ONS.

Figure 32: This '50-mile high street' illustration was produced by Royal Mail's Head of PR, James Eadie, for our joint Christmas 2005 marketing campaign. (*Source: James Roper Archive*)

John Lewis relaunched its online service as John Lewis Direct in 2005. Sales increased rapidly, rising by 75 per cent to more than £100 million in its 2004/5 full year, achieving over one million visits to the website in a week and almost reaching profitability. The following year John Lewis Direct marked its first million-pound day on 26 November 2006. Its sales for 2005/6 were up by almost another 70 per cent and by then the online business was fully in profit.

> *'Tesco.com has seen an increasing number of customers shopping for grocery and non-food items with us and during December [2005], 1 million customers chose to have a Christmas of convenience through us. We're helping to bring groceries to more remote places and our service now covers 98 per cent of the UK'*
>
> Laura Wade-Gery, Chief Executive, Tesco.com

* * *

IMRG was a primary focus for media reporting of Christmas shopping, ubiquitously featuring in press, TV and online coverage. The BBC were always honest and fair in their reportage – other media, not so much. The worst was the *Daily Mail* – or the *Daily Maul* as we designated it: a typical ploy was for a *Daily Mail* reporter to phone us in mid-December and say something like, 'Thanks for taking the call – it doesn't matter what you say, I'll write what I like.' Then the *Daily Mail*'s front-page headline would be something like, 'MISERY AT CHRISTMAS FOR ONLINE SHOPPERS' followed by made-up copy, attributed to us, about how millions of parcels would fail to arrive in time.

Pay For Performance (PFP): A New Future for Marketing

'Half the money I spend on advertising is wasted;
the trouble is I don't know which half'

John Wanamaker, nineteenth-century Philadelphia retailer

A step change took place in the first half of 2004 in how leading online merchants marketed themselves. From traditional spend on flat advertising space, droves of merchants migrated to 'pay for performance' (PFP) – with profound implications for everyone in the supply chain: retailers, media owners and manufacturers.

Traders had always been frustrated by having to rely on flat space ads at fixed cost, hoping that these would attract business but never actually knowing which marketing element was working and which wasn't. And if one component was particularly effective, how and why?

The PFP model had been evolving for around four years, but transformed in 2004 from 'accelerating trend' to 'standard practice'. For many merchants, PFP soon became the only way they would market themselves online.

And PFP was rapidly morphing into a 'Pay For Acquisition' (PFA) model, whereby merchants paid retrospectively only for sales achieved or new customers acquired.

PFP presented a whole new set of issues, opportunities and challenges: MEDIA OWNERS were expected to share risk; MERCHANTS could control costs much more tightly, and rapidly tune their efficiency and profitability in light of trading conditions observed in fine detail and in real time; MANUFACTURERS faced new dilemmas – *did they stick with traditional distributors who tied up high levels of stock and were unable to provide current sales and marketing intelligence, or did they switch to smart online distributors, and perhaps to using PFP themselves as a key element of the relationship?*

PFA encouraged a growing number of manufacturers, such as Panasonic, to bite the bullet and sell direct.

24 July: Internet Shopping Day (2001–2007)

On 24 July 2000 Neill Denny, the editor of Retail Week, suggested that IMRG should do something with the date: 'You should nominate today as Internet Shopping Day because 24/7 is what it's all about.' So for several years we did, launching ISIS on 24/7 Day 2001, as described earlier.

Figure 33: IMRG's 24/7 Day website logo. (*Source: James Roper Archive*)

> *'IMRG revealed the true potential of internet retailing to us through the 24/7 event. We did offer true value on the day [24 July 2004], but even so we were staggered by the response. We did 50 per cent of our previous month's turnover in one day! And 80 per cent of the orders were from new customers'*
>
> Paul Bond, Director, Voodooshoes.com, 2004

Two years later, in 2003, we ran the first of several annual 24/7 Day events celebrating all that was great about shopping online. At the time around 70 per cent of UK adults had never shopped online – the *Virtual Vending Virgins* as we dubbed them – and novice e-shoppers remained nervous, seeking confirmation that internet merchants were genuine and reliable before committing their order. We decided therefore to deploy 24/7 Day resources to help people find out about this new trading medium and give them good reasons to try it, while providing sound advice and guidance, some fun and, hopefully, an excellent experience.

*   *   *

2003: For 24/7 2003, IMRG organised media activities throughout the month of July, focusing on the big day itself – Thursday 24th. New internet users were encouraged with *great shopping offers from the best online merchants* to shop online for the very first time, while regular e-shoppers were invited to 'shop around the clock' with *time-limited offers* on the day and during the following week.

We built a dedicated 24/7 Day microsite to facilitate shopping promotions, communications, and a *Countdown Clock*. Dozens of merchants supported 24/7 Day with £12 million worth of prizes, special offers, limited edition items, exclusive bundles and gift vouchers – participants included Argos, Boots, BT, dabs.com, Debenhams, Empire Direct, Empire Stores, Figleaves, Game.UK.com, John Lewis, Kodak, La Redoute, Littlewoods, Royal Mail, Vertbaudet, Voodooshoes. com and many more. The 24/7 Day site promoted participants' offers, while the retailers symbiotically displayed the 24/7 Day logo with a reciprocal link. The 24/7 Day website attracted over a million visitors and the event drew extensive national TV and press media coverage.

Hitwise noted that merchants who offered 24/7 Day promotions enjoyed a huge increase in visits to their sites: traffic to online grocer, Ocado, who at the time partnered with Waitrose, was 115 per cent higher on 24 July than the previous day, Marks & Spencer, who offered customers the opportunity to win a £1,000 shopping spree on MarksandSpencer.com, was up 96 per cent, while MFI.co.uk saw a 46 per cent increase in response to their 'win a kitchen' offer.

2004: 24/7 Day in 2004 was a Saturday. That year we formed a partnership with the *Daily Mirror* and ran a campaign from the 9 to 24 July, introducing the 24/7 Day event to readers in advance and encouraging interactivity, to increase overall impact. Carol Vorderman, who was considered by many as being as *the internet authority* of the day, promoted 24/7 Day in her regular *Mirror* column in the three weeks leading up to the event. We took full- and half-page colour advertisements in the *Mirror* each day of the preceding week, culminating in a four-page centre pull-out section on Saturday the 24th.

The IMRG membership was asked to identify which of all British e-retailers they considered the best. Over 1,000 votes were cast during July, and seventy-six merchants were nominated. It was interesting to see who the professionals rated highest, and we were a little surprised that only three high street brands made the top ten but delighted that nineteen of the top twenty-five were all IMRG members. On 24/7 Day we announced that the top ten British E-Retailers had been voted as:

1   Amazon.co.uk
2   Tesco.com
3   figleaves.com
4   Argos.co.uk
5 = dabs.com, JohnLewis.com, lastminute.com, Play.com
9 = Ocado.com, CDWow.co.uk

Amazon.co.uk was the clear leader, taking 11 per cent of the votes, while Tesco. com ran a close second with 9 per cent. Punching well above its weight as usual, figleaves.com took 8 per cent of the votes, ahead of Argos with 6 per cent. Daniel Nabarro, chairman of figleaves.com said: 'We are flattered and excited to be voted number three by our peers.'

Dabs.com, the top electrical e-retailer, attracted eleven times as many votes as Dixons.co.uk, which ranked sixty-third. Dabs' marketing director, Jonathan Wall commented: 'We are really honoured to have been voted the top electrical e-retailer and ranked fifth overall in this recent IMRG poll.'

Ocado, at number nine with 3 per cent of the vote, had been delivering Waitrose groceries for less than two years from its purpose-built facility in Hatfield. 'It is a great privilege for us to be mentioned alongside Amazon and Lastminute as one of the best e-tailers in the UK, not least because we are such a young company', said Jason Gissing, one of Ocado's founders.

The combination of advertising and editorial worked reasonably well for our partner retailers and facilitators; however, linking with the *Mirror* led to the event being largely ignored by most of IMRG's other 350+ media contacts. The following year we skipped having a 24/7 Day event as 24 July 2005 fell on a Sunday, which would have been problematical for our retailers to adequately serve.

2006: For 24/7 Day 2006, a Monday, we branched out with a new GO GREEN, GO ONLINE campaign. Concern for the environment was mounting, and our aim was to provide a lightning conductor for interest in this topic, to focus research, and raise awareness of the huge potential that the internet-enabled marketplace presented for increasing efficiency and reducing waste.

A growing body of research from around the world was proving that shopping online was making a real contribution towards protecting the planet – reducing the amount of energy and materials used by making the sourcing and distribution of goods more efficient. With close to 10 per cent of all retail sales online, we thought it would be helpful to spread the word, as did our GO GREEN, GO ONLINE sponsors: ASOS.com, Debenhams.com, Dell, Get Safe Online, Kelkoo, Royal Mail, Worldpay and Zendor.

Research findings we highlighted included an OECD study indicating that use of internet retailing could eliminate the need for 12.5 per cent of retail-building space, saving the energy and materials needed to build, operate and maintain buildings. Other studies implied that internet shopping could use 40 per cent to 90 per cent less fuel than when customers drove their cars to the shops, and that customer mileage savings of 75 per cent–95 per cent had been recorded where food-shopping trips were replaced by deliveries to their home. An Ernst & Young study estimated that internet applications could reduce retail inventories by 25 to 35 per cent, while IBM suggested that the savings could be as high as 50 per cent. The GO GREEN, GO ONLINE campaign summarised the benefits as follows:

The green effects of internet shopping

✓ GREEN EFFECT 1: LESS VEHICLE MILES. Shopping is the most frequent reason for car travel in Great Britain, accounting for 20 per cent of all trips, and for 12 per cent of mileage. Efficient package delivery by van can replace inefficient personal driving to the shops; in the case of grocery shopping, this could reduce vehicle miles by 70 per cent or more. Internet

Plate 1: The 'Currys Cooker Selector' was one of the first interactive media in retail pilots in Europe, here being checked out by Chrissie Roper, in 1988. I had persuaded Currys, the home electronics and household appliances division of Dixons Retail plc, to commission the project from Convergent Communications while business development director there. (*Source: James Roper Archive*)

Plate 2: IMRG management team 1991: James Roper (left) with Chester Wallace and Dr David Best (right) of Touche Ross Management Consultants' (TRMC) Advanced Systems Division (latterly Deloitte). (*Source: James Roper Archive*)

Plate 3: The first IMRG Report, published on 27 September 1991, contained case study examples of the use of IMR, a set of good practice guidelines, and a summary of the findings of the original 1990/1 IMR research survey. (*Source: James Roper Archive*)

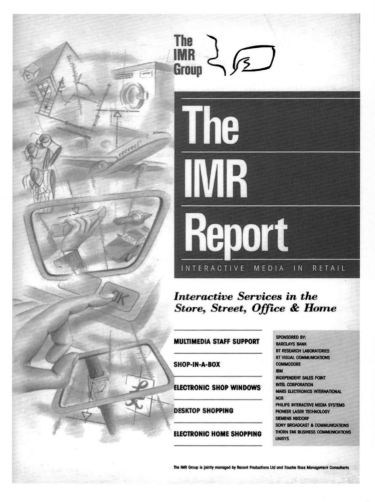

Plate 4: IMRG published its first website in 1994, as viewed here on the Netscape browser. (*Source: James Roper Archive*)

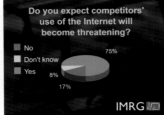

Plate 5: An IMRG Electronic Home Shopping workshop held in early 1997 posed a series of questions which delegates could vote on anonymously using handheld clickers. These slides show the results. For the third slide, the question 'Where will the threat be from?' was asked at the beginning, and then again at the end of the session – note the shift between the first and last votes as the retailers realised that their threat would come from new market entrants, not their own sector. (*Source: James Roper Archive*)

Plate 6: In 1997 IMRG helped to organise and lead a large-scale international 'Pathfinder' project called e-Christmas to kick-start cross-border e-retailing. *e-Commerce* magazine, Volume 1, Issue 3 of 1997 featured e-Christmas: IMRG's article, 'Jumpstarting Internet commerce in Europe' explained the argument for putting European merchants on the e-commerce map. (*Source: James Roper Archive*)

Europe@n Internet commerce

This year the festive season is different thanks to e-Christmas, an initiative aimed at jumpstarting Internet commerce in Europe. Many organisations, large and small, have committed resources, attracted by the opportunities for European merchants and determined to overcome any barriers in the region. For consumers the e-Christmas site is a new and convenient source of exciting Christmas presents from a range of famous European retailers. It is also a way of selecting the best gift for the right person whether it is a close friend or a relative. e-Christmas.com is packed with gifts from the fabulous to the frivolous, for him and her, young and old. It offers consumers the chance to buy online, and ship anywhere in the world, without wearing out shoe leather.

James Roper, Retail Expert, IMRG

Christmas is the most important time of year for retailers and consumers alike. It is the biggest sales bonanza of the calendar as buyers pound crowded streets with shopping lists. James Roper of UK electronic trade organisation, IMRG, explains the argument for putting European merchants firmly on the e-commerce map

Jumpstarting Internet commerce in Europe

But there is also a strong business argument for e-Christmas. Internet commerce is taking off rapidly in the US. In Europe, we are lagging behind. Some 14% of US households now use the web compared with only 2% in Europe. Among businesses the gap is much wider. Yet analysts predict that by 2000 the number of consumers, businesses and web sites in the US and Europe will be similar. If European consumers, coming to the net later than their US cousins, find US web services ready and willing to take their custom, the chances are we will see a growing e-trade imbalance in favour of the US, unless Europe has more to offer.

Commerce strategies

US dominance is not surprising. In this more advanced market, a growing number of companies are reporting intranet commerce turnover in excess of US$1 billion per annum. Many organisations are investing $1 million or more in their Internet commerce strategies. The US also has a number of other advantages. These include a single homogenous market, one language, one currency, a common approach to banking, fulfilment and marketing,

and a government which strongly encourages electronic commerce.

European online merchants face many challenges: different languages, currencies, taxes, shipping costs, and a minefield of bureaucracy. All this plus high risks and, so far, negligible sales prospects. Small wonder few European merchants are going online and millions of new European web users who wish to shop on the web are buying elsewhere.

Radical action

So what must Europe do, before it is too late? French Prime Minister, Lionel Jospin's decision to abandon the Minitel system, blamed for holding back adoption of the Internet in France, is one small step in the right direction. But more radical action is required. Europe urgently needs encouragement in the form of tax and investment incentives, standards, certificate authorities, an information channel for small and medium enterprises, codes of practice, training centres, and purposeful leadership from its governments.

For businesses and retailers it is essential to learn about online retail and the best way to support electronic commerce. Many have

had enough of theory and are crying out for an opportunity to gain practical experience. The e-Christmas initiative alone cannot address all of the issues, but it has resolved many of the key problems. It demonstrates the viability of Internet commerce in Europe today, and will generate data to support further electronic commerce investment. e-Christmas is also providing merchants of all sizes with the resources and the consumer base on which to build a successful online retail model. And if e-Christmas merchants achieve anything like the number of sales anticipated, the initiative will be a very loud wake-up call for Europe.

It is also important that new consumers are aware of the benefits of online shopping. The e-Christmas team believes that the best way to demonstrate this is by giving them an exciting and convenient online service. That is why the whole team has worked so hard to build the extensive range of gifts on offer at e-Christmas.com. I have already identified presents for some of my own hard-to-please friends and relations. I only hope the merchants haven't sold out before I get my order in.@

Plate 7: Amazon's first UK website as it appeared in November 1998, offering 1.2 million titles, six times more than the largest bookstores. As part of its expansion into Europe, Amazon had purchased the UK online bookseller Bookpages.co.uk a few months earlier, and promptly renamed it Amazon. co.uk. Simon Murdoch, Amazon's VP Europe, had established Bookpages in 1996 after being sacked by WH Smith. (*Source: James Roper Archive*)

Plate 8: 1 January 2000 – Tony Blair announced that the historic status of Greenwich as the home of time would be assured for the new millennium under IMRG's Greenwich Electronic Time (GeT) scheme, as reported here in *The Times* lead story on 28 December 1999. GeT, synchronised to Greenwich Mean Time (GMT), would be the universal time standard for internet users worldwide. 'It's a stroke of genius,' commented one senior Whitehall source. (*Used with permission from The Times / News Licensing*)

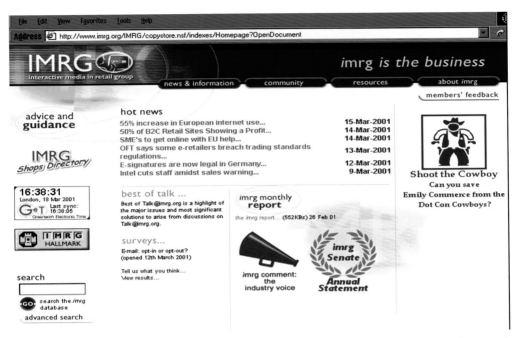

Plate 9: The IMRG website's homepage on 18 March 2001 included industry data, the Greenwich Electronic Time clock, and 'Shoot the Cowboy', an interactive game that gently teased merchants by highlighting the daft mistakes many of them were making. (*Source: James Roper Archive*)

Plate 10: In 2001 I advised the Barbadian government that the www.barbados.com website was owned by a privately funded start-up company incorporated in the State of Delaware, USA, that was using it to tout its vacation packages. (*Source: James Roper Archive*)

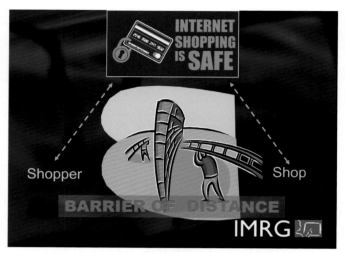

Plate 11: We used this slide to explain how the ISIS online shopping trust scheme, introduced by IMRG in 2001, gave people confidence that accredited sites and their services were honest, reliable and of good quality. The non-face-to face nature of the internet shopping medium, involving as it does both distance and the graphical representation of stores, goods and processes, requires triangulation with robust, independent verification. When a consumer saw an ISIS logo, they could click on it to view that organisation's ISIS accreditation certificate, which stated the registered company's name and internet address. The certificate also confirmed that the shop subscribed to the ISIS principles, had its site and service reviewed and monitored by IMRG, and had its Business, VAT and Data Protection registrations checked by IMRG. (*Source: James Roper Archive*)

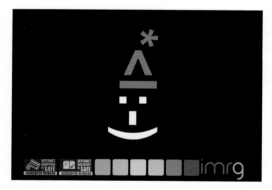

Plate 12: Christmas repunctuated! From 2003 there was a surge in online shopping each Christmas. Busy people with lots to buy and organise loved the convenience, just as long as they could remember the f*#*?ing password, which had to be at least eight characters long, mix both upper and lower case letters, and numbers, and include at least one keyboard symbol, eg @ # \ ] & ?, and of course be unique and changed often. (*Source: James Roper Archive*)

Plate 13: IMRG was constantly in the news in the run-up to and following each Christmas, as here on 21 September 2004. Feeding the media's insatiable appetite to know how many people were shopping online, what they were buying, the latest dates for safe pre-Christmas delivery, how many parcels would be sent out, and then revealing the post-Christmas hard data results, became our world from November through to mid-January. (*Source: James Roper Archive*)

Plate 14: Parcel delivery was always the Achilles' heel of e-retail – millions of people didn't shop online in 2004 because of the uncertainty and potential hassle associated with goods arriving when they were out. So IMRG formed a Delivery Forum that was instrumental in creating for the UK the most comprehensive, efficient and convenient suite of home delivery services available anywhere in the world. (*Source: James Roper Archive*)

Plate 15: 24/7 Day 2004 – centrespread of our four-page pull-out section in the *Daily Mirror* on Saturday, 24 July 2004. Note the ISIS logo, guaranteeing fair play. (*Source: James Roper Archive. Reprinted with permission from the Daily Mirror / Reach Publishing Services*)

Plate 16: Tom Dickson of Blendtec said his 'Will it blend?' viral social media campaign raised sales by 1,000 per cent. (*Source: Blendtec / James Roper Archive*)

Plate 17: In 2006 Littlewoods Shop Direct Group (rebranded as The Very Group in 2020) presented a small number of VIPs with limited edition iPods in lavish crystal cases. I was lucky enough to receive No. 1 of 50. Themed 'we're not who you think we are', the beautifully etched iPods were pre-loaded with high resolution images plus video from their latest fashion show. Shop Direct reported a 314 per cent increase in sales from mobile devices in late 2010 as their efforts to provide a 'slick and quick' mobile shopping experience paid off, with iPads and smartphones being amongst the *must-have* presents that Christmas. (*Source: James Roper Archive*)

Plate 18: GO GREEN, GO ONLINE. For 24/7 Day 2006 we placed full-page ads in the *Metro* and *London Evening Standard* on Monday, 24 July promoting our 'online is green' campaign. (*Source: James Roper Archive*)

Daily Mail

LIFESTYLE'S LAST-MINUTE GIFT GUIDE STARTS PAGE 41

NIGELLA'S CHRISTMAS EXPRESS

The Domestic Goddess's deliciously different guide to festive entertaining
SEE PAGES 56-57

THE YULE LOGJAM

Thousands of presents bought online won't arrive in time for Christmas

Alesha set to make £5m
SEE PAGE 11

HUNDREDS of thousands of families face bitter disappointment tomorrow because presents bought online have not been delivered.

Failures by internet firms, Royal Mail and private delivery companies have affected a huge range of Christmas gifts including computer consoles, designer goods and children's toys.

More than two million parcels and letters are estimated to have been

By **Luke Salkeld**

lost or delayed by Royal Mail alone. Many people who relied on the internet must decide today whether to spend even more on the high street to replace missing presents.

Hundreds more had to endure bitter cold over the weekend as they queued at depots to collect items after receiving 'failed delivery' notes.

Though all classes of package will have been delayed – including those posted by relatives and goods bought from mail order catalogues – experts say internet customers are the worst hit. Online Christmas

shopping was worth a staggering £1.8billion this year – around 15 per cent of all seasonal buys.

But as the boss of a major delivery firm admitted that vast numbers of packages would not arrive in time, there were predictions that the fiasco will produce a backlash against online shopping.

Complaints posted on internet messageboards highlighted the scale of the problem.

One angry Amazon customer reported that a £700 laptop computer had been left in plain view at his front door. Others told of receiving

Turn to Page 6

Plate 19: *The Daily Mail*'s annual e-retail whack – this example from Monday, 24 December 2007. (*Source: James Roper Archive. Reprinted with permission from the dmg media licensing*)

Plate 20: IMRG launched IMRWorld in 2008 as a definitive source of global e-commerce intelligence. IMRWorld's international partners included national e-commerce associations in Germany, France, USA, Holland, Belgium, Slovakia, and the European Commission. (*Source: James Roper Archive*)

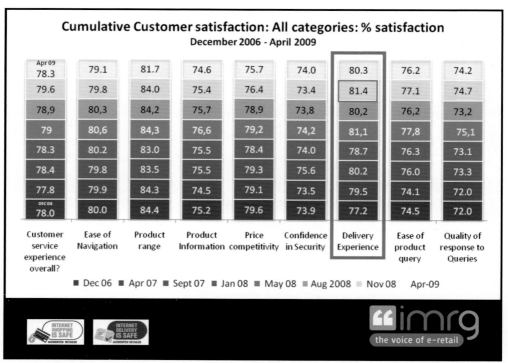

Plate 21: IMRG continuously monitored customer satisfaction with online shopping. This table records our findings from December 2006 through to April 2009, highlighting the delivery experience. IMRG and Metapack's introduction of IDIS Delivery Manager in November 2007 significantly raised fulfilment standards, however, satisfaction remained stubbornly static because whereas the industry delivery offer improved rapidly, so did consumers' expectations. Once an excellent service had been experienced, this became the shopper's new yardstick. (*Source: James Roper Archive*)

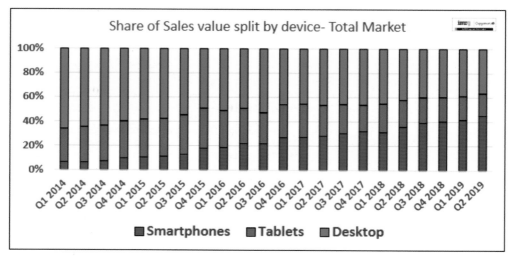

Plate 22: This chart shows e-sales revenue by device type from Q1 2014 to Q2 2019. The iPhone's launch in 2007 had unleashed the mobile trading genie – the explosive annual growth of m-commerce peaked at 359 per cent in May 2012. Initially, most sales were via tablets: in March 2014 tablets accounted for almost 80 per cent of mobile commerce. By 2016 mobile commerce had soared to account for the majority – 56 per cent – of UK online sales, up from less than 1 per cent in 2010. (*Source: IMRG / Capgemini*)

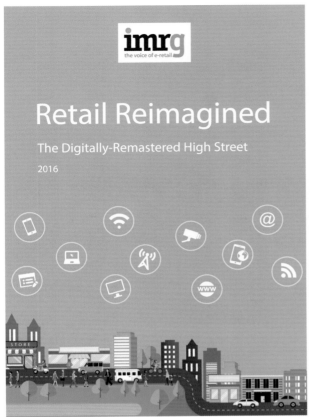

Plate 23: The Retail Reimagined report was commissioned from IMRG in 2016 as part of our work with the Future Retail Working Group (FRWG) to help towns and villages evolve sustainably in the digital age. The report was well received, published on the GREAT BRITISH HIGH STREET website, then ignored. (*Source: James Roper Archive*)

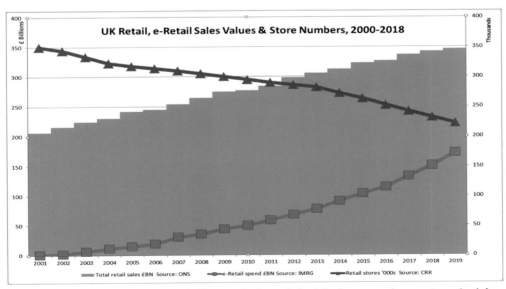

Plate 24: This chart shows the rise of UK e-retail sales and the fall of store numbers against a backdrop of total retail sales between 2000 and 2018. (*Source: ONS / IMRG / Centre for Retail Research (CRR) / James Roper Archive*)

Plate 25: In 2015, there was 428 million square feet of large warehouse space in the UK. By the end of 2020 that had risen by 32% – adding the equivalent of an extra 2,396 football pitches. (*Source: Teamjackson*)

Plate 26: At the European Commission, Brussels, 1 May 2013. I had many years' experience liaising with the EC, representing the UK in Brussels on e-commerce matters, speaking at or chairing EC events. It tended to be very frustrating and unproductive. (*Source: James Roper Archive*)

shopping also cuts out a large number of avoidable product movements between distribution depots and stores. In these ways, internet shopping contributes to reduced traffic congestion, air pollution and fuel use.

✓ GREEN EFFECT 2: LESS INVENTORY. The tendency towards 'pre-selling' online – i.e. taking orders for products before they are built, as famously implemented by Dell – enables producers to ascertain in advance of production what goods to make. This avoids the production of obsolete goods that sometimes simply get thrown away if they don't sell. Research on the US book trade showed that a third of best sellers are unsold due to overproduction. Pre-selling also enables new lines to be introduced without the delays often caused by having to first sell off old stock.

✓ GREEN EFFECT 3: LESS PRINTED MATERIALS: Many mail shots, catalogues, instruction manuals and other printed materials can be replaced by internet-delivered information. Often catalogues are out of date by the time they are rolling off the printing presses, prompting frequent republishing. And it has become the norm for instruction manuals to be printed in numerous languages, and therefore be much larger than necessary. The internet enables just the right information to be available in real time, on demand, wherever it is needed, thereby saving trees, paper production, printing and physical distribution.

✓ GREEN EFFECT 4: LESS PACKAGING: Packaging is the single largest category of municipal solid waste. Often packaging is large and of high quality simply because it has to 'sell' the product from off the shelf and communicate all of the product's attributes; just think of those big glossy software boxes with just a CD inside (and an inch-thick multi-lingual instruction book that is never read). And less packaging may be used when an item does not have to withstand numerous product movements. Internet shopping enables product information to be largely de-coupled from its packaging, and may enable the number of product movements – e.g. from manufacturer to distributor to warehouse to distribution centre to store to shelf to basket to car boot to home – to be significantly reduced. The internet shopping industry is working to develop highly efficient and, for some situations, returnable packaging.

✓ GREEN EFFECT 5: LESS WASTE. Internet technologies have a tremendous positive impact on procurement, manufacturing and distribution by compressing time and reducing costs throughout the supply chain. By enabling better communication between buyers and sellers, internet shopping helps extend product life cycles by helping to ensure that consumers get the right products in the first place, and by making repair information and spare parts easily accessible. And when consumers no longer need stuff, services like eBay and Amazon Marketplace enable the redistribution of second-hand items that might otherwise be thrown away – i.e. recycling.

✓ GREEN EFFECT 6: DEMATERIALISATION. Many retail products, such as music, entertainment, software, film, newspapers, dictionaries – and even money itself – are being 'dematerialised' – i.e. they are becoming digital and therefore downloadable. This is known as 'dematerialisation'. When this happens, the green effect of internet shopping on manufacture, packaging and physical product movement can be 100 per cent!

2007: 24/7 Day 2007 fell on a Tuesday. Building on the success of the GO GREEN, GO ONLINE campaign, this year we introduced *OnLine Green Awards* – the OLGAs (up-cycling the BAFTAs concept) – *'to inspire, encourage and reward individuals and companies who are using internet shopping to progress towards conservation of the earth's resources and / or a reduction in their carbon footprint'.*

IMRG, in conjunction with Heriot-Watt University, was working on a government-funded *Green Logistics* research project, looking at the environmental impact of internet retailing: comparing the carbon footprint of shopping online and shopping on the high street. On an average day, 2.3 million online shopping parcels were

Figure 34: The OnLine Green Awards—the OLGAs—were presented by IMRG at an all-day event at the Kensington Roof Gardens on 24 July 2007. (*Source: James Roper Archive*)

being delivered that year – but what was the impact of moving this parcel mountain each day in terms of logistics, road and vehicle use? We aimed to find out. Also, IMRG members were discussing and implementing many green initiatives. We felt that these needed to be recognised.

As well as retailers and suppliers – both large and small – OLGA award categories included a *Community Award, International Award, Green Thinker Award* and a *Grand Prix* for the best of the best.

The OnLine Green Awards—OLGAs: Winners 2007

Category	Sponsor	Winner
Small Retailer (Consumer Vote)	MSN	The Organic Delivery Company
Large Retailer (Consumer Vote)	HDNL	lastminute.com
Small Supplier	MSN	Giraffe Marketing (Hippo Box)
Small Retailer	GB Group	gizoo.co.uk
International Award	Shopping.com	Dell
Large Supplier	Post Code Anywhere	Home Delivery Network
Large Retailer	SecureTrading	Marks & Spencer
Grand Prix Award	PayPal	Tesco.com

Figure 35: The OnLine Green Awards (the OLGAs) winners 2007. (*Source: James Roper Archive*)

Thirty entries were submitted, and the OLGAs winners were chosen by 9,000+ consumers on MSN Shopping (Microsoft Network) and an independent panel of respected judges: Professor Alan McKinnon, Director of the Logistics Research Centre, Heriot-Watt University, EDINBURGH; Rory Cellan-Jones, BBC Technology Correspondent, LONDON; Aad Weening, Secretary General of the Brussels-based European Distance Selling Trade Association (EMOTA) from 1993 to 2007; Tim Danaher, Editor, *Retail Week* magazine, LONDON; and myself.

The winning initiatives ranged from small retailers www.footprintfriendly.com and Gizoo, both with 'eco-friendly' product ranges, to The Organic Delivery Company that sold food grown as local as possible, in season and affordable, to Marks & Spencer's five-year 'Plan A', a 100-point plan to go green, to Tesco's new electric van fleet that they described as 'blue on the outside, green on the inside'. Dell was recognised for its dedication to become 'the greenest technology company on the planet' and for taking the lead in setting an environmental standard for the computer industry. Home Delivery Network Limited was awarded for its multiple greening efforts while delivering over 110 million parcels throughout the UK in the previous year: the ratio of miles travelled to parcels it delivered, equated to an average of each parcel travelling about 600 metres.

*   *   *

In light of the global economic downturn that followed the financial crisis of 2007/8, with everybody focused on just trying to stay in business, we cancelled 24/7 Day 2008, then decided to discontinue the campaign altogether as unnecessary, the growth of online retailing having become so strong.

2005: Dual Pricing in Rip-off Britain

'The government has created mistrust of business with a misplaced campaign against "rip off Britain"'

John Clare, Dixons' CEO, addressing the CBI in London, 2003

Low prices, huge choice and rich information soon had consumers flocking online to shop in the early 2000s, particularly for high-ticket discretionary purchases such as LCD TVs, digital cameras and car GPS navigation systems, where savings of 15 per cent to 40 per cent were commonly available. In 2004 over £2 billion worth of electrical goods were sold online in the UK, an increase of 37 per cent on the previous year, and by that December there had been a fivefold growth in thirty-four months. When the peak Christmas trading season arrived the following year, 2005, fully 20 per cent of all electrical goods retail sales had migrated online.

In pre-internet Britain, retailers enjoyed some of the highest margins in the world, while their counterparts in Europe and the USA got by on much slimmer profits. Some brands became popular Aunt Sallys of consumer watchdogs and developed finely honed dodging skills. The government tried to tackle cartels with the UK Competition Act that came into force on 1 March 2000: this gave regulators tough powers to stop companies ripping off consumers, including the ability to impose fines of up to 10 per cent of their turnover for anti-competitive behaviour. But the manoeuvre had little real impact on the most unscrupulous businessmen who remained as slippery as oiled eels. The real problem was that there was not enough competition.

The consumer electrical goods sector was dominated and largely controlled by Currys (Dixons Group) and Comet, whose proposed merger was rejected by the Monopolies and Merger Commission (MMC) in May 1990 on the basis that while their combined market share would have been just under 25 per cent – the threshold that would trigger an MMC investigation – it would have been four times larger than its nearest competitor, Rumbelows. For some products, including microwave ovens, dishwashers and personal stereos, their combined market share rose to between 30 per cent and 40 per cent. Stanley Kalms, Dixons' chairman, who was fighting a hostile takeover bid by Comet owner Kingfisher Group at the time, said: '[This] is about a virtual monopoly in retail parks, the fastest growing sector of the business. Out of town there are only two competitors, Currys and Comet.' Trade Secretary Nicholas Ridley agreed, commenting that in the out-of-town sector, the combined group would control 70 to 80 per cent of the market.

There was also concern that the combined group's buying power 'would allow it to gain substantial discounts from manufacturers, and the lack of competition would mean it would not be under pressure to pass discounts on to the consumer'. Illustrating this point, a spat over the issue of monopoly pricing took place in the late 1990s between the world's leading computer chip manufacturer and the UK's leading electrical retailer. The chip manufacturer, who could then tell you a year in advance what their price for their products would be because they were utterly confident that they were able to control their marketplace, described the retailer's margins as being 'Ridiculous'. The retailer, who at the time probably controlled 50 per cent of UK home computer sales, countered by saying that it only made about 30 per cent profit on an average PC sale, one of its lowest margins. E-retail rapidly upended the cosy world of 'ridiculous profits' enjoyed by the few dominant traders.

Sparks fly, currently

The online electrical bargains that shoppers were snapping up in the early 2000s and which were fuelling the exponential growth of online shopping were seldom available from the major retailers, but instead came from a rapidly upcoming raft of smaller, and sometimes very small, traders with smart websites and low overheads, who were willing to operate on profit margins as low as 5 to 6 per cent.

Millions of people were perfectly happy to buy online electrical goods manufactured by reputable brands without first seeing the physical product. Legal

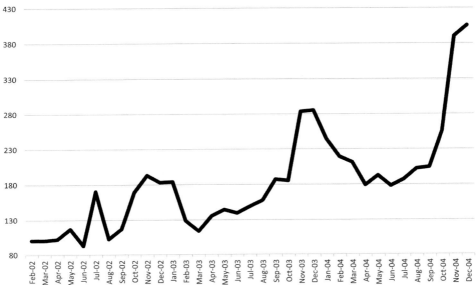

Figure 36: The IMRG Electricals Index—February 2002 to December 2004. Broken out as a sub-sector of the Total e-Sales Index in 2002, it registered fivefold growth in thirty-four months. (*Source: IMRG Capgemini Sales Index*)

protection gave consumers trading with EU e-retailers a seven-day cooling off period in which to return unsatisfactory goods. And in 2005, twelve million Britons had broadband connections with which to access the rich product information that was available on most consumer-goods manufacturers' websites.

So, while predictable, it was nevertheless shocking when, in the run-up to the Christmas trading peak 2005, a number of major electrical goods manufacturers introduced *Dual Pricing*, a new pricing structure scheme that had the effect of segmenting *high street* sales from *internet sales*. Dual pricing forced dealers to pay significantly more – typically 10 to 15 per cent – for their TVs and other goods if they sold them via the internet, deliberately making these dealers uncompetitive and killing their trade, thereby stifling competition and introducing the probability of price inflation.

Many online traders received very similar letters, *apparently independently*, from their major suppliers advising them of draconian changes *that had been made* to their Commercial Conditions, including increases in prices, corresponding new discounts for 'Face to Face Sales' and estimates of the percentages of their 'Non Face To Face Sales'. The letters demanded that merchants declared the proportion of their sales that were online and concluded that by continuing to trade they would be deemed to have read, understood and agreed to these new commercial terms.

'It's scandalous,' commented one affected dealer. 'This manufacturer, who we have worked with for many years, encouraged us to be innovative and trade online, and we've had a roaring success together. Now, out of the blue they have effectively stopped us trading. If other brands follow suit, we'll be out of business by the spring.'

'It's blatant market rigging,' commented another trader. 'We've lost £10 million due to [named electrical manufacturer].'

The Royal National Institute for the Blind also raised concerns that dual pricing discriminated against the UK's two million blind and partially sighted people, many of whom found online stores their only viable shopping outlets.

This scheme cynically positioned dual pricing as *rewarding* bricks-and-mortar retailers for having physical shops, rather than blighting internet traders for being efficient and increasingly popular with consumers.

The argument for dual pricing was that it cost more to run a physical shop than it did to run a virtual shop, which was neither true nor relevant. At the time, the costs of setting up and running a virtual shop *properly* – with rich information, good stock levels, convenient delivery options and first-rate customer service – were as high if not higher than that of a physical shop. A more pertinent point was that increasingly shoppers were inspecting goods in physical retail outlets in order to reach a decision on which to buy then purchasing the items more cheaply online – *free riding* by online retailers, as the Office of Fair Trading prejudicially described it.

But by then the internet was a fact of life and a central part of the everyday commercial environment which everyone was learning to work with: search engines were an inevitable consequence of the advent of the internet – product search engines did not undermine fair and efficient traders in any way. There was no compelling market or national economic reason to prop up the bricks-and-mortar distribution channel if it was becoming uncompetitive, particularly through an anomalous manufacturer-imposed subsidy.

The issue created a serious dilemma for IMRG, as our members included almost all the involved traders, both large and small. IMRG surveyed its membership: 70 per cent of respondents considered dual pricing to be **anti-competitive**; 4 per cent thought it was **simply restoring fair trading terms** to conventional retail channels; 84 per cent voted that IMRG should **name the electronics manufacturer identified as the instigator of dual pricing in a public statement**. Comments received included: 'Not fair', 'Canute economics', 'extremely short-sighted', 'pathetic attempt to stem the tide of the e-channel', 'it is myopic and ignores the consumer's desire for a multichannel service', 'has the look of manufacturers wanting to get *their share* of the lower cost of sales' and 'undermines confidence in the e-retail industry'.

IMRG also consulted its Senate, which took the view that IMRG should advise and assist whilst pointing out that the practice could be used for and against retailers. IMRG raised the issue with the Office of Fair Trading (OFT), Trading Standards Institute (TSI), Department of Trade and Industry (DTI) and the European Commission amongst others to gain clarity in legal and commercial terms as to Dual Pricing's sustainability if adopted as a commercial strategy by its members. The IMRG reserved its position pending the outcome of OFT, DTI, TSI and European Commission investigations.

Meanwhile, IMRG research indicated that dual pricing appeared limited to the UK and to the electrical sector, the practice having been initiated in 2004 by one particular manufacturer, since when others had followed suit, targeting mainly dealers who listed their products on price comparison sites such as Kelkoo, PriceRunner and Froogle. It was also apparent that other sectors and territories were keenly observing how this innovation was evolving – some in horror and some in hope.

Independent internet retailers were reluctant to speak out openly against the powerful electrical brands. One online retailer said to us on assurance of anonymity: 'Those who speak out find themselves penalised. You call up to order something from the manufacturers and it's always out of stock. Or orders go missing. That can be crippling at this peak time of year.'

The DTI declined to respond. The OFT eventually wrote back with a provisional view that 'dual pricing, in itself, does not raise significant competition concerns'. The Trading Standard Institute's Chief Executive, Ron Gainsford, took a dimmer view, expressing concern that at stake was most important consumer right of all, *the right to obtain the best possible deal*, and offered help from their PR department to get that story out. And a senior European Commission representative told IMRG: 'The scheme is either illegal or should be. We should look at this.'

The general assumptions were (1) that a small number of large electrical retailers and manufacturers had colluded to create the dual pricing scheme; (2) if left unchecked throughout the coming peak trading season, most or all of the UK's smaller electrical dealers would be wiped out by the following spring; and (3) pursuing redress through normal political and legal channels would probably, ultimately, be successful but take far too long to be of any help the threatened traders.

I discussed dual pricing with a fellow speaker at a European e-commerce conference, and it turned out that he was a highly experienced Nordic judge who had worked on numerous competition issues for the European Commission. The judge had seen this type of what he described as *prickly practice* many times before and suggested a range of ways with which the situation could be dealt. Over lunch a plan was formed whereby IMRG would make a public statement on the general subject of dual pricing including notification that, after a short delay, we would issue a second public statement on dual pricing but this time naming a manufacturer that had adopted this scheme – unless in the meantime the manufacturer confirmed their discontinuance of using it.

After passing this idea by the IMRG Senate – several of whom were extremely *unhappy* with it – an IMRG public statement on dual pricing was issued to 400+ media contacts and the IMRG membership. Copies of the statement were also sent by registered delivery to senior executives of all the leading electrical manufacturers.

The Trading Standards Institute helpfully invited IMRG to combine the release of our dual pricing statement with the launch of its *National Consumer Week*, to be held at the headquarters of the Department of Trade and Industry, 1 Victoria Street, London SW1 on Monday, 31 October 2005. The following is an extract of the statement:

ELECTRONICS GIANT INFLICTS NEW RIP-OFF SCHEME ON SHOPPERS

A major electrical consumer goods manufacturer has introduced a new scheme to deprive internet shoppers from getting competitive prices for its products. IMRG, the e-retail industry body, today warns this global brand that if it has not restored fair trading terms to all IMRG Members by the end of NATIONAL CONSUMER WEEK, it will be named, and its illicit and anti-competitive trading practices will be exposed.

IMRG's CEO, James Roper, commented: 'This serious abuse by a global brand of both its position and consumers' rights must be stopped immediately. Twenty-four million British consumers have embraced internet shopping. They are collectively investing £6 billion a year in PCs and internet connections that give them their own, personal shopping environments – their High Street at home. These consumers are directly bearing many of the costs previously carried by bricks-and-mortar shops, which is a major reason for internet shopping prices being highly competitive, so it is completely inappropriate to disadvantage them through Dual Pricing. IMRG has raised this as a matter of urgency with the Office of Fair Trading, and we are confident that we can rely on the Government, which has often proclaimed its commitment to "making Britain the best place in the world to trade electronically", to stamp down on this unhelpful innovation before it is copied by other manufacturers and adopted by other sectors, with dire consequences for consumers and the UK economy.'

IMRG recognises the profound and sometimes disruptive challenges that the internet can introduce, together with the severe commercial pressures that these may bring to bear. What is needed is for internet shopping to evolve as an effective, reliable and safe trading channel: this can only happen if all trading partners – manufacturers, retailers and carriers – are able to maintain reasonable profit margins that support adequate investment in their services, infrastructure and development. IMRG is working at industry level towards optimising the channel's commercial development for the sustainable benefit of all, and invites all interested parties to participate in this critically important process.

IMRG has so far refrained from naming the manufacturer in question, as it hopes that the company will respond positively of its own volition to the industry's request for it to correct its inappropriate behaviour. However, IMRG serves notice today through this statement that if the company does not restore fair trading terms to all IMRG Members by noon on 7 November 2005, IMRG will then publicly identify it and expose the illicit and anti-competitive trading practices it has deployed.

National Consumer Week 2005 coincided with the 400th anniversary of Guy Fawkes' plot to blow up the English Parliament and the king, James I, and IMRG did not have to wait long for fireworks. Phones rang off the hook with press and media enquiries demanding to know the name of the electrical manufacturer. IMRG

THE TIMES 60p

No. 68545 ■ TUESDAY NOVEMBER 15 2005 ■ www.timesonline.co.uk

Lose **6lb** in two weeks
THE CHRISTMAS PARTY DIET times2

Blair: action, not words, on poverty

Tony Blair has called on the US and the EU to cut farm subsidies and break the log jam in world trade talks. In his annual foreign policy speech he called on richer nations to honour promises made at the Gleneagles summit in July.
NEWS page 4

Metal mystery

A Chinese government copper trader has disappeared after apparently selling the metal short and exposing his country to massive losses.
NEWS page 6

Charity drive

Secondary schools in England will get £500 each for pupils to donate to charity under Home Office plans to encourage a culture of giving.
NEWS page 23

SUDOKU
SOLVE THE PUZZLE
times2

Wembley boost

England's 3-2 victory over Argentina has given the new Wembley Stadium its most successful day's takings.
SPORT page 80

Giant neighbours

A race of giant apes, 10ft tall and weighing up to 85 stone, may have lived alongside early humans, scientists say.
NEWS page 30

Higher offer

The Japanese company Nippon Sheet Glass is to raise its offer for Pilkington to 162p a share, *The Times* has learnt.
BUSINESS page 40

'We had similar riots 20 years ago without an imam in sight'
DAVID AARONOVITCH page 19

COMMENT 16 | WEATHER 65
BUSINESS 40 | TELEVISION &
REGISTER 61 | RADIO times2

End to online bargains as Sony forces prices higher

By Sean O'Neill

MILLIONS of internet shoppers face a "rip-off" Christmas after a decision by leading electronics companies to force up online prices for DVD players, hi-fis and similar products to high street levels.

Manufacturers, including Sony, are charging shopping websites wholesale prices between 10 and 15 per cent higher than their prices to high street stores, the trade group that represents online sellers says.

The rises mean that e-retailers will find it difficult to carry on undercutting prices in the high street. Manufacturers prefer traditional retail outlets because it allows them to "showcase" their goods.

Sony denies penalising internet shopping sites, arguing that it is rewarding stores that can demonstrate its products.

Internet traders will meet today to decide whether to "name and shame" the companies involved, which include the leading household names in home entertainment goods.

The Office of Fair Trading and the European Commission have already been asked to look into the pricing policies of Sony, the Japanese giant.

The Times has learnt that the practice of charging different prices to internet retailers and high street stockists — known

as dual pricing — was started by Sony and has been followed by other manufacturers.

The managing director of one website said that the electronics firms were too big for many of the independent website traders to argue with.

He said: "If you are seen to be a troublemaker it can have a detrimental effect on supplies. If they want to, they can just put you out of business.

"We are struggling to stay in business and some companies have already gone to the wall."

Sales of electronic goods on the internet have risen to 20 per cent of the total market over the past five years and total online shopping is expected to amount to £5 billion, or 9 per cent of all retail sales, this Christmas.

But the big retail names still have the largest share of the market and are understood to have exerted pressure on the manufacturers to offer them a better deal at a time of falling high street sales. Sony and the other manufacturers also have an interest in protecting the exclusive outlets that carry their brand names. There are around 100 Sony Centres in the UK which are independently owned but sell only Sony products.

James Roper, of the Independent Media in Retail Group (IMRG), the e-retailers indus-

try body, predicted that the electronics firms would face a backlash from millions of internet shoppers.

"For the major brand which has instigated this policy, this appears to be an extremely risky step which will upset a lot of consumers," said Mr Roper.

"I think they will get themselves into a horrible mess. We have researched this issue across 24 countries in Europe and there is no evidence of it happening anywhere else. Rip-off Britain is being treated to yet another world first.

"This is a serious abuse by a global brand of both its position and consumers' rights, and must be stopped immediately."

Bill Vestey, the company's UK spokesman, said: "Sony offers a common basic selling price to all resellers. This price is then affected by different types of discounts.

"Sony has a discount scheme that provides discounts for resellers that invest in building the brand and marketing our products in a way that provides the consumer with confidence in the Sony products' quality

Continued on page 2, col 3

Parents The bully, the bullied and the bystander
times2

Did one of Britain's greatest paint this?
NICK RAY

... or was it just an 'all-right amateur'?
NEWS page 3

Figure 37: *The Times* ran the dual pricing story that IMRG had seeded as its front-page leader on 15 November 2005. (*Image used with permission from The Times / News Licensing*)

declined to state any name but hinted that journalists could easily identify what was going on for themselves by looking online at the availability and prices of some popular electrical items. (Internally, we referred to the implicated manufacturers as STONY, MOANY, PHONEY and BONY.)

A media frenzy ensued, with all the major news services covering the story, and many naming Sony, Panasonic, Philips, Hitachi and Sharp as the culprits. IMRG was interviewed several times by TV and radio news channels. *The Times'* main front-page story on 15 November was headlined: 'End to online bargains as Sony forces prices higher'. The following day the *Financial Times* front-page leader read 'Online retailers accused' while its article on page three was titled 'Online retailers blow a fuse over dual pricing for electrical goods' and featured a quote from me: '*There will be a big backlash. Consumers will vote with their credit cards to show what they think.*'

None of the electrical manufacturers ever knew if they were *the one* being singled out for naming and shaming, however the issue of dual pricing in the UK electricals sector receded rapidly after all the publicity. Online electrical dealers soon reported that normal – or near normal – supplier service had been resumed. The online electrical retail sector continued to grow rapidly.

IMRG received many letters from electrical manufacturers' lawyers *placing Roper on notice*, but it never publicly identified any as being the one referred to in its anonymised public statement.

Deliverance! Where's My Stuff?

> '*NOBODY HOME: Thousands of failed deliveries are plaguing the otherwise booming online and home-shopping sector every week. So what's the solution?*'
>
> Alison Clements, Retail Week, 4 March 2005

Parcel delivery was always the Achilles' heel of e-retail. Millions of people didn't shop online in 2004 because of the uncertainty and potential hassle associated with goods arriving when they were out. So, we formed an IMRG Delivery Forum that would be instrumental in creating for the UK the most comprehensive, efficient and convenient suite of home delivery services available anywhere in the world.

The most active internet shoppers were cash-rich, time-poor working people who were almost always out during the day, when shippers typically attempted delivery. Consumers' high expectations of internet shopping were all too often dashed by delivery methods that had barely changed since the introduction of the *Penny Black* stamp on 6 May 1840. To cap it all, carriers would report leaving a 'you were out' card as a 'successful delivery', on the basis that they had got a man to the door. This was a huge problem for the e-retail industry and becoming intolerable.

Parcel delivery services in the 1990s remained largely on a 'take it or leave it' basis. Expectations were set by the mail order catalogue companies – your goods would probably turn up a week or two after you sent your order form off in the post, though they might take up to a month to arrive. At the turn of the new millennium, consumers' expectations of home parcel delivery could still be summarised as *untracked delivery*, and *up to 14 days, with no date specified*. In November 2000, the IMRG Mystery Shopper noted contentedly in their review of *Christmas Gifts Online* that most sites guaranteed delivery within a maximum of five working days.

The inadequacies of home parcel delivery services had been a low priority when the nascent e-retail industry's progress was blocked by so many other mountainous problems, but as online shopping took off, poor delivery became the pinch point in growth, continually rising as an issue of concern, ultimately topping our snagging list.

Shoppers' aspirations were set by the retailer's delivery offer, which was in turn heavily influenced by the carrier offer – 80 per cent of retailers were unable to handle international orders due to shipping challenges. Each of the stakeholder groups – *consumers, retailers, carriers* – expected another to take the decisive steps necessary to align home delivery with internet shoppers' needs, resulting in a strategic impasse. These quotes epitomised what IMRG were hearing:

> *I can't shop online because I'm always out when they deliver. The last time I had to traipse to a depot in the middle of nowhere on Saturday to get my stuff. Where's the convenience in that?*
>
> A shopper, 2004

> *The reason websites rarely offer time or date options is because few carriers are able to offer these services and if they do the cost is far too high. As a result, the number of customers who would actually be prepared to pay for them is too small*
>
> A retailer, 2004

> *We asked retailers what delivery services they wanted, then piloted the results – but they never want to pay a realistic price. New delivery services will only become cheaper when volumes are high. It's chicken and egg*
>
> A carrier, 2004

The Delivery Forum set out to accelerate progress through a sustained programme of positive pressure and guidance. Its inaugural meeting was held on 11 November at Kelkoo's offices at 1 London Bridge, with representatives attending from Arcadia, Axida, Collectpoint, Comet, Metapack, Royal Mail, Screwfix and Zendor. This working group was soon joined by all the leading carriers and many preeminent e-retailers, and went on to establish a *Delivery Charter*, standards and the *Internet Delivery Is Safe* (IDIS) trust scheme. IDIS was planned to be a *temporary* extension of ISIS – temporary because we aimed to fix the problem then close IDIS down.

Instrumental in the Delivery Forum were Colum Joyce, the ex-Head of Global Strategy at DHL, and Shiran Liyanage, publisher of the Internet Shoppers' Guides and previously Products Chief of Richard Branson's *Virgin Biznet*. Shiran, a trailblazer and stalwart of the e-commerce cause, had defined a set of service levels and values online shoppers should expect of delivery, which he shared with IMRG. Colum reviewed the documentation and proclaimed that he had 'never seen anything so comprehensive', so Shiran's model was adopted as the foundation on which we built our delivery standards.

The benefits we set out to unlock were these: CONSUMERS would spend more online more often; RETAILERS would be able to differentiate themselves from competitors, and gain significant bottom-line benefits through increased efficiency, higher volumes and lower customer churn rates; CARRIERS would be able to expand their revenues and service ranges (with new added value services) and increase profitability: while we predicted that the value of internet shopping would double within five years, we expected the value of e-retail delivery services to treble during the same period.

We were fighting an uphill battle. Most commercial carriers had previously sought to *minimise* the level of *Business to Consumer* (B2C) traffic they carried. In 2002/3, Parcelforce (the sister parcel delivery company to Royal Mail) even set about losing as much B2C work as it could by increasing prices significantly. This was because carriers prioritised *Business to Business* (B2B) delivery which gave greater consignment revenue (more parcels per delivery) and lower operating costs (deliveries concentrated in business areas during office hours) and therefore greater margins. B2C delivery was seen as less attractive because typically it involved single parcel deliveries to dispersed addresses, the recipient might not be at home, requiring repeated delivery attempts, drop densities were low in this emerging sector, and pressure for minimal costs.

Royal Mail rebrands itself *Consignia*

2001 was the strongest year yet for e-retail, so you might have expected anyone involved in shipping parcels to be focused on seizing growth opportunities. But in a move that nobody understood, Royal Mail spent its senior management time and £2 million on rebranding itself *Consignia*. 'The new name describes the full scope of what the Post Office does in a way that the words "post" and "office" cannot,' chief executive John Roberts told bemused customers. Sixteen months later, Roberts left, the meaningless name was a laughing stock and abandoned, and Royal Mail hoped the whole rebranding idea would be forgotten as soon as possible. I still cherish my *Consignia* pen, which is safely locked away in the IMRG archive.

Retailers were mainly reliant on postal operators which, supported by legal monopoly, were able to largely dictate rates (subject to price caps) and terms. Royal Mail's national, daily to-the-door service remained optimised for delivering information on paper – i.e. letters, not parcels. The situation was not helped by annual postal strikes – threatened or actual – in the run-up to Christmas each year.

Royal Mail was glacially slow to invest in services suitable for e-retail delivery and it was largely left to retailers and their carrier partners to innovate and invest in improvements in service quality and reliability. Some forward-thinking retailers did establish alternative delivery fleets for their own deliveries: Shop Direct Group in the UK (Home Delivery Network, later Yodel), and Otto in Germany (Parcelnet, later Hermes). Amazon became so frustrated with the inadequacy of delivery options that it would later set up Amazon Logistics, which by 2016 was delivering 80 per cent of Amazon's UK parcels.

Retailers were locked into carrier contracts and focused on operational efficiency, with little heed to customer convenience. The ramifications of uncertain delivery times and sketchy delivery information were considerable – deterring millions of people from shopping online at all.

* * *

Almost half of 100 e-retailers' websites that IMRG surveyed in 2005 gave the customer no delivery options at all, while seventeen of the sites with no options asked the customer to wait up to seven days or more. No specific delivery date could be chosen on 75 per cent of the sites inspected, and a similar proportion did not allow customers to specify a Saturday delivery. Overall, the average delivery charge was £4.26.[56]

NEED FOR CHANGE

- *More than half the adult population, or 26.1 million people, had something delivered in 2003, according to Verdict's 'Home Delivery and Fulfilment 2004', which valued the market at £34.7 billion*
- *About 50 per cent of UK households are unoccupied during normal working hours, according to industry estimates*
- *20 to 40 per cent of deliveries of items that do not fit into the letterbox fail first-time round*

Retail Week article extract: ONLINE RETAIL–HOME DELIVERY,
by Alison Clements, 4 March 2005

No such thing as free delivery: High street shops are expensive to run. Their overheads are self-evidently business costs, incurred in carrying out the operation of the enterprise; no shop would dream of charging customers just to walk in. Yet

Figure 38: IDIS: the internet delivery trust scheme—allied to the ISIS trust scheme. (*Source: James Roper Archive*)

many e-retailers struggled with the very idea of providing a free delivery service, even though this was patently also just *a cost of doing business*. The topic of *free delivery* was hotly debated for years, and retailers introduced all manner of devices to try to avoid, minimise or at least mitigate delivery costs, such as deploying minimum order values to trigger so-called *free* delivery.

The IDIS Delivery Trust Scheme – 2005

The IDIS (Internet Delivery Is Safe) trust scheme was publicly launched on BBC TV News on Tuesday 6 December 2005. IDIS was an extension of IMRG's general trust scheme, ISIS, that aimed to raise standards, particularly for the many retailers who – oblivious to the outcomes of their choices – still seemed to think that if a parcel left their warehouse and didn't come back, then all was well.

IDIS-accredited retailers at launch were Arcadia Group, BT, Carphone Warehouse, Comet, Co-op, dabs.com, Daxon, Empire Direct, Empire Stores, Figleaves.com, Firebox, Flatdeal, H. Samuel, IwantOneOfThose, JD Williams, Jomodo, La Redoute, Reebok, Richer Sounds, Schuh, Screwfix Direct, Signet, Trade Appliances, Vertbaudet, 24-7Electrical.co.uk.

IDIS was based on a delivery charter that identified, negotiated and documented key success factors, responsibilities and consequent activities in the delivery cycle. It set and monitored minimum commitments from all stakeholders so consumers buying from IDIS-accredited retailers knew that they could expect a predictable and positive shopping experience. For retailers, displaying the IDIS badge on their websites indicated that they were taking home delivery seriously and were investing in appropriate and reliable services.

IDIS DELIVERY CHARTER
AS AN ONLINE SHOPPER* WITH AN IDIS-ACCREDITED RETAILER, YOU HAVE THE RIGHT TO:

1. Clear delivery information before you place your order
2. Convenient delivery options
3. Notification of any delivery limitations / conditions
4. Charges that are complete and simple to understand
5. Access to information on your order progress
6. Delivery within the agreed time frame
7. Helpful support with failed / late / attempted deliveries
8. Your goods arriving in good condition
9. A clear returns process

*WITH RIGHTS COME RESPONSIBILITIES. AS AN ONLINE SHOPPER, YOU MUST:

- Check delivery details carefully
- Ensure all requested information is correct and complete
- Read and agree to the terms and conditions…

IF EFFICIENCY RATES RECORDED IN 2005 PREVAIL, IN 2006:

- *Half of the 7 million complaint calls will be delivery related*
- *£682 million of direct costs will be wasted due to largely avoidable home delivery inefficiencies and failures*
- *£1.26 of inefficiency cost will be imposed on every internet shopping shipment*

The Valuing Home Delivery project calculated the costs to all stakeholders of problematical parcel deliveries – including for the first time, to shoppers

Figure 39: IMRG's Valuing Home Delivery report was published in May 2006. It extrapolated that almost £700 million would be wasted due to largely avoidable home delivery inefficiencies and failures. (*Source: James Roper Archive*)

Valuing Home Delivery Report – 2006: When a delivery went wrong, it could cause considerable stress, inconvenience and cost for each of the stakeholder groups. But what exactly were the costs, and who bore them? Who cared?

To find out, the Delivery Forum researched the potential cost-benefit impacts of improving home delivery choice and convenience for the consumer, and in May 2006 published its findings in a seminal Valuing Home Delivery report.

Taking the UK home delivery performance recorded in 2005, we extrapolated the direct costs that would be dissipated as a result of largely avoidable home delivery inefficiencies and failures if performance remained unimproved in 2006. Sample data from an IMRG Merchant Survey, supplemented by generic industry data and conservative assumptions, extrapolated across the UK market, indicated that if home delivery performance remained unimproved, during 2006:

- 12 per cent of e-retail home deliveries would be 1ST TIME DELIVERY FAILURES, i.e. 65 million of the 540 million total;
- 2 per cent of e-retail home deliveries would be UNDELIVERABLE, i.e. 10.8 million of the 540 million total;
- £682 million of direct costs would be borne by Consumers, Retailers and Carriers due to internet shopping delivery inefficiencies and failures;
- £1.26 of inefficiency cost would be placed on every internet shopping delivery.

These annualised costs broke down across the stakeholders as follows:

- DIRECT COST TO CONSUMERS: 2,466 man-years of wasted time, valued at £12 per hour = £259 million
- DIRECT COST TO RETAILERS: £300 million due to 1ST TIME FAILURES & UNDELIVERABLES
- DIRECT COST TO CARRIERS: £123 million cost of delivery re-attempts.

Applying the results to the wider market, and factoring in conservative estimates for associated losses (sales, customer defection and the cost of marketing to replace customers lost due to delivery problems), IMRG estimated that £2 billion per annum of benefit was available by resolving delivery inefficiencies and failures that the IDIS trust scheme set out to address.

> *'To a business, its percentage of failed deliveries may seem low,*
> *but to each disappointed consumer, the failure is 100%'*
>
> *A parcel carrier, 2005*

Convenience and cost savings were primary drivers for online shoppers. But if delivery failure negated these benefits, the reason for shopping online was eliminated. We argued therefore that consumers' time, costs and frustration when things went wrong should be factored into the internet shopping delivery cost-benefit model.

For the first time, we calculated and publicised the costs to consumers of chaotic parcel delivery. Even when a delivery day was specified by the retailer, the standard

Consumer Costs of e-Retail Delivery Failure
Source: IMRG 2006

TIME CONSUMING TASK	TIME EXPENDED (minutes)	£ COST* (1 hour estimated to cost £12)
Follow up telephone calls	20	4
Waiting Time	40	8
Rearranging delivery / collecting parcel OR Cancelling order, making / managing claim, find and set up with new supplier	60	12
Total cost of an individual failure to a consumer *	**120 minutes per failure**	**£24 per failure***
Total cost of UNDELIVERABLES to all UK e-shoppers in 2006**	**2,466 man years p.a.**	**£259 million p.a.****

Figure 40: The costs to consumers of having to wait in for parcels or collect failed deliveries had been ignored by the online shopping industry until IMRG's Valuing Home Delivery report detailed and highlighted the issue. (*Source: James Roper Archive*)

model was for consumers to have to wait in and be available for half a day, *or even a whole day* to ensure receipt of their goods. However, for this exercise we excluded costs associated with ATTEMPTED DELIVERIES, i.e. deliveries that ultimately succeeded either through further delivery attempts or consumers collecting from depots. Instead, we exposed specifically the costs of UNDELIVERABLES, i.e. total delivery failures where the goods never arrived at all.

The figures were based on IMRG research and assumed that the 2 per cent 'undeliverable' rate recorded in 2005 remained constant in 2006 across the 540 million expected online shopping deliveries, i.e. that 10.8 million deliveries would fail completely.

The average shopper's time was valued at £12 per hour, which was less than the UK average wage.

Progress at last! The Valuing Home Delivery campaign attracted broad media coverage, raising awareness of the issues, and the situation finally began to improve. More retailers with their own delivery networks expanded to take on other retailers' deliveries. Other innovative retailers began investing in delivery as a service differentiator. Tesco introduced two-hour delivery slots for non-food items in September 2006, setting a challenging new benchmark.

Delivery service integrators emerged, notably Patrick Wall's company, Metapack, which enabled dynamic allocation of orders to the right carrier – this allowed retailers to hold contracts with multiple carriers and move seamlessly between them.

Peter Rowlands, proprietor of *Fulfilment Guide*, promoted IDIS through the *Fulfilment & e.logistics* magazine and website, and developed its online 'Guide to Suppliers' to reflect IDIS values / sponsorship / accreditation / performance indicators. This served as a solutions matrix, detailing all of the transporters and co-suppliers together with their service options.

Figure 41: IDIS Delivery Manager (IDIS DM), launched on 12 November 2007, enabled e-retailers of all sizes to offer their customers a variety of delivery options from multiple carriers, matching the services offered by the biggest and best retailers. (*Source: James Roper Archive*)

IMRG membership now included all of the main UK parcel carriers. We continuously monitored customer satisfaction with delivery – this remained stubbornly low because whereas the industry delivery offer improved rapidly, so did consumers' expectations. Once an excellent delivery service had been experienced, this became the shopper's yardstick.

Delivery to Home remained the firm preference in the UK, but less so in Germany and other markets, where alternative delivery points such as *lockers*, *In Store* and *to the workplace* gained popularity.

Amazon led the way as usual, constantly making parcel delivery more convenient, fast, predictable and affordable. Its delivery agents were rewarded for successful deliveries, not carding (leaving a card saying *sorry, you were out*), and would generally find an obliging neighbour or other way of getting goods safely to recipients.

Home Delivery Breakthrough: IDIS Delivery Manager – 2007

IMRG partnered with Metapack to create *IDIS Delivery Manager* (IDIS DM), a crucial breakthrough in home delivery management that would significantly raise the standards of e-retail fulfilment across the entire industry. What the e-retail industry had needed was more delivery choice and better communication – more choice, so that the shopper could choose the optimum delivery service for them, and better communication, enabling everybody in the delivery chain to know what was going on and avoid problems. IDIS DM empowered e-retailers of all sizes to offer their customers a variety of delivery options from multiple carriers and services. Launched on 12 November 2007 at the Office of Fair Trading as part of *National Consumer Week*, IDIS DM largely fixed the home parcel delivery problem, saving everybody time, cost and hassle.

> *'Even the best shopping experience can be totally negated by a bad delivery experience. With the IDIS Delivery Manager, our delivery options will be significantly better'*
>
> Nick Robertson, CEO and founder, ASOS

Whether the e-retailer was shipping twenty or 20,000 parcels a day, this new low-cost, on-demand, multi-carrier solution gave them a simple, automated toolset with which to select, price, present and manage a range of delivery options. IDIS DM also handled the back-end operations, out-bound communications and status reporting, freeing the retailer to focus on running their online shop.

Ron Gainsford, chief executive of the Trading Standards Institute (TSI) said: 'TSI welcomes this "IDIS Delivery Manager by Metapack" initiative that aims to bring industry-wide improvements to home delivery for online shoppers. With so many people now using the internet to shop, it's high time that such developments were introduced, in order to make home delivery as efficient and reliable as possible for all. IMRG's practical approach acknowledges that there are no easy answers, and sets out to bring all of the carrier industry's resources to bear on the problem.'

Metapack already provided delivery management solutions for several large retail clients including John Lewis, Dixons, B&Q and Comet. Now the same functionality was available for all IDIS-accredited retailers – even the very smallest – shipping any number of parcels a day at an easily affordable transactional price. The system could be set up in a day, was all web based, required no integration and could provide access to all of the UK's B2C carriers. It provided *delivery options at point of order* (i.e. the shopper could see the retailer's available delivery options for a specific item to their exact location before placing an order), *automatic carrier allocation*, an end to manual data entry, *label printing* and *manifesting*, and a full suite of customer service screens. There was a £100+VAT one-time set-up fee, and a pay-as-you-go charge that was directly related to the number of parcels despatched. Carriers that were already integrated into IDIS DM included Royal Mail, Parcelforce, Home Delivery Network, ANC, Business Post, DHL, GeoPost UK (Le Groupe La Poste / later DPD), LYNX (a UPS company), and Parcelnet (later Hermes). IMRG's aim was to make all significant delivery services that existed, or might emerge, available on IDIS DM.

ASOS' logistics manager, Stuart Hill, explained why they adopted IDIS DM. ASOS was the UK's largest online fashion and beauty store, attracting over one million visitors a week. With more than 53,000 product lines available and 500 new lines added each week, ASOS was the online shopping destination for many young women. Previously ASOS had a very limited delivery offer: just standard or next day, but the whole ethos of the business was about giving customers great choice. IDIS DM was the only solution available that gave ASOS exactly the multi-carrier flexibility and efficiency they needed, providing a level of sophistication that would be impossible for them to achieve in-house.

Hill said: 'There is real excitement right across the business about how IDIS DM gives us something new and different for our customers. Every department – customer care, operations, marketing, and so on – wins as a result of the flexibility, choice and control we now have over our fulfilment services.

'The steps are to use the system to dramatically improve our delivery offer. For example, the smart system will take a view of what is being ordered, the customer's profile and location, the day of the week and time of day, and then offer an optimised suite of available delivery options that best match her needs. Nobody will provide more convenient delivery options that ASOS.com.'

In September 2009, IDIS had 450 participating merchants.

*   *   *

Andrew Starkey became IMRG's Head of e-Logistics in 2009 and led the delivery programme brilliantly. Andrew's long career in logistics had included stints as a director at Royal Mail, Collectpoint, POSTCOMM, and Jersey Post International. He had been deeply involved with IMRG for many years and been instrumental in numerous IMRG initiatives, including production of the Valuing Home Delivery Reviews, managing our consumer surveys and developing IDIS. Now he took over from me in running the Delivery Forum at a time when logistics was more vital for the success of e-retail than ever before.

Andrew went on to develop the *IDIS Gold Standard for Home Delivery*, which IMRG launched in 2010. This enhanced standard indicated that a retailer enabled the probability of 100 per cent delivery success for every type of product it sold – including for items that did not fit through a letterbox and therefore might require access, specific arrangements, security and tracking.

*   *   *

Following the financial crisis of 2007/8 and through to 2014, consumers consistently sought delivery information before making their purchase, and came to expect real time information (tracking and pre-delivery alerts) pushed to their mobile devices. This drove up prices to pay for investment in capacity and technology to keep pace with the demands of the market.

UK consumers were increasingly reluctant to pay any premium for an enhanced service; their expectation was that many services that were historically considered 'added cost' should be included in the standard offer. The impact on a lot of retailers, especially through the recessionary years, was to change pricing strategies, passing more cost onto consumers and increasing free delivery thresholds.

Affordable *Same Day* services began to emerge, supported by technological developments, and enterprising retailers re-designing their supply chains and creating forward stock locations in appropriate markets.

Evolution of Returns: In the early 2000s the only options for Returns, apart from retailers with their own physical stores and delivery agents, was the Post Office. Typically Returns would take at least fourteen days and be untracked and unannounced to the retailer. By the time the goods were inspected and placed back into inventory, the consumer could be waiting up to twenty-eight days for a refund or replacement. This created a significant barrier to shopping online.

Starting around 2005, *Alternative Delivery Point* networks were developed in various markets – led by Germany, France and the Benelux countries – that provided a different route for returning parcels. In the UK, a similar network, Collect+, was set up in 2010 by Shop Direct Group (also owner of Yodel) to provide a competitive option to postal returns. UPS acquired Kiala (operating in Benelux and France) and established networks in the UK and Germany. Hermes (owned by Otto in Germany) replicated its German Parcelshop network in the UK. Also, retailers such as Amazon and ASDA began setting up locker box locations on commuter routes.

E-retail fulfilment improved steadily over the following years as important enhancements were introduced that today we all take for granted, including:

- Accurate advice of availability at time of order
- Estimated dispatch and delivery lead time at time of order
- In-transit updates to allow the consumer to anticipate delivery
- Delivery to a safe-place or neighbour
- The ability to increasingly specify or influence the delivery day and time
- Time slots for delivery – two hours but trending towards one hour.

Payment: Light at the End of the e-Payment Tunnel

'Online payment security is taken very seriously at dabs.com, which is why we became the first online retailer in the UK to implement the new 'Verified by VISA' initiative which adds an extra level of security to the online payment process'

Jonathan Wall, Marketing Director, dabs.com, 2003

A sign that all of the key players were finally coming together in a serious drive to implement robust e-retail payments came in April 2003 when we were able to report that all three major schemes – Visa, Mastercard and American Express – had joined IMRG. Online sales were rising rapidly, as was online fraud, driven largely by the success of chip and PIN securing payments on the high street.

Mastercard began extensively marketing its *SecureCode* in 2005. As Christmas 2006 approached it ran an advertising campaign online and placed advertorials in several UK national and regional newspapers. SecureCode cardholder registrations increased rapidly, and more card issuers came on board. By this time around 19,000 UK merchants had implemented SecureCode, including Dixons, Currys, dabs.com, John Lewis, Next, British Airways, LastMinute.com and British Midland. UK card Issuers supporting SecureCode included Royal Bank of Scotland Group, NatWest, Mint, HSBC, Barclays, HBOS and Lloyds. Global promotion of SecureCode brought on board 82,000 participating merchants worldwide, as well as over 3,000 issuers.

A new payment data standard came into force on 30 June 2005 that was being rolled out globally. All e-commerce merchants conducting more than 20,000 transactions per annum and with internal systems that processed, stored or transmitted cardholder information had to comply with the new *Payment Card Industry* (PCI) *Data Security Standard* or face significant fines. In extreme cases, uncomplying merchants could be banned from processing transactions using payment cards. The standard, sometimes referred to as the *Digital 12*, required merchants to address twelve areas of security.

* * *

The major problems associated with online payments were largely fixed by 2010, though individual countries often had significant differences. Sixty per cent of all global online payments were made by credit cards that used *Secure Sockets Layer* (SSL) encryption. The global market share of the major credit cards was: Visa – 53 per cent, Mastercard – 28 per cent, American Express – 0.95 per cent, Diners Club – 0.44 per cent. PayPal had 200 million users, including fifty-two million in Europe.

UK consumers used credit cards to pay for over 90 per cent of their online purchases according to Pago. Maestro, the leading international debit payment method, which was gaining ground in e-commerce in comparison with credit cards, was the only other payment method widely accepted by retailers in Britain, with a ten per cent share. PayPal was used, at least occasionally, by 46 per cent of UK online shoppers – some 21 million people. Cash on delivery accounted for less than 2 per cent of transactions, while the single transaction direct debit was almost extinct.

French consumers, meanwhile, preferred to use bank cards (including Carte Bleue, private cards or store cards). There were eight million PayPal account holders in France, the third highest number in a European country in 2010.

Germany presented a very different set of payment preferences to that of the UK. Credit card transactions were gaining popularity, having climbed to 38 per cent of transactions, including those facilitated by PayPal with its ten million German users. But there was still a high dependency on payments made directly from bank accounts: online bank transfer accounted for 31 per cent of payments, while one-off direct debits settled 24 per cent. Cash on delivery, which had earlier been the mainstay of catalogue payments, had shrunk to just 5 per cent.

Of the payment methods offered by German retailers, cash in advance topped the list of options at 68 per cent of internet trading sites, slightly ahead of the 67 per cent for credit cards. Fifty-nine per cent offered cash on delivery, while half accepted PayPal.

The Netherlands was unique in using iDEAL, the country's very own real-time bank transfer payment system that had an enormous 59 per cent market share of Dutch online shopping payments.

The Jersey Play: VAT and Tax Opportunism

> *'The implication that businesses are simply setting up on the Channel Islands to take advantage of this [VAT tax] relief is not true'*
>
> UK Treasury's conspicuously incorrect statement, 2010

Online retailers were quick to seize any opportunity that came their way to disrupt markets. A classic example was the exploitation of an EU

VAT tax loophole for importers that they massively overworked in the Channel Islands and elsewhere in the late 1990s, giving beneficiaries selling into the UK a price advantage of up to 17.5 per cent – rising to 20 per cent when the VAT rate increased from 4 January 2011.

EU value-added tax is a European Union tax adopted by the member states. It is paid to the government of the country in which the purchasing consumer lives. A VAT relief exemption was introduced in 1983[57] as a trade facilitation measure for retailers operating outside the EU whereby inexpensive items sold directly to consumers could be imported to EU countries without being liable for the local VAT. Known as *Low Value Consignment Relief* (LVCR), the intention of this regulation was to aid small businesses and avoid bureaucracy, acknowledging that the cost of collecting these duties would outweigh the revenue received. Each market could set its own limit and the UK did so at £18 / €22.

The Channel Islands – Guernsey and Jersey – are historically linked to the British Crown and have a special relationship with the UK, but are not part of the European Union: instead, they are a self-governing part of the customs territory of the EU and therefore do not charge VAT. Flower growers using Jersey's southern location to produce blooms ahead of the UK domestic flower growing season were just the kind of small businesses that LVCR was set up to help.

One such grower, *Flying Flowers*, which had been founded in 1965, spotted a wider mail order opportunity presented by LVCR and renamed itself *Flying Brands*. By 2001, Flying Brands had more than 30,000 active online buyers to whom it was selling audio books, vitamins, First Day Covers and new issue stamps in addition to flowers and bedding plants, reporting profits for that year up 20 per cent to £4.46 million on turnover of £32.8 million.[58]

The ability for Channel Island firms to sell goods at a considerably lower price than firms based on the UK mainland, which had to include the UK VAT rate of 17.5 per cent, had not gone unnoticed. A growing band of other traders followed suit, even though they had to ship goods as single orders rather than in bulk in order to fulfil the VAT threshold criteria. Leading this pack was Play.com.

Play.com was an online-only retailer founded in 1998 as Play247.com by Jersey residents Richard Goulding and Simon Perrée and based on the island. Rebranded Play.com in 2000, the company started out just selling entertainment products such a CDs and DVDs. It did this very well and grew rapidly, expanding to cover a wide range of products including video games, electronics, personal computers, T-shirts, clothing, tickets for events and much else. By November 2006, Play.com had become so successful that it was ranked second after Amazon.co.uk in the UK *Hot Shops List*, compiled by IMRG and Hitwise. In 2007 it achieved sales of £292.4 million. Bounding from strength to strength, in 2008, Play.com held a computer games show backed by Sony, Microsoft, Ubisoft, Activision and THQ amongst others. The following year it launched a branded VISA card in partnership with MBNA. At its peak, Play.com had fourteen million registered users and 500 employees.

In 2011, Play.com's owners – still Goulding and Perrée – were worth £160 million each and *again* on the Sunday Times Rich List, according to the *Jersey Evening Post*.[59] They were rumoured to have boasted that they wouldn't sell Play. com for less than a billion pounds. But LVCR, the energiser of its trading that supercharged its success, was less than secure.

By 2003 around 100 retailers – including giants such as Tesco and Amazon – had also set up bases in Jersey to sell low-cost items such as CDs, contact lenses, printer ink cartridges and books. Such sales were legal, but concerns were being voiced by the many retailers who were negatively affected by LVCR, and now these concerns were raised with the then EU Commissioner for the internal market and taxation, Frits Bolkestein, specifically following complaints by Leeds-based video games retailer Gameplay.com.

The UK government came under growing pressure from retailers and the Forum of Private Businesses to end the misappropriation of LVCR, and noted in the 2006 budget that the relief was costing the Exchequer around £85 million per year, hinting at changes if the exploitation continued. However, the government took no direct action at that time, leaving it to the Channel Islands governments to regulate the trade, and defending its position with the strange explanation that stopping LVCR would damage the UK Post Office. The IMRG Review of July 2005 noted that Jersey was considering closing the VAT loophole: Senator Frank Walker, president of the Channel Islands' policy committee, commented that *the loophole was unwelcome and damaging*.

Nothing much changed for several years regulation-wise, and in early 2010 the UK Treasury issued a statement to *The Guardian* that said: 'The implication that business are simply setting up on the Channel Islands to take advantage of this relief is not true. In fact exports from the Channel Islands account for a very small percentage of the CD/DVD market'.[60] But the Treasury statement was conspicuously wrong. By 2010, online stores operated by HMV, Tesco, Amazon, Play.com, Asda, WH Smith and Woolworths structured almost all of their CD and DVD transactions as personal imports from the Channel Islands. Their controversial VAT-free sales were rocketing, driving a third of CD sales online, threatening the futures of music stores, and costing the Exchequer an estimated £110 million per annum.

While the number of CDs bought online soared – by 18 per cent in 2009 alone – numerous high street stores failed, or disappeared altogether, including Fopp, Our Price, MVC, Music Zone, Virgin Megastores, Tower Records, Zavvi and Woolworths. The Entertainment Retailers' Association claimed that 1,600 shops selling music had closed in the past five years.

A *Guardian* article on 19 February 2010, *Boom in sales of tax-free CDs casts doubts on Treasury claims*,[60] quoted Mike Dillon who had run independent store Apollo Music in Paisley since the 1970s. Mr Dillon said that the last Christmas had been his worst, blaming unfair competition from VAT-avoiding online operators: 'The government has a duty to collect all the taxes that are applicable. Shops are shutting, people are losing their livelihoods, jobs they have had for years. It's absolute negligence.'

The article also quoted Alison Wenham, chief executive of the Association of Independent Music, representing small record labels and distributors, who said: 'This is a hidden disease within the music business. It is very simple to resolve, but what we are getting from government is denial of reality.'

In 2011, the UK government finally caved in with the Treasury Minister, David Gauke, announcing that from 1 April 2012, LVCR would no longer apply to goods imported from the Channel Islands, though the now-£15 threshold would continue to apply to other non-EU jurisdictions.[61]

Play.com was severely undermined by both the loss of its VAT-free status and the growth of music downloads. Play.com sold itself to Japan-based Rakuten in September 2011 for £25 million, then from March 2013 operated solely as an online marketplace. Play.com was entirely effaced by Rakuten.co.uk on 23 March 2015.

The User-Generated World: Web 2.0 – Social Media

'A brand is no longer what we tell the consumer it is – it is what consumers tell each other it is'

Scott Cook, co-founder of Intuit

Retailers were horrified when consumers' product reviews started to appear online in the late 1990s and actively tried to ban them. The audacious idea that a customer who had bought an item could tell every other prospective shopper that it was deficient or overpriced was appalling to them. It was the retailer's role to curate unique (and profitable) product lines that provided customers with a distinct collection, ideally unavailable elsewhere. Retailers knew best. Full stop.

In 1999, several consumer-review and rating sites appeared, such as rateitall.com, Epinions and deja.com, and some online-only retailers, notably Amazon and dabs. com, began heavily promoting customer reviews of products. By 2005, most shoppers read online reviews and considered them essential to their decision making.

Web 1.0: The first implementation of the internet, up to 1999, was described by Tim Berners-Lee as the 'read-only-web'. In this phase, which became known as the 'Web 1.0' era, users could only search for and read what was published online. Millions of static websites were posted but there was little active communication or information flow back from the consumer to the publisher. Online shops presented goods to potential customers, much as a catalogue or brochure did – adding a shopping cart application meant they could sell to anyone anywhere in the world, at least theoretically.

Web 2.0: From the late 1990s, the 'social web' or the 'read-write-publish' internet era – aka 'Web 2.0' – began to arrive, as exemplified by LiveJournal and Blogger. Innovations like *Blogs*, *Social Media* and *Video-Streaming* enabled the ordinary user, with no technical ability, to create and publish their own content for free with just a few clicks.

The first recognisable social media site, *Six Degrees*, was created in 1997. Named after the *six degrees of separation concept*, the Six Degrees site enabled users to upload a profile, list their contacts, and make friends with other users. A flotilla of social media platforms soon launched, offering web tools and new online communication tactics, most notably Blogger (1999 – acquired by Google in 2003), Wikipedia (2001), Myspace (2003 – acquired by News Corporation for $580 million in 2005), Facebook (2004), Flickr (2004 – acquired by Yahoo! for $22–25 million in 2005), YouTube (2005 – acquired by Google in 2006), Twitter (2006 – Facebook's attempts to buy Twitter in 2008 would fail). Suddenly millions of web surfers were using blog or social platforms to interact with each other and post items online.

BLOG

The term 'blog' was coined in December 1997 as a contraction of 'web log'. Blogger was launched in 1999 by Evan Williams, enabling any user to sign up and start posting their own blogs for free, with no technical ability required. By the end of 2008, 346 million people were reading blogs, and 184 million had started one of their own.

The term *social media* encompasses a continually evolving suite of online technologies, and the enormous diversity of services it would spawn defies definition. These Web 2.0 platforms introduced a myriad of new possibilities for online connections and activities. Most started out as undefined services for users to exchange posts with selected friends and communities – chat, gossip, share photos, discuss ideas, display self-curated content, modify each other's posts – the casual ephemera of social life. But as individuals took more of their everyday activities online, and novelty progressed to routine habit, Web 2.0 formed an entirely new medium through which people organised their lives.

The platforms quickly recognised the potential value of the data this connectivity produced as a by-product. Ways were found to code algorithms that turned user information into brand value and global marketing data. *Connectivity* was converted into monetising potential. Platforms interconnected, and a new infrastructure emerged: a vast ecosystem of connected social media.

As user numbers exploded after 2005, almost all the large influential platforms became commercialised, and many were taken over by big media corporations (the most notable exception being Wikipedia). Corporate owners remained cautious about exposing their profit motives to user communities, because it was the non-profit communal spirit of the ideological, early internet, in which selfless users collectively developed resources for the common good, that had caused the platforms to grow in the first place. Facebook launched on 4 February 2004 as a college student directory presenting photos and personal information, and in early 2008 its founder and CEO Mark Zuckerberg's stated primary interest was still *in building a really cool site* – social media sites were valued on their member numbers, with the assumption that profits would follow.

Facebook hired Sheryl Sandberg as its Chief Operating Officer in March 2008, recruiting her from Google where she was vice-president of global online sales and operations (and prior to that, chief of staff for the United States Secretary for the Treasury, Lawrence Summers). Sandberg held brainstorming sessions which concluded that advertising would be the main source of Facebook's monetisation, with ads *discreetly presented*. Having tweaked its advertising model to achieve profitability, in September 2009 Facebook announced that it had turned cashflow positive for the first time. When Zuckerberg became *Time* magazine's *Person of the Year* in 2010, he promised to make the world more open and transparent, persistently echoing the utopian spirit that had previously galvanised users. In early 2012, Facebook's profits had soared to $1 billion on revenue, up by almost 90 per cent at $3.71 billion.

As José van Dijck points out in *The Culture of Connectivity: A Critical History of Social Media*, social media platforms presented themselves as utilities transmitting communication and information, but far from neutrally channelling generic resources, they were customised services, programmed with specific objectives, the goal being making online sociality saleable. The largest platforms tended not to be presented as applications built to search, navigate and connect information on the WWW, but instead were conspicuously equated to the web itself.

Google and Facebook were the most successful at creating for themselves 'alternative' corporate ethoses while commoditising relationships, their coding technologies sanctifying user-generated content into *users' social capital*. Google transformed users' queries and knowledge into a universe of collegial answers. Facebook eulogised 'Likes' into the validation of personal status – exponentially enhancing (and exploiting) the natural human need to connect and create.

Casually clicking on a thumbs-up icon to *Like* something online was transmuted by social media coding technologies to take on an exalted value, with potentially far-reaching and long-lasting effects. The frivolous *Likes* of millions of web surfers, channelled by algorithms and amplified by automation, conferred great power and influence – conversely their absence could also censure and trigger suicides. Social media would indiscriminately convey huge caches of social capital to some – and then just as incomprehensibly nullify it.

Twitter mostly 'pointless babble'

Pear Analytics survey, August 2009

Pear Analytics, a US market intelligence firm, caried out a two-week study of random tweets in August 2009, placing each tweet in one of six categories: news, spam, self-promotion, pointless babble, conversation and pass-along value.[62] Out of the 2,000 tweets sampled, perhaps unsurprisingly the highest proportion (40.55 per cent) fell into the *pointless babble* category, which Pear described as the 'I'm eating a sandwich' type of tweet. *Conversational* tweets came second, while *pass-along value*, or re-tweets accounted for 8.7 per cent, a distant third. Fourth were *self-promotion* tweets at 5.85 per cent, followed at the bottom by *spam* and *news* at around 3 per cent each.

Self-promotion was far less than expected, given the flood of organisations joining Twitter to promote themselves. But the biggest surprise was *news* coming last, as Twitter was then being touted as the premier source of news and events.

'If you are not paying for it, you're not the customer; you're the product being sold'

This old marketing observation reappeared in various forms over several decades from the 1970s, describing media that delivers attention and demographics for advertisers, referring originally mainly to television

People would make immense efforts to accumulate Likes and Friends, for the empowerment their approbation implied. To retain attention and maintain the flow of likes, they had to post often, and their blogs, posts, tweets, or YouTube videos had to be interesting. The mass attention and rich demographic data produced by the collective efforts of millions of social media users was exactly what the platforms needed to attract advertisers' cash.

Businesses wanting to disseminate awareness of a product or brand soon learned that placing an advert on, say, Facebook's *News Feed* could deliver a vast number of views by social media users. Demographic data available about those users allowed specific audiences to be targeted. The users reached were then able to like, share and comment on an advert, thereby resending the advertiser's message on to their friends and beyond. Furthermore, users could add their opinions, and share their experiences, adding value and transparency to the original message. The type of audience an organisation was trying to reach would determine the social media sites they would use, but managing content across multiple media was no easy task for retailers: each of the social media forums required content to be tailored in a specific way, so maintaining brand consistency and continuity, as their content drifted out across multiple channels over which they had no control, became a major challenge.

Social media became a great equaliser: big brands could be outsmarted without making huge investments, and small brands could make big names for themselves. The smartest operators could grab attention without paying for advertising at all, by instead using engaging creative content that spread virally.

A pioneering example of viral social media marketing was the *Will it Blend?* Campaign, mentioned earlier (see *Colour Plates*), and first shown on YouTube in October 2006. Tom Dickson, the founder of the small company, Blendtec, demonstrated in a series of videos their blenders – especially the powerful $400 *Total Blender* – pulverising a mind-blowing array of everyday objects: golf balls, matches, mobile phones, toys, credit cards and more. The mesmerising videos were watched six million times in the first six days, garnering the company a ton of press and buzz. In the following decade Dixon uploaded a further 150 videos that as of November 2020 had more than 290 million views.

* * *

By early 2009, almost 75 per cent of European internet users were involved in some form of social media, according to eMarketer. Facebook, celebrating its fifth birthday, reported that more than 70 per cent of its 222 million users were outside the US, three billion minutes were spent on the site each day, and 850 million photos were added each month. Twitter had fifty-five million users per day and was one of the fastest growing sites in the UK, having seen a 974 per cent rise in traffic the previous year, according to Hitwise.

Microsoft reported that two-thirds of teenagers spent the majority of their time online visiting social networking sites, while Cyber Sentinel research revealed that the average teenager spent 31 hours a week online, of which up to nine hours was chatting to friends on forums and social networks. Half of teenagers surveyed by Bebo said they messaged as many as 250 friends on a regular basis.

Retailers, eager to follow the crowd, were piling into social networking. US retailer 1-800-Flowers.com became the first brand to produce a Facebook store in 2009. In the UK, upmarket lingerie brand Agent Provocateur launched a new social media campaign via Facebook, Flickr, Twitter and blog posts. Mothercare's social networking site, *Gurgle*, was a year old and had reached break-even, with 70,000 members in the UK and 500,000 visitors each month. Pizza Hut launched an online ordering application on Facebook. Ted Baker's new Facebook app allowed consumers to create outfits and then click through to the designer's website to make a purchase. Virgin Atlantic launched *Vtravelled*, a social community website aiming to tap into the 'inspirational' travel market by allowing visitors to organise and share their travel plans with friends and family. Waitrose launched *Mywaitrose.com* to drive interactivity with its customers, supplying tips from staff and the chance to swap ideas with Waitrose experts.

No traders embraced social media more enthusiastically than fashion retailers – ASOS, Boohoo and Missguided built their brands on their social networks. An eDigitalResearch social media study in 2011 that assessed seventy-two UK retail sites saw fashion retailers in all of the top spots, with well-established Twitter accounts and Facebook pages. Topshop and River Island led, recording large numbers of followers and high levels of customer engagement. ASOS came in third, with New Look and Next completing the top five rankings. Marks & Spencer's listed sixth.

ASOS had an online community channel on its website featuring blogs and profiles of members of the ASOS team. Ed Handasyde-Dick, Social Media Manager at eDigitalResearch commented, 'It is not surprising that brands aimed at a younger, more dynamic audience came out on top. We are beginning to see more content-driven marketing from many multichannel fashion retailers, such as in-house produced magazines, focusing on subjects that potential customers regularly talk about. It is only natural that consumers are turning to social media platforms to engage and identify with their favourite brands.'

Retailers' main use of social media was to interact with audiences to create awareness of their brand or service, hoping to create a two-way communication. The holy grail for retailers was to create a social commerce strategy that turned friends into customers and customers into repeat customers whilst building a rich community, combining conversation, collaboration and commerce, according to Hedley Aylott, founder and CEO of Summit Media.

In 2010 the most popular types of social media included: social networks (Facebook, LinkedIn); blogs, microblogs (Twitter); media-sharing sites (YouTube, Flickr); social bookmarking and voting sites (Digg, Reddit); news review sites (Yelp); virtual worlds (Second Life), and forums. Amazon, eBay, Groupon and Craigslist remained the leading trading and marketing social media sites.

Instagram, the US photo and video social networking service, launched in October 2010 and grew rapidly, registering one million users in the first two months, and ten million in a year. Instagram was acquired by Facebook in April 2012, and by June 2018 would have a billion users.

When Google-owned YouTube failed to turn into a significant social networking site despite its best efforts, Google launched Google+ in June 2011, its fourth foray into the online social space. However, even after strong initial take-up, low user engagement and design flaws led to Google+ being closed down in April 2019.

Social media reached a tipping point for retailers in 2011, with ramifications that could be either positive or negative. Information travelled fast among ever-connected consumers, and negative experiences disseminated quickly around large communities. Retailers who failed to monitor how their brand was being discussed on social media sites were missing opportunities to respond to and rectify sustained criticism. Several retailers provided a consumer forum through Facebook, allowing consumer complaints to be managed efficiently and conveniently.

In December 2011, 1.2 billion users worldwide – 85 per cent of the world's internet population over age 15 – logged on to a social media site, up from 6 per cent in 2007. By 2012, more than 100 million Twitter users were posting 340 million tweets a day.

Social media gave rise to 'influencers' who, with their alluring blogs, vlogs and vast communities of followers, accrued the power to shape opinions on anything from which lipstick to buy and what foods to eat, to organising global economic protests. Social media personalities and celebrities were employed by marketers to promote products, prompting the UK's Advertising Standards Authority (ASA) in 2013 to advise organisations to make clear if a message was a paid advert rather than just a personal opinion.

Some major brands, such as Domino's Pizza, would be completely transformed by social media. Domino's Pizza's adoption of digital marketing began with its use of social media to find fresh ideas on improving its business. In 2012 Domino's launched its 'Think Oven', a Facebook page where participants were encouraged to submit ideas in two categories: the *Idea Box* (for general ideas, e.g. new menu items, tips for going green, etc.) and *Current Project* (for specific things Domino's needed help with, e.g. 'New Domino's Uniforms'). The ideas that attracted the most amount of attention were rewarded with a monetary prize, and actually implemented with executive approval.

Following the success of social media initiatives, Domino's began a radical overhaul of the company's entire ethos, with a focus on creating an 'e-commerce company that happens to sell pizza'. To accomplish this, Domino's entire corporate structure was revised – beginning from the top down – to focus on digital sales and advertising.

* * *

The changes Web 2.0 wrought in the global media landscape are impossible to overestimate. In the previous industrial media paradigm, traditional media, such as TV, newspapers, radio and magazines, were one-way, static broadcast technologies, whereby one source would serve many viewers. For example, a magazine publisher would distribute expensive content to consumers that advertisers paid to insert their ads into. Or a television programme would be interrupted by commercials. Consumers, bombarded daily with a profusion of such interruptive mass advertising messages, each shouting for attention, became increasingly adept at blocking out and ignoring traditional advertising – for example, recording TV so as to be able to fast-forward through the ads. Social media obliged advertisers to rethink their marketing strategies and engage holistic marketing concepts that focused on building customer relationships with more creative, unpretentious and helpful messages, instead of in-your-face intrusions.

Social media differs from traditional media communications in many ways, including immediacy, legitimacy, reach, usability and permanence. Social media gave people a new sense of connectedness with either real or virtual communities.

Whereas social media was not so good at directly delivering retail sales – IMRG benchmark data in 2016 revealed it only drove 0.6 per cent of total e-retail revenue – as a tool for having conversations with customers, it was unparalleled. Over 80 per cent of British internet users were active on social media in 2016, with Facebook being the most popular platform, particularly amongst older generations. Younger audiences' demands from social media were different, with messaging being a key component, along with immediacy. Pinterest gained ground as a product discovery tool, with 93 per cent of its users in the UK saying that they used the service for this purpose.

* * *

Facebook remained the biggest social media site in 2019 with almost a third of the world's population – more than two billion people – using it every month.[5] More than sixty-five million businesses used Facebook Pages to promote their businesses, and it had six million advertisers. Most Facebook users – 94 per cent – accessed Facebook via its mobile app. Messenger was a feature within Facebook until 2011 when it was recast as a standalone app. Messenger, with 1.3 billion monthly users in 2019, had an expanded array of features enabling businesses to advertise, create chatbots, send newsletters and use a multiplicity of other ways to engage and connect with their customers.

The twenty most popular social media sites in 2019, according to Buffer.com were Facebook, with 2.23 billion monthly monthly active users (MAUs), YouTube – 1.9 billion MAUs, WhatsApp – 1.5 billion MAUs, Messenger (Facebook) –

1.3 billion MAUs, WeChat – 1.06 billion MAUs, Instagram – 1 billion MAUs, QQ – 861 million MAUs, Tumblr – 642 million MAUs, Qzone – 632 million MAUs, TikTok – 500 million MAU, Sina Weibo – 392 million MAUs, Twitter – 335 million MAUs, Reddit – 330 million MAUs, Baidu Tieba – 300 million MAUs, LinkedIn – 294 million MAUs, Viber – 260 million MAUs, Snapchat – 255 million MAUs, Pinterest – 250 million MAUs, Line – 203 million MAUs, and Telegram – 200 million MAUs.

Online (In)security

'It used to be expensive to make things public and cheap to make them private. Now it's expensive to make things private and cheap to make them public'

Clay Shirky, American writer, consultant and teacher on the social and economic effects of internet technologies and journalism

Early internet security threats were mainly a matter of adolescents causing mischief to impress their peers. By 2004 these pranksters had been replaced by criminals seeking to make serious money. Organised criminals were becoming increasingly technologically competent and had demonstrated that they were willing to buy in skills and expertise, or subcontract to specialists, where there was an advantage in doing so. It seemed inevitable that criminal use of hi-tech methods would only increase as businesses, banks and individuals became more reliant on IT and online transactions, and more and more potentially valuable data was stored on networks.

Consumers were not deterred from using the internet but became more wary and alert to what sort of things organisations would or would not send you via email. And there was very real cause for them to be concerned as the range and sophistication of online threats continued to increase.

'Passwords are like underwear: don't let people see it, change it very often, and you shouldn't share it with strangers'

Chris Pirillo, founder and CEO of LockerGnome, Inc., 2007

Gone phishing: 2004 was the year *phishing* – a burgeoning new form of larceny via identity theft (the impersonation of an individual for financial gain) – increased suddenly. The *Anti-Phishing Working Group*, a consortium of businesses and law enforcement officials, reported that 85 per cent of all reported phishing attacks during December (9,019) directly focused on banks and financial institutions, though the number of individual companies targeted was also growing. Attacks typically consisted of email messages that appeared to come from trusted companies which attempted to lure people to bogus websites where they were asked to divulge sensitive personal information – data that could be used to commit identity fraud.

Distributed Denial-Of-Service attack (DDoS attack): Extortion with a threat to bring down a website if a payment was not paid, also became increasingly common in 2004. Initially bookmakers and financial institutions were most commonly targeted. *Denial of Service* (DoS) is typically achieved by flooding the targeted server or resource with gratuitous requests in an attempt to overload systems and prevent legitimate requests being fulfilled.[63] In a *Distributed Denial of Service* attack (DDoS), the incoming traffic flooding victim originates from many different sources, effectively making it impossible to stop the attack by blocking a single source.

Thousands of DDoS attacks were reported in the following years. Even organisations as big as Amazon were vulnerable, as evidenced by a DDoS attack in October 2019 on Amazon's S3 – *Simple Storage Service* – which knocked out the websites of many client companies of the larger Amazon Web Services (AWS) by flooding specific domain names with phoney traffic.[64]

The botnet threat: An alarming development was the coming together of virus writers, spammers and organised criminals to use *botnets* – networks of compromised computers whose processing power and bandwidth could be abused to send out large volumes of spam and phishing emails. Botnets were the primary delivery mechanism for 70 per cent of spam and almost all phishing scams. Botnets greatly amplified their controllers' power and gave them almost total anonymity: they could be highly profitable, reputedly being rented out for just $10 per hour. People whose computers were infected with the remote access *Trojans* that controlled botnets were usually unaware that they were contributing to the problem.

Spyware and adware: *Spyware* and *adware* are general terms for software that performs certain functions such as advertising, collecting personal information, and delivering targeted content. Most spyware was included in free downloads of games trials, some search engines, file sharing and other applications. Any program that supplied a PC with ads that ran in a window other than a standard banner ad, had an adware – or spyware – component, generally an analysis and tracking programme that reported certain activities to the advertising providers' website.

This was not illegal, and could be positively helpful in identifying a user's preferences to an ad-serving website or network. For example, you might sign up for a free online service, but pay for that service by agreeing to receive targeted ads. If you understood the terms and agreed to them, you might have decided that it was a fair trade-off. You might have also agreed to let the company track your online activities to determine which ads to show you. But what spyware providers did with the collected information and what they were going to serve you with, was beyond your control.

Spyware could also contain code that would make remote changes to a computer that could be annoying and might cause the system to slow down or crash, change the browser's home or search page, or add additional browser components. Sometimes it could be difficult to change back to the initial settings.

Signs of a spyware infection were pop-up advertisements that appeared even when disconnected from the internet, if browser settings changed unexpectedly or if the browser suddenly displayed a new toolbar, and if the system was running slowly, or crashed more often. On a clean system, spyware could be kept at bay using a *firewall*, spyware protection software, and most of all, by observing responsible surfing behaviour. Like viruses, spyware was best removed by software that scanned and recognised certain code. Removal tools were provided free of charge by Microsoft and other suppliers, but for many people the whole matter was just too bamboozling to bother with: their inertia – and unprotected PCs – feeding the mischief-makers.

The fastest growing form of online crime in 2004 was CNP (card not present) fraud. There were counterfeit UK transactions costing £150.8 million according to the Association for Payment Clearing Services (APACS), though the risk management solutions company CyberSource suggested that the real costs could be much higher.

Andrew McClelland joined the IMRG team on 13 April 2004 as Head of Projects to lead our security programme and technology developments. Sixteen years on, Andrew remains closely engaged with IMRG as our Insight Expert, still fighting the good fight.

Later, as people's online activity went multi-device, wireless and mobile, security threats increased exponentially. And they were far more annoying and menacing on a mobile phone, with its limited screen space, battery life and connectivity.

The internet and e-retailing continued to be plagued by crime. Criminals switched to the internet from activities such as burglary because it was easy and largely risk-free – the overstretched and under-resourced police generally ignored it. Even when a thief was caught, the penalties for cybercrime were so lenient that they appeared to offer little deterrent.

By January 2017, fraud and online crimes made up almost half of UK's 11.8 million total number of reported crimes, according to ONS figures reported by the *Financial Times*.[65] Other ONS data showed a 39 per cent annual increase in fraud associated with UK-issued credit cards, cheques and online banking, of which the vast majority of cases were not reported to the police, who recorded only a 3 per cent rise. In September 2018 it was revealed that 96 per cent of cases reported to the UK's national fraud reporting centre, Action Fraud, remained unsolved, while Which? estimated that the police solved only 0.8 per cent of Action Fraud cases, far less than any other crime group.[66]

In January 2020, Mike Barton, former Chief Constable of Durham Police, speaking on BBC's *Question Time*, commented that half of all crime committed in the UK was actually online, adding that 'the people who cause that, who facilitate it, who allow it, are paying no tax', clearly alluding to giant tech companies such as Google and Facebook not paying their fair dues.[67]

Mobile

'Every once in a while a new product comes along that changes everything. ...Today Apple is going to reinvent the phone'

Steve Jobs, CEO, Apple Inc. at the iPhone One launch, 9 January 2007, San Francisco, California

Even before 2000 there was anticipation that smartphones would become important devices for e-retail transactions, yet little to confirm this materialised before 2007 when the first Apple iPhone arrived, followed in 2010 by the iPad. Together the iPhone and iPad unleashed a new re-energised phase of e-retail evolution. More than half of UK online sales were via mobile devices in 2016, as online shopping continued to power ahead with 17 per cent year-on-year growth. The iPhone became the most profitable product of all time, with sales approaching two billion in 2020.

Mobile phones had been invented in the 1940s, though they only arrived as a mass-produced consumer product in 1983 when Motorola launched its DynaTAC 8000X, effectively a car phone as it was far too bulky to fit in a jacket pocket. Rapid progress to make mobiles better, smaller and cheaper followed, led by Motorola, Nokia, IBM, Siemens, Blackberry and Sharp, amongst others. In 1992, the year that the number of BT-operated phone boxes across the UK peaked at 92,000, IBM created the first smartphone – the Simon Personal Communicator.

---

m-Commerce

Mobile commerce began in 1997 when two mobile phone-enabled Coca-Cola vending machines were installed in the Helsinki area in Finland. Payment was via SMS messages.
The first digital content sales via mobile – downloadable mobile ringtones – were introduced the following year, again in Finland.

The first mobile commerce (m-commerce) transactions were for cans of Coke in 1997: Coca-Cola installed two mobile-enabled vending machines in Helsinki, Finland, that allowed customers to pay by sending an SMS message. A year later we heard about the first digital content sales via mobile, also in Finland, when downloadable phone ringtones were made available.

An early sign that the internet was going mobile came in 1998 with the introduction of 3G, the third generation of mobile networks. This was seen as potentially a big deal for retailers because 3G's minimum information transfer rate of 0.2 megabits per second (Mbits/s) introduced much faster internet connectivity and therefore m-commerce, at least theoretically. However, it would be another decade before 4G arrived, in 2008, truly opening up the m-commerce floodgates.

Enormous interest in mobile telephones was fuelled in the late 1990s by Wireless Application Protocol (WAP) – an international standard that enabled mobile internet access, together with 'pocket PC commerce' applications that new WAP phones could run.

In January 1999, Vodafone bid $62 billion for and then merged with US-based wireless phone service provider AirTouch, to form Vodafone Airtouch Plc in June, setting the new enterprise on track to dominate the telecoms industry with its £350 billion valuation and fifty-four million customers across twenty-five countries. This was one of the three biggest takeovers in business history that took place around the turn of the millennium, each overtaking the last in size and scope of its potential repercussions, as newer, leaner organisations leveraged their value to buy into established businesses, sometimes competitors, sometimes not.

By 2000, 54 per cent of UK adults owned a mobile phone and the cost of using one had fallen by up to a third in the previous twelve months. Nokia dominated the handset market at this time, selling 126 million of its model 3310 phones that year alone.

Recall that BT Cellnet launched the world's first 'always-on' mobile network in June 2000 – GPRS mobile handsets that were permanently connected to the internet, so people could access email and websites without first having to dial into an internet service.

The e-retail talk of the time was all about WAP. Tesco was one of several retailers announcing WAP shopping services in the pipeline in 2000: its plan was to launch a service within a year, enabling customers to purchase anything from food to household goods, flowers to electronics, and to scroll through the latest offers, all from their WAP-enabled mobile phones. The first phase of Tesco's WAP project would roll out in the New Year 2001, with the sale of Tesco-branded mobile handsets.

Millions were being spent on advertising mobile internet and subsidising handsets, but for all the hype, the actual experience was terrible. Fewer than one in fifty adults were using mobile phones to access internet services, and even among regular internet users, wireless interactive take-up was running at under 5 per cent.

A global survey by the Boston Consulting Group in 2000 found that one in four owners of mobile devices stopped using m-commerce applications after the first few attempts. Sources of consumer frustration included high costs, slow speeds, awkward navigation, difficulties with typing text using a phone's tiny keypad, and unreliable service. And yet, 82 per cent of then current and potential users of m-commerce applications believed that the mobile device would become their personal travel assistant within the next three years. And 81 per cent predicted they would soon be using mobile devices to perform daily activities, such as sending emails, gathering information, and shopping.

Mobile phones were also ushering in a brand-new set of headaches for retailers. Typical of the type of problem on its way to Europe and already plaguing America was widespread validity checking of stolen credit cards on internet sex sites – if cards worked there, on the most sophisticated online payments systems available, they would work almost anywhere. And with the advent of mobile internet services, thieves were able to check a card's validity, minute by minute, then go shopping with confidence, either online or in the high street, knowing that their stolen payment card was not yet barred or registered on the *Hot Files*.

Unlike the telephone, where a young male voice claiming to be 'Mrs Smith' would ring warning bells at the merchant's call centre, you had no idea who was on the other end of an internet connection. It might not even be a person – it could just be a piece of software, such as one of the card number generators which were readily available on certain news groups, that would just keep hitting your online store until one worked.

At this time, Amazon.com was launching *Mobile Auctions*, a service that enabled net-capable phones to search for and bid on auction items, and track sales directly from a handset. Customers could also receive alerts via their handsets or pagers for status reports on their auctions. eBay had a similar cell phone alert system in place some three months earlier, and an auction paging service that had been operating since late spring of 1999.

There was a fuel crisis in September 2000 that put yet another log on the internet's fire by thrusting centre stage the woes of the petrol age. Campaigners protesting about the rising petrol and diesel fuel prices blocked oil refineries and other facilities, causing panic buying and some petrol stations to run out of supplies. As people and businesses cast around for alternatives to motor traffic with its relentless burdens of cost, congestion and pollution, their thoughts turned inevitably to electronic channels and how these might help. While the fuel crisis was a commercial disaster for most businesses, some online merchants made large gains from the many consumers who used delivery vans' fuel rather than their own to go shopping – thousands of customers tried e-shopping for the first time.

The primary relevant effect of the fuel crisis was to oblige people to examine new ideas and try new methods. The fuel strikes – themselves mobile phone-enabled phenomena – triggered surges in all forms of network traffic across Europe, with a tripling of conference calls and video conferences, and sent internet traffic through the roof.

Over forty million Britons (out of a total population of almost sixty million) now had cell phones. The tantalising promise of a forthcoming mobile commerce market excited the public and many entrepreneurs, yet little of consequence actually happened. The tentative steps towards m-commerce so far looked pretty wobbly and unlikely to have much effect on the shopping behaviour of richly facilitated Western consumers. For the next several years, IMRG closely followed and reported on mobile developments, holding at least one conference on the topic each year, but perpetually forecasting the market to be two years away.

* * *

In 2004 mobile phone use was rocketing, including the accessing of internet pages. UK users viewed 1.46 billion WAP pages via their mobile phones during May alone, according to figures from the Mobile Data Association (MDA). Some forty-seven million WAP pages were being viewed on a daily basis, having doubled in a year, and thirteen billion WAP page impressions were estimated for the whole of 2004. The MDA also said that a record twenty-five billion text messages has been sent from UK mobiles that year, double the 12.2 billion texts sent in 2001.

The first ever 'phonecast' gig by rock band, Rooster, was a sell-out when their forty-five-minute concert at a London venue on 2 November 2004 was broadcast by 3G mobile phone operator, 3. Some 1,000 fans paid £5 each for a ticket to hear the gig on their phones.

Handset makers were becoming highly excited about the revenue potential associated with multimedia-enabled smartphones, which, it was assumed, would put people in charge of content that they could store, listen to, watch and interact with on a variety of devices anytime, anywhere. Several companies in Europe and the US were experimenting with ways to download high-quality media files over cellular networks.

*   *   *

By 2005, the mobile phone was well established as a wallet, address book, organiser, scheduler, camera and ID card, and now 3G technology providers were promising broadband-speed wireless internet communication and video downloads direct to your pocket, car, holiday home or yacht.

UK mobile phone ownership exceeded that of PC penetration in the home for the first time, while worldwide more than 600 million 3G-enabled mobile phones sold that year into a global market of more than two billion.

iPhone (2007) and iPad (2010)

Then, after years of rumours and speculation, in 2007 Apple introduced the first iPhone – the *iPhone 2G*, later called the *iPhone 1* to differentiate it from subsequent models – which finally began to unlock mobiles' e-retail potential. While it wasn't the first smartphone, the iPhone turned out to be one of the most transformative technology innovations of the modern era, putting the internet in everyone's pockets.

Conceived by Apple's CEO Steve Jobs in 2005 as a breakthrough internet communicator with full web browsing and downloadable apps, Jobs bet the ranch on iPhone – all of Apple's resources were committed to developing iPhone, so, had it failed, the company had no other products in the pipeline that it could have fallen back on.

Jobs introduced the iPhone to the world at the Macworld Conference & Expo in San Francisco, California on 9 January 2007, then it was released for sale in the US on 29 June 2007. Although 3G had been around since 1998, as noted earlier, 3G wasn't available on the first iPhone, so users could only get online if Wi-Fi was available or if they were on AT&T's 2G *Edge* plan. The second-generation iPhone 3G, released on 11 July 2008, was the one that really heralded the modern smartphone age.

Before the iPhone, people hated their cell phones, which weren't so smart and were far from easy to use. Blackberry, the smartphone standard at the time, like Moto Q, Palm Trio, Nokia E62 and all the rest had button keyboards that occupied around 40 per cent of the front: some had a stylus as well. iPhone got rid of these, its user interface instead being a large touchscreen (3.5-inch, 160 ppi – huge by the standards of the day) that you navigated with a finger and multi-finger gestures. There was just one button to take you 'Home' from wherever you were.

In 2007 Apple would ship its 100-millionth iPod music player, so millions of people were already familiar with how iTunes automatically synched to their PC or Mac. iPhone synched in exactly the same way, taking all of the user's media, plus photos, contacts, calendars, notes, bookmarks and email accounts onto their phone.

iPhone One's OS10 software was at least five years ahead of any other phone, enabling the creation of desktop class applications and networking. It was far smarter and easier to use than the any other smartphone as well as being thinner, at 11.6 mm, and had a 2-megapixel camera built in.

People just loved the whole package. Many queued all night amidst scenes of chaos at stores around the world to buy iPhones at a starting price of $499 for the 4GB model and requiring a two-year contract. iPhone was an instant success, selling 1.39 million units by the end of 2007 and more than six million in a little over a year.

Initially, the arrival of the iPhone had little impact on Nokia's market dominance. While Apple was selling its first six million smartphones, Nokia sold over 450 million. But by June 2011, just four years later, Apple was making more mobile phones than Nokia, and in the following two years, Nokia's ranking as a smartphone maker fell from first to tenth. Apple iPhone sales peaked in 2015 at 231 million, by which time the Nokia smartphone brand had all but disappeared.

Three years after the iPhone was introduced, the iPad's launch kick-started a brand-new tablet market and gave another huge boost to mobile commerce. The first iPad was announced on 27 January 2010, then released for sale on 3 April. With a 9.7-inch multi-touch screen and a starting price of $499 for the 16 GB Wi-Fi model, media reaction to iPad was mixed – Apple fans, however, loved it and bought close to twenty million iPads within a year.

Shop Direct (Very and Littlewoods) reported a 314 per cent increase in sales from mobile devices in late 2010 as their efforts to provide a 'slick and quick' mobile shopping experience paid off, with iPads and smartphones being amongst the *must-have* presents that Christmas.

> *'The adoption rate of mobile is twice that of the internet,*
> *three times that of social media, and ten times faster than PCs'*
>
> *Emma Crowe, Somo, 2013*

Over the course of the next five years mobile platforms opened up a new 24/7 channel for the consumer, enabling them to browse, shop and research products at any time of day from almost any location, including in-store. In 2014, for the first time, more users accessed the internet from their mobile devices than desktop PCs. Younger generations had become *mobile first*, with millions saying that their smartphones never left their sides.

*   *   *

Speech recognition became a major growth-enabling factor for mobile commerce in the 2010s, saving people time and freeing their hands. By May 2016, 20 per cent of search queries on mobile devices were conducted via voice, and the number continued to grow.

Speech recognition has a long history stretching back to research at the Bell Telephone Laboratories (Bell Labs) in 1952, but for decades, progress remained slow. Google's first dip into speech recognition came in 2007, when systems still required a period of 'training' to learn the characteristics of an individual's speech. In the early 2010s a major breakthrough in speaker independence was achieved – within a few years human parity was being achieved by using multiple deep learning models to optimize speech recognition accuracy. Apple's virtual assistant, *Siri*, which uses voice queries and a natural-language user interface, was integrated into the iPhone 4S at its release in October 2011 and has since become an integral part of Apple's devices. Google Voice Search was released on 20 May 2012: it is now supported in more than thirty languages and used by hundreds of millions of mobile phone and PC users every day.

2007–2010: The Omnichannel Years

'The mouse is mightier than the sword'
Jo Evans, MD, IMRG

E-retail was booming as never before in 2007. At least it was until the global financial crisis of 2007/8 emerged as the US subprime mortgage market collapsed. This turned into an international banking crisis and the worst crash since the Great Depression of the 1930s – an estimated \$50 trillion was lost, equivalent to one year of global GDP. Growth in UK e-retail sales slowed from 40 per cent in the first half of 2008 to 15 per cent. Winds of change were blowing through the high streets – ill winds for the weak, indebted and stuffy traders they would clear away, but to a new generation of merchant venturers, these were trade winds.

Web 2.0 had been simmering in the background for years – now it was exploding. Three years on from the birth of a young geek's college project, 2007 became all about 'poking' people, constantly advising everyone of your status, counting your gazillions of friends, and putting GIFs on users' walls. Facebook – simultaneously

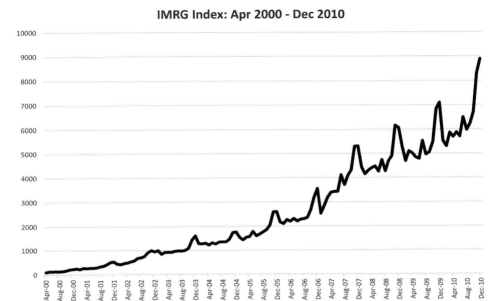

Figure 42: UK e-Retail Sales, April 2000 to December 2010. Note the steep rise in 2007 leading up to the global financial crisis, and how growth eased back over the next two years. (*Source: IMRG Capgemini Sales Index*)

the most influential and over-hyped internet phenomenon of the year, having been valued at anything up to $15 billion – was heralding a new era for the online shopping industry.

The IMRG Capgemini Sales Index recorded its highest sustained growth rate for four years – average year-on-year growth for Q2 2007 was 52.5 per cent. Online sales of electrical goods were a massive 92 per cent higher in June – Pixmania's Ulric Jérome, MD France & Northern Europe, explained why: 'June and July are key months for sales of electrical products on the internet, as people buy electronic items for their summer holidays: digital cameras, MP3s, laptops… Since the beginning of the year, we have seen that confidence in internet shopping has reached a very high level in the mindset of consumers. Our feedback shows that most UK customers are now coming directly to our web shop without first shopping / looking around in high street stores! The reality is that online retailers are able to secure more aggressive prices for their customers: this along with the vast quantity of product information available online and the ease of the buying process that avoids having to queue in stores is the winning mix of a smarter way to shop!'

'Logging on to the sales becomes new Christmas Day tradition'
The Independent headline, 26 December 2007

Many e-retailers were still failing to get the basics right in 2008, even now giving customers poor online experiences. Careless design and lazy implementation were

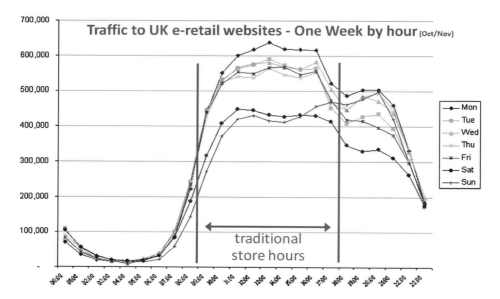

Figure 43: This chart shows the volume of traffic to e-retail stores by hour for one week in late 2008, revealing that more than a third of online shopping visits occurred outside of normal store opening hours. (*Source: IMRG / eDigitalResearch / James Roper Archive*)

the downfall of many a website, where shoppers were forced to play 'hunt the search function' or 'pin the price on the product' while their basket and the checkout disappeared and reappeared at random.

Bringing together search and merchandising techniques spawned a new concept known as 'searchandising', whereby retailers could deliver search results that took the customer to the product they wanted quickly (rather than landing on the website's home page) while cross-selling or up-selling to them at the same time. *Like that dress… how about these shoes?*

An IMRG survey of internet users revealed that half researched online either 'often' or 'always' before buying goods in all categories via *any* retail channel – and in some categories, such as books, DVDs and travel, this rose to 85 to 97 per cent. Respondents considered online prices to be competitive with or better than those in the high street. More than a third of all online shopping (38 per cent) took place outside normal shop hours, the peak being between 7 pm and 9 pm, when most high street shops were shut.

Also in 2008, the UK's first broadband service using fibre-optic cable was unveiled, and nearly twenty-five million people had smartphones. Amazon launched its Kindle eBook reader in the UK, a year after it first appeared in the US.

*   *   *

2009 was a wild ride for many retailers as they contended with a still bleak economy, desperate competitors and cautious, spoilt-for-choice consumers. As the ongoing recession bit even harder, domestic and economic hibernation was set to become a recurrent theme. The most popular New Year searches indicated that consumers were preferring to stay at home and 'cocoon' as well as stay home to shop. Forays for storage furniture and white goods suggested that householders were staying put, making the most of their existing properties, rather than moving. Equally popular were recipes, as entertaining at home replaced conspicuous spending in restaurants. Meanwhile, shoppers sought out cold weather clothing and heaters to beat the New Year's Arctic blast – an ominous meteorological metaphor for the business year ahead.

Cyberspace now had far wider implications for retailing than just being a £50 billion bright spot with double-digit sales growth: as well as a vital trading channel, the internet was a primary consumer influencer – a medium for discovery, research and reference; for help and support; for complaint and even retribution, where the disgruntled shared their experiences. For many, the internet had become their principal touchpoint for news, information, communication, acquisition and trade – their *omnichannel*.

Online shopping had become a fantastic boon for disabled people. Tesco had been notably active in ensuring that its website was accessible to disabled people with sight, audio and motor impairment restrictions. Nick Lansley, Tesco's head of R&D, had championed this activity and worked closely with IMRG, the RNIB and others on developing and applying best practice, such as appropriate design, navigation, text and colours, compliance with text readers, arranging for every image to have a text description, and having appropriate alt tags.

All of this was new and having a profoundly positive effect on many handicapped peoples' lives. I recall taking a phone call one day from a man who clearly had great

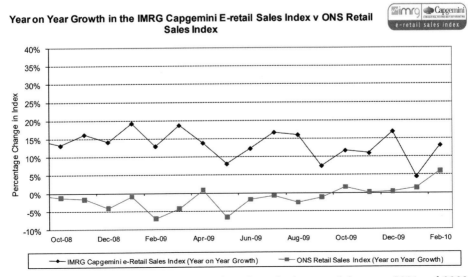

Figure 44: This chart compares online and total retail sales growth between 2001 and 2009. (*Source: IMRG / ONS / James Roper Archive*)

difficulty in speaking, who thanked me, profusely and personally, for helping him to do his Christmas shopping. I didn't understand what he meant at first. He went on to explain that for the first time ever he had, unaided, been able buy Christmas presents: online. It was very humbling.

There were over ten million registered disabled people within the UK, many of whom were eager online shoppers with significant spending power, just waiting for more accessible websites to be made available to them.

In 2009 we forecast that by 2020 around 90 per cent of all retail sales would be either on or influenced by a then ubiquitous internet, at which time the present online access methods and propositions would seem crude. We suggested that retailers who found themselves with time on their hands in a less than busy marketplace might take stock of their long-term prospects and make strategic investments that brought an e-business mindset into the centre of their operation.

The Great Recession

The Great Recession that started in 2008 stemmed from a mix of staggeringly irresponsible and frequently unethical behaviour by financial institutions, credit agencies, regulators, governments and consumers. Lax lending standards led to the US subprime mortgage crisis in which giant finance institutions including Bear Stearns and Lehman Brothers collapsed, then global markets immediately plummeted. On 18 September 2008 the US Treasury Secretary Henry Paulson and Federal Reserve Bank Chairman Ben Bernanke told President George Bush that they needed a trillion dollars by close of business or the financial system was done. A few days later Bush delivered a prime-time television address on a plan to provide $700 billion of *quantitative easing* to assist the troubled banks and shore up the US economy. World GDP was forecast to fall to its lowest rate since the Second World War.

Most people hadn't heard of quantitative easing (QE) before, but the term would be horribly familiar by late 2020. QE is a form of unconventional monetary policy in which central banks *print money* – as only they can – and use it to purchase securities from the open market. The goal is for banks to then lend and invest the new money to stimulate overall economic growth, but what actually happens is that banks hold on to much of it as excess reserves, and what money does get out to the broader economy pushes up the price of private equity and assets that are mainly owned by the wealthy. The average worker hardly benefits at all: instead, QE rewards the well-off, raising inequality and stoking public outrage that the central banks have been co-opted by the rich.

Caught up in the global spiral of turmoil, in late 2008 the Bank of England lowered the Bank Rate (which had been 14 per cent in 1990) from 5 per cent to 0.5 per cent to support UK economic recovery. This proved ineffective, so it too resorted to QE for the first time, in March 2009, when UK GDP was down to 2.4 per cent. Mervyn King, then Governor of the Bank of England, said, 'It's fair to say that in the Bank's 300-year history we have not seen measures of this kind enacted on this scale.' By July 2012 the Bank of England had applied £375 billion of QE.

In a June 2009 speech, US President Obama argued that a 'culture of irresponsibility' was an important cause of the financial crisis. He criticised executive compensation that 'rewarded recklessness rather than responsibility' and Americans who bought homes 'without accepting the responsibilities'.

Quantitative easing became the go-to lever for the world's major central banks to pull each time a new financial crisis emerged. But printing money was not nearly as effective as economists thought it would be and had serious unintended side-effects. The financial markets immediately became hooked on QE and its drug of free money. Public anger, that QE bailouts paid for by the working classes mainly enriched the wealthy, would go on to trigger a wave of populism that contributed to 2016's unexpected BREXIT *leave* outcome, and Donald Trump's surprise US Presidential victory, as voters used the ballot to reject government as they knew it.

Summing-up the Noughties

The 2000s was the decade when e-retail burst mainstream. Even as the Dotpocalypse dust was settling, consumers swarmed to plug in their newly available broadband connections. Millions took to email and shopping online despite media's constant scaremongering of the internet's perils. A raft of bold new traders emerged to service demand, their pioneering efforts hindered by dithering payments and carrier industries.

Nothing could impede e-commerce. Impenetrable barriers were bypassed. Legislators' daft laws were ignored. Trust – or rather lack of it – that had greatly inhibited progress was forged by IMRG's ISIS programme. E-retail proved resilient whatever the economic climate: when times were good, people shopped online to save time – when times were tough, they shopped online to save money.

Old school retailers continued to miss the boat, as upstart e-traders sailed off with their trade, especially at Christmas, when e-shopping came into its own. Black Friday pulled online buying ever earlier in the prime spending season, while 'pay for performance' (PFP) diminished advertisers' guesswork.

Social media went from nowhere to everywhere, with three-quarters of Europeans messaging by the end of the decade. The iPhone arrived and glued everything together, putting the internet in everyone's pocket, and globalization on steroids.

Disruptively devouring all it could, e-commerce subsumed key retail sectors, including travel, software, music and electrical goods.

The Great Recession of 2008 stalled UK e-sales growth briefly, but by the end of the decade the sector had trimmed its sails and was soaring again in new trade winds.

Part III

2010–2020

2010 saw more than half of UK consumers routinely shopping online. The IMRG Capgemini Sales Index marked its tenth anniversary, its ascendancy across the decade telling the story of e-retail success in awe-inspiring numbers. Online sales that had been worth less than £1 billion in 2000 had rocketed to £58.8 billion in 2010 – 5,772 per cent growth – a total value of some £250 billion across the period.

Three-quarters of the population now had internet access – there were 53 million internet users, out of a population of 62.76 million. Nineteen million UK homes (76 per cent) had broadband connections by the end of 2010.

Connectivity: Pledges Spun, Broken and Scrapped

'Oaths are but words, and words are but wind'

Samuel Butler, iconoclastic English author, 1835–1902

In 2009, BT had announced a £1.5 billion investment in superfast broadband networks with speeds of 100 Mbps. Half of the UK population already had broadband at home and media consumption was changing rapidly – e.g. music download sales overtook CDs.

That year the government had made the first of many connectivity pledges that, in the coming decade, would be broken or scrapped. The Labour government promised that all UK homes would receive 2 Mbps broadband by 2012, as set out by Lord Carter in his recommendations for Digital Britain. In 2011, the coalition government scraped Labour's pledge and instead promised to provide 'superfast broadband' of 24 Mbps to 90 per cent of premises by 2015. Two years later, this target was pushed back, the government of the day instead promising that 95 per cent of premises would have 'superfast broadband' by 2017. In 2015 Prime Minister David Cameron introduced a *universal service obligation* whereby broadband would be considered similar to other basic services such as water, electricity and mail. He claimed that this would guarantee broadband access to all by 2020, commenting: 'Just as our forebears effectively brought gas, electricity and water to all, we're going to bring fast broadband to every home and business that wants it. We're getting Britain – all of Britain – online, and on the way to becoming the most prosperous economy in the whole of Europe.'

Years of problems followed. BT and Ofcom continued to miss targets and the government abandoned yet more rollout pledges, claiming (implausibly) that some rural communities didn't want to be connected. Ofcom ordered BT to split from its Openreach division in 2016, thereby making it a fully independent company, before fining BT £42 million in March 2017 – the largest ever fine Ofcom imposed on a telco – for a 'serious breach' of regulations and undermining its rivals. BT was accused of abusing its Openreach monopoly, which generated almost 35 per cent of operating profits in 2016, particularly by underinvesting in the UK's broadband infrastructure, charging high prices and providing poor customer service.[68]

In February 2018, BT confirmed that it would be spending £3 billion to roll out faster broadband by 2020. Also in 2018, the Department for Digital, Culture, Media and Sports (DCMS) pledged that 'full-fibre' broadband should be fitted in all new homes and that all of the UK would have full-fibre broadband coverage by 2033, replacing the copper wire network that currently, as it were, delivered the service.

However, the government's own statistics suggested that only 4 per cent of UK premises then had a full-fibre link compared with 79 per cent in Spain and 95 per cent in Portugal. In mid-2018, it was reported that the UK had slipped from thirty-first to thirty-fifth place in the global broadband league tables, behind twenty-five other European countries.[69]

In early 2020 the government continued to make bold promises for nationwide ultrafast broadband while dodging specifics about how it would reach its increased target of five million connections per year (a huge ask) up from two million (probably viable), committed funding and the shortage of skilled engineers. The DCMS plan, dubbed *Building digital UK* (BDUK), now spoke of gigabit broadband rather than (unnecessary and probably impossible) 'full fibre', and clearing airwaves for future mobile broadband.

In Britain's aggressively competitive broadband market, prices were continually driven down, which made investment cases harder for commercial operators. But the government throwing cash at the problem risked creating market distortions – exactly the opposite of what Ofcom was trying to achieve. Nevertheless, public funding is inevitably required to help connect small and sparse communities, especially in rural areas, of which the UK has an abundance. Across the EU, an average of 42 per cent of people live in apartments, which are significantly quicker and cheaper to connect, compared with the UK where most people live in individual housing, and just 15 per cent live in apartments.[70]

In the Christmas week of 2020, with the Covid-19 pandemic raging and most people house-bound for months, UK MPs advised that the government was abandoning yet another broadband target – gigabit-capable connectivity for 85 per cent of the country by 2025 – as only a fraction of the £5 billion promised would be available. This meant that successive UK governments had either missed or rolled back every single one of the many broadband commitments made since 2009.

Ofcom said at the time that one gigabit speed broadband was then available a quarter of UK homes, but 600,000 people in towns and more rural locations would remain restricted to ten megabits per second or less, which was too slow for business use and would be slow for two or more users at home.

Who Would Be Last To Go Mobile First?

'The trend has been that mobile was winning. It's now won'
Eric Schmidt, CEO, Google, 2013

As disruptive technologies go, mobile proved to be a particularly effective one. The rapid take-up of mobile devices by the public thrilled consumers, developers and tech companies but dismayed retailers, brands and governments who had to completely rethink their strategies for marketing, trading and engagement.

Prior to the iPhone's arrival (in 2007), retailers had just about mastered selling to consumers via their desktop PCs. While the use of mobile phones had been growing fast for a decade, the transition of mobile commerce from vague concept to viable channel had been slow, and therefore safely ignored by most traders. Then suddenly, apparently out of the blue, mobile commerce arrived, and millions of consumers started trying to use their smartphones and tablets to shop online. Retailers were horrified to discover that the internet capabilities that they had invested in so heavily were hopelessly inadequate for serving the growing range of devices that were now trying to access them, with their motley assortment of screen sizes, interfaces and connection speeds: a website that looked fine on a desktop PC was likely to be completely useless on an iPhone.

Responsive Web Design (RWD) was the answer. This would give a consistent user experience across any internet device – desktop, laptop, tablet or mobile phone. RWD involved recognising the user's viewing environment – their device type, its performance and connectivity – and then reorganising content and design to suit on the fly. A website designed with RWD uses a fluid grid concept for page element sizing based on relevant units such as percentages instead of absolute units

Figure 45: Responsive Web Design (RWD) gave a consistent user experience across any internet device by using a fluid grid concept for page-element sizing based on relevant units such as percentages instead of absolute units like pixels. (*Source: James Roper Archive. Image used with permission from David Williams*)

like pixels. Achieving RWD was no trivial matter, and well beyond the capabilities of the website platforms that retailers had only recently built.

The Great Recession dragged on. Trading remained in the doldrums. Yet retailers were faced with the expense and disruption of having to *replatform* their entire internet capabilities – in other words to bankroll new technology for an uncertain, emerging, unpredictable future online marketplace – or risk being sidelined by those who did. Worse still, it was forecast that this trend of retailers having to serve different types of device would only expand with the coming of the *Internet of Things* (IoT) and a world in which shopping orders would arrive directly from proliferating ranges of office equipment, home appliances, vehicles, robots and buildings. And while traders were being urged to keep up with incessant change in mobile phone technology, where was the data to help fathom out what was actually going on and support the business case for such investment?

IMRG Index to the rescue – again! The IMRG Capgemini Quarterly Benchmarking Index was continually expanded to include new forms of data as they became available – and now mobile commerce was amalgamated, too. We soon confirmed m-commerce's growing significance: in the space of just two years, m-commerce rose from generating 0.4 per cent of UK e-retail sales at the beginning of 2010, to over 5 per cent at the end of 2011. This represented staggering growth of over 1,300 per cent.

IMRG created a dedicated monthly mobile commerce tracker – The *IMRG Capgemini m-Retail Index* – which launched as usual from a base line of 100 in January 2011, monitoring sales via mobiles devices (including tablets) from UK e-retailers. It tracked, year-on-year and month-on-month growth, average spend via type of mobile device, and mobile conversion rates that initially were only a quarter of those of desktops. Participating retailers received personalised monthly reports giving first and unique access to new data and business-critical intelligence, including detailed charts and tables.

Below are extracts from the *IMRG Capgemini m-Retail Index* report of April 2012 describing the explosive growth of m-commerce just four years after iPhone

---

IMRG Capgemini m-Retail Index report, April 2012

- 51 per cent of the UK population now have access to a smartphone
- 38 per cent of UK smartphone users have made a purchase via their mobile device, up from 23 per cent in 2010
- 8 per cent of Britons use tablets as their main means of accessing the internet
- 20 per cent of UK companies have a mobile-optimised website
- Over half of German e-retailers have a mobile platform
- eBay reported global sales of $5bn of goods via mobile devices in 2011.

The IMRG Capgemini m-Retail Index report of April 2012 recorded the explosive growth of m-commerce just four years after the release of the first iPhone, which was pivotal in unlocking the long-anticipated potential of mobile shopping

unleashed the mobile trading genie. The m-commerce market's year-on-year growth rate peaked at 359 per cent in May 2012.

'Mobile really is a game-changer. The shift to becoming the primary device of choice is well under way. …1 in 5 visits originate through a mobile device and, within a thriving multi-channel environment, we are starting to capitalise on the way that mobile 'glues' all our channels seamlessly together'

Adam Plummer, UK Head of E-commerce, The Body Shop

'The use of mobile devices and tablets as both research and transactional tools has soared over the past few years and, with over half of Britons now owning a smartphone, this trend looks set to continue'

Tina Spooner, Chief Information Officer, IMRG

Between January 2012 and March 2014, basket values fell while conversion rates rose, as mobile was being adopted as a mainstream shopping channel. In the initial phase of m-commerce development, most sales were via tablets. For example, the March 2014 m-commerce index reported that tablets accounted for 79 per cent of the mobile commerce sample (excluding travel), with just 21 per cent coming from smartphones. However, sales via smartphones were growing faster than via tablet devices. At the time, m-commerce was growing at three times the rate of total e-retail sales and accounted for a third of the UK online retail market.

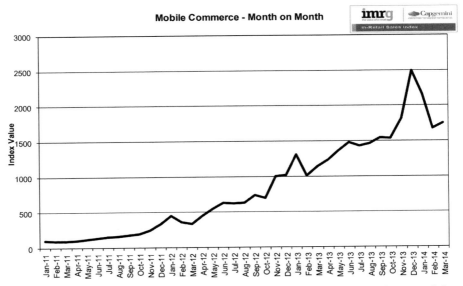

Figure 46: The chart shows the IMRG's UK Mobile Commerce Index (excluding travel) from January 2011 to March 2014. (*Source: IMRG Capgemini Sales Index*)

Smartphones accounted for all of the year-on-year gains in both traffic and baskets in Q4 2015, according to the Demandware Shopping Index, which measured digital commerce growth based on analysis of the shopping activity of over 400 million shoppers worldwide – more than 1,500 global retail sites then ran on the Demandware Commerce Cloud (now Salesforce).

A milestone was reached in 2016 when mobile commerce soared to account for the majority – 56 per cent – of UK online sales, up from less than 1 per cent in 2010 (Source: IMRG Capgemini e-Retail Sales Index). An astonishing 68 per cent of retail visits were via mobile devices. More than half (54 per cent) of UK consumers had used their smartphones to shop online for products, while 46 per cent had purchased goods via a tablet device.

*   *   *

Just as work and play separate weekdays from weekends, device preferences were clearly defined by the days of the week, with smartphones leading consistently throughout the day and evening at weekends.

By mid-2019, smartphones and tablets together handled an average of 63.5 per cent of all online sales value, and 75.9 per cent of all traffic. Smartphones scored a record share of sales in Q2 2019, accounting for 45.1 per cent of all online sales (by value). Shopping via tablets had peaked in late 2015, since when they steadily lost ground to smartphones.

The use of smartphones in shopping would continue to grow, boosted by advances in technology such as voice recognition and contactless payments, which enhanced consumers' ability to compare goods and prices wherever they were, including in the high street. The smartphone was becoming the shopping trolley in the consumer's pocket.

XB (Cross-Border): The Trillion Dollar Trade Route

'No borders, just horizons – only freedom'

Amelia Earhart, American aviation pioneer

By 2011, the e-commerce die was cast. The UK led the world in online shopping and had export values worth more than three times that of France or Germany, boosted by the global appetite for British fashion. Europe pipped North America as the largest e-commerce market in the world, with sales up 19 per cent to €246 billion.

The internet and e-commerce were major drivers for global and regional economies by 2011. The total world population reached seven billion, of which a third (2.3 billion) were internet users, according to Internetworldstats.com.

Global B2C e-commerce sales were estimated to have grown to $920 billion that year, an annual increase approaching 25 per cent. The leading country in B2C e-commerce remained the USA, followed by the UK and Japan. Asia-Pacific was witnessing rapid growth, particularly in China where e-commerce increased by more than 130 per cent that year.

The use of mobile internet and m-commerce was rising rapidly all over the world, in emerging as well as mature economies. The number of mobile subscriptions in late 2011 reached 5.9 billion or 85 per cent of the world population. Growth was led by China and India, which then had 30 per cent of all mobile subscriptions.

Britain had the largest internet economy in the G20 group of industrialised nations in 2010, accounting for 8.3 per cent of its total industry, compared to just 5.4 per cent in the US and 6.9 per cent in China. The Boston Consulting Group estimated that the UK's internet economy was worth £121 billion, more than £2,000 per person: if it was regarded as a sector in its own right, it would be the fifth biggest, behind finance, healthcare, construction and education.

*   *   *

As some domestic e-retail sectors looked to be approaching saturation, UK traders progressively speculated on growth overseas. Cross-border (XB) internet shopping was enabling a less capital intense and more rapid way of testing and growing businesses internationally. Leading the pack were ASOS and Wiggle, the Portsmouth-based bike seller, proving that consistently profitable XB trading was achievable.

Johnlewis.com also extended its delivery catchment during 2011/12 to cover overseas locations, initially within mainland Europe, the Nordic countries and Ireland. By late 2013 delivery had been extended to some thirty European countries, plus Australia, North America, New Zealand, Singapore and South Africa. Dedicated French and German language websites were developed to exploit the two largest and most developed EU e-commerce markets.

In 2012 there were a billion online shoppers worldwide. More than a third of global e-commerce was conducted in Europe, where XB sales were estimated to be worth around €32 billion, some 9 percent of online sales. 2013 saw global e-retail sales climb above a trillion dollars ($1,000 billion) for the first time.

But the internet economy remained a patchwork of uncertain rules, standards and practices, so there was much for retailers to get right if they wanted to maximise their chance to share in the borderless shopping spoils. And just as 'location' was the critical component of an offline proposition, 'trust' was the key factor online; get that wrong and you wouldn't sell much.

The UK was punching well above its weight. Britain was Europe's largest e-commerce exporter and had the largest e-trade surplus of any country, driven by fashion, according to a 2013 study by Google and OC&C Strategy Consultants: global e-commerce exports were worth $25 billion, of which UK fashion exports accounted for $1,220 million.

Of this $25 billion global XB trade, the US share was $11 billion, the UK's a huge $7 billion, while France accounted for $2 billion, Germany $2 billion, the Nordics $2 billion, and the Netherlands $1 billion. The calculations were based on parcels sent internationally using data from Google, Euromonitor, Metapack and OC&C analysis.

Britain generated over 30 per cent of all European e-commerce, and a growing number of international customers were buying from UK sites, encouraged by the huge choice of goods available, beneficial currency exchange rates, and the UK's reputation for good trustworthy service.

IMRWorld

IMRG had been strongly advocating XB trade ever since our involvement in the e-Christmas project way back in 1997. In the noughties we actively engaged with and then joined EMOTA (the European Multichannel and Online Trading Association), which elected me as vice-president in 2011. Each October, from 2006 to 2010, we took a delegation of up to thirty IMRG members to EMOTA's main annual event at SALON VAD (the *Vente à Distance* event) at the Grand Pallais, Lille, France.

In 2008 we created IMRWorld, a separate venture to provide a single point of access to the most recent research, surveys, reports, analysis and thought leadership from leading global experts in international e-commerce. IMRWorld was managed by IMRG as a free-of-charge service for and with e-commerce industry associations worldwide, funded by commercial sponsorship.

Leading IMRWorld with me were Colum Joyce, Director of Strategy, who was previously head of global e-business strategy at DHL, and Aad Weening, International Development, who had been Secretary General of EMOTA from 1993 to 2007. eDigitalResearch.com provided its survey tools, and Devon-based Createanet facilitated the website.

IMRWorld launched its website with a *World e-Commerce Dashboard* and *Interactive Data Maps* at SALON VAD 2008 in Lille. Our interactive maps provided information on the top forty e-trading countries accounting for almost three-quarters of global e-commerce, including their language, payments, broadband, top e-retailers, cross-border trade, incomes, online shoppers, basket sizes, GDP, competitiveness rankings, parcel deliveries, top product searches, business technology ranking, e-industry association and more.

Colum Joyce said at the at the launch: 'The IMRWorld Global e-Commerce Index is a major new information resource for e-commerce and business managers across the world. Covering 70 per cent of global e-commerce it provides what has always been missing for country, regional and global e-commerce strategy planners: clear, current, concise and comprehensive support information and data.'

IMRWorld had over two terabytes of business and country data and information compiled from over 400 worldwide sources, including national statistics, OECD, World Bank, European Commission, IMF, United Nations and regular IMRWorld's own surveys.

IMRWorld.org ran its own event in 2010 – **eBizEU.eu: e-Business Strategy Europe** – pitched as *The 'Davos' of the digital economy*, on 20 October at the Salle Eurotop, Lille Grand Palais, Lille, France. eBizEU was sponsored by ATG (now Oracle ATG). Nils Müller, CEO and founder of TrendONE, provided a visionary keynote address. Speakers included senior representatives from the EU Commission, Oxford University, 3 Suisses, Shop Direct Group, Pixmania, Nokia, Capgemini, Universal Postal Union (UPU), Swiss Post, La Poste, TNT, Metapack, Borderlinx, Euratechnologies, the Web Analytics Association, SND, and five national e-commerce industry associations. In four sessions panellists debated core questions relating to Europe's e-business strategy agenda. Audiences, attending both physically and virtually, were enabled to vote and voice their opinions.

During the IMRWorld's first two years of operation, the senior team presented at conferences in Brussels, Miami, Berne, Moscow, Beijing, Wiesbaden, Amsterdam, Berlin, Kiev, Copenhagen, Shanghai, London, Hanover, Monaco, New Orleans, Hong Kong and New York.

'Postal addressing' was one of several major challenges for XB traders that we focused on. IMRWorld teamed up with Charles Prescott as our US representative, together with his Global Address Data Association, which was working hard to fix the many international postal addressing problems.

The UK enjoys one of the best postal addressing systems in the world, so it surprised many British e-retailers that there were numerous address standards, and in many places no address standard. It was a shocking fact that four billion of the world's seven billion people had no address at all, precluding them from government services and healthcare, let alone online shopping.

Addressing created two specific challenges for cross-border e-retailers: firstly, offering the right fields in which the overseas customer could enter their address; secondly, being unable to check that a submitted address was correct before despatching the order – the retailer might therefore ship an order that had no possibility of being delivered, generating a frustrated customer as well as a cost. In Ireland, for example, there might be no road name and the address could be along the lines of 'the big white house on the corner'.

Charles Prescott is an experienced lawyer and government affairs expert, based in South Salem, New York, USA, with a substantial background in business development. Charles joined the US Direct Marketing Association in 1998 as Vice-President, International Business Development and Government Affairs, and was responsible for developing programmes to serve the growing multinational needs of its membership. In so doing, he became known as the DMA's 'Global Ambassador' to international agencies such as the OECD and UPU, and other DMAs around the world. As Charles would say: 'An address is *A Human Right*.'

* * *

In 2013 I passed the ownership of IMRG and IMRWorld to Justin Opie and Graeme Howe, two long-term allies of whose eCommerce Expo and other events IMRG had participated in over many years. I stayed on as IMRG's Chairman for five years, while Justin and his team took IMRG forward as strongly as ever, focusing on the index, data, and events. Thereafter, we agreed that my association with IMRG would be as its Founder Emeritus.

Jobs and the New Gig Economy

Jobs are always important, and e-commerce was being criticised for destroying them. IMRG instigated an *e-Jobs Index* in 2010 to discover to what extent this was true.

Retail was customarily the UK's largest private sector employer, and in 2010 still provided 2.9 million jobs – some 11 per cent of the total UK workforce. The John Lewis Partnership was the country's largest private employer, with 72,400 employees, while Alliance Boots was third. But over the previous five years employment in retail had fallen by 145,000 people, according to the BRC.

Our research revealed that more than 600,000 British jobs were either directly in or supporting the UK's 150,000 online retail businesses. It turned out that the growth in new e-jobs exceeded any losses they precipitated, and their pay rates were on average better too. Our counterintuitive findings made sense when you think about how e-commerce works: all the activities that have to take place to provide convenience for shoppers, and all the time and effort that previously consumers had to invest that was moved into paid work for others. Furthermore, 78 per cent of 160 e-retailers we surveyed expected to recruit more staff in the coming year. Since the first online retailers began trading in 1994, sixteen years earlier, the Compound Average Growth Rate (CAGR) of employment in online retail had been 19 per cent (18.9 per cent). If growth continued at that rate, we estimated that there would be approaching three million UK e-jobs by 2020.

eBay helped us with data for the e-Jobs Index. It surveyed 458 of its online retailers – all had annual turnovers of between £100,000 and £3.4 million on eBay alone – and their average number of employees was eight. eBay research also showed how internet trade was driving exports, by making it possible for SMEs to export around the world – 88 per cent of eBay's businesses sought growth by engaging in cross-border trade in the last quarter of 2008.

*   *   *

This was the start of the age of the *Gig Economy*, in which a large and growing section of the working population was operating in an entirely new way, enabled by technology and app-based devices. The gig economy involves the exchange of labour for money on a short-term and payment-by-tasks (known as gigs) basis via what in 2008 had been a cutting-edge form of employment agency – *gig platforms* – that would soon include Uber, Airbnb, PeoplePerHour, Deliveroo, Fiverr, TaskRabbit, AmazonFlex and AnyVan. Instead of being paid for the amount of time that they work, in the gig world people are paid a fixed fee for every task they complete, such as delivering a parcel or driving a taxi, resulting in people often working very long hours for not much money.

Uber, the American *mobility as a service* provider, arrived in the UK in 2012. For a short while Uber paid drivers a £10 bonus for each job they did, 'just to grab the market'. But soon the fares were going down and down, and drivers found themselves working seventy hours, eighty hours, even ninety hours a week, and still unable to make ends meet. By late 2015 Uber was the largest mobility platform in the world, worth $60 billion, more than General Motors.

The term 'gig' was coined in 1915 by jazz musicians to refer to their individual performances. When applied to the modern internet-enabled work model it indicates the one-off nature of the task the worker is hired to complete. In the aftermath of the 2008 financial crisis, widespread unemployment and underemployment led to a huge increase in demand for temporary work, as people sought to replace or supplement their income. A whole new gig economy rapidly emerged linking workers with jobs anywhere in the world via the internet, apps and smartphones. An ever-increasing range of gigs became available, from driving to bartending, teaching to technical support, consulting to babysitting.

The Conservative government constantly argued that it was supporting a large number of new UK jobs – David Cameron claimed in 2015 to have created a million new jobs, 1,000 a day since 2010 – with more people in work than ever before. But what sort of jobs were they?

The government talked up 'the flexible labour market in the UK that has allowed us to create these jobs', but this masked the huge jump in insecure work, zero-hours contracts and poverty wages: self-employment accounted for almost three-quarters of these million new jobs. Real pay fell for a dozen years and more after 2008 as inflation consistently outpaced wage rises

In 2016, an estimated 2.3 million people were working in the UK gig economy: by 2019 this had more than doubled to around 4.7 million, approaching 10 per cent of the working population – generally younger people – who were delivering gig work at least once a week.

But while the gig economy gives breadwinners new earning opportunities, and great flexibility as to how and when they work, it generally fails to provide job security, a pension, health insurance, paid sick leave or paid holidays. The successful organising of a series of general strikes in 2019 by Lyft and Uber drivers – initially in Los Angeles but which spread worldwide and to other platforms, protesting low wages, long hours, working conditions and lack of benefits – would challenge the lack of legislation supporting gig workers and eventually begin to secure basic employment rights for many.

Zalando and the A–Z of e-Commerce 'Death Stars'

'Don't be too proud of this technological terror you've constructed.
The ability to destroy a planet is insignificant next to the power of the force'

Darth Vader, the primary antagonist in the Star Wars movies

Would venture capital produce the 'ultimate retail weapon' like the fictional Death Star superweapon in the Star Wars movies, we asked in 2013. The e-retail arms race was escalating dramatically as investors ploughed billions of dollars into large disruptive start-ups, aiming for their new online enterprises to dominate entire market sectors. The dot.bomb lessons from the turn of the century seemed long forgotten. Speculators were back, but had they got their strategy and timing right, or would they just cause more market mayhem?

Zalando, the Berlin-based online fashion retailer, launched in October 2008 and achieved sales worth over a billion euros in 2012, double its 2011 revenues of €510 million.

Zalando started out in a shared apartment / office / warehouse on Berlin's trendy Torstrasse as a clone of Zappos, the US online shoe retailing pioneer (subsequently acquired by Amazon for $1.2 billion in 2009). Zalando had expanded from shoes – of which it claimed to sell 30,000 pairs a day – into general fashion and jewellery, offering a range of thousands of products from hundreds of brands. Most of Zalando's business was in Germany, Austria and Switzerland though it was rapidly expanding and by 2013 was selling across Europe through fourteen country-specific sites including to the UK, France, the Netherlands, Sweden, Denmark, Finland and Norway. But after four consecutive years of heavy losses, Zalando was repositioning itself as a digital platform and shopping mall, emulating Chinese tech companies.

Zalando was one of many start-ups by the Berlin-based Samwer brothers – Marc, Alexander and Oliver – who were best known for blatantly cloning (often down to the pixel) existing US businesses like Zappos, Airbnb, Facebook, Groupon and Pinterest, then blitzkrieging consumers with massive-scale traditional marketing, backed up by operational excellence, to ensure that their new brand rapidly achieved prominence in the marketplace. A number of these businesses had then been acquired by the original cloned company which was obliged to buy or be sidelined.

The Samwer brothers' first attempt as start-up founders was in 1999 when they approached eBay to start a German version and, after receiving no response, they did it themselves. Three months later they had sold their online auction platform, *Alando*, to eBay for $50 million. They weren't first to market, but what they had managed to do was execute well and, in doing so, proved to eBay that there was a market that couldn't be ignored. Just five years later the brothers had their next successful exit, selling their mobile SMS content company Jamba! to VeriSign for $270 million. Remember that annoying Crazy Frog? That was them.

Estimated to be worth around €3 billion, Zalando had attracted more than a billion euros worth of investment from a range of heavyweight backers including the Samwer brothers' own venture capital incubator, Rocket Internet (owning 44 per cent), Holtzbrinck Ventures (13 per cent), Tengelmann Ventures (8 per cent), Investment AB Kinnevik (16 per cent), DST Global (9 per cent), J.P. Morgan Asset Management (1 per cent), Quadrant Capital Advisors (1 per cent), as well as smaller stakes from Commerzbank, Sparkasse Mittelthüringen and KfW Bankengruppe. In August 2013, Danish fashion magnate Anders Holch Povlsen took a 10 per cent stake in Zalando from early-stage investors, becoming the third largest shareholder. Povlsen already had a significant stake in ASOS, which he would quietly raise from 6 per cent in 2010 to over 29 per cent in 2017, making his Bestseller fashion group the largest ASOS stakeholder.

Pundits assumed that Zalando had also been created to sell on, but had grown too fast and now the Samwer brothers were stuck with making it work. None of Rocket's other entrepreneurs had been nearly as successful as the guys who had founded and were then running Zalando: Robert Gentz and David Schneider. Flatmates at Germany's famous WHU – Otto Beisheim School of Management – Gentz and Schneider had connected over a common desire to start a company. Oliver Samwer, an alumnus of WHU who knew the pair from school events, hired them to work on his latest obsession: e-retail.

Zalando was certainly disrupting the already stressed retail marketplace; however, it was too early to tell what the lasting effect of this foray into fashion would be. Like Amazon had been for years, Zalando too was being ridiculed for 'buying' the market at too high a price and of having an unsustainable business model that would never be profitable. And Europe had idiosyncrasies that American e-retailers did not have to contend with: when Zalando launched its Italian site in 2011, some shoppers in the country – which had less than 60 per cent internet penetration – had to be taught how to open emails. It definitely risked overtrading as a result of growing too fast, and might face a natural bottleneck with suppliers or delivery services unable to cope with the demand it was creating. Its overstretched supply lines might fail causing reputation problems that would lose customers and undermine new customer recruitment.

One threat to the Samwer Brothers was their own social recklessness: their questionable business practices, such as unashamedly replicating others' hard work, risked alienating ethical consumers, and might well be drawn to the attention of those consumers by afflicted companies. Zalando was also dogged by negative press about poor staff working conditions and pay, and sharp marketing practices, such as telling shoppers that stock was running out when it wasn't.

So, would Amazon and Zalando be the A to Z of e-commerce *creators* – or *annihilators* – in Germany?

Amazon was by far the biggest online retailer in Germany with sales estimated to be worth more than €4 billion per annum, while Zalando was by far the fastest-growing German online retailer. Arguably these pioneers were good for the e-commerce market in Germany, where the take-up of online shopping had been relatively slow compared with, say, the Nordic countries or Britain. Many German consumers had been introduced to the benefits of shopping online by either Amazon or Zalando, which to an increasing degree were competing with each other. While this was good news for consumers it could be a nightmare for other retailers caught in the crossfire. For example, when Zalando emerged as a contender, Amazon's German fashion brand, Javari.de, began to offer a one-year return period, a two-week low-price guarantee and fast free shipping – a hard act to follow. On the other hand, Zalando was keen on selling at regular rather than predatory prices, and avoided dumping, whereby goods are sold in quantities that cannot be explained through normal market competition.

In 2013, we speculated that there were three possible outcomes. Zalando and similar e-retail 'Death Stars' might succeed, and their success would inevitably attract more venture capital seeking fast profit by capturing other market sectors, as Amazon has done but quicker. And as the US and Western European markets became saturated there would be plenty of other opportunities for replicating the model in less crowded, fast-growing markets in regions like Asia, South America and Eastern Europe.

Alternatively, this blitzkrieg model might fail due to the wafer-thin profit margins that extreme competition inevitably generates, rendering brands unable to adequately reward investors for the expensive capital they had staked. In this case there would be a real possibility of damage to the online sector if consumers and staff were severely inconvenienced or lost out, though competitors left standing would breathe a sigh of relief.

The third and worst possibility was somewhere in the middle, where a superweapon brand might limp on, destroying good and bad competitors alike, too big to close down but unable to progress, and not really adding any value to customers, themselves or the marketplace.

'Yes', was the answer to our earlier question: Would venture capital produce the 'ultimate retail weapon'?

Zalando began to flourish financially in 2014, as its forays into diverse European markets and now fourteen-million-strong customers base began to pay off. Zalando turned its first profit that year on sales of €2.2 billion and listed on the Frankfurt Stock Exchange. Sales grew strongly and steadily over the next six years.

2020 saw Zalando well established as Europe's largest online fashion retailer, with sales of nearly €7.9 billion. It was the highest-ranking online shop in Germany, offering its seventy million customers in seventeen European markets more than 650,000 fashion items from more than 3,000 brands. But its ambitions went further – much further.

Zalando set out to bridge online and physical retail. By 2018 it was selling products in its own brick-and-mortar stores, *Zalando Outlets*, in locations across Germany – Berlin, Frankfurt am Main, Cologne, Leipzig and Hamburg. In July, after two years of piloting, Zalando opened its first physical beauty store, the 'Beauty Station', in Berlin's Mitte district, in partnership with Estée Lauder.

Also in 2018 and much more significantly, Zalando began to roll out *Connected Retail*, a programme that enabled brands and brick-and-mortar retailers to become *Zalando fashion partners*. Connected retail partners could integrate their own e-commerce stock into the Zalando platform ecosystem, by either connecting their stock from warehouses and local stores, or by taking over order fulfilment. Via the partner programme, items were shipped directly from Zalando's partners to Zalando's customers. 'By connecting our partners' stock to our platform, we widen our assortment in depth and width, and can offer better product availability for the consumer,' said Carsten Keller, Zalando's Vice-President of Direct-to-Consumer.

Zalando estimated that it had been missing out on twenty to thirty million transactions each year – worth a billion euros in turnover – due to supply shortages in its own warehouses. Its plan was to turn Europe's high street shops into Zalando's stock pool – aiming to add 70,000 physical stores in the next three to five years. 'It is a massive stock pool we are tapping into,' Keller told Reuters.

2020 and Covid-19 brought skyrocketing Connected Retail sign-up rates. Over the course of the year, with the pandemic raging and all foot traffic lost due to lockdowns, the number of connected store partners more than quadrupled to over 2,600. In response to the crisis Zalando waived all commissions for new and existing partners and switched to weekly instead of monthly pay-outs to help traders maintain a continuous cash flow. Some of Germany's most traditional retailers reported fulfilling up to 2,000 orders per day through the Connected Retail programme. Then the partner programme was opened up to fifteen of the seventeen Zalando national markets.

Connected Retail was an integral part of Zalando's platform strategy of becoming *The Starting Point for Fashion and Lifestyle*. By supporting thousands of traditional shop owners during the Coronavirus crisis, Zalando brought forward the progress of that strategy by years.

All the investment money piling into the online retail market in the 2010s was bound to have a polarizing effect. But had it introduced the 'ultimate retail weapon'? Was the future of shopping to be each sector – or potentially all sectors – controlled by just one superpower brand?

The Death Star superweapon in the Star Wars movies was a gargantuan imperial space station armed with a planet-destroying superlaser; two were built and both were destroyed by the Rebel Alliance. Would retail reality mirror that of this fictional force? What was certain was that this venture capital success saga was yet another a hammer blow to the autonomy of independent traders and high streets.

The Attention Model and the Biggest Boycott in History

'If you're not confused, you're not paying attention'

Tom Peters, American writer on business management

The retail economy – both offline and online – is essentially centred on an 'attention model' whereby traders vie for customer attention in hopes of selling them what they might want. On the face of it, consumers had never had it so good, with the internet bringing more choice, information, services, convenience and better prices 24 x 7 x 365. Yet in 2016 there was clear evidence that many people were unhappy with aspects of digital innovation – particularly the behaviour of the $600 billion online advertising industry with its rampant appetite for bandwidth and intrusive tracking. Invasive adverts with enormous file sizes were damaging user experience, especially on mobile devices.

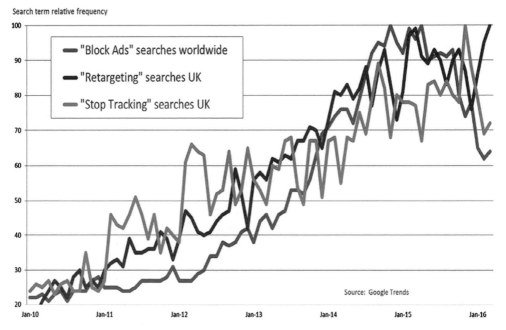

"Block Ads", "Retargeting" and "Stop Tracking" searches on Google

Figure 47: This chart shows the increase in Google searches for the terms 'Block Ads' (worldwide), 'Retargeting' (UK) and 'Stop Tracking' (UK) between January 2010 and March 2016. This time frame coincides with the explosion in what the trade calls 'adtech'—i.e. the tools and practices behind behavioural advertising. (*Source: James Roper research using Google Trends*)

The traditional analogue advertising model – blast it out as widely as possible and hope some of it sticks – once had us all drowning in email spam. This was largely being curtailed by 2016, when only half of all email was spam and filters removed much of what remained. But if spamming is about abusing other people's attention, the ethos of spam remained a huge problem that was getting worse as practitioners migrated to text, social media and other digital avenues to create and exploit vast algal blooms of linked content with catchy titles that fed on whatever was trending.

The arms race emerging between sellers and consumers in 2010 was evidence that relationships were becoming strained in the digisphere. Sellers were harnessing 'big data' to help them 'target', 'capture', 'track', 'manage' and 'lock in' customers.

Implicit in this mentality is the belief that customers are 'assets' to be 'controlled'. However, the internet had empowered consumers and given them independence. Citizens were hooked on their shopping freedom and wanted to be emancipated from systems built to control them. They preferred retailers to respectfully invite trade rather than try to coerce them.

Advertising pays for much of what you see, hear and read, but the trade-offs had become unbalanced. Advertising involves guessing what people want. Personalisation – better guessing with the help of big data – was seen as a superior form of advertising and had become a major theme in e-retailing, though this was an ambition of industry not consumers. In reality, personalisation all too often could end up being about advertisers latching on to almost any crumb of data or implied information scraped from a shopper's browsing trail, in a bid to be relevant.

From 2010 we saw explosive growth in what the trade called *adtech* – a catchall term for the tools and practices behind *behavioural advertising*: behavioural targeting, programmatic trading, deal ID, real-time messaging, clickstream data, retargeting, etc. *Retargeting* was the adtech tool most revealing of surveillance, whereby one ad turned up over and over again, at site after site, even though consumers disliked companies apparently spying on them in this creepy way. Marketing emails might also arrive to clutter up their already overfull inboxes: 'We couldn't help noticing...'

'Do not track' requests were simply ignored. The US Federal Trade Commission had seen the potential for digital applications to be used for surveillance and control, and in 2007 proposed to create a national 'Do Not Track'[71] list similar to the 'Do Not Call' phone list. In 2009, Mozilla created a prototype 'Do Not Track' add-in for its Firefox web browser. Soon Microsoft and Apple built support for Do Not Track into their browsers. Google followed suit in 2012. However, all this made little difference because Do Not Track was just a request in the form of an 'http header' signalled by the browser – a request that most publishers and advertisers chose to ignore.

Hence the arms race, with consumers acquiring tools to help preserve their autonomy, or at least give themselves some bargaining power. In 2015, software that blocked advertising was being used by more than nine million UK web users, 22 per cent of all those over 18 years old, up from 15 per cent the year before, according to the Internet Advertising Bureau.[72] The highest level of ad blocking was among the 18- to 24-year-old age group, at 47 per cent.

According to PageFair and Adobe's 2015 *Global Adblocking Report*, there were 198 million active AdBlock users around the world, having grown by 41 per cent globally in the previous twelve months, with annual growth rates of 48 per cent in the US and 82 per cent in the UK.

> *'By now the number [of AdBlock users] must be north of 200 million worldwide. If this be a boycott, it's surely the largest in human history'*[123]
>
> Doc Searls, 'The Intention Economy', 2012

There was an adtech bubble, although the industry and its clients were still largely in the denial stage and missing the point. A meeting of key global advertising stakeholders in early 2016 put forward a four-point plan to *rescue the credibility of the online advertising experience in the face of ad blocking, intrusive tracking, and poor metrics.*[73] They talked about seeing the collapse of the mechanism that had supported the diversity of content on the open web since the 1990s. They claimed *technology defeats ad blocking anyway.* One leading browser told its users that if they tried to opt out of ads in its browser settings, *'you'll still see ads by [us]–they just won't be based on your interests, your visits to advertiser websites or demographics'.*

The adtech bubble will probably burst eventually, but whether or not it does, the unprecedented consumer boycott of its practices marked a shift in the power dynamic, from suppliers to buyers. Citizens were learning how to use their newfound bargaining power to protect their interests and advance causes that concerned them. Advertisers were increasingly pressed to reorient their strategies from acquisition to retention, and to find new ways to reach and engage consumers.

Innovation is driven by a need to create more compelling value propositions in an increasingly connected and dynamic world. The adtech bubble drove advertisers to give more back to customers by spending their advertising budgets on assets that were actually useful to people rather than on brute force technology to browbeat them.

But in May 2019 the ethos of spam remained a huge problem: a staggering 326 billion spam emails were being sent on average each day from 247 countries and states – almost 85 per cent of emails sent worldwide.[74]

2014–2019: The Brexit Years

'Brexit means Brexit: The public made their verdict'

Theresa May, UK Prime Minister from 13 July 2016 to 24 July 2019

Five percent of store sales shifted online in 2014, and we forecast that a quarter of all retail sales would soon be online. IMRG membership then included 2,500 retail organisations and 130 solution providers – more than 85 per cent of the retailers we surveyed expected online growth to be in excess of 10 per cent in Q4. The second half of the 2010s would see the UK with the largest and most competitive e-commerce market in Europe.

Some 10,000 physical retail stores had been empty for more than three years in 2014, and tens of thousands more were at risk as their costs rose and productivity fell. Yet councils and landlords were still contributing to the demise of high streets by ignoring the fundamental transformation taking place in shopping.

2015 marked the fifteen-year anniversary of the IMRG Capgemini Sales Index: we estimated that £640 billion had been spent online in the UK during the 180 months since April 2000.

The average UK consumer owned 3.3 internet devices – half owned tablet computers, while three-quarters owned personal computers. The vast majority of consumers (85 per cent) went online at least once a day. Two-thirds went online while they watched TV: 63 per cent of those people used their smartphone to multiscreen, many others similarly used either a tablet or laptop.

More than half of British adults searched for goods on their smartphones in 2015. Half researched offline before they bought goods online; a quarter only researched their shopping purchases online.

IMRG had for many years published a quarterly table of the top-ranking e-retailers – in partnership with comScore. The fastest riser in the *IMRG comScore Top 50 Retailer Ranking* in November 2015 was online fashion retailer Boohoo, up

IMRG comScore Top 50 Retailer Ranking, November 2015

Movement YOY	Ranking July 2015	Ranking July 2014	Brand	URL
▷◁	1	1	Amazon	www.amazon.co.uk
▷◁	2	2	Argos	www.argos.co.uk
▷◁	3	3	Apple	www.apple.com
▷◁	4	4	Tesco	www.tesco.com
▲	5	6	Next	www.next.co.uk
▲	6	7	Marks and Spencer	www.marksandspencer.com
▼	7	5	Asda	www.asda.co.uk
▲	8	11	John Lewis	www.johnlewis.com
▷◁	9	9	Netflix	www.netflix.com
▲	10	14	B & Q	www.diy.com
▲	11	21	Currys	www.currys.co.uk
▲	12	18	EasyJet.com	www.easyjet.com
▼	13	12	The Train Line	www.thetrainline.com
▲	14	16	Thomson	www.thomson.co.uk
▼	15	8	ASOS	www.asos.com
▲	16	17	Expedia	www.expedia.co.uk
▲	17	22	Ryanair	www.ryanair.com
▼	18	15	Debenhams	www.debenhams.com
▼	19	13	AVG	www.avg.com
▼	20	10	National Rail	www.nationalrail.co.uk
▼	21	19	Boots	www.boots.com
▼	22	20	Sports Direct	www.sportsdirect.com
▲	23	25	New Look	www.newlook.com
▲	24	28	IKEA	www.ikea.com
▲	25	27	Lastminute.com	www.lastminute.com
▲	26	30	Homebase	www.homebase.co.uk
▼	27	26	Very	www.very.co.uk
▲	28	34	Screwfix.com	www.screwfix.com
▲	29	35	House of Fraser	www.houseoffraser.co.uk
▼	30	23	Telefonica O2	www.o2.co.uk
▲	31	33	British Airways	www.britishairways.com
▲	32	36	Hewlett Packard	www.hp.com
▲	33	37	Halfords	www.halfords.com
▲	34	41	Wickes	www.wickes.co.uk
▼	35	29	Sainsbury's	www.sainsburys.co.uk
▼	36	24	Ticketmaster UK	www.ticketmaster.co.uk
▼	37	32	Premier Inn	www.premierinn.com
▲	38	43	JD Sports	www.jdsports.co.uk
▲	39	47	National Express	www.nationalexpress.co.uk
▲	40	50	Carphone Warehouse	www.carphonewarehouse.com
▼	41	31	River Island	www.riverisland.com
▲	42	45	Boohoo	www.boohoo.com
▼	43	40	PC World	www.pcworld.co.uk
▲	44	53	Notonthehighstreet.com	www.notonthehighstreet.com
▼	45	44	Matalan	www.matalan.co.uk
▲	46	48	GAME	www.game.co.uk
▲	47	49	H&M	www.hm.com
▼	48	38	eDreams	www.edreams.co.uk
▲	49	52	BHS	www.bhs.co.uk
▼	50	39	Littlewoods	www.littlewoods.com

Figure 48: The fastest riser in the IMRG comScore Top 50 (November 2015) was online fashion retailer Boohoo, up eleven places to thirty-seven compared to its ranking a year earlier. The Top 50 tracked visitors to retailers selling goods and services within the IMRG Capgemini Index Classification—it was published quarterly and based on comScore's MMX online audience measurement technology. This list recorded UK visitors from desktops and laptops in September 2015. (*Source: James Roper Archive*)

eleven places to thirty-seventh compared to a year earlier – we would hear a lot more about Boohoo later. The table below shows that there was very little movement in the top eight e-retailers – Amazon.co.uk always took the top spot, and each of the other seven leaders had become highly adept at holding on to their lofty position.

This decade was overshadowed by Brexit which brought much conflict, uncertainty and volatility. In early 2013 David Cameron promised to renegotiate Britain's membership of the European Union if his Conservative Party won a majority at the next general election. Following his winning re-election in May 2015, Cameron led the campaign to stay in the EU and called the Brexit Referendum, asking the British electorate whether the country should remain a member of the EU, or leave. The poll took place on 23 June 2016. The result was close: 51.9 per cent of the votes cast were in favour of leaving the EU, but there were stark differences across the UK – only 38 per cent of Scottish voters chose 'leave'. Cameron resigned the following day, and although the result was not legally binding, the Conservative government promised to implement the result.

The BREXIT referendum's unexpected *leave* vote brought a huge economy shock: the pound collapsed and $2 trillion was wiped out across global markets. In response, the Bank of England applied a further £70 billion of quantitative easing (QE).

Following the Great Recession of 2008, in 2010 the UK's new Conservative Chancellor George Osborne had introduced an austerity programme to reduce the government budget deficit. This included sustained reductions in public spending on welfare, schools, local government, the police, courts, prisons, the arts and culture – and an increase in VAT to 20%.

Ordinary working-class people had made the biggest sacrifices following the 2008 crash. Yet as the self-defeating austerity programme dragged on for years, UK billionaires' wealth more than doubled, from £150bn in 2010 to £350bn in 2016, by which time Britain's richest 1 per cent had more than twenty times the wealth of the poorest twelve million people. A frustrated electorate used the momentous Brexit referendum to reject the status quo and, as the UKIP (UK Independence Party) leader Nigel Farage described it, 'stick two fingers up' at Britain's politicians.

Further stirring up resentment, the so-called Panama Papers of 2016 and Paradise Papers of 2017 were giant leaks exposing the rogue offshore finance dealings of rich and powerful people and companies around the world. Tens of millions of financial and legal records were divulged to journalists, exposing a system that enabled crime, corruption and wrongdoing, hidden by secretive offshore companies. Major banks had steered the creation of hard-to-trace companies in tax havens – or *offshore financial centres* as the industry prefers to call them – such as the Isle of Man and the British Virgin Islands. Multinational corporations' tax engineering was exposed, such as Apple's $2 trillion stashed offshore in Jersey. One journalist commented: 'the whole industry is rotten and has lost its compass and its values for what is right and wrong.'

Cameron's resignation, in June 2016 after the Brexit vote, brought an abrupt end to his six-year premiership. The Conservatives generally preferred to leave financial matters to the banks and markets to sort out, but when Theresa May took over as the new PM, she immediately made a host of bold economic pledges. 'We're coming after you,' she warned dysfunctional markets, rip-off firms and tax-dodging multinationals 'that treat tax laws as an optional extra'. She tried to introduce new workers' protections and clamp down on CEO pay, and in 2018 announced that she was ending the decade of austerity. But when May resigned in March 2019, little had been achieved – her economic legacy was a country transfixed by Brexit and treading water amid rudderless political uncertainty.

Governments around the world continued to pour enormous quantities of QE money into the system. People with private equity got incredibly wealthy, and the super-rich got super-richer.

But QE was not stimulating the real economy, or promoting genuine, durable and inclusive economic growth, and governments were still not listening to the people. Philip Hammond who served as Chancellor of the Exchequer from 2016 to 2019 explained: 'We always have to remember the markets, the international investment communities which are so important for the UK's prosperity.' In 2019, Hammond responded to a UN report which argued that fourteen million people in the UK were living in poverty and 1.5 million were destitute, by saying he 'rejects the idea that there are vast numbers of people facing poverty in this country... I think that's all nonsense'.

The whole sorry Brexit saga would drag on for 1,652 days from the vote to the UK actually leaving the EU single market and customs union at 11 pm on 31 December 2020. Even then, many years of further negotiations and uncertainty were anticipated.

* * *

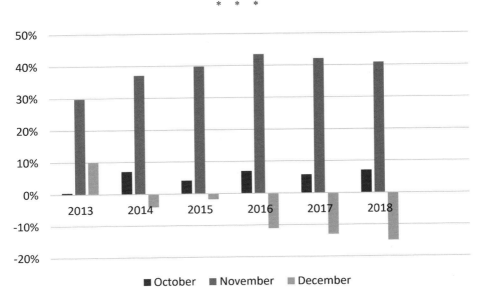

Figure 49: This chart shows the month-on-month online sales growth rates, October to December, 2013–2018, and how e-retailers successfully pulled sales earlier each year. (*Source: IMRG Capgemini e-Retail Sales Index*)

As the decade rolled on online shopping continued to grow steadily, rising by 15.9 per cent in 2016. In 2017 around 93 percent of the UK's 65.5 million population were internet users and 87 per cent shopped online – over 57 million e-shoppers. The biggest growth in January 2017 was recorded by department stores, which saw their online sales increase by almost a fifth year-on-year.

In 2018 physical stores experienced a very tough year from start to finish, while online retail displayed a lopsided pattern: strong growth in the first half of the year collapsed in the second half, culminating in a rise of just 3.6 per cent for December, the lowest increase ever recorded for any December in the IMRG Index's eighteen years.

Black Friday remained volatile, refusing to settle down into a consistent pattern. It was a day, then a weekend, then a week – and now, for many e-retailers, was the entire month of November as they desperately attempted to pull sales forward.

But the e-retail growth trend was a general decline, raising questions as to whether online as a trading platform had plateaued and was beginning to run out of steam. Growth remained subdued in 2019 until better Christmas trading generally helped overall annual growth for the year come in at 6.7 per cent, though still the lowest recorded in nineteen years. E-retail was not in a strong position heading into 2020.

2020 (MMXX): e-Dominance

> *'Even before the Covid-19 pandemic, there are few retailers that wouldn't have predicted the continued growth of e-commerce relative to physical shops. But what would have previously been a gradual upward climb in demand has, with the outbreak of Covid-19, turned into a trajectory more reminiscent of scaling Everest.'*
>
> James Bailey, Waitrose & Partners executive director, August 2020

As we turned to our new 2020 diaries, IMRG was recording online retail sales growth at around 5 per cent per annum. More than half of Britain's shopping was already either on or influenced by the internet, but e-retail's growth trend had been declining for years and in 2019 was at an historic low. Then the Covid-19 pandemic precipitated an abrupt mass shift to digital that brought a punishing year of painful restructuring to the retail sector. 2020 would be the worst year for the high street in a quarter of a century, with more than 16,000 store closures and 180,000 job losses.

A subdued e-trading pattern continued in the early months of 2020. Then in March, when the first pandemic lockdown was introduced, the growth trend line reached for the sky as there were few other options for buying stuff. From July, as things

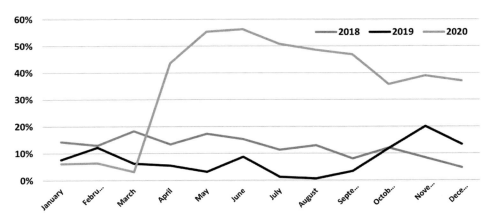

Figure 50: Year-on-year growth in UK online sales, 2018 to 2020. (*Source: IMRG Capgemini Sales Index*)

started to open up again, the rate of growth gradually eased, but then rebounded in November as the second lockdown was introduced in England.

UK e-sales exceeded £112 billion in 2020, according to Statista. IMRG recorded online sales for the year up 37 per cent, a near sixfold increase on that of 2019 and the highest annual growth rate since 2007. After several years of plateauing, mobile commerce sales climbed a vertiginous 73 per cent: 52 per cent of all web traffic came from mobile devices.

Multichannel retailers, with their physical stores shut, performed significantly better than their online only counterparts, with e-sales growth of 57 per cent vs 9.1 per cent. Category winners included garden and electricals, though with people confined to their homes this proved to be a dismal year for clothing sales.

2020 was a boom time for small e-retailers (<£10 million turnover), whose sales were up 100 per cent, on average, every month from May. A likely reason for small traders doing so well was because of the strain the large retailers (£100m+) found themselves under – in some categories, demand was so high that their websites buckled under the load in the early months of the pandemic, explained IMRG's strategy and insight director, Andy Mulcahy. Also, as shoppers flocked online, some found the large retailers were either limiting orders for high-demand items or were out of stock. In such cases, people would have searched on Google for additional options and come across the smaller retailers. Another reason was that larger retailers restricted marketing (emails, AdWord spend, etc) due to excessive site traffic, so smaller retailers had greater visibility online.

*   *   *

At the start of 2020 Amazon.com overtook Walmart as the biggest retailer on the planet.[75] Amazon's founder, Jeff Bezos, was the richest person in the world – again – with a net worth estimated to be $115 billion, even after an expensive divorce and having lost $10 billion in one year.[76] The world's third-largest retailer, after

Walmart, was the Chinese e-commerce giant Alibaba, its founder, Jack Ma, ranking #19 on the Bloomberg Billionaires Index with wealth of $45.9 billion.[77] Alibaba's core business was selling goods online to its 654 million active retail customers, but it had also invested heavily in areas including entertainment, logistics and payments. Its revenues had grown 51 per cent to $56 billion in fiscal 2019.

Meanwhile, Forbes was asking: 'Will 2020 be the year Sears finally goes out of business[78]?' Sears, Roebuck and Co., colloquially known as Sears, had been the largest retailer in the US in the 1980s and earlier. Founded in 1892, the company had completed its 110-storey Sears Tower headquarters in Chicago in 1974, then the world's tallest building. But tough decades followed, and despite creating *Prodigy*, the pre-web online portal referred to earlier, and earnest attempts to trade online, the once-mighty retailer's dominance faded to the point where Sears filed for Chapter 11 bankruptcy in 2018, using the process to shed debt and evade liquidation. Sears entered 2019 with 489 full-line department stores – by the close of 2020 less than forty remained.

Retailers comprised just 1.9 per cent of the FTSE 100 in early 2020, down from a peak of 8.4 per cent in 1986. Marks & Spencer had been ejected from the FTSE in late 2019, while at the start of 2020 supermarket chain Morrisons and DIY conglomerate Kingfisher were at risk of expulsion, having fallen near the bottom with market valuations of £4.1 billion and £4 billion respectively. If they were to drop out, only four bricks-and-mortar retailers would remain – Tesco, Sainsbury's, JD Sports and Next.[79]

*   *   *

Coronavirus disease 2019 (Covid-19) is an infectious respiratory disease that was first identified in Wuhan, Hubei, China in December 2019. The Wuhan Municipal Health commission made the first public announcement of a pneumonia outbreak of unknown cause on 31 December 2019, confirming twenty-seven cases – by then thousands of Chinese people had developed symptoms. The World Health Organisation (WHO) confirmed the human-to-human transmission capability of the disease and its pandemic potential on 20 January 2020. By the end of the year there would be eighty-five million confirmed cases of Covid-19 recorded worldwide, and 1.82 million lives lost to the virus.

Italy and the UK both had their first confirmed cases on 31 January 2020, joining twenty-two other countries outside China with confirmed infections. At the time, all of the 304 official deaths had occurred within China. On 19 March, Italy overtook China as the country with the most Covid-19 deaths. By 26 March, the United States had overtaken Italy as the country with the highest number of confirmed cases in the world – a lamentable lead it would keep and massively extend.

*   *   *

The pandemic triggered the worst economic crisis since the Great Depression of the 1930s. Global economic shutdowns, panic buying, and supply disruptions led to mass hysteria. A major and sudden global stock market crash, referred to as the *Coronavirus Crash*, began on 20 February and ended on 7 April. Market instability intensified in the first half of March with multiple severe daily drops, the largest occurring on 16 March with falls of 12–13 per cent in most global stock markets. In just four trading days, the Dow Jones Industrial Average (DJIA) plunged 6,400 points, about 26 per cent. The crash signalled the start of the international Covid-19 Recession.

To help mitigate the panic, banks and reserves around the world cut their interest rates and offered yet more unprecedented quantitative easing support to calm the markets. Just as after the 2008 crash, the US took the lead with President Trump announcing on 16 March a fiscal stimulus package, with the government purchasing $500 billion of Treasury securities and $200 billion of mortgage-backed securities, and adding that it would buy bonds in 'the amounts needed to support smooth market functioning'. The European Central Bank bought three-quarters of a trillion euros worth of securities.

On 19 March the UK announced £200 billion of new QE and cut interest rates to an all-time low of 0.1 per cent. In June and November, further tranches of QE worth £100 billion and £150 billion were announced. By late 2020 the Bank of England had printed £895 billion to prop up the UK economy since starting down the QE route during the Great Recession of 2008.

* * *

In March, the UK government imposed a stay-at-home order, banning all non-essential travel and contact with people outside one's home, and shutting almost all schools, businesses, venues, facilities and places of worship – including all non-essential shops. People with symptoms, and their households, were told to self-isolate, while the elderly and medically vulnerable were instructed to shield themselves. A Coronavirus Act 2020 was passed on 19 March giving the government emergency powers not used since the Second World War. On 20 March the government announced a furlough scheme, backdated from 1 March, whereby any employer could apply for a grant to cover 80 per cent of the wages (up to £2,500 per month) of employees who were not working but *furloughed* and kept on the payroll. The retail sector would furlough more employees than any other.

Mothercare was 2020's first major retail casualty, shutting its physical UK stores for good in the early days of the pandemic, following its collapse into administration in November 2019. Having opened in 1961, at its peak in 2017 the retailer had 150 UK stores. Mothercare's demise lost 2,500 jobs, however, its products remained available in Boots stores.

Laura Ashley went into administration on 17 March, with 2,700 job losses, after rescue talks were scuppered by the pandemic. It was acquired by the Gordon Brothers investment firm and was hoped would make a return through a partnership with Next.

Beales, the historic department store chain, founded in 1881, closed its doors for the last time in March, as did Carphone Warehouse, when it permanently shut all of its 531 UK stores, affecting almost 3,000 staff. Brighthouse, the rent-to-own retailer also tumbled into administration that month, closing 240 stores and putting 2,400 jobs at risk.

*   *   *

Lockdown! Prime Minister Boris Johnson announced a strict lockdown across the country from Monday 23 March, telling people to stay at home, only shop for basic necessities, exercise once a day, and only travel to and from essential work. Most shops had to close and would remain so for the next eighty-four days – twelve weeks – when non-essential retailers would be allowed to reopen in England on Monday 15 June as long as safety measures were in place, including plastic screens at tills and floor markings for social distancing.

The bricks-and-mortar shops deemed non-essential and forced to close included clothing, books and electricals stores, car showrooms, hairdressers and markets, whether they were indoors or outside. Shops defined as essential and allowed to stay open were mainly food retailers, pharmacies, DIY stores and petrol stations.

But with some 300,000 confirmed cases of Coronavirus in the UK, shopping was not like it had been before lockdown.[80] Social distancing took away the social, fun experience of shopping. Shops looked different, with two-metre distance markings, arrows on the floor showing which way to walk, hand sanitising stations, shop assistants wearing masks and visors, Perspex barriers at tills, and continual cleaning of shopping baskets and door handles. Shopping became a solitary exercise, with people advised to go shopping on their own, seating areas removed to discourage gathering, and cafes, restaurants and hotels closed. Customers touching goods that they were not going to buy was largely forbidden. Many shoppers were irritable – already fed up with weeks of lockdown, they were now frustrated by the abnormal rules, delays and endless queues.

With no tourists, fewer commuters and many people reluctant to use public transport, footfall in central London plummeted 63 per cent on an annual basis in March according to Retail Gazette,[81] citing Springboard data. Across the nation high streets were badly affected, with footfall dropping 41 per cent year-on-year, while shopping centre footfall fell 25.4 per cent. 'The annual change represented an unprecedented decline in retail footfall that was three times greater than the worst result we have ever previously recorded,' said Springboard insights director Diane Wehrle. Then shopping destination footfall deteriorated even further as the public became accustomed with the safety rules, declining 73 per cent year-on-year in May. Even in June, when lockdown easing allowed some shops to reopen mid-month, the downturn was 57 per cent.[82]

As people were asked to stay at home, more and more headed online to shop, most notably for groceries. People were stockpiling food, many items were restricted and supermarket online delivery slots were all full. Tesco, the UK's biggest supermarket, warned that it could not meet online demand, despite increasing its online shopping capacity by more than a fifth, so most food would still need to be purchased in-store.

Oasis and Warehouse fashions brands went into administration on 15 April. All of their ninety-two stores and 437 concessions closed, resulting in 1,800 job losses – the brands were subsequently sold to the online fashion group Boohoo. Cath Kidston, the retro retail label, closed all of its sixty stores when a rescue deal brokered for the business closed on 21 April: more than 900 jobs were cut.

Whereas e-retail sales generally were higher, the sun wasn't shining across all the online checkouts; a deep divide emerged between e-retailers' fortunes, depending largely on what they were selling. Three product sectors reported large year-on-year growth for April – Home & Garden, Electricals and Health & Beauty (71 per cent, 102 per cent and 82 per cent respectively). Electricals reported its best month since July 2007.

Meanwhile, Clothing, which had always represented a significant portion of the overall online retail market, posted a heavy year-on-year fall of –24 per cent, which was by far the worst performance IMRG had recorded for the sector since it began tracking it in February 2002. Online sales of T-shirt bras, tracksuit bottoms, slippers and bathroom products rose, as customers adapted to a 'stay-at-home lifestyle', while barely any suits or ties sold. Brands like New Look, ASOS and Boohoo capitalised on the shift to online shopping, pushing leisurewear and pyjamas instead of the summer dresses, chunky heels and bikinis they would normally be selling ahead of the summer holiday period.

The government extended the job furlough scheme by four months in May. At that time a quarter of the UK workforce, about 7.5 million people, was covered by the scheme, which was costing £14 billion a month.

People used to shopping online did so more, while millions adopted it for the first time, particularly the older community who were most at risk from Covid-19. Yodel, one of the UK's biggest parcel carriers handling more than 150 million parcels a year, said that it had to adapt quickly in March, even partnering with taxi firms at one stage to help deliver the extra packages. 'It's like Christmas every day for us,' said Mike Hancox, Yodel's chief executive. Consumers being out when a delivery was attempted was no longer a problem – they were always in.

ONS statistics only recorded part of what we considered to be online shopping, but even by its narrow definition online sales as a proportion of all UK retail sales hit a record high of more than 30 per cent in May, before falling back to 28 per cent in July.

The pandemic acerbated trends in the retail landscape that was already experiencing widespread revision. Retailers brought forward or ramped up their e-commerce plans as store closures and sharp declines in discretionary consumer spending crippled nonessential retail. Many retailers had to make tough choices, including temporarily or permanently closing doors, and furloughing or shedding employees: hundreds of shops that closed 'temporarily' under the lockdown rules would never reopen.

Radical changes were being made to facilitate online trading. Automotive retailer, Vertu Motors, reported in a BBC *Breakfast* interview on 26 May that people were doing far more on the internet, and their online sales had gone up considerably. 'We sold 650 cars last week as a group without a single test drive and

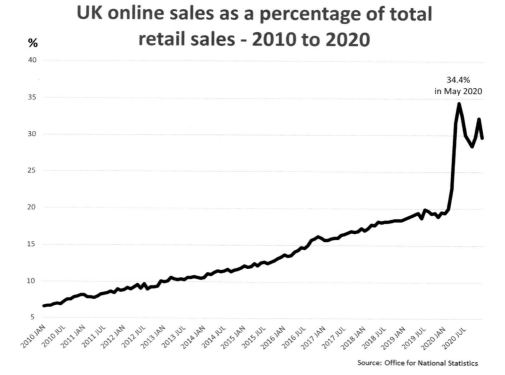

UK online sales as a percentage of total retail sales - 2010 to 2020

Source: Office for National Statistics

Figure 51: Online sales as a proportion of all UK retail sales was just 6.6 per cent in January 2010 according to ONS calculations (and its narrow definition of e-retail categories), rising to a record high of more than 34 per cent in May 2020. (*Source: ONS*)

not one person coming into a showroom,' said Robert Forrester, chief executive of Vertu Motors.[83] On 1 May the DVLA confirmed that car buyers could take unaccompanied test drives on a car dealer's trade plates,[84] and other restrictions were relaxed to enable salesrooms to sell cars using *click-and-collect* services. But despite all efforts, new car sales for the year fell to a thirty-year low, a decline of 29 per cent and the biggest one-year fall since the Second World War, according to the Society for Motor Manufacturers and Traders (SMMT). Some 1.6 million new cars were registered in 2020, the lowest number since 1992, as millions of journeys were replaced by Zoom, Skype, Teams and Viber video calls. Overall, the SMMT said the Covid-19 crisis had cost the car industry some £20 billion.[85]

Total retail sales in May were 5.9 per cent lower than a year earlier. The Centre for Retail Research (CRR) advised that 2,123 stores operated by 38 large- and medium-sized retailers had fallen into administration in the first half of 2020. These firms employed 49,200 staff.

In June, with infection rates falling, the government relaxed some Coronavirus restrictions as part of an effort to try to boost the economy. In mid-June some non-essential retailers reopened after the first lockdown. The third most-read BBC *Business* news story that month was a guide to which shops had reopened:

John Lewis kicked off by opening thirteen branches in stages; Next was initially reopening just twenty-five of its 500 stores; Debenhams was opening fifty stores in England; Topshop was reopening all of its English stores and selected ones in Northern Ireland…

But this respite was already too late for many retailers. Monsoon and Accessorize fashion brands were bought out of administration on 11 June by their founder, Peter Simon, in a deal that resulted in the closure of thirty-five stores and 545 job losses. TM Lewin, the shirtmaker, called in the administrators on 30 June and closed all its sixty-six outlets permanently, with the loss of about 600 jobs.

* * *

On 9 July, John Lewis advised that between 60 and 70 per cent of its sales would be made online both that year and next, compared with 40 per cent before the Coronavirus crisis. Additionally, that having struggled to manage competition from online rivals and slower consumer spending, they would be permanently closing eight of their department stores, potentially cutting 1,300 jobs. John Lewis department stores in Birmingham and Watford would not reopen after the Coronavirus lockdown eased, and it would additionally shut down its *At Home* stores in Croydon, Newbury, Swindon and Tamworth, and travel sites at Heathrow airport and London St Pancras.

Also on 9 July, Boots reported that 4,000 jobs would go – some 7 per cent of its workforce – at its head office and stores, many from the forty-eight of its Boots Opticians practices that it was closing, out of a total of over 600.[86] The company said sales across all Boots UK outlets were down 50 per cent in the third quarter, and around 70 per cent at Boots Opticians. In September, the boss of Boots, Seb James, said that Christmas would be much more online, so they had tripled their online capacity.

It was officially announced in August that the lockdown had pushed the UK into recession for the first time in eleven years, between April and June, during which time the number of people in work fell by 220,000, according to the ONS. Retail had been one of the hardest hit sectors of the economy.

'Shopping may never be the same,' said M&S chief executive Steve Rowe on 18 August, the day he announced 7,000 jobs would be cut over the following three months.[87] The pandemic had driven several changes for M&S, including a shift to online, and its customers buying more casual clothing. M&S said that online shoppers were then browsing earlier in the day, between 15:00 and 17:00. And as more customers worked from home, desktop visits were up 38 per cent in comparison with the same period the previous year.

IMRG reported in August that its membership community had almost doubled to over 17,000 since the start of lockdown as sellers flooded to trade online. John Lewis's online Christmas shop opened that month after a summer spike in searches by customers.

Edinburgh Woollen Mill Group, the fashion group with 21,500 staff, owned by the billionaire entrepreneur Philip Day, fell into financial crisis in October. Its brands – Edinburgh Woollen Mill, Ponden Mill, Peacocks, Jaeger, Austin Reed and Jacques Vert – followed each other into administration, cutting 860 jobs.

The prime minister announced on 31 October that England was to be put under a second lockdown on 2 November for one month, bringing further disruption to everyone's lives and livelihoods. Pubs, gyms, and non-essential retailers would close again, but schools, colleges and universities could stay open. Although a further lockdown was widely anticipated, the short two-day notice left many thousands of shops scrambling to adapt in what would normally be the key run-up to the Christmas trading period – the closure time included Black Friday, further benefitting online shopping.

At the beginning of November, the government announced that it would extend the furlough scheme to the end of March 2021. Furlough was later extended again to the end of April 2021.

Marks & Spencer announced its first loss in ninety-four years as a publicly listed company in November, as clothing sales slumped. In the six months to 26 September, the retailer made a loss of £87.6 million, compared with profits of £158.8 million in the same period a year earlier. Steve Rowe commented that the firm's performance had been 'much more robust than at first seemed possible'. In August M&S announced a sales slide of 16 per cent, largely impacted by lower clothing and home sales. Between July and September, clothing sales in its city stores were down by 53 per cent.

On 5 November, Sainsbury's said it would cut 3,500 jobs and close 420 Argos stores. Argos had already announced (on 30 July) that after forty-eight years it was axing its catalogue, which comedian Bill Bailey jokingly described as 'The laminated book of dreams'. The encyclopaedia-like catalogue was first launched in 1972 and at its peak was Europe's most widely read publication, with only the Bible in more homes across the UK.

December 2020 arrived heralding one of the blackest weeks for the British High Street in which both Arcadia and Debenhams would fail and imminently cease to exist as companies. Each was a British retail institution that had withstood recessions, depression and wars, but succumbed finally to the twin threats of the internet and pandemic shutdowns. Both had been key anchor stores in city centres for decades, but fell behind fashion trends, whilst locked into long leases with rising rents, and underperforming online sales. Debenhams' and Arcadia's brands had been some of the few sizeable anchor tenants left after the demise of Woolworths, BHS and others, leaving councils around the country pondering the future of their town centres.

As the busiest shopping period of the year began after a monthlong lockdown in England, Debenhams started closing-down sales in its 124 stores. With no rescue deal agreed, on 1 December it announced plans to liquidate. Some 4,000 head office and store staff had already gone as a result of its second administration in a year; its 12,000 remaining staff faced an uncertain future.

Arcadia had collapsed into administration the previous day, on 30 November, affecting 13,000 jobs. Sir Phillip Green's fashion group brands including Topshop, Miss Selfridge and Dorothy Perkins were being auctioned off. The plus-size label

Evans' online operations had already been sold, but all its outlets were to close, meaning hundreds of job losses. Arcadia had previously cut 500 head-office jobs in the summer.

* * *

In December, just as everyone was looking forward to spending Christmas in *family bubbles* and putting 2020 behind them, there was yet another piece of bad news: a new and extremely contagious variant of Coronavirus – the Kent strain – was spreading from the southeast of England and replacing other versions of the virus. In response to this alarming news dozens of countries banned UK arrivals and France shut its border with the UK for forty-eight hours, which led to serious freight disruptions and thousands of lorry drivers having to spend Christmas in their cabs, stuck in queues near Dover.

Prime Minister Boris Johnson had been heavily criticised throughout the year for not reacting quickly enough to the pandemic, and for last-minute public notification of new government rules. The plan had been to allow up to three UK households to mix indoors for five days between 23 and 27 December. But on 19 December, with cases of the Kent strain rising dangerously, there was yet another frantic government announcement imposing new harsh Tier 4 restrictions from the following day, and scrapping plans for *Christmas bubbles* completely.

On 23 December, the UK reported 39,237 confirmed Covid-19 cases, the highest in any one day since the start of the pandemic, and 744 new deaths, the most fatalities since 29 April. It was also announced that another new variant of Coronavirus, discovered in South Africa, had reached the UK. On the last day of 2020, the UK reported 55,892 new Covid-19 cases, yet another daily high.

* * *

2020 was the worst year for high street job losses in twenty-five years (6). Fifty-four major UK retailers failed, affecting 5,214 stores. There was a total of 16,045 store closures. Retailers shed 182,564 jobs during the year – 3,400 jobs vanished a week – according to the Centre for Retail Research (CRR). Of these, 71,811 jobs were lost through retailers falling into administration (such as Arcadia, Edinburgh Woollen Mill Group and Debenhams), and a further 11,986 fell victim to company voluntary arrangement (CVA) deals, a controversial insolvency procedure used to close loss-making stores and secure rent cuts – CVAs were by entered by companies including River Island, Clarks and New Look.

A further 92,921 jobs were sacrificed through *rationalisation* as part of cost-cutting programmes by large retailers and small shops shutting for good, up 18.3 per cent on 2019, the CRR said. The total number of overall retail jobs lost in 2020 was up by almost a quarter on the 143,128 lost during 2019. Professor Joshua Bamfield, a director at the CRR, warned up to 200,000 retail jobs could disappear in 2021. According to the real estate adviser Altus Group, 436,000 business premises in England were closed on 31 December 2020 under Tier 3 and Tier 4 restrictions, including 310,504 non-essential shops, 37,581 pubs and 27,028 restaurants.

On a brighter note, after months of bad-tempered wrangling an eleventh-hour Brexit deal was finally agreed on Christmas Eve, 1,645 days after the UK voted to leave the EU, and 328 days after we actually departed. Just days before the status quo was set to disappear, the shape of our relationship with our nearest foreign neighbours was drawn up and agreed, with both sides claiming victory as a spin battle commenced. The agreement avoided an acrimonious end to the Brexit transition period that might have soured relations not only with Europe, but also with Joe Biden's incoming US administration. Both sides welcomed the agreement with warm rhetoric.

E-grocery sprouts up

> *'As a result of Covid-19, we have seen years of growth in the online grocery market condensed into a matter of months; and we won't be going back'*
>
> Tim Steiner, Chief Executive, Ocado, July 2020

The Coronavirus crisis and lockdowns saw a massive jump in demand for online grocery deliveries as people sought to minimise trips to supermarkets. In August, Tesco announced that online sales which had taken twenty years to reach 9 per cent of its trade took just twenty weeks to nearly double to 16 per cent, and that in response it was creating 16,000 new permanent posts.

After years of tentative growth, the online grocery shopping sector had substantialised in 2016 when Amazon teamed up with Morrisons to offer fresh and frozen goods, and Sainsbury's acquired Argos, which itself had joined forces with eBay to provide a bigger range of fulfilment services. But in 2020, the switch to internet shopping amid the Coronavirus lockdown led to a 'permanent redrawing' of the retail landscape, according to online grocer Ocado's chief executive Tim Steiner in July.[88] Ocado was the fastest-growing grocer in the UK, thanks to a 50/50 partnership with Marks & Spencer that had been formed in 2019: its sales during the first half of 2020 jumped 27 per cent to more than £1 billion. Ocado would begin delivering M&S grocery products in September, when its deal with Waitrose expired – this would trigger another sharp rise in Ocado's sales.

Ocado's technology provided retailers with the infrastructure and software to build their online service and compete with giants such as Amazon. Ocado was still losing money, having incurred the costs of opening its first two customer fulfilment centres abroad, for Casino in France and Sobeys in Canada, while increasing capacity in the UK, though the loss was smaller than the £147.4 million posted in the same period the previous year. Ocado had also cut overseas deals with ICA Group in Sweden, Kroger in the US, and Coles in Australia, and enjoyed robust share price growth in recent years. After raising £1 billion through an equity and bond issue in June, Ocado said it had £2.3 billion in cash on its strong balance sheet so was well placed for the future.

Ocado had been operating for twenty years, but in most of those years struggled to make money. A former Tesco chief executive once described the firm as a 'charity' because of the losses it had racked up. And when it was revealed in February 2019 that Marks & Spencer had spent £750 million to buy a 50 per cent stake of Ocado's retail arm, M&S shares fell by 12 per cent as investors raised concerns that it had overpaid for access to Ocado's technology and delivery network. M&S's food division had long struggled to grow its market share, held back by its absence from the fast-growing online market. The Ocado deal would enable M&S to leap directly to the cutting edge of digital technology and inherit a state-of-the-art distribution channel for its 6,000 product lines including ready meals, groceries and fresh produce. At the time of the deal, M&S had recently confirmed plans to axe 7,000 jobs as part of a turnaround strategy that chairman Archie Norman and chief executive Steve Rowe were implementing – a strategy that would seem prescient by late 2020.

More than three quarters of people in the UK did at least some online grocery shopping, Waitrose reported in August.[89] A Waitrose poll of 2,000 people across the UK found that 77 per cent shopped for groceries online, compared with 61 per cent the year before. The data indicated that a quarter of Britons were shopping online for groceries at least once a week – double the number a year earlier – while one in five said they had not considered it before Covid-19. The biggest shift was among over-55s where regular online shopping nearly trebled. 'Because online shopping quickly becomes habitual, these changes are irreversible,' proclaimed James Bailey, Waitrose & Partners executive director.

In September, Waitrose said that it was delivering some 170,000 weekly food orders, up from 60,000 pre-lockdown, and that demand was rising since its partnership with online grocer Ocado had lapsed in August.

In late September there was a seismic shift in the grocery retail landscape when Ocado became the UK's most valuable retailer, as investors continued to bet on the firm. Ocado's stock market value overtook that of Tesco following the launch of the M&S grocery service, and having reported a 50 per cent jump in third quarter sales. Ocado was valued at £21.7 billion, more than Tesco's £21.1 billion, despite having only 1.7 per cent of the UK grocery market, compared with Tesco's 26.8 per cent share, according to analyst, Kantar.[90]

Morrisons, Britain's fourth biggest supermarket, announced on 30 September that it was creating 1,000 new jobs to pick and pack orders from more than fifty stores to fulfil online orders for its services on Amazon.[91]

October brought another change in the grocery sector when the supermarket chain Asda returned into UK majority ownership for the first time in two decades. Following a failed £7.3 billion merger between Asda and Sainsbury's that had been blocked by the regulator on competition grounds in April, the US retail giant, Walmart, sold Asda to billionaire brothers from Blackburn for £6.8 billion. This consortium, consisting of brothers Zuber and Mohsin Issa and private equity firm TDR Capital, took a majority stake in Asda. The Issa brothers already owned EG Group, which had more than 5,200 petrol stations across the UK and Europe.

Online grocery shopping surged 70.3 per cent over the year, according to Barclaycard, which tracked almost half of all credit and debit card spending.[92] Online's share of grocery sales at UK supermarkets doubled to 15.5 per cent in December, according to Nielsen.

Back in 1996, IMRG reported on a survey of British Social Attitudes that found 64 per cent of those polled did not like going to the supermarket, and around 40 per cent would be interested in direct shopping from home. But the supermarkets wanted to get people into their stores where they were bound to buy more than they planned, so largely neglected the public's enthusiasm for home delivery. How times had changed – in 2020 every supermarket was scrambling to meet the demand from consumers who en masse were clamouring for grocery delivery slots.

Royal Maelstrom

Royal Mail blamed 'high demand' for delivery delays in the run-up to Christmas 2020. But scores of retailers including John Lewis, Boots and HMV blamed Royal Mail, as it continued to squander its serendipitous online opportunities. 'We could not possibly have anticipated this level of packets and parcels, it seems to be intensifying every day,' commented Terry Pullinger, deputy general secretary of the Communication Workers' Union in December.[93]

Royal Mail's trading update of 8 September said it expected to make a material loss in 2020 despite seeing parcel deliveries rise by more than a third during lockdown.[94] Antiquated working practices that were still holding it back included sorting parcels manually and workers signing on by hand, and it had yet to remove old letter-sorting machines 'unneeded when letter volumes had halved since [peaking in] 2004'. Historic underinvestment in automation, legacy operations, a heavily unionised workforce and a watchful regulator made it difficult for Royal Mail to shift from letters to parcels, as its trading update noted: 'We are failing to adapt our business to fundamentally lower letter volumes and are holding on to outdated working practices and a delivery structure that no longer meets customer needs.' Meanwhile competitors cherry-picked the easy and most profitable parcel delivery traffic, leaving Royal Mail to fulfil the many unprofitable conditions of its *Universal Service Obligation* such as conveying post to the Outer Hebrides. RM also had to deliver large volumes of items coming in from China at well below cost, because China was still classed as a *developing country* for postal interchange purposes.

Royal Mail might have evoked more sympathy had it not recruited Rico Back as its chief executive with a lavish £6 million *golden hello* in 2018, and then agreed a £1.4 million exit package after he suddenly quit less than two years later, having reportedly been running the business from his luxury penthouse family home overlooking Lake Zurich in Switzerland since just after the first lockdown on 23 March. During Back's tenure, a string of disappointing trading updates had sent Royal Mail's shares crashing 66 per cent, and the firm lost its prized FTSE 100 status.

John Lewis undersold

John Lewis had for many years been the darling of UK shoppers with its ethos of trust, family feel, outstanding value, brilliant staff who would always go out of their way for you, and its 'never knowingly undersold' price promise, which meant that you didn't have to shop around so much to find the best price. It had also been an early adopter of online shopping, achieving impressive results as noted earlier. But at the start of 2020 JLP announced its third year of declining profits. Its results for the 2019/20 year ending 25 January revealed a profit of just £123 million, down from £370 million for 2016/17.

Andy Street had become managing director of John Lewis shortly before *The Great Recession* of 2008, having joined the firm as a trainee at their Brent Cross store in 1985. Street was applauded for his bold efforts to recover the brand's fortunes after the economic crash; during his tenure in the top job, he oversaw a 50 per cent increase in gross sales to over £4.4 billion. A notable triumph was Street's introduction of John Lewis' famous Christmas television adverts, which became an annual tradition of British culture, their appearance signalling the countdown to Christmas had begun. Instead of being a product catalogue like other retailers' Christmas adverts, John Lewis would spend £7 million a year lavishly telling memorable, heart-warming, emotional stories that focused on family values and trust. The adverts had a profoundly positive impact on the perception of the John Lewis brand, increased 'golden quarter' revenue, and also set the bar for all Christmas advertising.

But Street had also embarked on an aggressive store expansion plan, that would come to be seen as big miscalculation. In a decade, John Lewis almost doubled its department store portfolio, including building large shops in Cardiff, Leeds, Exeter, Oxford, York and Birmingham: The John Lewis Grand Central department store in Birmingham's Bull Ring, which cost £35 million, opened in 2015 and would close permanently less than five years later. Andy Street, who meanwhile had resigned from John Lewis in 2016 to become Mayor of the West Midlands – which includes Birmingham – commented at the time, 'We are astounded by the decision to press ahead with the closure of the Birmingham store,' describing it as a 'dreadful mistake'.

By late 2020 the John Lewis Partnership, including Waitrose, was in deep trouble, dragged down by the dire performance of the department store chain. All of its main rivals – Debenhams, House of Fraser and Beales – had fallen into administration.

John Lewis, the eponymous founder of the retail chain, had opened the first store in Oxford Street, London, in 1864. The John Lewis Partnership entered 2020 with fifty John Lewis & Partners shops plus one outlet and 337 Waitrose & Partners shops across the UK, along with the johnlewis.com and waitrose.com websites. Dame Sharon White, a career civil servant with no previous retail experience, became Chairman of the John Lewis Partnership on 4 February 2020, taking over from Sir Charlie Mayfield who had held the position since 2007. On doing so she signed a document promising to abide by JLP's constitution which set out the partnership's ultimate purpose as being the 'happiness of all its members, through worthwhile and satisfying employment in a successful business'. Also, that the retail group needed to make 'sufficient profit from its trading operations to sustain its commercial vitality' and 'distribute a share of those profits each year to its members'.

The following month Covid-19 forced John Lewis to temporarily close all its stores, from 24 March. JLP also announced a 'significant' reduction of its £500 million planned investment for the year. Over 2,000 John Lewis staff were already temporarily working in its Waitrose stores to cope with large grocery demands due to the Coronavirus outbreak. Bad news stalked John Lewis throughout the spring and summer as it was compelled to permanently close department stores and axe hundreds of jobs.

On 17 September Dame White had the unenviable task of reporting that JLP had crashed to a £635 million loss for the first half of its financial year. The bulk of the loss was a £500 million write-down due to a reassessment of the value of its department stores: the John Lewis website was handling 60 per cent of the company's sales, up from half that amount before the pandemic, therefore its department stores, as properties, were deemed to be worth far less than before. However, excluding one-off charges, the group made an underlying loss of just £55 million in the six months to the end of July, only slightly worse than a year earlier. Dame White described this as 'a creditable performance in the circumstances' and better than anticipated, adding, 'The pandemic has brought forward changes in consumer shopping habits which might have taken five years into five months.'

All the John Lewis department stores had been closed for months, sales for the period were down 10 per cent, to £1.9 billion, and its operating profits had almost halved.[95] The calamitous results put the company on track to make its first annual loss since the partnership was set up by John Spedan Lewis in 1920, and forced it to scrap its staff bonus for the first time in sixty-seven years, since 1953. In 2020 John Lewis closed eight department stores, announced more than 3,000 redundancies, and set out to remove a further £300 million of annual costs by restructuring its head-office operations. After ninety-five years, John Lewis also dropped its 'never knowingly undersold' price promise, an untenable policy in the internet age.

Arcadia's dystopia

Sir Philip Green, once known as the 'King of the High Street' was facing his biggest challenge yet in November 2020. The latest saga in the tycoon's colourful career saw his Arcadia retail empire teetering on the brink of collapse.

Arcadia had been one of the most talked-about brands on the high street, but long before Coronavirus, Green's brands were struggling against newer, online-only fashion retailers such as ASOS, Boohoo and its sibling Pretty Little Thing. Green was well known for being averse to electronic gadgets – in 2005 I asked him if he was ever going to start selling his clothes online. 'We've got a man working on that somewhere,' he replied. In its accounts for the year to 1 September 2018, Arcadia reported a £93.4 million pre-tax loss compared with a £164.6 million profit in the previous 12 months: the accounts also noted that sales dipped 4.5 per cent to £1.8 billion.

Arcadia fell into administration on 1 December 2020, the biggest retail failure of the Coronavirus pandemic, putting 13,000 jobs at risk. Arcadia Group stores by brand, including concessions in places such as Debenhams, were Dorothy Perkins (427 stores), Wallis (293), Burton (282), Miss Selfridge (191), Topshop (179), Outfit (98), Evans (88), and Topman (78) [Source: Savills, Local Data Company].[96] Administrators from Deloitte were brought in to handle the colossal demise.

The business had persuaded its landlords to lower its rents in June, but it was not enough to steady the ship. Adding to the uncertainty facing the thousands of Arcadia staff was an estimated £350 million hole in the company's pension fund, which had 10,000 members.

Green had earlier been branded as the 'unacceptable face of capitalism' for selling BHS – which was also burdened with a huge pension deficit – to former racing driver Dominic Chappell for £1 in 2015.

Green had first become a household name in 2000 when he bought BHS, then known as British Home Stores, for £200 million. BHS had once been one of Britain's best-known retailers, but by 2000 the department store chain was faded and dowdy. BHS remained the weakest link in Green's expanding portfolio of retail brands, and by 2015 was losing £1 million a week when Chappell's consortium, Retail Acquisitions, bought BHS for the token sum. In his year of ownership, Chappell was paid £2.5 million from BHS, mostly as fees for consultancy provided by another of his companies, the soon-to-be bankrupt finance firm Swiss Rock Limited. BHS went bust thirteen months later, in April 2016, with the closure of 164 stores, the loss of 11,000 jobs, and a £571 million pension deficit.

Back in 2005, Green's company had raised eyebrows when it paid a £1.2 billion dividend to the owner of Arcadia – his English wife, Christina Green. Since she was a resident of Monaco, she paid no tax in the UK. The following year, Green was made a Knight Bachelor in the 2006 Queen's Birthday Honours 'For services to the Retail Industry'.

Unsurprisingly, Sir Philip was heavily criticised for agreeing to the £1 BHS sale – he and his family had collected £586 million in dividends, rental payments and interest on loans during their fifteen-year ownership of BHS. In April 2016, Angela Eagle, then the shadow business secretary, said of the deal: 'in this situation, it appears this owner extracted hundreds of millions of pounds from the business and walked away to his favourite tax haven, leaving the Pension Protection Scheme to pick up the bill.' Green eventually agreed a *voluntary* £363 million cash settlement with the Pensions Regulator to plug the gap in the BHS pension scheme.

On 5 November 2020 Dominic Chappell was sentenced to six years in jail for tax evasion. A Southwark Crown Court jury found him guilty of failing to pay tax of around £584,000 on £2.2 million of income he received after buying BHS for £1. The court heard that the 53-year-old spent the money on two yachts, a Bentley and a holiday in the Bahamas. In sentencing, the judge said Chappell had engaged in a 'long and consistent course of conduct designed to cheat the revenue'. Adding, 'You are not of positive good character. Your offending occurs against a backdrop of successive bankruptcies.'

Sir Philip Nigel Ross Green prided himself on having worked his way to the top, despite having been born on 15 March 1952 into a well-to-do family in Croydon,

Surrey, that made its money from a series of petrol stations. He attended Carmel College, the now-closed exclusive boarding school, nicknamed the 'Jewish Eton', then left school aged 15 with no O-levels and began working on the forecourt of one of the petrol stations that his mother managed. He went on to learn business basics as an apprentice for a shoe importer before setting up his own first business importing and selling jeans at age 23.

'He had a very mixed track record of starting up companies, and closing them down, working with other people, falling out with people,' commented Stuart Lansley, the author of an unauthorised biography of Green. 'He travelled a lot, learning about the supply chain, but he certainly wasn't a household name.' Buying BHS in 2000 marked the moment when Green *arrived*. 'He borrowed very large sums of money, invested a little bit himself, and bought up companies that were relatively cheap, because they weren't doing very well,' Lansley explained. 'He turned them around, paying off his debt, and then tripling – quadrupling – the money he put in, in a matter of a couple of years. Two years later, he copied that model when he bought the retail empire Arcadia [for £840 million], which owned brands such as Burtons, Dorothy Perkins, Miss Selfridge, and of course, Topshop and Topman.'

Green is notoriously stubborn. His resistance to change, and insisting he knew best, was at the heart of Arcadia's demise. As many have said, he was not really a retailer: he was a shrewd financier – a money man.

Green's most ambitious move had been in 2004, when he put together £10 billion, much of it from investment banks, to make an offer for Marks & Spencer – an offer that even impressed Sir Stuart Rose, then his rival and boss of Marks & Spencer.

Arcadia Group's brands would have new owners early in 2021: ASOS bought Topshop, Topman and Miss Selfridge in a deal worth £330 million, closing seventy shops forever, and putting 2,500 jobs in jeopardy. Boohoo bought Dorothy Perkins, Wallis and Burton for £25 million, closing 214 shops and laying 2,450 jobs at risk.

Debenhams' demise

Debenhams had prospered for more than two centuries and been one of the largest and most historic store chains in the world. On 1 December 2020 Debenhams announced it was winding down after 242 years. All of its 124 department stores, which were rented rather than owned, would close and all 12,000 employees were likely to lose their jobs.

Debenhams had been struggling financially since before the financial crisis; it had been in administration since April, for the second time in two years. Successive restructurings had failed to find a winning formula. Hopes of a last-ditch rescue were finally crushed when the last remaining bidder, JD Sports, withdrew – Sir Philip Green's Arcadia had been Debenhams' biggest concession operator and when Arcadia went into administration the risks for JD became just too great. The company had already trimmed its store portfolio and cut about 6,500 jobs since May as it struggled to stay afloat.

Founded in 1778 as a single high-end draper's shop at 44 Wigmore Street in London's West End, Debenhams went on to become one of the largest retailers in the UK with, at one point, more than 200 large stores in eighteen countries.

But department stores were hard hit by changes in spending habits, their income down 17.2 per cent in 2020 according to Barclaycard. This, together with the pandemic and the loss of concessions such as Oasis, Warehouse, and the Arcadia brands that had a big footprint in Debenhams with sections set aside for their clothes, proved unsurvivable.

Department stores, the once formidable cornerstone of any successful high street or shopping centre, became an anachronism, their format facing an existential threat. Debenhams' protracted 'death spiral' ended in collapse, and the venerable brand being sold to the fifteen-year-old online upstart Boohoo for a knockdown £55 million just weeks later – but only the brand would survive: 12,000 jobs and all 166 shops would be lost, leaving a fourteen-million-square-foot hole in the high street.

Boohoo's crocodile tears

Boohoo, the self-proclaimed *young girl's fashion best friend*, and one of the fastest-growing UK companies, had a momentous yet mixed year in 2020. Fashion sales to its thirteen million active international customers remained strong and it snapped up a sextet of iconic but struggling British fashion brands – Oasis and Warehouse, and then Debenhams, Dorothy Perkins, Wallis and Burton as noted above. However, its shares almost halved in June over exposure of gross violations of UK work rules at its suppliers.

Boohoo's annual results to 29 February 2020 reported total revenue of £1,235 million, up 44 per cent on 2019. International sales had grown 51 per cent, while its UK trade was up 39 per cent. And despite the initial impact of Covid-19, Boohoo said its sales in the three months to May 2020 had risen by 45 per cent: worldwide sales were £368 million in the quarter to May 2020, while in the UK, which accounted for half of its total revenue, sales were up 30 per cent to £183 million. Eleven per cent of Britain's 18- to 24-year-olds had purchased something from Boohoo for themselves in the previous three months, according to polling firm YouGov in May. Boohoo predicted 'another year of strong profitable growth' which would outdo analysts' expectations.

Boohoo had been founded in 2006 by Mahmud Kamani and his business partner Carol Kane, who previously supplied high street rivals such as Primark and New Look. With Kamani and Kane as joint chief executives, the online-only fashion retailer set out to sell own-brand clothing, shoes, accessories and beauty products aimed at 16- to 24-year-olds.

The Kamani family behind Boohoo became one of the richest in the country in March 2014 after selling a £240 million stake in the online business, which was valued at £560 million when the company floated, debuting on AIM to become a PLC. The Manchester-based Kamani family still owned 44 per cent of the company after the listing. Kane said at the time that Boohoo was differentiated from the likes of ASOS as all of its clothes were own brand and its price points were lower, with an average price tag of £17. 'Our customer is 16–24 years old and at the value end of the market. When we worked in the high street, we were the go-to fashion team,' she said.

Boohoo's business model, known as *test and repeat*, was built around market testing a wide range of items on its site, then reordering those proving popular. By manufacturing half of its goods in the UK, it could offer turnaround times for new styles of about four to six weeks – much faster than for goods shipped from, say, the Far East.

Boohoo launched *BoohooMAN* in 2016. That December it acquired a majority stake in *PrettyLittleThing*, with Boohoo purchasing a 66 per cent of the business at a cost of £3.3 million, the existing management team retaining the remaining shares. PrettyLittleThing had been co-founded in 2012 by Umar Kamani and his brother Adam Kamani.

Nasty Gal, a US retailer based in Los Angeles, was acquired by Boohoo in 2017 out of Chapter 11 bankruptcy for $20 million (£15 million). Nasty Gal had been founded in 2012 by Sophia Amoruso who is widely credited with popularising the term 'girl boss'. Previously, Nasty Gal had been named 'fastest growing retailer' by *Inc.* magazine, in 2012.

2019 saw Boohoo group expanding its target age range upwards from 16- to 40-year-olds as it added brands Coach and Karen Millen, the latter aimed at *driven and career-minded women in their 30s and 40s*. Boohoo also acquired MissPap in March 2019: John Lyttle, CEO of Boohoo Group plc said at the time: 'MissPap is a brand with great potential which can leverage the group's expertise.'

Boohoo explained that its social media strategy and 'flexible supply chain', largely based in the UK, were what drove its growth, allowing the quick turnaround and promotion of what some were criticising as 'fast fashion' items. More than half of Boohoo's 36,000 garments were made in the UK, especially Leicester, London and Manchester. It was reported that Boohoo bought 75–80 per cent of all the clothing made in Leicester after other retailers such as ASOS reduced the amount they sourced from the city over concerns about working conditions. Customers could order items from Boohoo up to midnight for next-day delivery, including on Sunday.

The term *fast-fashion* is used to describe companies selling clothes very cheaply – clothes that are often disposed of quickly as trends change, at a cost to those making the clothes for very low wages and causing pollution and waste. Boohoo's low prices and rapid turnover drew in customers wanting to continually update their wardrobe – something that became more important in the age of Instagram. 'There's this perception on social media that you always have to be changing your outfit, so of course to do that, you buy fast fashion,' commented Barbara Adeniken, a London-based social media pundit.

Rather than rely on traditional marketing, Boohoo focused on winning over young women, in particular, via Instagram influencers, bloggers, student campus tours and events such as shoots with reality TV contestants from the hit summer show *Love Island*. Boohoo claimed to have ten million social media followers worldwide at the end of 2020 – including over seven million Instagram and three million Facebook followers.

Poor working conditions and illegal wages had become issues of great concern in the UK's garment industry, and following *Sunday Times*' allegations about one of its supplier's failures to protect workers in Leicester, Boohoo's shares lost 46 per cent of their value by mid-July 2020.

The *Sunday Times* report revealed that Boohoo brand, Nasty Gal, was paying its workers at Jaswal Fashions as little as £3.50 an hour, far less than the minimum wage of £8.72 for over 25-year-olds. Others had reported Boohoo suppliers for breaching social distancing guidelines and forcing furloughed workers to come to work. An investigation by *The Guardian* in December 2020 traced Boohoo's supply chain to factories in Pakistan where workers claimed they were being paid as little as £47 pounds per month and ordered to work shifts of as long as twenty-four hours without receiving full overtime pay.

Philip Dunne expressed incredulity that on 8 July 2020 Boohoo said publicly it was 'shocked and appalled' by allegations of illegal working practices at one of its suppliers: a year earlier the Environmental Audit Committee, of which Dunne was chairman, had questioned Boohoo co-founder Carol Kane about exactly such malpractice in Leicester. 'It is shameful that it took a pandemic and the ensuing outrage about working practices in their supply chain for Boohoo finally to be taken to task for turning a blind eye,' Dunne said.

But investors continued to place their bets on Boohoo. Its share price had risen more than 800 per cent in five years, including a 12 per cent increase in 2020. As the year closed, the fifteen-year-old Boohoo set about adding the once mighty Arcadia brands to its vast collection, which would soon encompass Pretty Little Thing, NastyGal, Karen Millen, Oasis, Warehouse, Debenhams, Dorothy Perkins, Wallis and Burton.

ASOS: not a retailer – a destination

'TO BE THE #1 DESTINATION FOR FASHION-LOVING 20-SOMETHINGS WORLDWIDE'

The ASOS vision

ASOS had a strong 2020, adding millions of fashion-loving 20-something customers from around the world. Its profits quadrupled to £142.1 million in the year to 31 August, up from £33.1 million in the same period the previous year, as it traded through Coronavirus lockdowns with store-based rivals closed. Earnings benefitted from cost-cutting, and buyers returning fewer items amid the pandemic. Sales rose 19 per cent to £3.26 billion while customer numbers jumped up 3.1 million to 23.4 million.

Shares in ASOS, which had doubled over the year, closed in early October at 5,378 pence, valuing the business at £5.4 billion – more than twice the market capitalisation of Marks & Spencer, Britain's biggest clothing retailer by sales.

In the four months to 31 December, ASOS' total retail revenue climbed by 23 per cent to just over £1.3 billion after UK retail sales increased by 36 per cent to £554 million. International sales growth was also strong with sales up 18 per cent, 13 per cent and 15 per cent in the EU, US and the rest of the world respectively.

Nick Beighton, ASOS' chief executive, commented: 'We are really pleased with the strong performance we have delivered, which is testament to both the strength of our multi-brand model and the hard work of our people.' During this period, the retailer's active customer base increased by 1.1 million to 24.5 million.

ASOS said the growth offset the impact of existing customers having fewer occasion-led reasons to shop due to the Coronavirus pandemic. But it also said it was worried about unemployment hitting young customers, singling out those in their twenties, for whom life was unlikely to return to normal for 'quite some time'.

Within weeks of the year's end the self-proclaimed *fashion destination* would, for a paltry £330 million, acquire the collapsed Arcadia's premium brands – Topshop, Topman, Miss Selfridge and the athleisure brand HIIT.

Would the ASOS deal for Arcadia's brands impact on the clothes Britons wear due to its migrating large numbers of fashion decisions from stores to the internet? *The Guardian*'s associate fashion editor, Jess Cartner, argued that it would, by prompting people to buy clothes that were more brightly coloured, stretchier and made of cheaper fabrics: bright colours, because these grab attention onscreen, and stretchier, because it's easier to visualise what these hit-or-miss buys will look like when worn, as opposed to tailored clothes which rely more on fit. And as quality fabrics don't matter so much when they can't be felt, cheaper options were likely to prevail.

Amazon: king of the e-jungle

> *'[Amazon] is now the key enabler for most of
> Western society during this crisis'*
> Christopher Rossbach, Chief Investment Officer, J. Stern & Co., July 2020

The biggest retail winner from the Covid-19 pandemic was Amazon. Its global net sales in 2020 rocketed 38 per cent to $386 billion: $263.5 from the US, Amazon's main market, $29.6 billion from Germany, its second largest market, and $26.5 billion from the UK, which ranked third, as reported by Statista.

Amazon's UK online sales climbed 24 per cent in the first quarter, the fastest pace in four years, and Bezos was quick to invest heavily to grab market share while lockdowns closed most traditional shopping outlets. Antitrust regulators were already investigating the company, but Amazon was now deemed in the pandemic to be an essential distribution channel for society – Bezos compared his workers to Covid-19 first responders – and gambled that strengthening Amazon's position would be unlikely to provoke a backlash.

> *'Brands are absolutely terrified to be reliant on Amazon right now,
> but they have no other choice. Amazon has been the one place where
> brands in all categories have said we have to double down'*
> Josh Cowan, account manager at Amazon marketing experts Streiff Marketing and a
> former Amazon.com buyer, May 2020

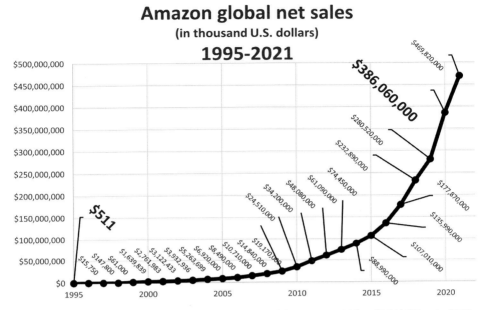

Amazon global net sales
(in thousand U.S. dollars)
1995-2021

Figure 52: Amazon's annual net sales increased from $511,000 in 1995 to $386 billion in 2020. (*Source: Amazon.com Annual Reports / James Roper Archive*)

'Amazon wins business from reluctant brands after Coronavirus closes stores,' the *Seattle Times* reported on 5 May 2020.[97] Before the pandemic, some 45 per cent of brands didn't sell products on Amazon at all, according to a survey conducted by Feedvisor, a seller of pricing software used by online retailers. And more than one-third said they didn't need Amazon to reach customers. Many brands and wholesalers kept Amazon at arm's length because they were concerned it would squeeze their margins, collect precious customer data, and copy their most popular products. Brands also wanted to avoid alienating their brick-and-mortar channel partners by selling via the world's largest online retailer, but many of these stores were now closed, and even the stores that were open had only meagre sales. Amazon was suddenly attracting a broad range of new vendors as they were forced to overcome their aversion to trading through its marketplace. And given that many of the traditional retail outlets were not expected to survive the pandemic, it seemed likely that Amazon would hang on to much of the new business.

Amazon announced that by the end of the year it would create 10,000 new UK jobs, paying a minimum of £9.50 per hour, to meet growing demand.[98] This would take its total permanent UK workforce to more than 40,000, quadrupling its UK staff in five years. It was additionally recruiting 20,000 seasonal posts for the festive season. Worldwide, Amazon's full-time staff numbers were approaching 800,000 in 2020.

At a time when many people were losing their jobs, announcements of thousands of new posts were welcome. But the rise and rise of Amazon had been mirrored by the decline and recent fall in overall retail employment. As Amazon was adding

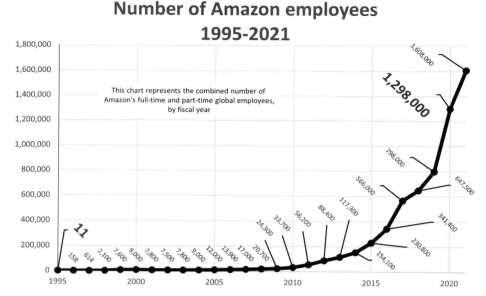

Figure 53: Amazon's staff numbers increased from eleven in 1995 to 1,298,000 in 2020. Source: Amazon.com Annual Reports / James Roper Archive.

30,000 jobs in five years, the ONS advised that there were 106,000 fewer total retail jobs over the same period which didn't even include the Covid impact, the BBC's Simon Jack reported.

Despite spending billions of dollars gearing itself up to operate through the Coronavirus crisis, Amazon still delivered a huge increase in profits during the second quarter of 2020. Amazon recorded global sales of nearly $89 billion for its Q2 ending 30 June – up 40 per cent, and working out at more than $10,000 a second, 24 hours a day. Net income for the three months was $5.2 billion, double what it earned the previous year, then an all-time quarterly record, and far higher than analyst's expectations. Amazon shares climbed by 5 per cent, valuing the business at $1.5 trillion.[99]

*   *   *

Amazon had charted its path to retail domination through efforts to make annual subscription to Amazon Prime a must-have for every household. First introduced in 2005 as a premium shipping service, by January 2020 Prime had signed up more than 150 million subscribers who were enticed by its free / fast delivery, streaming music and video, and ever-growing catalogue of other services.

When Bezos had launched Prime in 2005, Walmart generated more in profits than Amazon did in sales. Fifteen years later, Amazon was worth three times as much as Walmart, with a market capitalisation rivalled only by Apple, even though Walmart's annual sales of $514 billion in 2019 were almost twice the $280 billion generated by its online rival.

Wall Street assigned the massive premium to Amazon because of its five-year growth rate of 22 per cent and its domination online, already accounting for 40 per cent of all e-retail in America before Covid-19 arrived. Walmart ranked a distant second with just 5 per cent.[100]

It had taken seven years for Amazon to generate its first profit – a modest $5 million in the fourth quarter of 2001, on revenues of a little over $1 billion. In 2019, the company made $10 billion in profits, powered by its lucrative cloud computing business, up sharply from $3 billion the year before, and amply exceeding Walmart's $6.7 billion bottom line.

* * *

Amazon was charged with abusing its market power and EU competition rules on 10 November 2020. The European Commission accused Amazon of using its dominant position by using data on third-party sellers that traded on its marketplace to gain advantage in Germany and France. It also launched a fresh investigation into possible preferential treatment of sellers that used Amazon logistics and delivery services.

Amazon was not the only huge tech-sector company in the crosshairs of government enforcers looking to reign them in – or even to break up the giants whose technologies had disrupted retail ecosystems and much else. While the tech companies differed by region, the issue was global. Chinese authorities had concerns about the dominance of Alibaba and JD.com which together accounted for roughly three-quarters of Chinese e-commerce. As of September 2020, Alibaba had 881 million mobile monthly active users – more than half of China's population. US authorities were taking action against Google's dominance in the biggest antitrust suit in the US since a case against Microsoft in the late 1990s. The US Department of Justice described Google as a 'monopoly gatekeeper of the internet': Google had a 92 per cent share of the global search market, while Microsoft Bing ranked second with less than 3 per cent. Governments everywhere had concerns about Facebook, by far the biggest of the social media networks with 2.74 billion active users – a third of the world population – and reaching 59 per cent of everyone using social networks. Many Democrats – the US political party that was about to regain power – harboured grievances with Facebook dating back to 2016, when it failed to stop Russian hackers from using the platform to covertly influence the presidential election in Donald Trump's favour.

Google and Facebook accounted for around 60 per cent of total digital advertising spending in 2020, and digital accounted for around half of global ad spending.

Summing-up the 2010s

The 2010s was the decade when digital rose to dominate retail. Everyone had a mobile phone, i.e. a shopping trolley in their pocket or handbag, and millions automatically reached for theirs when they wanted to buy anything. For many, queueing at tills was either a thing of the past or something they had never experienced.

The UK led the e-retail world, especially in cross-border trade where its fashion icons were blazing the trail. Amazon and Zalando invested fortunes developing overwhelming vending superpowers – the ultimate retail weapons – against which resistance was largely futile.

An arms race emerged between sellers using 'big data' to corner customers, and internauts who were having none of it. The Twitterati and Blogger communities were accused of hijacking journalism with their opinionated take on news, while slacktivists 'tweeted', 'shared' and 'liked' their countless unbridled opinions on global warming, Donald Trump, China's vast economic initiatives, and anything else that fleeted across their transitory attention spans.

E-retail made steady progress throughout the decade, but when Covid arrived in 2020, closing off most other means of buying stuff, online shopping suddenly became the go-to marketplace – society's essential distribution channel. While the Covid-19 pandemic may have been a passing phase, it superaccelerated the take-up of e-commerce, and recast permanently the retail landscape.

Part IV

Buckle Up

Blunders and Worse

> *'There's no chance that the iPhone is going
> to get any significant market share'*
> Steve Ballmer, CEO, Microsoft, 2007

E-commerce has always been the source of a torrent of bungles, mix-ups, unexpected outcomes, errors of judgement, undesired consequences, failures, missed opportunities, outright catastrophes, crime and mischief. Here are some classics.

In e-commerce's formative phase, many mishaps were to do with unrealistic expectations, technobabble, and people backing soon to be obsolete technology – like the laserdiscs mentioned earlier. Systems became overloaded, as when Virgin Trains' 50 per cent ticket price offer on 5 February 2001 crashed their website for two days. Many foul-ups were down to simple operator error, aka *finger trouble*, and those pesky roving decimal points. Typical of this batch of bungles were the March 2001 glitch in Hilton's central reservation system that enabled several dozen travellers to book Hilton Mexico City Airport Hotel rooms for a nightly room rate of zero, and United Airlines' numerous snafus in 2001 that it initially refused to honour whereby it sold thousands of flights at either random or giveaway prices – 123 lucky travellers purchased round trips from Chicago to Bombay for $140 instead of the normal price of $4,000.

Lloyds TSB that year sent a mail shot to 4,000 of its customers including names, addresses and credit card details. Unfortunately, many of the letters had the personal details of customers living at other addresses. The mistake happened during a promotion to sell customers insurance against fraud.

Autobytel posted the car deal of the decade when on 22 April 2002 it offered a Hyundai car for sale at −**£91,460** (a minus figure), advertising that they would pay customers munificently to take these vehicles away. And despite initial denials, Compaq Australia eventually admitted that it did in fact process customers payments of just one cent for laptops on 9 May.

On 19 March 2003 the Amazon.co.uk website was crippled by demand for HP iPaq Pocket PDAs that it accidentally offered for sale for £7.32 instead of the usual price of between £299 and £330. That same month, Lastminute.com charged one client £27 million for a four-night hotel stay in Venice: the shocked holidaymaker commented, 'I only wanted to book one room, not to buy the whole hotel.'

US Airways became the low-cost carrier of all time over a weekend in April 2005 when it started selling international flights to some US cities for $1.86 plus fees. Meanwhile in the UK, one happy Homebase customer bought five Bush 28-inch televisions in August 2005 *'as they were so cheap'* at only £0.49 each: the next day he received an email confirming the order, and the £2,45 was taken out of his account – however, a follow-up letter advised that Homebase were sorry but could not complete the order.

Hamleys toyshop faced a retailer's nightmare in December 2006 – a shortage of toys for sale at Christmas – after a website loophole allowed customers to claim a cumulative 60 per cent discount. 'It's like the Vikings have been to Hamleys,' reported one shopper. 'If you get on to their site, it's been emptied and pillaged.'

Mobile phone giant O2 reportedly lost £500,000 in July 2007 after an internet blunder forced them to give away over 3,000 handsets. Customers who bought a £149 Samsung X830 phone from O2's website were also offered a free year-long movie pass. But confusion over the wording in India, where the webpages were put together, led to customers being offered the phone for free as well.

'There's just not that many videos I want to watch'

Steve Chen, CTO and co-founder of YouTube expressing concerns about his company's long-term viability, 2005

Blockbuster no doubt later questioned its decision to turn down an offer from Netflix to buy their company for $50 million in 2000 because the CEO was not interested in such a 'very small niche business' that was losing money. Blockbuster Video, founded in 1985, was an iconic brand in home video and games rental services that had 9,094 stores at its peak in 2004. Blockbuster failed to transition to the digital marketplace and filed for bankruptcy in 2010, by which time Netflix had twenty million subscribers and $2.16 billion in revenue.

Kodak's Click-Ups

As well as making bumbling mistakes, many organisations missed conspicuously obvious commercial opportunities – Kodak did both. In 2002, Kodak's lack of attention to its e-retail operation was exposed when gross mishandling of what started out as the simple miskeying of a camera price for its UK website turned into a legendary disaster. A decade later, in 2012, having been for a century the world's dominant photographic film and equipment company, Kodak was forced into bankruptcy: Kodak had simply failed to keep up with the digital revolution, despite being well aware of its implications and having had many opportunities to be its vanguard.

The first prototype of a digital camera was created in 1975 by a Kodak engineer, Steve Sasson. Kodak later invested billions of dollars in technology to take digital pictures, yet it resisted developing digital cameras for the mass market for fear of damaging its core film business. Kodak also made a prescient purchase in 2001 when it acquired a photo sharing site called Ofoto; however, instead of spearheading the online photo revolution, it tried to use Ofoto to get more people to print digital images. Kodak's hesitancy to fully embrace the transition to digital, for fear of cannibalising its strongest product lines, ultimately led to its demise.

Kodak's UK e-retail debacle began on New Year's Eve 2001, when Kodak prepared a *January Sale* offer for its shop@kodak website. What was intended to have been a 10 per cent discount on £329 package – a DX3700 digital camera together with a 32mb memory card plus inkjet paper – was incorrectly posted at a price of £100 plus a delivery charge of £4.99.

A handful of consumers saw the ad and placed orders. The Kodak site issued automatic email responses, confirming receipt and acceptance of the orders. It wasn't long before Kodak staff spotted the error and contacted those who had placed orders, advising them that the offer had been made in error and that their orders would not be fulfilled.

One of those consumers took umbrage at the way Kodak had handled the situation and placed a brief notice on a newsgroup. Two things about this posting were significant: firstly, the timing – it was deliberately posted late on a Friday afternoon which reduced the likelihood of Kodak being alert to any short-term response; secondly, the URL given was a direct link to the page containing the £100 offer – not to the front of the Kodak site where visitors would normally go, and via which one would only see the corrected price tag. The link went directly to the cached page – known as 'deep linking'. Users were astonished to find that the page

Figure 54: On New Year's Eve 2001, Kodak's website presented a mispriced 'January Sale' offer. Thousands of orders were placed for £100 cameras [not £329] before Kodak finally took down the original order page. (*Source: James Roper Archive*)

was still there and accessible, and that it took orders which were responded to with 'acceptance' emails. It was at this point that it all went horribly wrong for Kodak.

Word spread by email like wildfire, and 'some thousands' of orders were placed for the £100 cameras during the next few days before Kodak realised it still had a problem and finally took down the original order page.

Many companies over the years had found themselves in similar predicaments, and experience showed that the best way to deal with the problem was to acknowledge the fault and sell the 'readily available stock' at the advertised price. Kodak did not do this. Instead, Kodak issued an email statement to those who had placed orders flatly refusing to fulfil them. This seriously irritated many of the consumers involved. The situation was not helped by the fact that one of the phone numbers given on the email was wrong, while the only one given that worked didn't for long – it was a mobile phone, of which the battery soon ran out and its owner did not have a charger with her.

Before long, a number of the exasperated would-be customers approached the press, and a media merry-go-round began involving, amongst many others, BBC's *News*, *Watchdog* and *Working Lunch*, the *Financial Times*, *The Guardian*, the *Mirror*, *The Independent*, *The Sun*, Silicon.com and *The Register*.

At around the same time, one of the IT-savvy shoppers whose order had been bounced, Dominic Watts, looked at available domain names that might be relevant to the issue, and bought the first one he saw – kodakcamera.co.uk – for £6.79. What started as 'a bit of a laugh' for the father of three from Croydon, quickly spiralled into something altogether more serious. And as one of the 5,000 people who had tried to buy the camera, Dom admitted: 'This Kodak thing enraged me.' His Kodak camera protest website became the focus for a month-long campaign by consumers in search of fair play.

Kodak eventually caved in to pressure on 31 January 2002, agreeing to honour its £100 deal *'to all of our customers who ordered the camera and accessories'* – even though it maintained that the price tag was a mistake. The fiasco had already cost Kodak weeks of negative media publicity and at least £2 million, with many further compensation claims in the pipeline from people who had given up and bought other cameras.

After filing for bankruptcy in 2012, Kodak jettisoned many of the businesses that had made it famous – such as its personal film business, that included 105,000 photo kiosks, and its photographic paper operations – and re-emerged in 2013 as a much smaller, consolidated company focused on serving commercial customers.

* * *

But the biggest missed e-commerce opportunities are indubitably Yahoo! and Excite's failures to acquire Google when they had the chance in the late 1990s.

Google co-founders Larry Page and Sergey Brin approached Yahoo! in 1998, offering to sell their PageRank system for $1 million, as the duo wanted to focus on their studies at Stanford. Yahoo!, which then defined the internet, showed no interest as it wanted users to spend more time on its own platform, not less. In fact,

Yahoo! did not want users to leave its platform at all: as well as having directories that were designed to answer questions, it also let users view email, shop and even play games – which seemed to work well for them at that time.

PageRank, named after Larry Page, is an algorithm designed by Brin and Page that ranks websites in order of relevance: its aim is to get users to the best results fast. But these were the days before the online world realised the importance of third-party online advertising revenue – before Google built its own pay-per click service called AdWords and used PageRank to power its success.

The following year, Excite, one of the original internet portals, also turned down the chance to acquire Google for petty cash. In early 1999 Brin and Page were still willing to sell PageRank and approached Excite's CEO, George Bell, who rejected their asking price. One of Bell's colleagues then talked the pair down to $750,000, but Bell rejected that too. Whoops. In 2020 Google, aka Alphabet, was worth $1 trillion.

Data breaches

'To err is human; to really screw things up you need a computer'

Anonymous

People have always fouled things up, but computers do it much faster and with a great deal more efficiency. And when computers become networked this exponentially accelerates the potential for unexpected digital outcomes, mischief and crime, especially when it comes to the administration of the internet age's 'new oil' – data.[101]

As soon as the internet was formed it began to produce vast quantities of data as a by-product of what it was and did. Exploitation of this data soon spawned large, profitable businesses, such as Yahoo!, Amazon and Google. Everyone became increasingly reliant on data, so you might have expected its custodians to appropriately cherish, secure and protect these valuable if intangible assets. Most didn't. By the turn of the millennium tens of thousands of organisations were being hit with data breaches – relentless waves of security calamities that just kept on coming. Between January 2005 and May 2008, there were 227,052,199 individual records containing sensitive information involved in security breaches in the US alone, according to the Privacy Rights Clearinghouse.

Data breaches are incidents in which sensitive, protected or confidential data is potentially viewed, stolen or used by an unauthorised individual. There have been data breaches for as long as people and organisations have kept records and held personal information, but when computers and the internet came along, the ways in which data could end up in the wrong hands multiplied. Some data breaches are unintentional – people can accidentally send data to the wrong email or *share address*, servers can be misconfigured, files may not be properly deleted or disposed of. Negligence and errors account for 17 per cent of breaches according to Verizon's 2018 Data Breach Investigation Report.[102] But the report also advised that most breaches are deliberate and financially motivated, with 28 per cent involving insiders.

Devices such as laptops, smartphones and data storage media can be lost or stolen. However, the most common and damaging breaches are cyber-attacks, where hackers use ransomware, malware, phishing, social engineering, skimming or other related techniques to gain access to sensitive information, or blackmail victims.

In late 2002, Tower Records exposed the personal data of millions of US and UK shoppers at its online store, including email addresses, phone numbers, home addresses and past purchases. A site redesign glitch allowed anyone to view its database of customer orders dating back to 1996. More than three million such records were exposed.

In 2003, AOL, then the world's biggest internet service provider, had a list of its ninety-two million customer account 'screen names', email addresses, zip codes and telephone numbers stolen by one of its software engineers, 25-year-old Jason Smathers, who sold it for $28,000 to a spammer. The spammer, Sean Dunway, of Las Vegas, NV, used the list to promote his own internet gambling business, then sold it on to other spammers for $52,000. These spammers collectively sent out some seven billion unsolicited emails. 'I know I've done something very wrong,' a contrite Smathers told the judge as he was sentenced to a year and three months in prison.

2005 was the year when data breaches began to really boom, and witnessed the first breach to compromise more than one million credit cards. In a cyber break-in of the company's database, DSW Shoe Warehouse of Columbus, Ohio, had 1.4 million records stolen, including card numbers and account names, driver's licence and bank account numbers. The Federal Trade Commission – whose own chairwoman, Deborah Platt Majoras, had been one of the victims – charged that DSW unnecessarily held on to sensitive customer data that it no longer needed, and stored the information in multiple files, increasing the risks to consumers. Regulators also accused DSW of failing to use adequate or readily available security measures to limit access to its computer networks and to detect break-ins. Thousands of organisations would have similar charges levied at them in the following years.

From individuals reusing woefully deficient passwords such as *12345*, *password* or *letmein*, to the US Military sending back a defective hard drive for recycling that contained unencrypted records of veterans' details including millions of Social Security numbers dating back to 1972, it seemed that nobody was immune to data imprudence. The many eminent casualties included one of the world's largest credit bureaux, Equifax, the European Central Bank, Facebook, Twitter, JP Morgan Chase and Uber. The NHS admitted losing a laptop containing up to 8.6 million patient records in 2011 – the breach having then been unreported for three weeks. Even the quintessential digital security vendor, RSA Security, had its *SecureID* authentication tokens compromised in March 2011, when a cyberattack stole an estimated forty million employee records.

One landmark incident, in March 2008, involved a leading US payments processing company, Heartland Payment Systems, which was then handling 100 million credit card payments per month for more than 175,000 mostly small- to mid-sized retailers. An SQL injection of spyware exposed 134 million credit cards from accounts it had processed. The breach was discovered in January 2009 when Visa and Mastercard notified Heartland of suspicious transactions. The company paid out an estimated $145 million in compensation for fraudulent payments and was barred from processing the payments of major credit cards until May 2009 due to being deemed out of compliance with the Payment Card Industry Data Security Standard (PCI DSS). The vulnerability to SQL injection was well understood and security analysts had warned retailers about it for several years, yet this remained the most common form of attack against websites at the time.

Sony's PlayStation Network had seventy-seven million accounts hacked on 20 April 2011, including twelve million with unencrypted credit card numbers, in what was viewed as the worst gaming community breach of all time. The PlayStation Network site was down for a month, with estimated losses of $171 million. Hackers were able to access full names, passwords, email addresses, home addresses, purchase history, credit card numbers and download login details. In 2014, Sony agreed to pay a preliminary $15 million settlement in a class action lawsuit over the breach.

eBay had a cyberattack in May 2014 that exposed names, addresses, dates of birth and encrypted passwords of all of its 145 million users. eBay reported that hackers had accessed the company systems using the credentials of three corporate employees and had complete insider access for 229 days. It asked customers to change their passwords, but advised that financial information, such as credit card numbers, was not compromised as these were stored separately. The breach had little impact on revenues which continued to rise in line with analyst's expectations.

Marriott International suffered a huge breach when data on some 500 million customers was stolen by cyberthieves in 2014–18. Marriott's acquisition of Starwood Hotels in 2016 had brought with it a band of data thieves who remained in the system and undiscovered till September 2018. Personal data stolen included passport numbers, credit card numbers and their expiration dates.

Yahoo!, which had been founded by Stanford University students Jerry Yang and David Filo in January 1994 to soon become the first popular directory and online search engine on the web, suffered the world's biggest data breach to date in 2013/14 which impacted all of its three billion user accounts, though this only came to light in late 2016 during negotiations for Yahoo! to sell itself to Verizon. It was ultimately revealed that groups of hackers at various times had accessed names, dates of birth, email addresses, phone numbers, passwords, security questions and answers. Four men, including employees of the Russian Federal Security Service, were indicted by the US for their involvement in the attack. Yahoo! had been the dominant internet company in the 1990s with its value peaking in 2000 at $100 billion. The breaches cost Yahoo! an estimated $350 million of its sale price to Verizon – $4.48 billion.

The UK government plumbed a new and possibly all-time low when the Cabinet Office accidentally published the wrong 2020 New Year Honours list containing more than 1,000 recipients full house and email addresses. The 1,097 honours recipients included high-profile celebrities, such as Sir Elton John and cricketer Ben Stokes, senior police officers and politicians, and the former director of public prosecutions, Alison Saunders. Meanwhile, government ministers were announcing that they were set to place tech companies – such as Facebook and Google – under a statutory *duty of care*, whereby senior executives would personally face fines and the threat of criminal prosecution for failing to protect people who use their services.

The European Commission: Cookies, anyone? GDPR?

Q: *How do you justify passing laws that it is not technically possible to comply with?* James Roper, CEO, IMRG, 2007
A: *That's your problem.* Viviane Reding, European Commission Vice-President & Commissioner for Justice, Fundamental Rights and Citizenship (formerly Commissioner for Information Society and Media)

The EC tried to ban cookies, having failed to understand what they are or do. (Cookies are text files that every website uses to help organise and store browsing information, authentication, preferences and much more – some websites, including the EC's, use hundreds of cookies.) Instead, the EC introduced the so-called *cookie law* (the e-Privacy Directive) which forced all websites in the EU to gain *informed consent* before they could store or retrieve information on a visitor's web-enabled device. That is, all websites except the EC institutions' own, which they originally proposed would remain at liberty to track your browsing activity without informing you. As these cookie consent dialogues took vastly different shapes, the average user wouldn't be able to tell an 'Allow cookies? Yes/No' dialogue from a 'Install malware? Yes/No' one.

The well-meaning but breathtakingly stupid cookie law condemned everyone for years to an impaired internet, a nightmare of *I accept* pop-ups that people almost immediately became conditioned to dismiss without reading, frustration, much wasted time, a huge cost to the online industry – and zero improvement to privacy.

I attended a FEVAD dinner in Paris in 2007 at which the guest of honour was Viviane Reding, European Commission Vice-President & Commissioner for Justice, Fundamental Rights and Citizenship (formerly Commissioner for Information Society and Media). FEVAD is the French e-commerce industry association, and at the time Reding was planning *further enhancements* to the cookie law. I asked Commissioner Reding how she could justify passing laws that it was not technically possible to comply with? 'That's your problem', she replied, which neatly characterised the relationship between the European Commission and the e-commerce industry.

By then I had had many years' experience of liaising with the EC, representing the UK in Brussels on e-commerce matters, speaking at or chairing EC events, battling against its constant outpouring of absurd ideas. On several occasions I had served as the lead reviewer of the EC's international ESPRIT (European Strategic Programme for Research and Development in Information Technology) programmes – one of these being *Virtual Reality Shop*, which kicked off in 1997, decades before its ambitions would become technically feasible.

The EC had always struggled with e-commerce, rarely understanding the technology it regulates, and seemingly incapable of providing constructive leadership or competent administration. The EC posed a major threat to Europe's digital future.

It wasn't that there was no need for new legislation, good internet governance and enforcement – clearly there was, as the catalogue of crimes, incompetence and delinquency we have looked at earlier testifies. Modern technology had opened up pathways to violate privacy on a scale grander than previous generations could even have imagined. But European e-retailers were already at a disadvantage compared with their US competitors in having less access to venture capital and addressing smaller markets with language, currency and idiosyncratic legislative challenges. Instead of assisting, the EC was hobbling European websites and slapping intrusive warnings all over them. EC-imposed legislative burdens, red tape, tax and logistical complexities killed many SMEs and start-ups.

Thousands of other European merchants opted to mitigate the strain by trading via marketplaces, such as eBay, Amazon, Etsy, Rakuten, etc., for the simplicity, marketing and protection they offered, handing yet more profit to foreign businesses. It also gave these marketplace hosts crucial insight into what products were selling most quickly and profitably – aka trade secrets – information that they could then use to commandeer the most rewarding trade.

The EU data legislation evolved over time, with each iteration more draconian than the last. It started out with a Data Protection Directive in 1995, which created a country-by-country patchwork of data laws. In 2002 the ePrivacy Directive was introduced to regulate the use of online tracking technologies, and from 2013 compliance became mandatory. The whole lot was replaced in May 2018 by the eighty-eight-page General Data Protection Regulation (GDPR) that toughened up everything with more enforcement, sanctions and fines.

GDPR requires organisations to safeguard personal data and uphold the privacy rights of anyone in EU territory. It includes seven principles of data protection that must be implemented and eight privacy rights that must be facilitated.

But GDPR has been roundly criticised as a case of regulatory failure: it impairs user browsing experience; it is ineffective in increasing the awareness about online tracking; it is also a failure from the enforcement perspective as none of the policing agencies has the financial or organisational muscle to take on the powerful tech companies most likely to require their attention.

These are just a handful of the jaw-dropping confusions, missed opportunities, crimes and absurdities that e-commerce has presented so far. Many more will surely follow.

Unruled e-Britannia

> '...we must be utterly mad, as a country, to leave it to the
> Americans to make money from a great British invention'
>
> Boris Johnson, Mayor of London, 2010 (speaking of the Harry Potter novels)

The Elector of the Rhineland Palatinate declined to invest in Johan Gutenberg's unpropitious printing machine because there was no demand for printed copies of manuscripts due to the low literacy rate (as well as the unacceptable threat to the large workforce of monks who copied manuscripts).

Britain seemed similarly ambivalent about monetising its technological inventions and other crucial innovations that had made e-commerce possible – the first modern computer, the microchip, the World Wide Web, HTTP, the first web browser, supercomputers, laptop computers, the RSA cipher, the Linux kernel, fibre optics, liquid crystal displays, cash machines, micro TVs, teletext, SMS text messaging, touchpads, the MP3 audio player, ARM architecture that powers every smartphone....[103] As trade moved online, the British government lounged on the sidelines, occasionally administering suggestions.

None of the world's governments had a great track record with the digisphere, their interventions all too often focused on grabbing headlines, short term, overly cautious or bungled. Yet only governments could seize many of the huge opportunities that the internet presented to nations. We could not understand why the British government squandered the following notable three.

IMRG Recommendation to Government No. 1: Control the '.UK' domain
Internet domains are administrative entities. Domain name and address spaces came into being in 1981. The .uk top-level domain was assigned to Andrew McDowell of University College, London – it was the first country code delegation.

Douglas Alexander became Britain's e-Commerce Minister on 11 May 2001 and asked IMRG what we thought the UK should do. My main recommendation to him was for the government to take control of '.UK', Britain's *uniform resource locator* (URL) – i.e. the country code top-level domain for the United Kingdom, colloquially named *web address*. Specifically, I proposed that users of the *.UK* URL should be required to conform to British standards and comply with UK law. Furthermore, that the UK should establish terms and conditions and a code of practice for those registering and using a .UK domain, as well as its second-level domains – e.g. '.co.uk'. I advised that doing so would set the '.UK' mark as the *gold standard* for online trading, boost UK registered businesses, generate revenue from associated services (such as finance, insurance, security and shipping), and provide a wealth of intelligence about the online marketplace.

The recommendation was ignored. Instead, allocations of the .UK URL remained on a *first come, first served* basis – anyone could buy any name (***.uk) that was not already registered and then use it for whatever they liked. There were no territorial restrictions and applicants need not have any connection to the UK. As a result, millions of .uk domains were acquired by foreign entities, attempting to give the impression that they were British and trustworthy, when often they were neither. As of 2020, .UK is the fourth most popular country code top-level domain with over 113 million registrations.

Governments are the only viable contenders to ordain such mechanisms, but successive administrations around the world have shied away from the area, seeing it as a political minefield.

The government's neglection of this .UK domain control recommendation, together with its rejection of IMRG's allied plan for *TrustUK (an e-commerce trading framework with identity verification and trustworthiness validation)* has pushed thousands of British (and international) traders into the welcoming arms of Google, Amazon, eBay, Etsy, Rakuten, Alibaba and the many other intermediaries that provide validity through triangulation with their trusted brands. As well as handing vast power and profit to these foreign businesses, such intermediaries are granted crucial market intelligence – information that can be used to identify and expropriate lucrative trade opportunities at will.

IMRG Recommendation to Government No. 2: Greenwich Electronic Time (GeT)

Figure 55: IMRG's Greenwich Electronic Time logo, 2000. (*Source: James Roper Archive*)

I was in Sydney in October 1999 giving the keynote address for an Australian e-commerce conference. While there I was introduced to Alex Allan who was about to take up the new UK e-Envoy post, mentioned earlier. I told Allan about our ideas for launching *Greenwich Electronic Time* (GeT) on 1 January 2000, as a *joint government and industry initiative to develop and make available essential e-commerce time tools.* The advent of the New Millennium provided an obvious trigger moment for the UK to capitalise on GMT by launching a new time framework and toolset for global e-commerce – every email message and electronic commerce transaction has a timestamp. He liked the idea and asked me to work it up as a proposal that he might take to the prime minister, Labour's Tony Blair.

Time is the most accurately measured entity known to man. Greenwich Mean Time (GMT) was originally set up to aid naval navigation when travel around the globe started to open up with the discovery of the 'New World' (America) in the fifteenth century. GMT had been accepted as the universal standard for time measurement in 1884, but GMT was largely taken for granted and had virtually no profile on the internet in terms of it being a 'British contribution to global order'.

And almost everyone wrongly assumed that GMT remained the global Time Standard. But GMT had been relegated as *only a Time Zone* used by the UK and a few other countries (e.g. South Africa), the *Time Standard* having been usurped in 1967 by Coordinated Universal Time (aka UTC, based on the oscillation of caesium-133 atoms rather than the earth's rotation). GMT and UTC *share the same time* in practice, but the latter is maintained by the Bureau International des Poids et Mesures (BIPM) based in Paris.[104] After intense French lobbying, UTC had been accepted as the *Standard* for civil time and time zones worldwide.

The International Meridian and Time Standard

The Paris meridian runs though the Paris Observatory in France's capital city – longitude 2°20′14.02500″ East – and was a long-standing rival to the Greenwich meridian as the prime meridian of the world.

By the 1870s there was pressure to establish a prime meridian for worldwide navigation and to unify local times for railway timetables – in the US one table showed 100 local times varying by over three hours. At the request of the US president, Chester A. Arthur, the International Meridian Conference was held in October 1884 in Washington D.C. to determine a prime meridian for international use. This resulted in fixing the Greenwich meridian as the common zero of longitude and *standard of time reckoning* throughout the world: the resolution passed 22 – 1, though France abstained.

The French did not accept the Greenwich meridian as the beginning of the universal day until 1911. Even then France refused to use the name 'Greenwich', instead using the term 'Paris Mean Time, which was GMT retarded by 9 minutes and 21 seconds'. Paris Mean Time was switched to CET (Central European Time) in 1940, while France was under German occupation. France legally adopted 'Coordinated Universal Time' (UTC) as its time standard in 1978.[128]

It had become clear that accurate timing was a prerequisite of online organisation and security – precise recording of when an event happened was an essential element of any digital audit trail; root-cause analysis, intrusion analysis and so forth. In the computerised world when things happen very fast across multiple time zones, the fleeting moments when two people might both own something at the same time, or the split seconds in a handover when nobody actually owned an item, were opportunities for corruption, chaos and crime. How many times in a second could a switch be made, or an automated process sell a piece of software or intellectual property online? Who would be responsible? Whose insurance and legal jurisdiction would apply?

At the end of the 1990s no holistic internet timeframe or tools existed. Merchants' computer clocks were hopelessly inaccurate and their timestamping of communications and transactions capricious. Customers and suppliers in different parts of the world / time zones were typically confused by and often conflicted over 'time windows' for responses, deliveries or service calls.

During the final weeks of 1999, IMRG complied with Alex Allan's request. We worked the GeT concept into a detailed, actionable proposal, secured several sponsors, acquired the URL – *www.get-time.org* – and created a GeT website. Following several more discussions with Allan and communications people at No 10 as Christmas approached, no commitment was forthcoming from the government, so we assumed a lack of interest and my wife and I went on holiday to Barbados to see 2000 in with family and friends.

Early on 28 December 1999 I received a slightly panicked phone call from IMRG's office manager, Gareth Donovan, to say that the lead story on *The Times* newspaper's front-page was that Tony Blair would announce Greenwich Electronic Time on New Year's Day 2000.

> *'The GeT website will turn GMT into a user-friendly e-commerce tool. Because of the Greenwich connection, it will be clearly branded as a UK service to global business, underlining the leading role UK companies are playing in the online marketplace.'*
>
> Tony Blair, British Prime Minister, 1 January 2000

Blair's unexpected announcement of Greenwich Electronic Time in the midst of the Millennium celebrations was immediately picked up by mainstream media worldwide and kicked off a hectic round of activity for us. GeT was 'owned' on behalf of government by the e-Envoy's Office, and Alex Allan led the official GeT launch at the Royal Opera House in London on 23 January 2000. IMRG initiated a comprehensive ongoing programme of work to position GMT as 'Internet Time – The Pulse of Electronic Commerce'.

> *'An accurate, easily available time standard on the Internet is a valuable tool for all involved in electronic commerce. Trusted time stamps will be the way forward for E-business all over the world and this venture and supporting infrastructure puts the UK at the forefront of Internet development.'*
>
> Alex Allan, the UK Government's E-Envoy

Patricia Hewitt, then Minister of State for E-Commerce at the Department of Trade and Industry, recorded a video outlining her support for GeT. The UK's *Time Lord* – Dr John Laverty, Head of Time Metrology at the National Physical Laboratory – oversaw the programme from a scientific perspective. LINX (London Internet Exchange) engaged the ISP industry and led the development and management of the GeT Network of time servers – atomic clocks, accurate to three one-thousandths of a second, that were GeT's reference point – and the NTP (Network Time Protocol) infrastructure. Law firm, Olswang, provided legal advice and registered the Trademark. Nominet, the official registry for UK domain names, assisted with the management of domains.

IMRG and the many other involved organisations all freely gave their time and resources to the GeT initiative. In addition, IMRG raised more than £400,000 in cash from commercial sponsors including BT, CyberSource, DHL, Forrester Research, Grey Interactive UK, Interflora, NetBenefit, Thomas Cook, Timex, UUNET and Video Arts.

> *'To validate digital transactions, it is imperative to have a reliable, accurate to the second, time source and GeT will provide this to the business and Internet communities. As part of GeT we are also working towards achieving a method of authenticating time stamps, which will be a major step forward for e-Business the world over.'*
>
> Keith Mitchell, Executive Chairman, LINX (ISP's London Internet Exchange)

Throughout the year a core working party representing numerous contributing organisations worldwide applied hundreds of man-hours to overcome the many technical, logistical and political challenges which GeT encountered. A range of downloadable GeT time tools was developed and distributed internationally to 40,000 online businesses and consumers free of charge, including a five-time zone 'desktop clock' and a 'website clock'. In addition to this, an evolving portfolio of time-oriented instruments and other collateral to help and support global communication, synchronisation, commerce and education was planned and being developed.

One of the problems GeT encountered was a bug in the Microsoft browser, Internet Explorer. This caused unpredictable behaviour and could display times on the same screen that were out of synch with each other by nine seconds or more. It was a significant issue as IE was then used by more than 80 per cent of web surfers, and illustrated yet again the need for accurate online time tools. Keith Mitchel, executive chairman of the London Internet Exchange (LINX), was quoted in *The Independent* on 1 August 2000, saying: 'You would have to ask Microsoft why their version of their own software doesn't do what their published details say it will. I don't know why it doesn't.'

To our bewilderment and considerable disappointment no further UK government endorsement or support for the GeT enterprise was forthcoming all year. Polite conversations continued. Proposals were requested, then ignored. We were just blanked. This of course undermined IMRG's attempts to raise the funds necessary to take GeT forward into 2001 when £50,000 was needed to build GeT's 2002 global Daylight Savings Tables.

During the week between Christmas 2000 and New Year 2001, a deeply frustrated IMRG was compelled to issue a statement that the GeT programme would be terminated permanently due to lack of government support.

As world trade migrated to the internet in the digital millennium, the GMT time standard was surely Britain's second most important contribution to this sphere of evolution, after the English language. But the major opportunity for the UK to capitalise on GeT was ignored by Labour's landslide government. Network Time Protocol (NTP) service, though essential for all internet commerce, remained a volunteer sport for years, while GMT was consigned forever to be a mere synonym for UTC.

IMRG Recommendation to Government No. 3: Digital High Street Pathfinder

IMRG understood better than most what was happening to Britain's high streets due to e-retail's proliferation, as well as what could be done to help them transition sustainably into the digital age. We had for years been centrally involved in trying to develop a national strategy for town centres, and a new vision for their futures.

In 2013 the government set up a *Future High Street Forum* under the direction of the Department of Communities and Local Government (DCLG), comprised of leaders from private business, government and trade, and tasked with addressing the health of UK High Streets. Within this a *Digital High Street Board* (DHSB) was formed in April 2014 to further its work and, in particular, to look forward and recommend strategic initiatives to improve our High Streets in the context of a digital future – 'likely to be a dominant factor affecting the future vibrancy of the High Streets'. John Walden, then chief executive of Home Retail Group PLC (the parent company of Argos, Habitat and Homebase) was elected chairman and he invited me to join the DHSB.

Digital High Street Advisory Board

Membership

Chair: John Walden, Chief Executive, Home Retail Group PLC

Private business
Argos
BT
Facebook
Google
Hammersons
IBM
John Lewis
Lloyds Banking Group
M&S
Post Office
Sainsbury's
Telefonica
Tesco Metro
Westfield

Public sector
Department for Business Innovation & Skills (BIS)
Department for Communities & Local Government (DCLG)
Dartford Borough Council
Innovate UK (formerly Technology Strategy Board)

Trade bodies
Association of Convenience Stores (ACS)
Association of Town and City Management (ATCM)
British Retail Consortium (BRC)
British Independent Retailers Association (BIRA)
British Council of Shopping Centres (BCSC)
GSMA (Mobile Network Operators Association)
IMRG (UK's Online Retail Association)

Figure 56: The Digital High Street Advisory Board was formed in 2014 to address the health of UK High Streets. (*Source: James Roper Archive*)

I argued that our starting point had to be much better intelligence. Whereas digital was forcefully reshaping the economy, we were unable to quantify how and to what degree. The significant omnichannel components, interdependencies and effects were not identified or measured in the round: there was no holistic digital evidence matrix; there were no comprehensive digital valuation models, or even definitions and terminology. Reliable intelligence to support long-term planning for digital-induced structural change was unavailable. IMRG proposed a *measurement and value workstream* to look into this. The DHSB approved the idea, and Walden asked me to lead it.

The central issue was that town centres had traditionally relied on income from retail trade which had been diminishing for years and would not return. Towns therefore needed to attract replacement income and modify themselves to meet society's evolving requirements.

After numerous meetings, and months of unproductive effort, the DHSB produced a 'Digital High Street 2020' report in March 2015 that was published on the *GREAT BRITISH HIGH STREET* website. The report had no noticeable effect and the DHSB fizzled out.

* * *

IMRG carried on with the *measurement and value* work, and this was picked up in 2016 by another government-led initiative – the Future Retail Working Group (FRWG) – which was examining innovation from a national perspective to identify where greater collaboration could enlighten our understanding and inform planning. The FRWG was trying to help towns and villages evolve sustainably in the digital age, and in this context commissioned me to write the *Retail Reimagined* (see *Colour Plates*) report. My report offered a view on how cooperation between impacted stakeholders could optimise the next phase of retail innovation. It argued that if nothing was done to enable local goods to become visible and buyable online, no amount of promotion was going to bring back vibrant high streets.

The key idea IMRG put forward in this report was for the nation's high streets to establish a collective online marketplace – and thereby an ability to earn a share of the colossal and fast-growing online advertising revenues. Digitally remastered high streets could offer advertisers a lifeline, enabling them to reach people while they were in leisure / shopping mode, rather than be compelled to spend their promotional budgets with foreign digital marketing channels – Google, Facebook, Instagram, Twitter, Amazon…

Such a *high street e-marketplace* would enable advertisers to engage with communities through the provision of local services and by supporting native issues that consumers are interested in and care about. Advertisers could also recruit local businesses and residents to be their ambassadors. Citizens could tell advertisers what they are interested in and thereby attract new resources to support the social and cultural functions that underpin society, which in the past high streets had funded out of retail profits.

This serendipitous convergence would create a vital opportunity for communities to take control of rather than remain subservient to e-commerce. However, the report pointed out, consumers would be unable to seize the opportunity alone: if the managers of government and major institutions did not also take responsibility for the common good, then nobody else could or would.

The *Retail Reimagined* report concluded with four recommendations for making high streets and the goods within them discoverable online and digitally accessible: a goal, a plan, metrics and a project.

a) GOAL: Agree what good high streets should look like and do
- **SWOT Analysis:** Describe the nature and scale of the digital threat and opportunity for a representative selection of locations – competitivity, skills / jobs, revenues, infrastructure…
- **Ambitions:** Identify the ambitions of and issues faced by stakeholders, for example, policy decisions on high street issues, logistics planning or mobile commerce standards…
- **Visualise** the UK and its typical places when optimum digital integration has been achieved – (jobs, opportunities, trade, lifestyle, health, global image…)
- **Trade:** Define how the UK's high streets could operate as a collective online marketplace (to make their goods and services discoverable online)

b) PLAN: Stakeholder inclusive, informed discussion and planning
- **Marketplace:** Specify a national collective online marketplace of high streets – a holistic framework of elements and their interdependencies
- Develop a nesting set of detailed action plans for a representative selection of locations (a prerequisite for this is unambiguous terminology for omnichannel and its interconnected constituent parts)
- Estimate the resources, timescale and approach needed to achieve a range of outcomes

c) METRICS: A holistic digital value matrix to measure dynamics
- **Digital High Street Data Panel:** Establish a panel comprised of relevant experts to guide measurement and monitoring
- **Standards:** Define new e-commerce measurement standards based on consumer spending (not just traditional goods and services) to enable consistent comparisons
- **Digital Evidence Matrix:** Develop a digital evidence matrix as a mechanism for managing (collecting, analysing and reporting) multiple and complex data flows and interdependencies to inform decision making, together with boilerplate equations for a representative selection of places: this must be unbiased, trusted, affordable and credible
- **Value Model:** Create a 'digital high street value model' to benchmark behaviour and performance: e.g. footfall, influencers, smart device usage, showrooming, social media interactions, changes in leisure activities

d) PROJECT: Action to deliver digitally remastered high streets
- **Digital Hub:** Create a High Street Digital Hub as a resource to agree standards and disseminate knowledge, best practice, tools and skills training
- **Boxed Solutions:** Provide a suite of Plug & Play 'solutions in a box' that empower SMEs and citizens with digital knowledge, standards, tools and skills
- **Marketplace:** Invite tenders for an online marketplace of high streets
- **Connectivity:** Decent, affordable broadband in the high street should become a universal right

At the same time, we initiated a *Digital High Street Pathfinder Programme* to investigate the 'marketplace' concept, which I believed was the key to the whole thing (many thanks to East Lindsey District Council, Louth merchants and Loughborough University for boldly supporting our efforts). Digital could be the gateway to a new vision of growth for town centres, but a new structural model and *thought process* was needed to unlock the potential. Without support most SMEs were shut out from competing online by the cost and complexity of digital services. Our idea was for *Pathfinder Towns* to cluster digital innovation and short-circuit progress, creating solutions and tools that could be replicated nationwide.

In preparing for the *Retail Reimagined* report, we undertook research to better understand consumers' changing needs in a digitally connected world, and how this altered the relationship between shoppers, retailers and town centres. We developed a valuation framework for measuring and contextualising the digital impact on high streets. We ran a workshop on *Retail, Digital and Place Data* with a group of stakeholders in *The Innovation Space* at the Department for Business, Innovation & Skills (BIS). All this brought together stakeholders to find new ways of understanding and measuring the digital economy with a view to helping high streets refocus appropriately.

We surveyed 1,000 consumers around how their retail and high street behaviour was evolving, and what more they would like from their shopping experience, using the Toluna research panel.

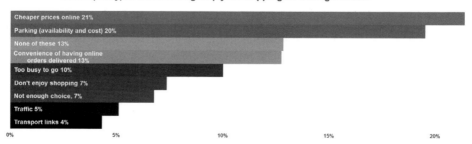

Figure 57: Shoppers said that high prices and onerous parking were their main reasons for avoiding shopping in the high street in 2016. (*Source: IMRG survey of 1,000 consumers by www. toluna-group.com, 2016 / James Roper Archive*)

When asked the purpose of their last visit to a high street retailer's store, less than a third in our survey (30 per cent) bought anything, while the majority (68 per cent) were either just checking prices, researching or out for a stroll.

A third (34 per cent) of the survey told us that the primary thing that stopped them shopping in the high street was e-retail – cheaper prices and the convenience of home delivery in particular.

In IMRG's 2016 consumer survey, only 20 per cent of respondents thought that locally available goods which showed up in online searches were competitively priced, while over half (52 per cent) believed that they either didn't show up at all, or if they did were not competitive.

IMRG's *Retail Reimagined* report was well received, published on the *GREAT BRITISH HIGH STREET* website, then ignored.

*   *   *

'It's supposed to be automatic, but actually you have to press this button'

John Brunner, British author of science fiction novels and stories

The UK government didn't appear to understand the long-term implications of ungoverned digital intervention. And IT in general seemed to elude the UK government's grasp. One of 'the worst and most expensive contracting fiascos' in public sector history was how the failed £9.8 billion attempt to upgrade the NHS computer system in England was described by the Public Accounts Committee: launched in 2002, the scheme was effectively abandoned in 2011, though it was still racking up large future costs.[105]

Time and again huge UK government IT projects went the same way – such as changes to the benefits system. In June 2020, the UK's Covid-19 contact tracing app fiasco was described as 'a masterclass in mismanagement' after the government ditched the plan it had previously lauded as 'world-beating'[106] – at one point an astonishingly elementary error by Public Health England lost thousands of positive Covid-19 results because the archaic version of Excel XLS (dating back to 1987) that it tried to use was incapable of pooling the large number of swab test logs.

Reaffirming governments' lack of even a sketchy cognisance of IT, the EU–UK Brexit trade deal struck on Christmas Eve 2020 referenced the decades-old Netscape browser and Mozilla Mail as 'modern' services (the last major release of Netscape Communicator was in 1997) yet ambassadors from the twenty-seven EU member states unanimously approved it, as did the UK Parliament.

Meanwhile the giant tech companies' profits soared, enriched by copious revenues earned from unruled e-Britannia.

High Streets Reimagined – *Again…*

'A nation of shopkeepers'

Adam Smith, 'The Wealth of Nations', London, 1776

High Street is the most common road name in the UK – there are more than 5,000 of them. The name apparently emerged in the twelfth century, when the word 'high' came to indicate elevated status – the high street being the most important thoroughfare in a place, its main commercial area and the very heart of town and village life.[107] These marketplaces were originally established on average some 16 miles apart, as eight miles was about the distance people could walk in a day to visit them. Over time the term high street became a metonym for retail trade. For generations, retail was the nation's largest private employer, and provider of the bulk of most high streets' income.

The Great Exhibition of 1851 was a celebration of the best of British craftsmanship in the mighty Crystal Palace in Hyde Park. The sight of so many goods under one roof inspired William Whiteley to build London's first department store, Whiteleys, a mile away in Bayswater. Shopping came of age in Edwardian times thanks to the riches of the Empire, and its popularity was championed by the Suffragettes who supported tea shops and department stores as respectable places for women to go on their own.

Britain's 1,500 town and city centres were always at the forefront of innovation and fashion – their high streets weathered centuries of disruptive change. The 1938 book *High Street* (with gorgeous illustrations by Eric Ravilious)[108] provides an interesting snapshot of what was then considered to be its role and value in that golden period, just before the Second World War. It describes the art of displaying goods conveniently for selling, and how each trade had its own shop and distinguishable style. 'Its own kind of cart for delivering goods – a baker's cart is quite different from a milkman's: its own costume – you will never see a grocer in a butcher's blue apron,' it explains. 'What makes a shop so exciting as a thing to look at is the quantity of goods, arranged in order – the happy effect of crowds of the same things packed in colourful patterns.'

Even then the personal and local character of high street shops was disappearing with the arrival of multiple stores and their ready-made shop fronts and fittings, bringing better goods to more people at lower prices. Increasing levels of pre-packaging and branding ushered in self-service, changing how many shops operated, but not displacing them as the place of trade.

Mail-order catalogue shopping gained market share in the twentieth century, offering an ever-expanding range of goods, but with slow delivery, and seasonal editions that were out of date as soon as they were printed, they presented only a minor threat to the all-powerful high streets. Throughout its history catalogue shopping never exceeded 5 per cent of the retail market.

Britain's first supermarket opened on 12 January 1948 – a Co-op in Manor Park, East London – and its format soon proliferated. Supermarkets presented a more significant challenge to high streets, as many would set up out of town, attracting footfall away.

High streets' fortunes began to decline in the 1950s as personal incomes rose and the population became more urbanised and mobile. Multiple-shop organisations flourished, spawning formulaic high street clones, making town centres predictable and monotonous. Avaricious chains overpriced goods in sectors they dominated, fostering ill will that online traders would later exploit.

Shopping's next golden age arrived in the 1960s when Britain became affluent again, mass production and disposable culture really took off, and families acquired cars. Cars had a hugely detrimental effect on the high street as they enabled shoppers to drive to out-of-town retail malls and supermarkets, and to buy and carry more than a few days' provisions at a time. Cars also brought parking chaos, so were diverted onto ring roads to avoid town centre congestion, diminishing high streets' passing trade. Retail parks and large multi-purpose malls sprang up all over.

The 1964 Resale Prices Act abolished the anti-competitive practice of *Minimum Resale Price Maintenance* through which manufacturers and retailers had set the retail price of their goods in the UK. This opened the way for buying in volume and slashing prices, helped lower the cost of living, and was a critical turning point in the growth of supermarkets.

Investors and institutions acquired swathes of retail locations across the country to financially exploit the perennial retail cash cow, but decades of sucking out profits and putting little or nothing back in ruined many high streets and blighted neighbourhoods. From being most people's only trading option, high streets became just one of several, with waning appeal.

Sunday shopping had been illegal, with a few exceptions, until in December 1993 when Parliament voted – by just eighteen votes – to allow it. This changed the British way of life as Sunday soon became the second biggest trading day.

In 1950 there had been 404,845 retail organisations of which 376,446 (93 per cent) had only one establishment, according to that year's *Great Britain Census of Distribution* report. Of the UK's 529,648 shops, 71 per cent were accounted for by these single-unit retailers who handled 48 per cent of total retail sales.

By 1990, as the *World Wide Warehouse* loomed, the number of retail outlets had already dropped by 36 per cent from the 1950 tally, to 338,248. However, retailing still employed some 2,347,000 people – 6.4 per cent of Britain's fifty-seven million population.

*   *   *

For fifty years, the primary thrust of the retail industry had been based on economy of scale: bigger self-service superstores and lower prices. Retailers had made shopping convenient for themselves, but less so for the consumer who was required to provide time, effort and transportation to find, buy and then carry home their goods. Opening hours, parking and transport proximity all inconvenienced shoppers. *Loyalty cards* were another irritation for many people; consumers wanted choice and value, not a relationship with an outdated, corporate behemoth.

Pre-internet, a trip to the high street would often be triggered by a single need, which would then spawn a string of additional transactions with different trades. Triggers for 'trip chaining' as this was known, might include picking up a paper, going to the bank, renting a DVD or posting a letter, all of which became declining behaviours as consumer adoption of PCs and smartphones provided digital alternatives.

Convenience, choice and the ability to compare offers propelled online shopping's popularity, while the lookalike high streets with their perpetual sales looked tired. Digital innovation also reduced the range of goods that stores could profitably sell by making some obsolete and dematerialising others. At the time of writing almost 95 per cent of UK adults own a smartphone that almost certainly contains a camera, clock, calculator, dictionary, compass, calendar, address book, music player, mail service, bank, encyclopaedia, maps, video and sound recorder, library, photo album, pedometer, torch and all sorts of other things (sat nav, tape measure, spirit level, guitar tuner, metronome…) that previously were individual products or services sold out of retail floor space that is no longer viable for that purpose. Similarly, the way media – newspapers, books, music, movies, videos and games – is consumed changed, making other types of store space obsolete. People took to spending their disposable money on digital downloads, experiences and social media, routinely taking several weekend breaks during the year, and longer holidays.

Many businesses and some entire industries would become redundant, as the manufacturers of photographic film and video cassettes discovered. Olympus quit the camera business after eighty-four years in 2020, blaming the arrival of smartphones for shrinking the market for separate cameras: standalone camera sales fell 84 per cent between 2010 and 2018 according to LENSVID.[109]

Online shopping started with the sale of a CD, a format that it subsequently replaced and wiped out: how many other goods and services will digital innovation consign to oblivion, or subsume as just part of its ensemble? The idea of a clock that doesn't know the time will soon seem absurd.

* * *

Digital developments barely impacted high streets at all in the decade following the first secure internet transactions. Some retail locations attempted to block mobile phone signals in order to prevent shoppers accessing the internet, until this was made illegal in 2006 under section 68 of the Wireless Telegraphy Act.[110]

While online gradually drilled itself into the very core of retailing with relentless insistency, taxation, in the form of business rates, car parking and other charges, continued to hammer high streets. Worst hit were the secondary and tertiary high street locations, such as run-down manufacturing districts and seaside towns. In these places, crashing property prices, social issues, loneliness, obesity and health problems due to boredom and lack of exercise ensued.

'A nation of online shoppers'

Observable fact, 2020

Only governments had the ability to shape such wholesale change at the confluence of science, technology, society and policy, but the authorities didn't appear to even understand the basic issues let alone know what to do to mitigate the digital shock for those being debilitated.

Nothing would have helped high streets more than levelling the taxation playing field. Multinationals were routinely accused of dodging taxes, but if – as they claimed – they paid all the taxes that they were legally obliged to, the responsibility for disparities lay squarely with the governments that failed to adjust tax legislation in light of contradistinctive market conditions.

A series of half-hearted attempts to revive town centres had almost no perceptible effect. The UK's high streets were flying blind in a digital fog.

> **'Independents are a key component of our high streets, and this is seen both in the fact they represent a majority [65 per cent in 2016] of the units but also the diversity and vibrancy they can bring along with their direct connection to local economies'**
>
> *Matthew Hopkinson, Director, Local Data Company, 2016*

American Express (Amex) initiated the *Small Business Saturday* event (the day after Black Friday) in the US in 2010 to encourage consumers to shop locally. The following year, Small Business Saturday was adopted by the Senate with unanimous consent, and by 2014, the one-day event attracted an estimated $14.3 billion extra spending with small businesses.

Such promotional programmes – and there were many – were helpful in a tactical sense to breathe life back into struggling high streets. However, in 2015, data from the Local Data Company (LDC) and British Independent Retailers' Association (BIRA) showed that high streets needed much more help. UK independent shops were opening at their slowest rate in seven years: most of those that did open were either e-cigarette shops or American restaurants. Independent retailers still accounted for 65 per cent of shops in Britain's top 500 town centres, however the net increase in shop openings in 2015 was just +117 shops (+0.11 per cent).

Michael Weedon, Deputy Chief Executive of BIRA, commented: 'Within the figures we see a powerful rebalancing away from product-based retail towards service providers, leisure operators and convenience operators.'

> The product that online you can find and buy in seconds from a distant seller may be available in your local shop, but this nearby stock is likely to be undiscoverable online.

Small businesses in particular were disadvantaged in, if not precluded from, the digital marketplace by their lack of knowledge, skills, tools and poor connectivity. The effect of this handicap was that their goods were undiscoverable online.

*   *   *

Britain's town centres had for decades been dominated by soulless service offices – banks, building societies, insurance agents, estate agents – an overabundance of edifices that add very little social value to our traditional meeting places, but could financially outgun local traders to acquire the prime locations. In 2020 even the soulless edifices were being digitally sidelined and their physical manifestations rendered superfluous – leaving places entirely hollowed out and desolate.

Add to this a toxic broth of brutalist architecture, uninspired town planning, and mercenary traffic wardens, and you produce a culture in which town centres die. Layer Covid-19 on top – even temporarily – and you get high street extinction events.

Yet above the mundane street-level facias in almost any UK place is evidence of interesting, individualistic and often elegant buildings just waiting to be rediscovered, refurbished, reloved. Amid the slew of 2020's store closures, there was a sliver of positive news; as more people worked from home, they were spending more money locally and rediscovering their local high streets and independent stores. Smaller neighbourhood shopping areas were faring much better than large cities and shopping centres during the pandemic.

Many factors influence high streets. More people worked from home and had flexible employment in 2018 – a YouGov survey found that just 6 per cent of people still worked the traditional workplace hours of 9 am to 5 pm. The growing circular economic trend whereby we make less and recycle more leads away from the disposable era to one in which our possessions are upgraded and repaired and last longer. And while *Remote Additive Manufacturing* (3D Printing) is not mainstream today, it is likely to disrupt traditional commerce in the future. The future of 'ownership' may change: some products may be transmuted to *subscriptions*, or *digitally enabled services*.

The boom in online shopping is massively accelerating progress in automation, both in warehouses where robots are getting better at picking and packing, and in the delivery process – expect more delivery robots on the streets.

The normalisation of e-grocery shopping is particularly intimidating for high streets. As this vast retail domain moves online, the inseparable twin drivers – growing critical mass of e-trade, and greater parcel drop densities – may further improve the efficiency of home delivery to such an extent that it generates a *transaction black hole* capable of sucking in almost all shopping for physical items.

*   *   *

Shops are to shopping what typewriters are to writing

Yet for most people the term 'shopping' takes on meaning far beyond the simple exchange of goods and money. The ancient history of trading is evident in archaeology dating back more than 10,000 years. Shopping is central to the human condition, inseparably enmeshed in all manner of human behaviour – socialising, discovering, browsing, buying, bartering, relaxing, news gathering, eating, gossiping and a thousand other things.

Shopping embodies emotions and aspirations, and may serve as exercise, entertainment, therapy, personal expression, stress relief, contact sport, a pastime or a drug.[111] It incorporates all kinds of activities, from getting a few groceries at the corner shop to a day out with family or friends. Shopping can be a joy or a chore, treat or torture – occasionally all at the same time.

Women and men shop differently, presumed to be a result of functional anthropology, stemming from the time when women as gatherers would work together in groups, while men as hunters would go out alone to remain quiet. Men get bored shopping after just twenty-six minutes, while women tire of it only after two hours, according to a Quidco study of 2,000 Britons in 2013.[112]

People try to rethink the shop, believing that it can be reinvented in some way so as to make it fit for purpose in a digital future. This confuses the facts – people are sociable and have always lived in groups and had meeting places, so shops sprang up where people congregated. What is needed is for towns and villages to be re-established in vogue and recentred back to their natural position – at the heart of the 'attention model' where traders vie for customer attention in hopes of selling them what they might want.

If the nation's high streets were to be digitally remastered as a collective online marketplace, and thereby enabled to compete for retail trade (as customer touchpoints rather than warehouses) and earn a share of the huge and growing online advertising revenues, this would offer everyone a lifeline back to consequential social normality: advertisers could reach people while they were in leisure / researching mode, and support native issues – communities could regain attractive nearby destinations, and reasons to visit them.

'Location, loc@tion, l@c@ti@n'

The three things that matter in retail... updated apocryphal aphorism

Shopping is the stuff of life. Yet its primary form that had endured for centuries was vanishing in a generation. Carelessly ungoverned, high streets were abandoned to their fate. The role of high streets will always evolve. What was abundantly clear in 2020 was that they would need far less space for storing products, and more for services, social interaction and leisure.

Dot, Dot, Dot…

The train now arriving at platforms three, four,
five and six… is coming in sideways

Brilliant innovators created the amazing digisphere and the world embraced it. Snake oil salesmen, racketeers and fools corrupted and abused it. Money men and accountants used it to plunder civilisation's treasures and find ingenious ways to eliminate paying taxes. Governments proclaimed they would regulate it when they should have been directing it – then didn't. A wealthy elite used it to accumulate vast fortunes at the expense of billions of ordinary people who were left dispirited and frustrated. If 'the economy' is the term we use to describe the systems we employ to turn assets into human welfare, basically, it was being hijacked via abuse of digital innovation. So, what next?

As we journey toward the metaverse world of 2050, with its infinity of as-yet-undreamed-of possibilities, it is appropriate to consider what we have – and haven't – learned in the past thirty years of digital revolution.

Three tectonic shifts in the form of human locomotion have already happened – from legs, to wheels, to electrons – but the biggest is yet to come: virtualisation.

In virtual reality's five-dimensions – identity, presence, space, time, cloud – avatars roam computer-generated universes, slaying dragons and trading non-fungible tokens (NFTs) with their holographic pals. All is possible and impossible. Everything and nothing is remote. VR unleashes a leap forward for mankind. It unlocks a new approach in which existing resources will be leveraged in new ways. The value of virtual assets will soon transcend all others.

But don't give up on reality just yet. And will pirates be allowed to steal the treasure again?

Web 3.0, 4.0, 5.0 and counting…

'I have a dream for the Web [in which computers] become capable
of analysing all the data on the Web – the content, the links, and
transactions between people and computers. A 'Semantic Web'…'

Tim Berners-Lee, 1999

We looked earlier at the first two implementations of the web – Web 1.0, the 'read-only-web' era up to 1999, and then Web 2.0, the 'read-write-publish' phase that gave us Blogs, Social Media and Video-Streaming.

Web 3.0 – the third *'Semantic'* iteration of the web – involves online applications and websites getting smart by learning and becoming more intelligent. Amazon's website demonstrates this when it recommends '*frequently bought together*' items as you place an order: its algorithm having looked at what others have bought after buying the item you just ordered. Tim Berners-Lee set out his vision of the Semantic Web in 1999, in the above quote, adding that when this emerged, 'the day-to-day mechanisms of trade, bureaucracy and our daily lives will be handled by machines talking to machines. The "intelligent agents" people have touted for ages will finally materialize.'

Web 3.0 is also about connecting people with devices, and devices with each other, and became known as the *Internet of Things* (IoT). Examples of IoT include online thermostats, doorbells and security systems, though the big idea is that eventually pretty much everything will be interconnected.

The goal of the Semantic Web is to make internet data and *meaning* machine-readable, thereby enabling computers to manage concepts, relationships between entities, and categories of things. Furthermore, Web 3.0 moves away from the centralisation of services like search, social media and chat, towards the incorporation of semantic metadata (granular data and its meaning), Artificial Intelligence, 3D graphics, Extended Reality, and ubiquity beyond screens.

With Web 3.0 we are entering yet another internet revolution, with vast new boundaries, new experiences and behaviour, and complications that will render much of what has gone before obsolete. But there is yet more.

Bypassing Web 4.0, a term which some used to describe *mobile internet* developments, because *mobile* was effectively swept up as part and parcel of the Web 2.0 development phase, we skip forward to Web 5.0 – the next phase of internet development.

Web 5.0 conceptually represents '*The Emotional / Telepathic / Blockchain Web*', or the '*read-write-execution-concurrency*' Web. Although Web 5.0 is still developing and largely undefined, its general direction is toward symbiotic interaction between humans and computers, a coherent web that communicates with us like we communicate with each other. Web 5.0 will be very powerful and fully executing – making decisions and then actioning them without human interventions.

> *'AI is likely to be either the best or worst thing to happen to humanity'*
>
> *Stephen Hawking*

* * *

In 2020 e-commerce remained a teenage industry, with a lot of growing, and growing-up, still to do. Extreme advances in technology had already transformed retailing, markets and auctions, however further major advances were foreseen on all fronts: AI-powered marketeers will soon know what we need and want before we do, while armies of delivery robots and drones will whizz about gratifying the whims of citizens shopping in cornucopian virtual showrooms and malls. We'll attend holographic concerts in our living room, holiday on distant planets, and 3D-print new body parts using our own stem cells.

But will 'the gulf between superfluous wealth and abject poverty' that Martin Luther King denounced, just get wider than ever if we continue to ignore 'the danger of the profit motive'?

Cloud-cuckoo-land economy

'Money is like muck, not good except that it be spread'

Francis Bacon, English philosopher (1561–1626)

Global economic inequality was out of control in 2020. Nothing increased its eccentricity more than technology, which was where the real money was being made. The world's four most valuable companies were Apple, Microsoft, Amazon and Alphabet (Google) according to the 2020 Hurun Global 500.[113] Worth $2 trillion, Apple led the great armada of buoyant US tech stocks sweeping across the planet, their values boosted by surges in demand for tech goods and services amid the pandemic. In September, Apple Inc. was reported to be more valuable than the entire FTSE 100.

By contrast, London-listed companies wallowed. The FTSE was down 22 per cent from its 2020 high of 7,675 in January.[114] 'The FTSE 100 is a dinosaur, full of rather lumbering old-world stocks with precious little growth to offer,' commented Neil Wilson, chief market analyst for Markets.com. With the exception of Ocado, 'there is no tech to speak of,' he added. 'Whilst the US has Zoom, we have BT and Vodafone. The US boasts Netflix and Amazon – the FTSE can muster ITV and Sainsbury's.'

Britain, however, was identified as by far the biggest enabler of global corporate tax dodging, helping multinationals like Google and Amazon funnel $500 billion dollars away from state coffers, according to a Tax Justice Network report of May 2019.[115] Six of the world's top ten tax havens were British Empire-related, in the Caribbean, the Channel Islands and Asia.

A wealthy elite, enabled by digital advancements, accumulated vast fortunes. On the final day of 2020, the Bloomberg Billionaires Index showed that eight of the ten wealthiest people in the world made their money from technology, and despite the Covid-19 pandemic, the wealth of these ten had collectively increased by 23 per cent, or $1.3 trillion, during the year, aided by the boost given to markets by unprecedented stimulus efforts by governments and central bankers.

Amazon boss Jeff Bezos was the richest man on the planet with total net worth of $192 billion. Bezos owned about 11 per cent of Amazon, the world's largest retailer, already down from the 16 per cent share he had held before a 4 per cent stake was transferred to MacKenzie Bezos in 2019 following the couple's divorce. Amazon controlled about 40 per cent of the e-retail market. Bezos' net worth increased $76.9 billion during 2020.

Elon Musk came a close second in the wealth stakes with net worth valued at $167 billion accumulated from ventures including SpaceX and Tesla, assets which had gained a whopping $140 billion during the year.

Microsoft founder Bill Gates was the third richest, with a total net worth of $131 billion, up $18.2 billion in 2020.

Facebook's Mark Zuckerberg ranked fifth, with $103 billion, up $24.7 billion in the year, while Google co-founder Larry Page listed seventh, his stack worth $81.9 billion, up $17.2 billion.

Eighth was Steve Ballmer, who had made most of his $80.2 billion while at Microsoft – his boodle had increased in value by $22 billion that year. Ninth was Google's other co-founder, Sergey Brin, with $79.3 billion, up $16.6 billion.

Completing the top ten was Oracle Corporation's Larry Ellison with a net worth valued at $79.2 billion, that had soared by $20.4 billion in 2020.

All of the world's ten richest people were men and all but one was American. Of the two whose wealth didn't stem from technology, one was Frenchman, Bernard Arnault, chairman and CEO of the world's largest luxury-goods manufacturer, LVMH Moët Hennessy Louis Vuitton (whose goods were bought by the wealthy), who ranked fourth with a net worth valued at $115 billion, up $9.28 billion. The other was business tycoon Warren Buffett, ranking sixth with $87 billion, the only one of the ten whose net worth had fallen during 2020, down by $2.3 billion.

Between 18 March 2020, and 12 April 2021, the collective wealth of American billionaires leaped by $1.6 trillion, or 55 per cent, from $2.95 trillion to $4.56 trillion, according to Inequality.org.[116]

* * *

Tax systems are designed and administered by national governments. They developed at a time when cross-border flows of goods, services and capital were much less important than they are today.

In 1995, observers had noted that, once online cash transactions became a reality, governments would find it difficult to tax assets. 'I just don't see how they could collect taxes. It's an international system, highly complex and totally unregulated,' commented Rob Tristani, a systems engineer with the US Army missile command. A spokesman for the UK Treasury said that the department was not aware of any problems.

In 1998, US President Bill Clinton proposed a solution: permanently ban taxes on electronic transmissions across borders. Astonishingly, World Trade Organisation (WTO) diplomats agreed to keep internet business duty free for at least a year while they studied Clinton's proposal, which aimed at keeping markets open in light of financial turmoil that had affected Asia. Wrapping up a three-day WTO meeting in Geneva in May, representatives said keeping markets open was a key solution, so agreed to consider the US drive for a *permanent* WTO accord to keep cyberspace trade tax free. Developing countries resisted a quick accord, saying they needed to understand all the implications. But they agreed on the standstill while negotiators in Geneva worked on a more detailed agreement to be presented at the next ministers' meeting, in 1999.

The WTO had been created in 1995 to *lift the lives of ordinary citizens*. Its formation amounted to the biggest tax cut in history, worth $76 billion a year. Just four years later, world trade was up 25 per cent.

Clinton, speaking to the 1998 WTO gathering, urged the ministers to follow his no-tax stance. His stated aim was to pursue an ever-more-open global trading system, tapping in full the new potential of the Information Age to encourage the free flow of information and commerce on the internet: 'In an era in which product life-cycles are measured in months, and information and money move around the globe in seconds, we can no longer afford to take seven years to finish a trade round, as happened during the Uruguay Round [that had founded the WTO], or let decades pass between identifying and acting on a trade barrier. In the meantime, new industries arise, new trading blocs take shape, and governments invent new trade barriers every day'.[117]

The following year, at the 1999 WTO conference in Seattle, the 135 member states unanimously decreed that e-commerce would remain duty and tax free for the next two years. This moratorium was regarded as a major benefit for businesses and consumers alike, and also as a measure to involve even more countries in e-commerce.

The tax and duty moratorium on electronic transmissions as a general principle continues at the time of writing (December 2020), though the issue and its impacts are increasingly complicated due to the emergence of cloud infrastructure, developments in Internet of Things (IoT) and the emergence of *Remote Additive Manufacturing* (3D printing).

* * *

Since the Great Recession of 2008, the world's four major central banks had spent $20 trillion on quantitative easing (QE), though showering the banks with cash, in the biggest monetary policy stimulus the world has ever seen, was not having the desired effect. Instead of stimulating the real economy, QE was ultimately benefitting the most privileged in society. The wealth of UK billionaires had trebled, to almost £600 billion, while average UK house prices had gone up 60 per cent in twelve years. Spiralling housing costs hit the poor hardest, and for most young people the idea of owning a home had become a receding hallucination. Meanwhile, nurses battling the Covid-19 pandemic and key workers who hold our society together were going to foodbanks.

An ex-City trader commented: 'In the crashes – stocks have gone up. We have the bizarre situation where the consequence of economic collapse and crisis is repeatedly a massive increase in stock and asset prices – and who owns these? Mainly its wealthy people.'

The real economy, in which people live and work, appeared to be just a sort of sideshow for the City of London – its stock market a slot machine with shiny buttons. Median real UK earnings were lower than in 2008 while the poverty rate of working households was at a record high. Many people thought that the political establishment had failed them and that we needed to rethink the economy. But no such reevaluation was in prospect – taxing the wealthy had been out of fashion since the 1970s.

Ben Phillips has helped bring global attention to the inequality crisis. In his book *How to Fight Inequality* he explains how, around 2015, governments and establishment institutions across the world suddenly shifted en masse and said that they agreed that inequalities are recognised as harmful and dangerous. Mainstream economists, the IMF, the World Bank, the Organisation for Economic Co-operation and Development (OECD) and even the World Economic Forum all concurred. Every United Nations member state signed up to the UN Sustainable Development Goals in 2015, pledging to reduce inequality. But since then, not much changed, and rich countries continued to block progress on tackling tax dodging and reforming trade.

Phillips notes that the 'Patriotic Millionaires' in the US – a group of super-wealthy individuals supporting calls for greater equality – have set out powerfully that their wealth is not only a product of individual effort but is shaped by unfair regulations designed in their interests, and that their wealth now perpetuates itself. They talk of how a more equal society would be a better one: 'We want to live in a country that has a basic sense of fairness, and where millionaires don't get special treatment just because they're rich.'

'Inequality is the root of social evil,' said Pope Francis. And he's bang on the money, says Phillips. If we don't fix this we'll end up with an even more volatile society, massive violence, huge economic damage and the undermining of democracy – a world in which everyone hates each other.

* * *

The phrase *cloud cuckoo land* was coined by the fourth-century-BC Greek playwright Aristophanes in the whimsical play *The Birds*, and came to mean a realm of fanciful or impractical, idealistic notions. Cloud computing creates its very own *cuckoo land* in which amorphous nesting sets of digital services enable cloud controllers to freeload on the work of others to feed their ravenous corporate offspring – and then to further parasitise society by dodging taxes.

Others flocking together to feather their nests in bird land included the chief executives of Britain's biggest companies. They earned about 120 times that of a typical UK worker, up from around fifty times at the turn of the millennium, and twenty times in the early 1980s, according to Luke Hildyard, director of the High Pay Centre.[118] The bosses of Britain's biggest companies earned more in three days than the average worker's annual wage.

The great wealth divide was the result of a system that gave more wealth to the privileged few than to everyone else. The world's richest 1 per cent had more than twice the wealth of the other 6.9 billion people according to an Oxfam report, *Time to Care*, published in January 2020.[119] The report said that governments were massively under-taxing the wealthiest individuals and corporations and failing to collect revenues that would help tackle poverty and inequality.

* * *

The thing about computers is their ability to share learning and become more intelligent. If I learn to drive a car, it doesn't mean that my son can drive – he has to acquire the ability for himself. But teach one computer something and potentially all computers can know it. This bionic leverage generates awesome superfluous wealth for those controlling computer technology, resulting in ever more extreme concentrations of power. And as Lord Acton famously pronounced in 1887, power tends to corrupt, and absolute power corrupts absolutely.

All this raised questions about what truly matters to society, and deep concerns about the governance of the economy. What effects was the endless pursuit of profit and wealth having on social cohesion, crime, public health and wellbeing – and the planet? Who was prioritising what, and why?

It was starkly obvious that Earth's finite natural resources could not meet man's insatiable capitalist demands, driven by population growth, wealth creation and technology.

The digisphere is a foreign country

'We are now all connected to the internet, like neurons in a giant brain'

Stephen Hawking

In just thirty years the internet reinvented retailing in its own image and hired a new cast. Online shopping turned consumer choice from not so much to EVERYTHING, shrank prices and elevated acquiring stuff from an unpredictable chore to a reliable cinch, available anytime, anywhere.

The transilience inevitably brought disruption and downsides – lost shops, jobs, lifestyles, social capital – and ghost high streets haunting once-busy town centres. Nevertheless, the percentage of Britons saying they were 'very' or 'fairly' satisfied with their lives rose from less than 86 per cent in 1990 to over 91 per cent in 2020, according to Eurobarometer.

Few in 1990 would have believed that a start-up internet bookseller could, in just a quarter of a century, become the world's largest retailer, and its founder the richest man on earth. Fewer still could have imagined the turbulence that would buffet our everyday lives as the physical and virtual worlds began to blend. The culminating digisphere is a foreign country; a strange, ethereal cosmos rising out of the mists of human ingenuity; a place that any previous age would have regarded magical. We will need to learn to wield the awesome new powers we find here with great care, and tarry a while before we all feel completely at home in this new augmented stomping ground.

Epilogue

We knew that e-commerce would blow the doors off the traditional retail model, with inevitable consequences for shops and town centres. But none of us imagined that so many of the incumbent political and business leaders would just stand idly by – unwilling or unable to respond – as a tsunami of unprecedented developments approached and then began to overwhelm their worlds. Carelessly ungoverned, high streets, once-stalwart enterprises and entire workforces, as well as the police and enforcement agencies, were abandoned to their fate, sacrificed to the gods of 'progress'.

We have come a long way since the days of secretaries tippexing on their new-fangled computer screens, yet equitable distribution of the benefits that e-commerce and digital empowerment is making possible, is still not happening. Why is this? Does it matter? Can anything be done about it?

The primary reason for inertia is of course that those in power are, unsurprisingly, happy with the status quo. A secondary explanation is short-termism. But the ever-increasing extreme concentration of power, together with the snowballing pace of change, oblige us to look beyond the short term, and expand our notions of time, or risk calamity.

In the mid-1990s IMRG targeted organisations that would obviously be impacted by e-commerce, none more so than Royal Mail, then Britain's most trusted brand. In a series of meetings with Kate Pitts, Strategy Manager–Future Business, Royal Mail Group Plc (then the Post Office Research Group), we outlined how letters would be replaced by emails and shopping was heading online, requiring more parcels to be delivered. Pitts explained that she had no budget to look at this, but would be happy for IMRG to do research and report to her on the potential. Great, I thought, and prepared a detailed case. A good while after its submission, Pitts came back explaining that, while e-commerce was interesting, it was just too small and insignificant to bother her board with. She wrote to me enclosing a token of her appreciation – a Penny Black stamp – clarifying that it was 'a real one and I thought would be a reminder of our heritage at a time when we are really starting to look forward. Still impossible to deliver it except by post though!'

Was this irony, or its opposite – wrinkly? Imagine how different the UK e-commerce landscape could have been if Royal Mail had seized its many opportunities: to become Britain's e-trust scheme; to meet the demand for parcel delivery and new warehousing; to provide a virtual marketplace for the nation's high streets.

We eventually stopped even trying to convince people of e-commerce's potential on the basis that if they didn't get it, that was their problem. It was either too early, or unimportant, we were told. Politicians were too busy, or felt is best to leave it to market forces: Whitehall's got this covered.

As one IMRG member put it: 'It's the old "I can't be bothered to understand the real issues, and anyway, the Civil Service has handed down the research to such junior juniors that nothing vaguely technical is ever going to hit my desk, so let's just go with what a few slick, overpriced consultants tell us, rather than listening to people actually in the business" scenario.'

Governments' laissez-faire approach left the development of the digisphere to the giant companies whose technologies enable it, resulting in everyone else scrambling to remain relevant in a fast-changing world. Unbridled social media amplifies absurdity and legitimises guile. Online crime is rampant and goes unchecked. Young people are alienated and depressed, deprived of the relative economic security of previous generations. Around the world, humans driven by poverty or greed are destroying habitats and inflicting suffering on animals and each other. What should be bringing prosperity is instead all too often bringing misery. We need new politics, and far better leadership. Will we get them? Let's hope so.

Works Cited

1. INTEL. Over 50 Years of Moore's Law. *https://www.intel.co.uk*. [Online] [Cited: 31 January 2020.] https://www.intel.co.uk/content/www/uk/en/silicon-innovations/moores-law-technology.html.

2. T. Berners-Lee/CN, R. Cailliau/ECP. https://www.w3.org/Proposal.html. *w3.org*. [Online] 12 November 1990. [Cited: 19 February 2020.] https://www.w3.org/Proposal.html.

3. News Shopper: Charlotte Ikonen. Nostalgic look back at UK high street shops like Woolworths. *https://www.newsshopper.co.uk*. [Online] 17 July 2021. [Cited: 13 November 2021.] https://www.newsshopper.co.uk/news/19436786.nostalgic-look-back-uk-high-street-shops-like-woolworths/.

4. Retail Gazette. UK retailers' store profit margins have halved in the last 8 years. *https://www.retailgazette.co.uk/*. [Online] 23 October 2019. [Cited: 23 January 2020.] https://www.retailgazette.co.uk/blog/2019/10/uk-retailers-store-profit-margins-halved-last-8-years/.

5. Buffer. 21 Top Social Media Sites to Consider for Your Brand. *buffer.com*. [Online] 2019. [Cited: 15 December 2020.] https://buffer.com/library/social-media-sites/.

6. Cenre for Retail Research. The Crisis in Retailing: Closures and Job Losses. *https://www.retailresearch.org/*. [Online] 23 February 2021. [Cited: 23 February 2021.] https://www.retailresearch.org/retail-crisis.html.

7. Chicago Tribune. FLORSHEIM, VIDEO MAKE PERFECT FIT. *https://www.chicagotribune.com*. [Online] 5 November 1986. [Cited: 16 February 2021.] https://www.chicagotribune.com/news/ct-xpm-1986-11-05-8603230457-story.html.

8. Archive, James RJ Roper. James R J Roper's personal archive of e-retail evolution.

9. Invention of the integrated circuit. *Wikipedia*. [Online] [Cited: 18 February 2020.] https://en.wikipedia.org/wiki/Invention_of_the_integrated_circuit.

10. Computer History Museum. 13 SEXTILLION & COUNTING: THE LONG & WINDING ROAD TO THE MOST FREQUENTLY MANUFACTURED HUMAN ARTIFACT IN HISTORY - by David Laws. *computerhistory.org*. [Online] 02 April 2018. [Cited: 16 February 2020.] https://computerhistory.org/blog/13-sextillion-counting-the-long-winding-road-to-the-most-frequently-manufactured-human-artifact-in-history/?key=13-sextillion-counting-the-long-winding-road-to-the-most-frequently-manufactured-human-artifact-in-history.

11. Semiconductor Industry Association. Industry Impact. *Semiconductor Industry Association*. [Online] 2020. [Cited: 17 February 2020.] https://www.semiconductors.org/semiconductors-101/industry-impact/.

12. Deloitte. *Semiconductors – the Next Wave*. s.l. : Deloitte, 2019.

13. Lean, Tom. A brave new world: the 1980s home computer boom. *https://www.historyextra.com*. [Online] [Cited: 19 February 2020.] https://www.historyextra.com/period/20th-century/a-brave-new-world-the-1980s-home-computer-boom/.

14. New York Times. Strong Growth in PC Industry, Reports Say. *https://www.nytimes.com*. [Online] 27 April 1997. [Cited: 19 February 2020.] https://www.nytimes.com/1997/04/28/business/strong-growth-in-pc-industry-reports-say.html.

15. Wikipedia. Iridium satellite constellation. *Wikipedia*. [Online] [Cited: 17 February 2020.] https://en.wikipedia.org/wiki/Iridium_satellite_constellation.

16. The sound of dial-up internet. *willterminus*. [Online] 8 November 2008. [Cited: 19 April 2020.] https://youtu.be/gsNaR6FRuO0.

17. Li, Wei. The First Search Engine, Archie. *http://people.lis.illinois.edu/~chip/projects/timeline/1990archie.htm*. [Online] 20 September 2002. [Cited: 19 February 2020.] http://people.lis.illinois.edu/~chip/projects/timeline/1990archie.htm.

18. PC World - Christopher Null. The 50 Best Tech Products of All Time. *https://www.pcworld.com/*. [Online] 2 April 2007. [Cited: 19 February 2020.] https://www.pcworld.com/article/130207/article.html.

19. Wikipedia. Mosaic (web browser). *https://en.wikipedia.org*. [Online] [Cited: 19 February 2020.] https://en.wikipedia.org/wiki/Mosaic_(web_browser).

20. CERN. Home of the First Website. *http://info.cern.ch/*. [Online] [Cited: 19 February 2020.] http://info.cern.ch/.

21. Web Server Survey. *https://news.netcraft.com*. [Online] Netcraft. [Cited: 19 February 2020.] https://news.netcraft.com/archives/category/web-server-survey/.

22. BBC. Minitel: The rise and fall of the France-wide web. *https://www.bbc.co.uk/news*. [Online] 28 June 2012. [Cited: 21 February 2020.] https://www.bbc.co.uk/news/magazine-18610692.

23. Wikipedia. Bildschirmtext. *Wikipedia*. [Online] [Cited: 21 February 2020.] https://en.wikipedia.org/wiki/Bildschirmtext.

24. Shopify. History of Ecommerce. *https://www.youtube.com/user/shopify*. [Online] 26 November 2015. [Cited: 20 February 2020.] https://www.youtube.com/watch?v=eGyhA-DIYvg.

25. BBC. Online shopping: The pensioner who pioneered a home shopping revolution. *https://www.bbc.co.uk/news/*. [Online] 16 September 2013. [Cited: 20 February 2020.] https://www.bbc.co.uk/news/magazine-24091393.

26. New York Times - Petyer H Lewis. Attention Shoppers: Internet Is Open. *https://www.nytimes.com/*. [Online] 12 August 1994. [Cited: 20 February 2020.] https://www.nytimes.com/1994/08/12/business/attention-shoppers-internet-is-open.html.

27. Timmons, Craig Kanarick and Otto. Welcome the The "First" Banner Ad. *http://thefirstbannerad.com/info.html*. [Online] 1994. [Cited: 19 February 2020.] http://thefirstbannerad.com/.

28. Harvard Business Review - Joe McCambley. Stop Selling Ads and Do Something Useful. *https://hbr.org/*. [Online] 12 February 2013. [Cited: 19 February 2020.] https://hbr.org/2013/02/stop-selling-ads-and-do-someth.

29. Interactive Advertising Bureau (IAB). First Quarter 1999 Internet Advertising Revenues Double Over First Quarter 1998. *https://www.iab.com/*. [Online] 3 May 1999. [Cited: 5 June 2020.] https://www.iab.com/news/first-quarter-1999-internet-advertising-revenues-double-first-quarter-1998/.

30. Barclays Bank. Shopping through the ages – Part Two. *https://www.home.barclaycard/about-us/our-story-so-far/50-years-of-stories/shopping-through-the-ages-part-two.html*. [Online] 5 November 2020. https://www.home.barclaycard/about-us/our-story-so-far/50-years-of-stories/shopping-through-the-ages-part-two.html.

31. Mueller, Milton L. *Ruling the Root: Internet Governance and the Taming of Cyberspace*. Cambridge, MA : MIT Press, 2002. ISBN: 9780262632980.

32. Symbolics.com. The Big Internet Museum. *symbolics.com*. [Online] [Cited: 27 January 2020.] http://symbolics.com/museum/.

33. Verisign. Internet Grows to 294 Million Domain Names in the First Quarter of 2015. [Online] 30 June 2015. [Cited: 27 January 2020.] https://investor.verisign.com/news-releases/news-release-details/internet-grows-294-million-domain-names-first-quarter-2015?releaseid=920138.

34. BITLAW. DOMAIN NAME DISPUTES. *https://www.bitlaw.com*. [Online] [Cited: 30 January 2020.] https://www.bitlaw.com/internet/domain.html.

35. Wikipedia. Sex.com. *https://en.wikipedia.org.* [Online] [Cited: 30 January 2020.] https://en.wikipedia.org/wiki/Sex.com.

36. Mozilla stomps IE. *snafu.de.* [Online] 4 October 1997. [Cited: 13 January 2019.] http://home.snafu.de/tilman/mozilla/stomps.html.

37. BBC News. Business: The Economy. *BBC News - http://news.bbc.co.uk/.* [Online] 18 November 1998. [Cited: 6 June 2020.] http://news.bbc.co.uk/1/hi/business/216594.stm.

38. Freeserve and ten years of boom and bust. *BBC News.* [Online] 22 September 2008. [Cited: 6 June 2020.] https://www.bbc.co.uk/blogs/technology/2008/09/freeserve_and_ten_years_of_boo.html.

39. www.wired.com - Frank Rose. Sex Sells. *www.wired.com/.* [Online] 01 December 1997. [Cited: 15 November 2021.] https://www.wired.com/1997/12/sex-3/.

40. SFGATE. Startups Fetch Record Financing / Kestrel and Pets.com top venture capital list in Bay Area. *SFGate.com.* [Online] 11 August 1999. [Cited: 15 January 2020.] https://www.sfgate.com/business/article/Startups-Fetch-Record-Financing-Kestrel-and-2913482.php.

41. Business Insider. "Spam" is from a Monty Python sketch. *youtube.com.* [Online] 12 February 2017. [Cited: 24 January 2020.] https://www.youtube.com/watch?v=zLih-WQwBSc.

42. BBC News. EU businesses count spam costs. *http://news.bbc.co.uk/.* [Online] 15 July 2003. [Cited: 26 January 2020.] http://news.bbc.co.uk/1/hi/business/3068627.stm.

43. European Commission. Fighting spam, spyware and malicious software: Member States should do better, says Commission. *https://ec.europa.eu/commission/presscorner.* [Online] 27 November 2006. [Cited: 26 January 2020.] https://ec.europa.eu/commission/presscorner/detail/en/IP_06_1629.

44. European Commission's Information Society and Media. Legal analysis of a Single Market for the Information Society. [Online] November 2009. [Cited: 25 January 2020.] http://ec.europa.eu/information_society/newsroom/cf/document.cfm?doc_id=838.

45. The Guardian. Tony Blair's full speech. *https://www.theguardian.com.* [Online] 7 March 2000. [Cited: 8 June 2020.] https://www.theguardian.com/uk/2000/mar/07/tonyblair.

46. Geek.com. Kibu.com kloses. *Geek.com.* [Online] 10 March 2000. [Cited: 26 February 2020.] https://www.geek.com/news/kibucom-kloses-564896/.

47. BBC News. Net shopping 'pitfalls' warning. *http://news.bbc.co.uk.* [Online] 12 Octoner 2000. [Cited: 26 February 2020.] http://news.bbc.co.uk/1/hi/business/965243.stm.

48. Drapers - Kirsty McGregor. How Asos founder Nick Robertson built a £1.4bn business. *www.drapersonline.com.* [Online] 20 December 2017. [Cited: 28 February 2020.] https://www.drapersonline.com/how-asos-founder-nick-robertson-built-a-14bn-business/7028171.article.

49. ASOS PLC. ASOS PLC ANNUAL REPORT & ACCOUNTS 2010. *www.asosplc.com.* [Online] 32 March 2010. [Cited: 28 February 2020.] https://www.asosplc.com/~/media/Files/A/ASOS/results-archive/pdf/AnnualReport2010.pdf.

50. BBC News. EU businesses count spam costs. http://news.bbc.co.uk/. [Online] 15 July 2003. [Cited: 26 February 2020.] http://news.bbc.co.uk/1/hi/technology/3120628.stm

51. BBC News. Asos profits plunge 87% after difficult year. *https://www.bbc.co.uk/news.* [Online] 10 April 2019. [Cited: 28 February 2020.] https://www.bbc.co.uk/news/business-47877688.

52. COMPUTERWORLD. https://www.computerworld.com/article/3412338/a-history-of-uk-broadband-roll-out--bt--openreach-and-other-major-milestones.html#slide1. *COMPUTERWORLD.com.* [Online] 23 July 2018. [Cited: 15 January 2020.] https://www.computerworld.com/article/3412338/a-history-of-uk-broadband-roll-out--bt--openreach-and-other-major-milestones.html#slide1.

53. Steven J. Murdoch and Ross Anderson, University of Cambridge, UK. Verified by Visa and Mastercard SecureCode: or, How Not to Design Authentication. *https://www.cl.cam.ac.uk/.* [Online] 2010. [Cited: 14 November 2020.] https://www.cl.cam.ac.uk/~rja14/Papers/fc10vbvsecurecode.pdf.

54. BBC News. Banks 'too often blaming customers' for fraud. *www.bbc.co.uk/news*. [Online] 12 December 2020. [Cited: 12 December 2020.] https://www.bbc.co.uk/news/business-55286037.

55. Committee of Advertising Practice. The Cap Code. *https://www.asa.org.uk/*. [Online] 1997. [Cited: 10 June 2020.] https://www.asa.org.uk/uploads/assets/47eb51e7-028d-4509-ab3c0f4822c9a3c4/The-Cap-code.pdf.

56. Snow Valley. [Online]

57. EUR-Lex. Council Directive 2009/132/EC. *https://eur-lex.europa.eu/*. [Online] 19 10 2009. [Cited: 21 January 2020.] https://eur-lex.europa.eu/legal-content/EN/ALL/?uri=CELEX:32009L0132.

58. Investegate. Flying Brands Limited - Final Results. *https://www.investegate.co.uk*. [Online] 12 February 2002. [Cited: 21 January 2020.] https://www.investegate.co.uk/ArticlePrint.aspx?id=200202120700303094R.

59. Jersey Evening Post. Play.com owners move up Sunday Times rich list. *https://jerseyeveningpost.com/*. [Online] 7 May 2011. [Cited: 22 January 2020.] https://jerseyeveningpost.com/news/2011/05/07/play-com-owners-move-up-sunday-times-rich-list/.

60. The Guardian. Boom in sales of tax-free CDs casts doubt on Treasury claims. *The Guardian*. [Online] 19 February 2010. [Cited: 21 January 2020.] https://www.theguardian.com/business/2010/feb/19/tax-free-cd-boom-casts-doubt-on-treasury-claims.

61. BBC. VAT free loophole to be closed by UK Treasury. *https://www.bbc.co.uk/news/*. [Online] 8 November 2011. [Cited: 27 February 2020.] https://www.bbc.co.uk/news/world-europe-15642336.

62. Campaign. Twitter mostly 'pointless babble' says study. *https://www.campaignlive.co.uk*. [Online] 13 August 2009. [Cited: 3 December 2020.] https://www.campaignlive.co.uk/article/twitter-mostly-pointless-babble-says-study/926942.

63. CISA. Understanding Denial-of-Service Attacks. *https://www.us-cert.gov/ncas*. [Online] November 2009. [Cited: 27 January 2020.] https://www.us-cert.gov/ncas/tips/ST04-015.

64. The Register. Amazon is saying nothing about the DDoS attack that took down AWS, but others are. *https://www.theregister.co.uk/*. [Online] 28 October 2019. [Cited: 23 January 2020.] https://www.theregister.co.uk/2019/10/28/amazon_ddos_attack/.

65. Financial Times. Fraud and online crimes make up almost half of UK's 11.8m total. *ft.com*. [Online] 19 January 2017. [Cited: 24 January 2020.] https://www.ft.com/content/03e8674e-de47-11e6-9d7c-be108f1c1dce.

66. Which? Exclusive: more than 96% of reported fraud cases go unsolved. *which.co.uk*. [Online] 24 September 2018. [Cited: 15 December 2020.] https://www.which.co.uk/news/2018/09/exclusive-more-than-96-of-reported-fraud-cases-go-unsolved/.

67. BBC Question Time. Question Time. *bbc.co.uk*. [Online] 23 January 2020. [Cited: 24 January 2020.] https://www.bbc.co.uk/iplayer/episode/m000dlzb/question-time-2019-23012020.

68. Wikipedia. *Openreach*. [Online] [Cited: 17 January 2020.] https://en.wikipedia.org/wiki/Openreach#cite_note-3.

69. BBC. Broadband speeds in UK slip down global league table. *bbc.co.uk*. [Online] 10 July 2018. [Cited: 15 Januray 2020.] https://www.bbc.co.uk/news/technology-44778017.

70. ISPreview. The Challenges of Boris Johnson's 2025 Full Fibre for All UK Pledge. *ISPreview*. [Online] 3 August 2019. [Cited: 17 January 2020.] https://www.ispreview.co.uk/index.php/2019/08/the-challenge-of-boris-johnsons-2025-full-fibre-for-all-uk-pledge.html/2.

71. Wikipedia. Do Not Track. *https://en.wikipedia.org*. [Online] [Cited: 1 March 2020.] https://en.wikipedia.org/wiki/Do_Not_Track.

72. IAB.uk. New IAB UK research reveals latest ad blocking levels. *https://www.iabuk.com/press-release/new-iab-uk-research-reveals-latest-ad-blocking-levels*. [Online] 11 November 2015. [Cited: 1 March 2020.] https://www.iabuk.com/press-release/new-iab-uk-research-reveals-latest-ad-blocking-levels.

73. AdAge. AS TECHNOLOGY DEFEATS AD BLOCKING, ONLINE ADS MUST IMPROVE. *https://adage.com*. [Online] 25 March 2016. https://adage.com/article/global-news/technology-defeats-adblocking-industry-responds/303270.

74. Talos. TOTAL GLOBAL EMAIL & SPAM VOLUME FOR DECEMBER 2019. *https://talosintelligence.com/*. [Online] 26 January 2020. [Cited: 26 January 2020.] https://talosintelligence.com/reputation_center/email_rep#top-senders-ip.

75. Forbes. GLOBAL 2000 - The World's Largest Public Companies. *https://www.forbes.com/*. [Online] 15 May 2019. [Cited: 2 March 2020.] https://www.forbes.com/global2000/#20735da0335d.

76. Bloomberg. Bloomberg Billionaires Index. *https://www.bloomberg.com*. [Online] 2 March 2020. [Cited: 2 March 2020.] https://www.bloomberg.com/billionaires/.

77. Bloomberg Billionaires Index #19. *https://www.bloomberg.com/*. [Online] 2 March 2020. [Cited: 2 March 2020.] https://www.bloomberg.com/billionaires/profiles/jack-y-ma/.

78. Forbes. Is The Sears Death Watch Entering Its Final Stages? *https://www.forbes.com*. [Online] 2 January 2020. [Cited: 2 March 2020.] https://www.forbes.com/sites/warrenshoulberg/2020/01/02/is-the-sears-death-watch-entering-its-final-stages/#630c5a6a1925.

79. *Footsie sheds shops.* The Sunday Times - Sam Chambers. 1 March 2020, London : The Sunday Times, 2020, Vols. Business - P 3.

80. BBC News. Coronavirus: Five ways shopping will be different from now on. *https://www.bbc.co.uk/news*. [Online] 12 June 2020. [Cited: 17 June 2020.] https://www.bbc.co.uk/news/business-53005123.

81. Retail Gazette. Footfall plummets up to 63% in wake of Covid-19 crisis. *https://www.retailgazette.co.uk*. [Online] 23 March 2020. [Cited: 5 October 2020.] https://www.retailgazette.co.uk/blog/2020/03/footfall-plummets-63-wake-covid-19-crisis/.

82. BBC. Retailers report sales jump in June, says trade body. *https://www.bbc.co.uk/news/business*. [Online] 14 July 2020. [Cited: 8 October 2020.] https://www.bbc.co.uk/news/business-53397953.

83. Forrester, Robert. Chief Executive, Vertu Motors. *BBC Breakfast - https://youtu.be/sWQY22UNhfw*. BBC Breakfast, London : BBC TV, 26 May 2020.

84. CarDealer. *https://cardealermagazine.co.uk*. [Online] 1 May 2020. [Cited: 10 October 2020.] https://cardealermagazine.co.uk/publish/dvla-confirms-car-buyers-can-take-unaccompanied-test-drives-trade-plates/191239.

85. BBC News. UK new car registrations in 2020 sink to 30-year low. *https://www.bbc.co.uk/news/business*. [Online] 6 January 2021. [Cited: 6 January 2021.] https://www.bbc.co.uk/news/business-55551315.

86. BBC. Coronavirus: John Lewis and Boots to cut 5,300 jobs. *https://www.bbc.co.uk/news*. [Online] 9 July 2020. [Cited: 9 October 2020.] https://www.bbc.co.uk/news/business-53348519.

87. BBC News. Coronavirus: Shopping may never be the same, says M&S. *https://www.bbc.co.uk/news*. [Online] 20 May 2020. [Cited: 8 October 2020.] https://www.bbc.co.uk/news/business-52724901.

88. Ocado says switch to online shopping is permanent. *https://www.bbc.co.uk/news*. [Online] 14 July 2020. [Cited: 8 October 2020.] https://www.bbc.co.uk/news/business-53402767.

89. The Independent. MOVE TO ONLINE GROCERY SHOPPING DURING PANDEMIC IS 'IRREVERSIBLE' AS THREE QUARTERS OF UK EMBRACE IT. *https://www.independent.co.uk*. [Online] 20 August 2020. [Cited: 8 October 2020.] https://www.independent.co.uk/life-style/online-grocery-shopping-irreversible-coronavirus-waitrose-survey-a9679166.html.

90. BBC News. Ocado overtakes Tesco as most valuable UK retailer. *https://www.bbc.co.uk/news/business*. [Online] 30 September 2020. [Cited: 11 January 2021.] https://www.bbc.co.uk/news/business-54352540.

91. Sky News. Morrisons creates 1,000 new jobs for Amazon tie-up. *https://news.sky.com*. [Online] 30 September 2020. [Cited: 11 January 2021.] https://news.sky.com/story/morrisons-creates-1-000-new-jobs-for-amazon-tie-up-12085882.

92. BBC News. Spent less, saved more: What we bought this year. *https://www.bbc.co.uk/news/business*. [Online] 31 December 2020. https://www.bbc.co.uk/news/business-55494105.

93. Christmas post delays blamed on 'high demand'. *https://www.bbc.co.uk/news/business*. [Online] 18 December 2020. [Cited: 10 January 2021.] https://www.bbc.co.uk/news/business-55364955.

94. Royal Mail set for 'material loss' despite jump in parcels. *https://www.bbc.co.uk/news/business*. [Online] 8 Septemner 2020. [Cited: 8 September 2020.] https://www.bbc.co.uk/news/business-54068885.

95. The Guardian. Suffering John Lewis stands at a crossroads on the high street. *https://www.theguardian.com/business*. [Online] September 19 2020. [Cited: 8 October 2020.] https://www.theguardian.com/business/2020/sep/19/suffering-john-lewis-stands-at-a-crossroads-on-the-high-street .

96. BBC News. Topshop owner Arcadia goes into administration. *https://www.bbc.co.uk/news/business*. [Online] 30 November 2020. [Cited: 2 December 2020.] https://www.bbc.co.uk/news/business-55139369.

97. The Seattle Times / Bloomberg. Amazon wins business from reluctant brands after coronavirus closes stores. *https://www.seattletimes.com*. [Online] 5 May 2020. [Cited: 5 October 2020.] https://www.seattletimes.com/business/amazon-wins-business-from-reluctant-brands-after-coronavirus-closes-stores/.

98. BBC News. Amazon to create 7,000 UK jobs. *https://www.bbc.co.uk/news*. [Online] 3 September 2020. [Cited: 8 October 2020.] https://www.bbc.co.uk/news/business-54009484.

99. ft.com. Amazon doubles quarterly profit despite Covid-19 costs. *https://www.ft.com*. [Online] 30 July 2020. [Cited: 9 October 2020.] https://www.ft.com/content/7a42b1d8-9ca7-4827-aaae-729fdb7637f5.

100. *Walmart readies rival to Prime*. The Sunday Times - Danny Fortson. 1 March 2020, London : The Sunday Times, 2020, Vol. Business P 3.

101. Digital Guardian. The History of Data Breaches. *https://digitalguardian.com*. [Online] 1 December 2020. [Cited: 16 December 2020.] https://digitalguardian.com/blog/history-data-breaches.

102. Verizon. 2018 Data Breach Investigations Report. *https://enterprise.verizon.com/*. [Online] April 2018. [Cited: 27 January 2020.] https://enterprise.verizon.com/resources/reports/DBIR_2018_Report.pdf.

103. Wikipedia. List of English inventions and discoveries. *https://en.wikipedia.org*. [Online] [Cited: 22 February 2020.] https://en.wikipedia.org/wiki/List_of_English_inventions_and_discoveries.

104. Buckle, Anne. The Difference Between GMT and UTC. *https://www.timeanddate.com/time/gmt-utc-time.html*. [Online] Time and Date AS, 2020. [Cited: 01 December 2020.] https://www.timeanddate.com/time/gmt-utc-time.html.

105. BBC News. NHS IT system one of 'worst fiascos ever', say MPs. *https://www.bbc.co.uk/news*. [Online] 18 September 2013. [Cited: 19 January 2021.] https://www.bbc.co.uk/news/uk-politics-24130684.

106. MIT Technology Review. The UK's contact tracing app fiasco is a master class in mismanagement. *https://www.technologyreview.com*. [Online] 19 June 2020. [Cited: 19 January 2021.] https://www.technologyreview.com/2020/06/19/1004190/uk-covid-contact-tracing-app-fiasco/.

107. BBC History Extra - Rupert Matthews, historian and author. High street. *www.historyextra.com*. [Online] 15 March 2011. [Cited: 17 December 2020.] https://www.historyextra.com/period/high-street/#:~:text=In%20the%20vast%20majority%20

of,main%20commercial%20or%20shopping%20thoroughfare.&text=The%20name%20
seems%20to%20have,more%20important%2C%20status%20than%20others..

108. Ravilious, J M Richards and Eric. *High Street*. London : V&A Publishing; Facsimile edition (5 Mar. 2012), 1938. 1851776893 / 978-1851776894.

109. LENSVID. *https://lensvid.com*. [Online] 11 February 2019. [Cited: 26 June 2020.] https://lensvid.com/gear/technology/what-happened-to-the-photography-industry-in-2018/.

110. Ofcom. Radio frequency jammers. *https://www.ofcom.org.uk*. [Online] 2006. [Cited: 22 June 2020.] http://www.legislation.gov.uk/ukpga/2006/36/section/68.

111. TIME - Brad Tuttle. The True Meaning of Shopping. *https://business.time.com/*. [Online] 14 December 2010. [Cited: 18 March 2020.] https://business.time.com/2010/12/14/the-true-meaning-of-shopping/.

112. Daily Mail - Marth de Lacey. Trying to impress a man? Steer clear of the sales. Men get bored shopping after just 26 MINUTES... women after 2 hours. *https://www.dailymail.co.uk*. [Online] 5 July 2013. [Cited: 18 March 2020.] http://www.dailymail.co.uk/femail/article-2356781/Men-bored-just-26-MINUTES-shopping--women-2-hours.html.

113. Hurun. 2020 Hurun Global 500. *https://www.hurun.net/en-US/Info/Detail?num=E6VM7L8L4I15*. [Online] 12 January 2021. [Cited: 13 January 2021.] https://www.hurun.net/en-US/Info/Detail?num=E6VM7L8L4I15.

114. BBC News. Apple more valuable than the entire FTSE 100. *https://www.bbc.co.uk/*. [Online] 2 September 2020. [Cited: 2 September 2020.] https://www.bbc.co.uk/news/business-53996191.

115. The Independent - Ben Chapman. UK by far the biggest enabler of global corporate tax dodging, groundbreaking research finds. *https://www.independent.co.uk/*. [Online] 28 May 2019. [Cited: 13 March 2020.] https://www.independent.co.uk/news/business/news/uk-corporate-tax-avoidance-havens-justice-network-dodging-a8933661.html.

116. A Third of U.S. Billionaire Wealth Gains Since 1990 Have Come During Pandemic, Chuck Collins. *Inequality.org*. [Online] 15 April 2021. [Cited: 15 April 2021.] https://inequality.org/great-divide/billionaire-pandemic-profit-surges/.

117. World Trade Organization. UNITED STATES Statement by H.E. Mr. William J. Clinton, President . *https://www.wto.org*. [Online] May 1998. https://www.wto.org/english/thewto_e/minist_e/min98_e/anniv_e/clinton_e.htm.

118. BBC News. FTSE 100 chief executives 'earn average salary within 3 days'. *https://www.bbc.co.uk/news/*. [Online] 6 January 2021. [Cited: 13 January 2021.] https://www.bbc.co.uk/news/business-55551314.

119. Oxfam. Time to care. *https://www.oxfam.org*. [Online] 20 January 2020. [Cited: 29 December 2020.] https://www.oxfam.org/en/research/time-care.

120. AIR & SPACE MAGAZINE - Craig Mellow. The Rise and Fall and Rise of Iridium. *https://www.airspacemag.com*. [Online] September 2004. [Cited: 17 February 2020.] https://www.airspacemag.com/space/the-rise-and-fall-and-rise-of-iridium-5615034/.

121. BBC News. VAT free loophole to be closed by UK Treasury. *BBC News*. [Online] 8 November 2011. [Cited: 22 January 2020.] https://www.bbc.co.uk/news/world-europe-15642336.

122. ASOS Plc. About. *https://www.asos.com*. [Online] [Cited: 28 February 2020.] https://www.asos.com/about/who-we-are/?ctaref=aboutus|whoweare.

123. Doc Searls on "The Intention Economy: When Customers Take Charge". *The Berkman Klein Center for Internet & Society at Harvard University*. [Online] 11 June 2012. [Cited: 1 March 2020.] https://cyber.harvard.edu/events/2012/05/searls.

124. The New Yorker Collection 1993. https://www.plsteiner.com/cartoons#/newyorker. *https://www.plsteiner.com/*. [Online] 5 July 1993. [Cited: 7 March 2020.] https://www.washingtonpost.com/blogs/comic-riffs/post/nobody-knows-youre-a-dog-as-iconic-internet-cartoon-turns-20-creator-peter-steiner-knows-the-joke-rings-as-relevant-as-ever/2013/07/31/73372600-f98d-11e2-8e84-c56731a202fb_blog.html.

125. Internet Advertising Bureau UK. New IAB UK research reveals latest ad blocking levels. *https://www.iabuk.com.* [Online] 11 November 2015. [Cited: 17 June 2020.] https://www.iabuk.com/press-release/new-iab-uk-research-reveals-latest-ad-blocking-levels.

126. Wired. BargainFinder. *https://www.wired.com/1995.* [Online] 18 January 1995. [Cited: 2 November 2020.] https://www.wired.com/1995/10/bargainfinder/.

127. Retail Economics. UK RETAIL STATS & FACTS. *https://www.retaileconomics.co.uk.* [Online] 23 February 2021. [Cited: 23 February 2021.] https://www.retaileconomics.co.uk/library-retail-stats-and-facts.

128. John H. Seago, P. Kenneth Seidelmann and Steve Allen. LEGISLATIVE SPECIFICATIONS FOR COORDINATING WITH UNIVERSAL TIME. *Science and Technology, American Astronautical Society, 113: 41.* [Online] 2012. [Cited: 2 May 2020.] https://www.ucolick.org/~sla/leapsecs/seago.pdf.

Index